FIX-IT and FORGET-IT® Lightly

FIX-IT and FORGET-IT ®
Lightly

Healthy, Low-Fat Recipes for Your Slow Cooker

New York Times bestselling author
Phyllis Pellman Good

Good Books

Intercourse, PA 17534
800/762-7171
www.goodbks.com

An independent consulting firm calculated the nutritional analysis that follows each recipe. Although the analysts and editors have attempted full accuracy, many variables (including variations related to particular brands, to the refinement of products, and to the exact amounts of ingredients, as well as whether they are cooked or raw) could result in the analyses being approximate.

Because many factors influence your health, please check with your health-care expert before making substantial changes in what you eat.

Cover design and illustrations by Cheryl Benner
Design by Dawn J. Ranck

FIX-IT AND FORGET-IT LIGHTLY
Copyright © 2004 by Good Books, Intercourse, PA 17534

International Standard Book Number: 1-56148-431-8 (paperback edition)
International Standard Book Number: 1-56148-432-6 (comb-bound paperback edition)
International Standard Book Number: 1-56148-433-4 (hardcover gift edition)
Library of Congress Catalog Card Number: 2004012021

Printed in the United States of America.

Library of Congress Cataloging-in-Publication Data
Good, Phyllis Pellman
  Fix-it and forget-it lightly : healthy, low-fat recipes for your slow cooker / by Phyllis
Pellman Good.
      p. cm.
   Includes index.
ISBN 1-56148-433-4 (hardcover) — ISBN 1-56148-431-8 (pbk.) — ISBN 1-56148-432-6
(plastic comb) 1. Electric cookery, Slow. 2. Quick and easy cookery. 3. Low-fat diet—
Recipes. I. Title.
  TX827.G64 2004
  641.5'884—dc22   2004012021

Table of Contents

About
Fix-It and Forget-It LIGHTLY

Yes, now you can have it all: Food from your slow cooker that is scrumptious, quick, easy to prepare—and low-fat!

This volume in the best-selling *Fix-It and Forget-It* tradition gives you more than 500 new and revised recipes that are mouth-watering but guilt-free. Now you can choose healthy, light dishes, fix them quickly, and then forget about them until mealtime.

We work at portion control here . . .

You'll notice that our serving sizes are quite modest. So if you'd like to manage your weight, *Fix-It and Forget-It LIGHTLY* will help with portions and healthy ingredients.

Ideal slow-cooker sizes . . .

The ideal slow-cooker size given with each recipe is just a suggestion. I went big in most cases so that you aren't faced with a pot that's running over. (On the other hand, be aware of the fact that your food may get too dry if your pot is less than half full.)

Some raw vegetables stand up and take a lot of room. As they cook, they quiet down and sink together. So some recipes with an abundance of uncooked vegetables suggest a larger cooker than other recipes which yield the same number of servings.

Slow cookers are great for carry-in meals and pot-lucks. But who wants an overflowing pot in the back of a vehicle? So, again, I tilted toward the larger size.

Cooking times do vary . . .

New slow cookers are generally faster than old ones. If your cooker is relatively new, go with the lesser amount of cooking time when a range of times is given.

Mark up this cookbook!

When you've found the perfect cooking time for a recipe—write it in your cookbook. When you've discovered the right size slow cooker for a recipe, write that next to the recipe. And when you've made a tasty and compatible go-along for a dish, note it next to the recipe. (In fact, send us your adaptations, innovations, and combinations, if you like. We may want to include them in a future edition of *Fix-It and Forget-It LIGHTLY.*)

Personalize this cookbook—and it will be your companion in the kitchen and in your effort to eat healthfully.

Calculating the nutritional analyses . . .

The recipe analyses are based on the lesser amount of an ingredient when a range of amounts is given. Optional ingredients are not included in the analyses. Only those items on a recipe's list of ingredients are part of that recipe's analysis. (If a recipe's procedure or Notes suggest serving it with pasta or potatoes, for example, those foods are not calculated in the analysis.)

Why is *Fix-It and Forget-It LIGHTLY* such a friend?
- Its pages are packed with recipes.
- Its recipes call for just a few ingredients—and they're readily available.
- Many of the recipes are offered in multiple variations. Find the one that suits your taste—and the ingredients you have on hand.
- Preparations are easy; the ingredients are reasonably priced.
- Everybody eats well and healthfully—without the cook being under pressure.
- Little fuss. Lots of flavor!

Feast healthfully. Your family and friends—your waistline and your heart—will thank you!

— Phyllis Pellman Good

Chicken and Turkey Main Dishes

One-Pot Easy Chicken

Jean Robinson
Cinnaminson, NJ

Makes 6 servings
(Ideal slow-cooker size: 6-quart)

6-8 medium-sized potatoes, quartered
1-2 large onions, sliced
3-5 carrots, cubed
1 tsp. garlic salt
¼ tsp. black pepper
5 lbs. chicken, skin removed (quarters or
    legs and thighs work well)
1 small onion, chopped
¾ tsp. black pepper
2 tsp. whole cloves
2 tsp. garlic salt
1 Tbsp. chopped fresh oregano
1 tsp. dried rosemary
½ cup lemon juice

1. Mix together potatoes, sliced onions, carrots, 1 tsp. garlic salt, and ¼ tsp. black pepper in bottom of slow cooker.
2. Rinse and pat chicken dry. In bowl mix together chopped onions, ¾ tsp. black pepper, cloves, and 2 tsp. garlic salt. Dredge chicken in seasonings. Place in slow cooker over vegetables.
3. In small bowl mix together oregano, rosemary, and lemon juice. Pour over chicken.
4. Cover. Cook on low 6-8 hours, or until vegetables are soft and chicken juices run clear.

Per Serving: 470 calories (200 calories from fat), 22g total fat (6g saturated, 0g trans), 215mg cholesterol, 1120mg sodium, 50g total carbohydrate (7g fiber, 7g sugar), 82g protein, 100%DV vitamin A, 40%DV vitamin C, 10%DV calcium, 30%DV iron.

This is a lifesaver when the grandchildren come for a weekend. I get to play with them, and dinner is timed and ready when we are.

Lemon Garlic Chicken

Cindy Krestynick
Glen Lyon, PA

Makes 4 servings
(Ideal slow-cooker size: 3½-quart)

1 tsp. dried oregano
½ tsp. seasoned salt
¼ tsp. black pepper
4 chicken breast halves, skinned and
　rinsed
2 Tbsp. butter or margarine
¼ cup water
3 Tbsp. lemon juice
2 garlic cloves, minced
1 tsp. low-sodium chicken bouillon
　granules
1 tsp. minced fresh parsley

1. Combine oregano, salt, and pepper. Rub all of mixture into chicken. Brown chicken in butter or margarine in skillet. Transfer to slow cooker.
2. Place water, lemon juice, garlic, and bouillon cubes in skillet. Bring to boil, loosening browned bits from skillet. Pour over chicken.
3. Cover. Cook on high 2-2½ hours or low 4-5 hours.
4. Add parsley and baste chicken. Cover. Cook on high 15-30 minutes, until chicken is tender.

Per Serving: 180 calories (60 calories from fat), 7g total fat (2g saturated, 0g trans), 65mg cholesterol, 430mg sodium, 5g total carbohydrate (0g fiber, 1g sugar), 24g protein, 0%DV vitamin A, 4%DV vitamin C, 2%DV calcium, 6%DV iron.

Chicken and Sun-Dried Tomatoes

Joyce Shackelford
Green Bay, WI

Makes 8 servings
(Ideal slow-cooker size: 6-quart)

1 Tbsp. olive oil
3 lbs. boneless, skinless chicken breasts,
　cut in 8 serving pieces
2 garlic cloves, minced
½ cup white wine
1½ cups fat-free, low-sodium chicken
　stock
1 tsp. dried basil
½ cup chopped, sun-dried tomatoes, cut
　into slivers

1. Heat oil in skillet. Add several pieces of chicken at a time, but make sure not to crowd the skillet so the chicken can brown evenly.
2. Transfer chicken to slow cooker as it finishes browning.
3. Add garlic, wine, chicken stock, and basil to skillet. Bring to a boil. Scrape up any bits from the bottom of the pan.
4. Pour over chicken. Scatter tomatoes over the top.
5. Cover. Cook on low 4-6 hours.

Per Serving: 320 calories (70 calories from fat), 8g total fat (2g saturated, 0g trans), 145mg cholesterol, 230mg sodium, 2g total carbohydrate (0.5g fiber, 1g sugar), 54g protein, 0%DV vitamin A, 0%DV vitamin C, 4%DV calcium, 15%DV iron.

Greek Chicken

Judy Govotsus
Monrovia, MD

Makes 8 servings
(Ideal slow-cooker size: 6-quart)

6 medium-sized potatoes, quartered
3 lbs. chicken pieces, skin removed
2 large onions, quartered
1 whole bulb garlic, minced
1/2 cup water
3 tsp. dried oregano
1 tsp. salt
1/2 tsp. black pepper
1 Tbsp. olive oil

1. Place potatoes in bottom of slow cooker. Add chicken, onions, and garlic.
2. In small bowl mix water with oregano, salt, and pepper.
3. Pour over chicken and potatoes. Top with oil.
4. Cover. Cook on high 5-6 hours or on low 9-10 hours.

Per Serving: 430 calories (70 calories from fat), 8g total fat (2g saturated, 0g trans), 145mg cholesterol, 430mg sodium, 31g total carbohydrate (4g fiber, 3g sugar), 56g protein, 0%DV vitamin A, 30%DV vitamin C, 6%DV calcium, 20%DV iron.

Twenty-Clove Chicken

Nancy Savage
Factoryville, PA

Makes 6 servings
(Ideal slow-cooker size: 4-quart)

1/4 cup dry white wine
2 Tbsp. chopped dried parsley
2 tsp. dried basil leaves
1 tsp. dried oregano
pinch of crushed red pepper flakes
20 cloves of garlic (about 1 head)
4 celery ribs, chopped
6 boneless, skinless chicken breast halves
1 lemon, juice and zest
fresh herbs, optional

1. Combine wine, dried parsley, dried basil, dried oregano, and dried red peppers in large bowl.
2. Add garlic cloves and celery. Coat well.
3. Transfer garlic and celery to slow cooker with slotted spoon.
4. Add chicken to herb mixture. Coat well. Place chicken on top of vegetables in slow cooker.
5. Sprinkle lemon juice and zest in slow cooker. Add any remaining herb mixture.
6. Cover. Cook on low for 5-6 hours or until chicken is no longer pink in center.
7. Garnish with fresh herbs if desired.

Per Serving: 170 calories (30 calories from fat), 3.5g total fat (1g saturated, 0g trans), 75mg cholesterol, 90mg sodium, 7g total carbohydrate (2g fiber, 1g sugar), 28g protein, 4%DV vitamin A, 10%DV vitamin C, 6%DV calcium, 10%DV iron.

Note: For browned chicken, sauté uncooked breasts in large skillet in 1 Tbsp. olive oil over medium heat. Cook for 5 minutes on each side, or until golden brown. Then proceed with steps above.

Lemon Chicken

Judi Manos
West Islip, NY
Joette Droz
Kalona, IA
Cindy Krestynick
Glen Lyon, PA

Makes 6 servings
(Ideal slow-cooker size: 5-quart)

6 boneless, skinless chicken breast halves
1 tsp. dried oregano
1/2 tsp. seasoned salt
1/4 tsp. black pepper
1/4 cup water
3 Tbsp. lemon juice
2 garlic cloves, minced
2 tsp. chicken bouillon granules
2 tsp. fresh parsley, minced

1. Pat chicken dry with paper towels.
2. Combine oregano, seasoned salt, and pepper. Rub over chicken.
3. Brown chicken in a nonstick skillet over medium heat.
4. Place chicken in slow cooker.
5. Combine water, lemon juice, garlic, and bouillon in skillet. Bring to a boil, stirring to loosen browned bits. Pour over chicken.
6. Cover. Cook on low 3-4 hours.
7. Baste chicken. Add parsley.
8. Remove lid and cook 15-30 minutes longer, allowing juices to thicken slightly.
9. Serve chicken and juices over rice.

Per Serving: 150 calories (30 calories from fat), 3g total fat (1g saturated, 0g trans), 75mg cholesterol, 320mg sodium, 1g total carbohydrate (0g fiber, 0g sugar), 27g protein, 2%DV vitamin A, 4%DV vitamin C, 2%DV calcium, 6%DV iron.

Note: If you want to make sure the chicken absorbs the flavors of the sauce as fully as possible, cut it into 1-inch cubes just before placing in slow cooker.

Dill-Lemon Chicken

Vera Schmucker
Goshen, IN

Makes 4 servings
(Ideal slow-cooker size: 4-quart)

1 cup fat-free sour cream
1 Tbsp. fresh dill, minced
1 tsp. lemon pepper seasoning
1 tsp. lemon zest
4 boneless, skinless chicken breast halves

1. Combine sour cream, dill, lemon pepper, and lemon zest in a small bowl. Spoon one-fourth of the sour cream-lemon-dill mixture into bottom of slow cooker.
2. Arrange chicken breasts on top in a single layer.
3. Pour remaining sauce over chicken. Spread evenly.
4. Cover. Cook on low 3-4 hours or until juices run clear.

Per Serving: 200 calories (35 calories from fat), 4g total fat (1.5g saturated, 0g trans), 80mg cholesterol, 230mg sodium, 10g total carbohydrate (0g fiber, 5g sugar), 30g protein, 8%DV vitamin A, 0%DV vitamin C, 10%DV calcium, 6%DV iron.

Healthy Chicken

Carla Koslowskay
Hillsboro, KS

Makes 8 servings
(Ideal slow-cooker size: 6-quart)

3½ lbs. chicken pieces or whole chicken, cut up
2 cups skim milk
5 cups rice or corn cereal, finely crushed
1 tsp. salt
½ tsp. black pepper

1. Remove skin from chicken. Dip in milk.
2. Put crumbs in a plastic bag. Drop chicken pieces into bag to coat with cereal. Shake well.
3. Place chicken pieces in slow cooker. Sprinkle with salt and pepper.
4. Cover. Cook on high 3½-4 hours.

Per Serving: 480 calories (120 calories from fat), 14g total fat (4g saturated, 0g trans), 165mg cholesterol, 480mg sodium, 26g total carbohydrate (0.5g fiber, 5g sugar), 59g protein, 4%DV vitamin A, 0%DV vitamin C, 15%DV calcium, 15%DV iron.

"Baked" Chicken

Eileen Eash
Carlsbad, NM

Makes 8 servings
(Ideal slow-cooker size: 5- or 6-quart)

3 lbs. chicken pieces
1 cup flour
1 tsp. salt
½ tsp. coarse black pepper
¼ tsp. garlic powder
1 tsp. Montreal chicken seasoning
1 Tbsp. parsley flakes
2 Tbsp. canola oil
1 cup water

1. Remove skin from chicken. Rinse. Pat dry.
2. Combine remaining ingredients, except water.
3. Toss chicken pieces with seasoned flour mixture.
4. Brown chicken lightly in skillet in oil.
5. Place in slow cooker. Pour water around the outside wall of the cooker.
6. Cover. Cook on low 6-8 hours.

Per Serving: 350 calories (60 calories from fat), 7g total fat (2g saturated, 0g trans), 145mg cholesterol, 450mg sodium, 12g total carbohydrate (0g fiber, 0g sugar), 54g protein, 2%DV vitamin A, 2%DV vitamin C, 4%DV calcium, 15%DV iron.

Slow-Cooker Barbecued Chicken

Charlotte Shaffer
East Earl, PA

Makes 6 servings
(Ideal slow-cooker size: 3- or 4-quart)

1 lb. frying chicken, cut up and skin
   removed (organic or free-range, if
   possible)
10¾-oz. can condensed tomato soup
¾ cup onion, chopped
¼ cup vinegar
3 Tbsp. brown sugar
1 Tbsp. Worcestershire sauce
½ tsp. salt
¼ tsp. dried basil

1. Place chicken in slow cooker.
2. Combine all remaining ingredients and pour over chicken, making sure that the sauce glazes all the pieces.
3. Cover. Cook on low 6-8 hours.

Per Serving: 170 calories (40 calories from fat), 4.5 total fat (1g saturated, 0g trans), 45mg cholesterol, 550mg sodium, 16g total carbohy-drate (0.5g fiber, 11g sugar), 17g protein, 6%DV vitamin A, 20%DV vitamin C, 2%DV calcium, 10%DV iron.

Barbecued Chicken Breasts

Jeanne Allen
Rye, CO

Makes 8 servings
(Ideal slow-cooker size: 3- or 4-quart)

8 boneless, skinless chicken breast halves
8-oz. can low-sodium tomato sauce
8-oz. can water
2 Tbsp. brown sugar
2 Tbsp. prepared mustard
2 Tbsp. Worcestershire sauce
¼ cup cider vinegar
½ tsp. salt
¼ tsp. black pepper
dash of garlic powder
dash of dried oregano
3 Tbsp. onion, chopped

1. Place chicken in slow cooker sprayed with non-fat cooking spray. Overlap chicken as little as possible.
2. Combine remaining ingredients. Pour over chicken.
3. Cover. Cook on low 6-8 hours or on high 3-4 hours.
4. To thicken the sauce a bit, remove the lid during the last hour of cooking.

Per Serving: 170 calories (30 calories from fat), 3g total fat (1g saturated, 0g trans), 75mg cholesterol, 470mg sodium, 7g total carbohydrate (0.5g fiber, 5g sugar), 27g protein, 2%DV vitamin A, 4%DV vitamin C, 2%DV calcium, 8%DV iron.

Chicken Breasts with Rosemary

Marla Folkerts
Holland, OH

Makes 4 servings
(Ideal slow-cooker size: 3- or 4-quart)

4 boneless, skinless chicken breast halves
  (4 ozs. each)
1½ tsp. balsamic vinegar
1 tsp. minced garlic
1 Tbsp. grated lemon rind
¼ tsp. salt
⅛ tsp. black pepper
½ cup dry white wine, or reduced-sodium
  chicken broth
1 tsp. finely chopped fresh, or ½ tsp.
  dried, crumbled rosemary leaves
½ cup fresh tomato, diced

1. Place chicken breasts in slow cooker.
2. Mix vinegar, garlic, lemon rind, salt, pepper, and wine. Pour over chicken.
3. Cover. Cook on low 6 hours or on high 3 hours.
4. One-half hour before the end of the cooking time, stir in rosemary and fresh tomato.

Per Serving: 170 calories (30 calories from fat), 3 total fat (1g saturated, 0g trans), 75mg cholesterol, 210mg sodium, 3g total carbohydrate (0.5g fiber, 1g sugar), 27g protein, 4%DV vitamin A, 8%DV vitamin C, 2%DV calcium, 6%DV iron.

Southwestern Chicken

Joyce Shackelford
Green Bay, WI

Makes 6 servings
(Ideal slow-cooker size: 6-quart)

2 15¼-oz. cans corn, drained
15-oz. can black beans, rinsed and drained
16-oz. jar chunky salsa, divided
6 boneless, skinless chicken breast halves
1 cup low-fat shredded cheddar cheese

1. Combine corn, black beans, and ½ cup salsa in slow cooker.
2. Top with chicken. Pour remaining salsa over chicken.
3. Cover. Cook on high 3-4 hours or low 7-8 hours.
4. Sprinkle with cheese. Cover 5 minutes for cheese to melt.

Per Serving: 370 calories (50 calories from fat), 6g total fat (2g saturated, 0g trans), 75mg cholesterol, 1210mg sodium, 43g total carbohydrate (7g fiber, 7g sugar), 39g protein, 6%DV vitamin A, 10%DV vitamin C, 15%DV calcium, 20%DV iron.

Note: This dish goes well with rice.

Barbara Jean's Special Chicken

Barbara Jean Fabel
Wausau, WI

Makes 4 servings
(Ideal slow-cooker size: 3-quart)

1 yellow onion, thinly sliced
14-oz. jar marinated artichoke hearts, drained
14-oz. can low-sodium peeled tomatoes
6 Tbsp. red wine vinegar
1 tsp. minced garlic
1/2 tsp. salt
1/2 tsp. black pepper
4 boneless, skinless chicken breast halves

1. Combine all ingredients except chicken in slow cooker.
2. Place chicken in cooker, pushing down into vegetables and sauce until it's as covered as possible.
3. Cover. Cook on low 4-6 hours.
4. Serve over rice.

Per Serving: 270 calories (80 calories from fat), 8g total fat (1g saturated, 0g trans), 75mg cholesterol, 900mg sodium, 18g total carbohydrate (4g fiber, 4g sugar), 31g protein, 4%DV vitamin A, 30%DV vitamin C, 6%DV calcium, 6%DV iron.

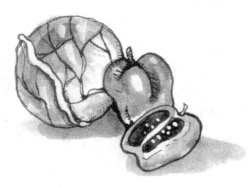

Chicken and Apples

Jean Butzer
Batavia, NY

Makes 6 servings
(Ideal slow-cooker size: 5- or 6-quart)

6-oz. can frozen orange concentrate, thawed
1/2 tsp dried marjoram leaves
dash ground nutmeg
dash garlic powder
1 onion, chopped
6 skinless, boneless chicken breast halves
3 Granny Smith apples, cored and sliced
1/4 cup water
2 Tbsp. cornstarch

1. In a small bowl, combine orange juice concentrate, marjoram, nutmeg, and garlic powder.
2. Place onions in bottom of slow cooker.
3. Dip each chicken breast into the orange mixture to coat. Then place in slow cooker over onions.
4. Pour any remaining orange juice concentrate mixture over the chicken.
5. Cover. Cook on low 6-7 hours.
6. Add apples and cook on low 1 hour longer.
7. Remove chicken, apples, and onions to a serving platter.
8. Pour the sauce that remains into a medium saucepan.
9. Mix together water and cornstarch. Stir into the juices.
10. Cook over medium heat, stirring constantly until the sauce is thick and bubbly.
11. Serve the sauce over the chicken.

Per Serving: 240 calories (30 calories from fat), 3g total fat (1g saturated, 0g trans), 75mg cholesterol, 65mg sodium, 24g total carbohydrate (2g fiber, 19g sugar), 28g protein, 2%DV vitamin A, 20%DV vitamin C, 4%DV calcium, 6%DV iron.

Note: You can also thicken the sauce by adding cornstarch and water mixture to sauce in the slow cooker. Cook on high 10-15 minutes until thickened.

Cran-Apple Chicken

Joyce Shackellord
Green Bay, WI

Makes 6 servings
(Ideal slow-cooker size: 5- or 6-quart)

6 boneless, skinless chicken breast halves
1 cup fresh or frozen cranberries
1 green apple, peeled, cored, and sliced
1 Tbsp. brown sugar
1 cup unsweetened apple juice or cider

1. Place chicken in slow cooker.
2. Sprinkle with cranberries and apples.
3. Mix brown sugar and apple juice. Pour over chicken and fruit.
4. Cover. Cook on low 6-8 hours.

Per Serving: 190 calories (30 calories from fat), 3g total fat (1g saturated, 0g trans), 75mg cholesterol, 65mg sodium, 13g total carbohydrate (2g fiber, 11g sugar), 27g protein, 0%DV vitamin A, 20%DV vitamin C, 2%DV calcium, 6%DV iron.

Sweet 'n Sour Chicken Over Rice

Carol Eberly
Harrisonburg, VA

Makes 6 servings
(Ideal slow-cooker size—5 quart)

1 lb. baby carrots
1 medium onion, cut into wedges
6 boneless, skinless chicken breast halves
20-oz. can unsweetened pineapple chunks
1/3 cup brown sugar
1 Tbsp. low-sodium soy sauce
2 tsp. chicken bouillon granules
1/2 tsp. salt
1/2 tsp. ground ginger
1/4 tsp. garlic powder
3 Tbsp. cornstarch
1/4 cup water
3 cups cooked long grain enriched rice

1. Layer carrots and onion in slow cooker. Top with chicken.
2. Drain pineapple, reserving juice. Place pineapple chunks over chicken.
3. Mix together pineapple juice, brown sugar, soy sauce, chicken bouillon, salt, ginger, and garlic. Pour over top.
4. Cook on low 6-7 hours.
5. Combine cornstarch and water. Gradually stir into slow cooker.
6. Cook 30 minutes longer or until sauce is thickened.
7. Serve over rice.

Per Serving: 330 calories (20 calories from fat), 2.5g total fat (0.5g saturated, 0g trans), 35mg cholesterol, 760mg sodium, 59g total carbohydrate (3g fiber, 29g sugar), 17g protein, 200%DV vitamin A, 20%DV vitamin C, 4%DV calcium, 15%DV iron.

Sweet 'n Sour Chicken Over Potatoes

Dorothy VanDeest
Memphis, TN

Makes 8 servings
(Ideal slow-cooker size: 5 quart)

3 medium-sized potatoes, peeled and
   sliced thin
4 whole chicken breasts, skinned and
   halved
1 cup orange juice
2 Tbsp. brown sugar
1 tsp. dried basil
1/4 tsp. nutmeg
2 Tbsp. cider vinegar
dried parsley flakes
17-oz. can pineapple chunks in water,
   drained
chopped fresh parsley

1. Place sliced potatoes in slow cooker.
Arrange chicken breasts over potatoes.
2. Combine orange juice, brown sugar,
basil, nutmeg, and vinegar. Pour over chicken.
3. Sprinkle dried parsley flakes over
chicken.
4. Cover and cook on low 8-10 hours.
5. Remove chicken breasts and potatoes
from sauce and arrange on a warm platter.
6. Add pineapple chunks to sauce remaining
in slow cooker. Cook on high until they are at
serving temperature.
7. Pour sauce over chicken and potatoes.
Garnish with chopped parsley.

Per Serving: 180 calories (15 calories from fat), 1.5 total fat
(0g saturated, 0g trans), 35mg cholesterol, 40mg sodium,
25g total carbohydrate (3g fiber, 10g sugar), 15g protein,
8%DV vitamin A, 30%DV vitamin C, 2%DV calcium,
8%DV iron.

Orange Chicken Leg Quarters

Kimberly Jensen
Bailey, CO

Makes 8 servings
(Ideal slow-cooker size: 5- to 6-quart)

4 chicken drumsticks, skin removed
4 chicken thighs, skin removed
1 cup strips of green and red bell peppers
1/2 cup fat-free, low-sodium chicken broth
1/2 cup prepared orange juice
1/2 cup ketchup
2 Tbsp. soy sauce
1 Tbsp. light molasses
1 Tbsp. prepared mustard
1/2 tsp. garlic salt
11-oz. can mandarin oranges
2 tsp. cornstarch
1 cup frozen peas
2 green onions, sliced

1. Place chicken in slow cooker. Top with
pepper strips.
2. Combine broth, juice, ketchup, soy sauce,
molasses, mustard, and garlic salt. Pour over
chicken.
3. Cover. Cook on low 5-6 hours.
4. Remove chicken and vegetables from slow
cooker. Keep warm.
5. Measure out 1 cup of cooking sauce. Put in
saucepan and bring to boil.
6. Drain oranges, reserving 1 Tbsp. juice. Stir
cornstarch into reserved juice. Add to boiling
sauce in pan.
7. Add peas to sauce and cook, stirring 2-3
minutes until sauce thickens and peas are
warm. Stir in oranges.
8. Arrange chicken pieces on platter of
cooked white rice, fried cellophane noodles, or
lo mein noodles. Pour orange sauce over chicken
and rice or noodles. Top with sliced green
onions.

Per Serving: 170 calories (40 calories from fat), 4g total fat (1g saturated, 0g trans), 45mg cholesterol, 520mg sodium, 18g total carbohydrate (2g fiber, 11g sugar), 16g protein, 10%DV vitamin A, 30%DV vitamin C, 4%DV calcium, 10%DV iron.

Super Easy Chicken

Mary Seielstad
Sparks, NV

Makes 4 servings
(Ideal slow-cooker size: 4-quart)

4 frozen boneless, skinless chicken breast halves
1 pkg. dry Italian dressing mix
1 cup warm water or chicken stock

1. Place chicken in slow cooker. Sprinkle with dressing mix. Pour water over chicken.
2. Cover. Cook on low 8-10 hours, or until juices run clear.

Per Serving: 160 calories (30 calories from fat), 3g total fat (1g saturated, 0g trans), 75mg cholesterol, 650mg sodium, 6g total carbohydrate (0g fiber, 4g sugar), 27g protein, 0%DV vitamin A, 0%DV vitamin C, 2%DV calcium, 6%DV iron.

Company Chicken

Jeanne Allen
Rye, CO

Makes 6 servings
(Ideal slow-cooker size: 6-quart)

1 envelope liquid Butter Bud mix
6 boneless, skinless chicken breast halves
6 fat-free mozzarella cheese slices
10³/4-oz. can cream of mushroom soup
¹/4 cup water
6-oz. package stuffing mix

1. Prepare liquid Butter Bud mix according to package directions.
2. Place chicken breasts in slow cooker sprayed with non-fat cooking spray.
3. Top each breast with a slice of cheese.
4. Combine soup and water. Pour over chicken.
5. Toss the stuffing mix, its seasoning packet, and prepared Butter Buds together. Sprinkle over chicken breasts.
6. Cover. Cook on low 6-8 hours or on high 3-4 hours.

Per Serving: 350 calories (60 calories from fat), 7g total fat (2g saturated, 0g trans), 80mg cholesterol, 1310mg sodium, 30g total carbohydrate (1g fiber, 3g sugar), 39g protein, 0%DV vitamin A, 0%DV vitamin C, 45%DV calcium, 10%DV iron.

Note: For additional seasoning, add 1 tsp. dried sage to Step 5.

Spicy Italian Chicken

Ilene Bontrager
Arlington, KS

Makes 6 servings
(Ideal slow-cooker size: 5-quart)

1 medium-sized onion, chopped
1/2 cup fat-free Italian dressing
1/2 cup water
1/4 tsp. salt
1/2 tsp. garlic powder
1 tsp. chili powder
1/2 tsp. paprika
1/4 tsp. black pepper
6 boneless, skinless chicken breast halves
2 Tbsp. cornstarch
2 Tbsp. cold water

1. Spray the inside of the slow cooker with nonfat cooking spray. Combine all ingredients except chicken, cornstarch, and water in slow cooker.
2. Add chicken. Turn to coat.
3. Cover. Cook on low 4-5 hours.
4. Remove chicken and keep warm.
5. In a saucepan, combine cornstarch and cold water.
6. Add cooking juices gradually. Stir and bring to a boil until thickened.
7. Pour sauce over chicken and then serve over noodles or rice.

Per Serving: 180 calories (30 calories from fat), 3.5g total fat (1g saturated, 0g trans), 75mg cholesterol, 550mg sodium, 7g total carbohydrate (0.5g fiber, 3g sugar), 27g protein, 2%DV vitamin A, 0%DV vitamin C, 2%DV calcium, 6%DV iron.

Note: The flavor of the chicken improves if you marinate it in the Italian dressing for a few hours before cooking.

Chicken and Veggie Bake

Sara Puskar
Abingdon, MD

Makes 8 servings
(Ideal slow-cooker size: 4-quart)

8 boneless, skinless chicken breast halves
black pepper to taste
1 tsp. garlic powder
16-oz. bottle fat-free Italian salad dressing, divided
2 15-oz. cans whole potatoes, drained
1 lb. frozen Italian veggies, or green beans
8-oz. can water chestnuts, optional

1. Sprinkle chicken with pepper and garlic powder.
2. Put chicken in bottom of slow cooker. Pour half of salad dressing over meat, making sure that all pieces are glazed.
3. Add potatoes, vegetables, and water chestnuts. Pour remaining salad dressing over, again making sure that the vegetables are all lightly coated.
4. Cover. Cook on high 4 hours or on low 7-8 hours.

Per Serving: 200 calories (35 calories from fat), 3.5g total fat (1g saturated, 0g trans), 75mg cholesterol, 480mg sodium, 12g total carbohydrate (3g fiber, 2g sugar), 29g protein, 50%DV vitamin A, 4%DV vitamin C, 4%DV calcium, 10%DV iron.

Chicken Italiano
Mary C. Casey
Scranton, PA

Makes 6 servings
(Ideal slow-cooker size: 4-quart)

2 large whole boneless, skinless chicken
  breasts, each cut in 3 pieces
3/4 tsp. salt
1/4 tsp. black pepper
1/2 tsp. dried oregano
1/2 tsp. dried basil
2 bay leaves
26-oz. jar low-sodium meatless spaghetti
  sauce

1. Place chicken in bottom of slow cooker.
2. Sprinkle seasonings over chicken.
3. Pour sauce over seasoned meat, stirring
to be sure chicken is completely covered.
4. Cover. Cook on low 6 hours or on high
3 1/2-4 hours.
5. Serve over pasta.

Per Serving: 120 calories (30 calories from fat), 3.5g total
fat (0g saturated, 0g trans), 25mg cholesterol, 820mg
sodium, 10g total carbohydrate (2g fiber, 5g sugar), 11g
protein, 10%DV vitamin A, 6%DV vitamin C, 4%DV
calcium, 6%DV iron.

Note: You may substitute 2 1-lb. cans of diced
tomatoes, undrained, for the spaghetti sauce. Or
use 2 cups diced fresh tomatoes and 1-lb. can
crushed tomatoes for the spaghetti sauce.

Jane's Slow-Cooked Italian Chicken
Dorothy VanDeest
Memphis, TN

Makes 8 servings
(Ideal slow-cooker size: 5 quart)

3 lbs. boneless, skinless chicken breast
  pieces
1 pkg. dry Italian dressing mix
10 3/4-oz. can 98% fat-free cream of
  mushroom soup
4-oz. can mushrooms, drained
8 ozs. fat-free sour cream or fat-free plain
  yogurt

1. Place chicken in slow cooker.
2. Mix together Italian dressing mix, soup,
and mushrooms. Stir into chicken.
3. Cook on low 6-8 hours.
4. With a slotted spoon, lift chicken out of
cooker. Place in a covered dish and keep
warm. Combine cooking juices with sour
cream or yogurt in slow cooker. Cover and
heat until warmed through.
5. When ready to serve, place chicken on
bed of rice or noodles and pour sauce over top.

Per Serving: 340 calories (70 calories from fat), 7 total fat
(2.5g saturated, 0g trans), 150mg cholesterol, 750mg
sodium, 11g total carbohydrate (0g fiber, 4g sugar), 55g
protein, 4%DV vitamin A, 0%DV vitamin C, 8%DV
calcium, 10%DV iron.

Zesty Chicken Breasts

Barb Yoder
Angola, IN

Makes 6 servings
(Ideal slow-cooker size: 4-quart)

6 chicken breast halves
2 14½-oz. cans diced tomatoes, undrained
1 small can jalapenos, sliced and drained, optional
¼ cup reduced-fat, creamy peanut butter
2 Tbsp. fresh cilantro, chopped, optional

1. Remove skin from chicken, but leave bone in.
2. Mix all ingredients, except chicken in medium-sized bowl.
3. Pour one-third of sauce in bottom of slow cooker sprayed with non-fat cooking spray. Place chicken on top.
4. Pour remaining sauce over chicken.
5. Cover. Cook on high 3-4 hours or on low 6-8 hours.
6. Remove from slow cooker gently. Chicken will be very tender and will fall off the bones.

Per Serving: 230 calories (60 calories from fat), 7g total fat (1.5g saturated, 0g trans), 75mg cholesterol, 650mg sodium, 11g total carbohydrate (4g fiber, 5g sugar), 31g protein, 8%DV vitamin A, 10%DV vitamin C, 10%DV calcium, 8%DV iron.

Parmesan Chicken

Karen Waggoner
Joplin, MO

Makes 8 servings
(Ideal slow-cooker size: 4- or 5-quart)

8 boneless, skinless chicken breast halves (about 2 lbs.)
½ cup water
1 cup fat-free mayonnaise
½ cup grated fat-free Parmesan cheese
2 tsp. dried oregano
¼ tsp. black pepper
¼ tsp. paprika

1. Place chicken and water in slow cooker.
2. Cover. Cook on high 2 hours.
3. Mix remaining ingredients. Spread over chicken.
4. Cover. Cook on high 2-2½ hours.

Per Serving: 180 calories (35 calories from fat), 4g total fat (1g saturated, 0g trans), 75mg cholesterol, 400mg sodium, 4g total carbohydrate (0.5g fiber, 2g sugar), 28g protein, 2%DV vitamin A, 0%DV vitamin C, 8%DV calcium, 6%DV iron.

Baked Chicken Breasts

Nadine L. Martinitz
Salina, KS

Makes 6 servings
(Ideal slow-cooker size: 4- or 5-quart)

3 whole chicken breasts, skin removed and halved
10¾-oz. can low-sodium condensed cream of chicken soup
½ cup cooking sherry
4-oz. can sliced mushrooms, drained
1 tsp. Worcestershire sauce
1 tsp. dried tarragon leaves
 or dried rosemary
¼ tsp. garlic powder

1. Rinse chicken breasts and pat dry. Place in slow cooker.
2. Combine remaining ingredients and pour over chicken breasts, making sure that all pieces are glazed with the sauce.
3. Cover and cook on low 8-10 hours or on high 4-5 hours.
4. Serve over mashed potatoes or noodles.

Per Serving: 340 calories (70 calories from fat), 7 total fat (2.5g saturated, 0g trans), 150mg cholesterol, 750mg sodium, 11g total carbohydrate (0g fiber, 4g sugar), 55g protein, 4%DV vitamin A, 0%DV vitamin C, 8%DV calcium, 10%DV iron.

Chicken Delicious

Janice Crist
Quinter, KS

Makes 12 servings
(Ideal slow-cooker size: 6-quart)

12 boneless, skinless chicken breast halves
¼ cup lemon juice
1 tsp. salt
½ tsp. black pepper
¼ tsp. celery salt
¼ tsp. paprika
10¾-oz. can fat-free, low-sodium cream of mushroom soup
10¾-oz. can fat-free, low-sodium cream of celery soup
⅓ cup dry sherry, or white wine
grated fat-free, low-sodium Parmesan cheese

1. Mix together lemon juice, salt, black pepper, celery salt, and paprika in medium-sized bowl. Stir in mushroom and celery soups and sherry or wine.
2. Dip each chicken breast half in seasoned soup mixture, then place chicken pieces in slow cooker.
3. When all chicken is in cooker, pour remaining soup mixture over chicken. Sprinkle with cheese.
4. Cover. Cook on low 8-10 hours.
5. Serve with rice.

Per Serving: 160 calories (35 calories from fat), 3.5g total fat (1g saturated, 0g trans), 75mg cholesterol, 470mg sodium, 2g total carbohydrate (0g fiber, 0g sugar), 27g protein, 0%DV vitamin A, 0%DV vitamin C, 2%DV calcium, 6%DV iron.

Ruth's Slow-Cooker Chicken

Sara Harter Fredette
Williamsburg, MA

Makes 6 servings
(Ideal slow-cooker size: 4-quart)

6 boneless, skinless chicken breast halves
10¾-oz. can fat-free, low-sodium
cream of mushroom soup
1 pkg. low-sodium dry mushroom soup
mix
¼-½ cup fat-free sour cream
4-oz. can mushrooms, drained

1. Stir together mushroom soup and dry soup mix. Dip each chicken breast half in mixture and then place in slow cooker.
2. Pour remaining soup mix over chicken pieces.
3. Cover. Cook on low 6-8 hours.
4. Just before serving, stir in sour cream and mushrooms. Cover. Turn cooker to high and heat for 10 minutes.
5. Serve over noodles.

Per Serving: 200 calories (45 calories from fat), 5g total fat (1.5g saturated, 0g trans), 75mg cholesterol, 620mg sodium, 8g total carbohydrate (0g fiber, 1g sugar), 28g protein, 0%DV vitamin A, 0%DV vitamin C, 4%DV calcium, 6%DV iron.

Note: Leftover sauce makes a flavorful topping for grilled hamburgers.

Chicken "Delite"

Rose Hankins
Stevensville, MD

Makes 8 servings
(Ideal slow-cooker size: 5- or 6-quart)

8 boneless, skinless chicken breast halves
1 cup onion, chopped
½ cup celery, chopped
2 chicken bouillon cubes
2 cups water
2 cups steamed rice
¼ cup fresh parsley

1. Combine all ingredients except rice and fresh parsley in slow cooker.
2. Cover. Cook on low 8 hours.
3. Add steamed rice and parsley, stir, and cook for 10 minutes.

Per Serving: 130 calories (15 calories from fat), 2g total fat (0g saturated, 0g trans), 35mg cholesterol, 340mg sodium, 14g total carbohydrate (0.5g fiber, 2g sugar), 15g protein, 2%DV vitamin A, 2%DV vitamin C, 2%DV calcium, 6%DV iron.

Note: You can substitute brown rice or pasta in place of the steamed rice.

Apricot Mustard Chicken

Lee Ann Hazlett
Delavan, WI

Makes 6 servings
(Ideal slow-cooker size: 5- or 6-quart)

11½-oz. can apricot nectar
2 Tbsp. Dijon mustard
1 clove garlic, minced
¼ tsp. fresh ginger, grated
¼ tsp. cayenne pepper
¼ tsp. ground allspice
¼ tsp. turmeric
¼ tsp. ground cardamom
6 boneless, skinless chicken breast halves
4 cups prepared couscous or wild rice
   (blended is good, too)

1. Combine all ingredients except chicken and couscous in slow cooker.
2. Add chicken, turning it to make sure all sides are covered in sauce.
3. Cover. Cook on low 5-6 hours or on high 2½-3 hours.
4. Remove chicken and arrange over warm couscous or rice. Pour the sauce over the chicken and serve.

Per Serving: 300 calories (35 calories from fat), 4g total fat (1g saturated, 0g trans), 75mg cholesterol, 200mg sodium, 33g total carbohydrate (2g fiber, 8g sugar), 31g protein, 15%DV vitamin A, 2%DV vitamin C, 4%DV calcium, 10%DV iron.

Mandarin Orange Chicken

Ann VanDoren
Lady Lake, FL

Makes 4 servings
(Ideal slow-cooker size: 3- or 4-quart)

4 boneless, skinless chicken breast halves
1 medium-sized onion, thinly sliced
¼ cup orange juice concentrate
1 tsp. poultry seasoning
½ tsp. salt
11-oz. can mandarin oranges, drained,
   with 3 Tbsp. juice reserved
2 Tbsp. flour

1. Place chicken in slow cooker.
2. Combine onion, orange juice concentrate, poultry seasoning, and salt. Pour over chicken.
3. Cover. Cook on low 4-5 hours.
4. Remove chicken and keep warm. Reserve cooking juices.
5. In a saucepan, combine 3 Tbsp. reserved mandarin orange juice and flour. Stir until smooth.
6. Stir in chicken cooking juices. Bring to a boil. Stir and cook for 2 minutes to thicken.
7. Stir in mandarin oranges. Pour over chicken.
8. Serve with rice or pasta.

Per Serving: 240 calories (30 calories from fat), 3.5g total fat (1g saturated, 0g trans), 75mg cholesterol, 360mg sodium, 25g total carbohydrate (1g fiber, 20g sugar), 28g protein, 10%DV vitamin A, 30%DV vitamin C, 4%DV calcium, 10%DV iron.

Golden Chicken and Noodles

Betty B. Dennison
Grove City, PA

Makes 8-10 servings
(Ideal slow-cooker size: 5-quart)

2 10¾-oz. cans 98% fat-free cream of
  chicken soup
½ cup water
¼ cup lemon juice
1 Tbsp. Dijon mustard
1½ tsp. garlic powder
¼-½ tsp. black pepper, according to your
  taste preference
6 large carrots, sliced
8 boneless chicken breast halves
8 cups hot, cooked egg noodles
parsley, if desired

1. Combine cream of chicken soup, water,
lemon juice, mustard, garlic powder, pepper,
and carrots in slow cooker.
2. Cut the chicken breast halves into
quarters or smaller chunks. Stir into mixture in
cooker.
3. Cover. Cook on low 6-7 hours.
4. Serve over egg noodles.

Per Serving: 450 calories (90 calories from fat), 10g total fat
(2.5g saturated, 0g trans), 130mg cholesterol, 740mg
sodium, 51g total carbohydrate (3g fiber, 5g sugar), 37g
protein, 200%DV vitamin A, 10%DV vitamin C, 6%DV
calcium, 25%DV iron.

*Note: If you prefer a thicker sauce, and if you are
willing to add a few more calories and carbs to
your meal, remove the cooked chicken from the
slow cooker after Step 3. Keep warm. Remove ½
cup cooking juices from cooker and allow to cool
for a few minutes. Stir 2-3 Tbsp. flour or
cornstarch into juices until smooth. Then stir
back into juices in cooker. Cover and cook
another 15 minutes, until juices are thickened.
Stir in chicken and serve.*

Oriental Chicken

Donna Lantgen
Rapid City, SD

Makes 6 servings
(Ideal slow-cooker size: 5- or 6-quart)

6 boneless, skinless chicken breast halves
½ cup light soy sauce
½ cup honey
2 Tbsp. sesame seeds, optional

1. Mix together soy sauce, honey, and
sesame seeds, if desired.
2. Place chicken in slow cooker, spooning 2
Tbsp. of soy-honey-seeds mixture over each
breast. Pour any remaining sauce over top
after all chicken is in the cooker.
3. Cook on low 4-6 hours, or until meat
juices run clear.

Per Serving: 170 calories (15 calories from fat), 1.5g total
fat (0g saturated, 0g trans), 35mg cholesterol, 740mg
sodium, 25g total carbohydrate (0g fiber, 22g sugar), 15g
protein, 0%DV vitamin A, 0%DV vitamin C, 2%DV
calcium, 6%DV iron.

Low-Fat Glazed Chicken

Martha Hershey, Ronks, PA
Jean Butzer, Batavia, NY

Makes 6 servings
(Ideal slow-cooker size: 4 quart)

6-oz. can frozen concentrated orange juice,
  thawed
½ tsp. dried marjoram
¼ tsp. nutmeg
¼ tsp. garlic powder
6 skinless chicken breast halves
¼ cup water
2 Tbsp. cornstarch

1. Mix orange juice concentrate with marjoram, nutmeg, and garlic powder.

2. Dip chicken breasts in sauce. Place in slow cooker.

3. Pour remaining orange juice mixture over chicken.

4. Cover and cook on low 6 hours or on high 3-4 hours.

5. Remove chicken from slow cooker and keep warm on a platter.

6. Pour remaining liquid in a saucepan.

7. Mix the cornstarch in water and pour into saucepan. Cook until thickened.

8. Pour sauce over the chicken and serve with rice or noodles.

Per Serving: 130 calories (15 calories from fat), 1.5g total fat (0g saturated, 0g trans), 35mg cholesterol, 35mg sodium, 13g total carbohydrate (0g fiber, 11g sugar), 14g protein, 2%DV vitamin A, 30%DV vitamin C, 2%DV calcium, 4%DV iron.

Notes:

1. To add texture and flavor, add 3 Granny Smith apples, cored and sliced, immediately following Step 4. Continue cooking 1 more hour on low. Then remove chicken and apples and keep warm while proceeding to Step 6.

2. If you are not concerned about sodium intake, you may increase the garlic powder to ¹/₂ tsp., or add ¹/₂ tsp. salt to Step 1.

Coq au Vin
Nancy Savage
Factoryville, PA

Makes 6 servings
(Ideal slow-cooker size: 4- or 5-quart)

4 slices turkey bacon
1¹/₂ cups frozen pearl onions
1 cup fresh, sliced, button mushrooms
1 clove garlic, minced
1 tsp. dried thyme leaves
¹/₄ tsp. coarse ground black pepper
6 boneless, skinless chicken breast halves
¹/₂ cup dry red wine
³/₄ cup fat-free, low-sodium chicken broth
¹/₄ cup tomato paste
3 Tbsp. flour

1. Cook bacon in medium skillet over medium heat. Drain and crumble.

2. Layer ingredients in slow cooker in the following order: onions, crumbled bacon, mushrooms, garlic, thyme, pepper, chicken, wine, and broth.

3. Cover. Cook on low 5-6 hours.

4. Remove chicken and vegetables. Cover. Keep warm.

5. Ladle ¹/₂ cup cooking liquid into small bowl. Allow to cool slightly.

6. Turn slow cooker to high. Cover.

7. Mix removed liquid, tomato paste, and flour until smooth.

8. Return tomato mixture to slow cooker.

9. Cover. Cook 15 minutes or until thickened.

10. Serve over egg noodles, if desired.

Per Serving: 230 calories (45 calories from fat), 5g total fat (1.5g saturated, 0g trans), 80mg cholesterol, 230mg sodium, 11g total carbohydrate (2g fiber, 4g sugar), 31g protein, 6%DV vitamin A, 6%DV vitamin C, 4%DV calcium, 15%DV iron.

Delicious Chicken & Vegetables

Tina Goss
Duenweg, MO

Makes 6 servings
(Ideal slow-cooker size: 4- or 5-quart)

1 cup fresh mushrooms, sliced
2 carrots, sliced
2 onions, sliced
2 celery ribs with leaves, cut in 1" sections
6 boneless, skinless chicken breast halves
1 tsp. salt
1/2 tsp. black pepper
dash of red pepper flakes
1 cup water
1/2 cup white wine
1/2 tsp. dried basil
2 tsp. dried parsley

1. Combine mushrooms, carrots, onions, and celery in slow cooker.
2. Lay chicken breasts on top.
3. Mix together salt, black pepper, red pepper flakes, water, and wine. Sprinkle with basil and parsley.
4. Cover. Cook on high 3½-5 hours.
5. To serve, place chicken in center of platter. Using slotted spoon, place vegetables around the chicken. Serve remaining broth in a gravy bowl.

Per Serving: 190 calories (30 calories from fat), 3.5g total fat (1g saturated, 0g trans), 75mg cholesterol, 470mg sodium, 7g total carbohydrate (2g fiber, 4g sugar), 28g protein, 100%DV vitamin A, 2%DV vitamin C, 4%DV calcium, 8%DV iron.

Note: If you'd like more vegetables, add another 1/2 cup mushrooms, 1 more carrot, 1 more onion, and an additional celery rib. You may need to add another hour to the cooking time so that the vegetables are done to your liking.

Smothered Chicken

Marilyn Mowry
Irving, TX

Makes 4 servings
(Ideal slow-cooker size: 4- or 5-quart)

4 boneless, skinless chicken breast halves, each 1/4 lb. in weight
flour as needed (about 3 Tbsp.)
1 Tbsp. vegetable oil
1/2 tsp. salt
1/4 tsp. black pepper
2 cups carrots, cut in 1/2" diagonal slices
1 cup onion, cut in 1/4" slices
1 garlic clove, minced
2 4-oz. cans mushrooms, drained
1/4 cup flour
14½-oz. can fat-free, low-sodium chicken broth
1 Tbsp. fresh thyme, chopped, or 1 tsp. dried thyme
chopped fresh chives, optional

1. Dredge chicken in flour to coat. Saute in hot oil in skillet, just until browned. Season with salt and pepper.
2. Combine all ingredients except fresh thyme and fresh chives in slow cooker
3. Cook on low 6-8 hours or until vegetables are tender. Stir in fresh herbs and serve.

Per Serving: 310 calories (70 calories from fat), 7 total fat (1.5g saturated, 0g trans), 75mg cholesterol, 930mg sodium, 26g total carbohydrate (6g fiber, 7g sugar), 34g protein, 250%DV vitamin A, 10%DV vitamin C, 6%DV calcium, 20%DV iron.

Note: You may skip Step One for a healthier meal.

Slow-Cooked Chicken & Mushroom Stew

Joette Proz
Kalona, IA

Makes 4 servings
(Ideal slow-cooker size: 4- or 5-quart)

10¾-oz. can 98% fat-free cream of
   mushroom soup
half a soup can water
4 boneless, skinless chicken breast halves
½ tsp. salt
¼ tsp. black pepper
½ lb. fresh medium-sized white
   mushrooms, or a variety of mushrooms,
   including portabella, cut-up
1 cup baby carrots
2 ribs celery, cut into small pieces
½ tsp. garlic powder

1. Combine soup and water in slow cooker.
2. Cut chicken into 2" chunks. Sprinkle
with salt and pepper. Place in slow cooker.
3. Add mushrooms, carrots, celery, and
garlic powder. Stir gently to mix.
4. Cover. Cook on low 6-8 hours or until
chicken is done and internal temperature
reaches 170°.
5. Serve with rice.

Per Serving: 230 calories (50 calories from fat), 5g total fat
(1.5g saturated, 0.5g trans), 75mg cholesterol, 900mg
sodium, 14g total carbohydrate (2g fiber, 4g sugar), 30g
protein, 150%DV vitamin A, 8%DV vitamin C, 6%DV
calcium, 10%DV iron.

*Note: If you're a mushroom lover, double the
amount of mushrooms! You may want to increase
the salt, pepper, and garlic powder if you add
mushrooms.*

Roasted Chicken

Kristen Allen
Houston, TX

Makes 4 servings
(Ideal slow-cooker size: 4- or 5-quart)

1 medium-sized onion, cut in 8 pieces
1 lb. frozen, boneless, skinless chicken
   breasts
3-4 carrots, peeled and cut into 4 pieces
2 potatoes, cleaned and cut into chunks
4 ribs celery, each cut into 4 pieces
1 pkg. herb-with-garlic dry soup mix
10¾-oz. can 98% fat-free cream of
   mushroom soup

1. Place onions on bottom of slow cooker.
Place chicken on top.
2. Add carrots, potatoes, and celery.
Sprinkle dry soup mix over all.
3. Spread mushroom soup over top.
4. Cover. Cook on low 6-8 hours.

Per Serving: 460 calories (70 calories from fat), 8g total fat
(2.5g saturated, 0.5g trans), 100mg cholesterol, 1070mg
sodium, 53g total carbohydrate (5g fiber, 7g sugar), 42g
protein, 200%DV vitamin A, 20%DV vitamin C, 8%DV
calcium, 15%DV iron.

Chicken Dinner

Doris Perkins
Mashpee, MA

Makes 4 servings
(Ideal slow-cooker size: 5- or 6-quart)

4 medium-sized potatoes, cut into chunks
4 carrots, sliced
1 large onion, chopped
4 cabbage wedges
1 can cream of mushroom soup
1/2 cup water
4 boneless, skinless chicken breast halves

1. Layer vegetables in bottom of slow cooker.
2. In small bowl, mix together soup and water. Spoon half of mixture over vegetables.
3. Place chicken over soup and vegetables.
4. Add remaining diluted soup.
5. Cook on high for 4 hours or on low for 7-8 hours, or until vegetables are done.

Per Serving: 530 calories (80 calories from fat), 9g total fat (2.5g saturated, 0g trans), 80mg cholesterol, 780mg sodium, 76g total carbohydrate (18g fiber, 20g sugar), 41g protein, 300%DV vitamin A, 200%DV vitamin C, 30%DV calcium, 35%DV iron.

Note: If your diet allows, you may want to add 1 tsp. salt and 1/2 tsp. black pepper to soup and water mixture in Step 2.

Chicken and Vegetable Casserole

Cindy Krestynick
Glen Lyon, PA

Makes 8 servings
(Ideal slow-cooker size: 5-quart)

8 boneless, skinless chicken breast halves
2 cups potatoes, peeled and quartered
3-4 carrots, peeled and cut in chunks
1 onion, chopped
1 rib celery, chopped
1 cup frozen lima beans
1 1/3 cups water
1/2 tsp. salt
1/4 tsp. black pepper
10 3/4 -oz. can cream of chicken soup

1. Rinse chicken. Pat dry. Place in slow cooker.
2. Add potatoes, carrots, onion, celery, lima beans, water, salt, and pepper.
3. Pour cream of chicken soup over all.
4. Cover. Cook on low 3-4 hours.

Per Serving: 190 calories (35 calories from fat), 4g total fat (1g saturated, 0g trans), 40mg cholesterol, 500mg sodium, 20g total carbohydrate (4g fiber, 4g sugar), 17g protein, 100%DV vitamin A, 10%DV vitamin C, 4%DV calcium, 10%DV iron.

Note: Add more vegetables if you like.
If you are not concerned about your sodium intake, you may want to increase the salt to 3/4 tsp. and/or add 1/2 tsp. seasoning salt or Mrs. Dash's seasoning in Step 2.

Chicken Soft Tacos

Kristen Allen
Houston, TX

Makes 6 servings
(Ideal slow-cooker size: 5- or 6-quart)

1-1½ lbs. frozen, boneless, skinless
chicken breasts
14½-oz. can low-sodium diced tomatoes
with green chilies
1 envelope low-sodium taco seasoning

1. Place chicken breasts in slow cooker.
2. Mix tomatoes and taco seasoning. Pour over chicken.
3. Cover. Cook on low 6-8 hours.
4. Serve in soft tortillas. Top with salsa, low-fat shredded cheddar cheese, guacamole if your diet allows, and fresh tomatoes.

Per Serving: 100 calories (20 calories from fat), 2.5g total fat (0.5g saturated, 0g trans), 50mg cholesterol, 300mg sodium, 2g total carbohydrate (0.5g fiber, 1g sugar), 18g protein, 0%DV vitamin A, 0%DV vitamin C, 2%DV calcium, 4%DV iron.

Chicken and Rice

Batty Chalker
Dalhart, TX

Makes 6 servings
(Ideal slow-cooker size: 4-quart)

10¾-oz. can cream of chicken soup
1 pkg. dry onion soup mix
2½ cups water
1 cup long grain rice, uncooked
6 ozs. boneless, skinless chicken breast
tenders
¼ tsp. black pepper

1. Combine all ingredients in slow cooker.
2. Cook on low 5-6 hours.
3. Stir occasionally.

Per Serving: 140 calories (35 calories from fat), 4g total fat (1g saturated, 0g trans), 20mg cholesterol, 520mg sodium, 16g total carbohydrate (0.5g fiber, 1g sugar), 8g protein, 4%DV vitamin A, 0%DV vitamin C, 2%DV calcium, 4%DV iron.

Marinated Chicken Tenders

Elsie Schlabach
Millersburg, OH

Makes 8 servings
(Ideal slow-cooker size: 6-quart)

3 lbs. chicken tenders
15-oz. bottle fat-free Italian salad dressing
1 Tbsp. vegetable oil
2½ cups flour
½ tsp. salt
½ tsp. Lawry's Seasoned Salt

1. Rinse chicken. Pat dry.
2. Cut chicken tenders into 1" square pieces and place them in a 9 x 13 pan.
3. Pour Italian dressing over meat and marinate for at least 3 hours.
4. Place flour and seasonings in sturdy plastic bag. Add one-third of the cubed chicken. Toss until all pieces are well coated.
5. Remove chicken (reserve flour mixture in plastic bag). Brown in vegetable oil in skillet. Remove chicken with slotted spoon. Place in slow cooker.
6. Repeat steps 4 and 5 with remaining chicken.
7. Cover. Cook on low 2-3 hours.

Per Serving: 410 calories (80 calories from fat), 9g total fat (2.5g saturated, 0g trans), 145mg cholesterol, 990mg sodium, 24g total carbohydrate (1g fiber, 4g sugar), 56g protein, 0%DV vitamin A, 0%DV vitamin C, 6%DV calcium, 15%DV iron.

Curried Chicken

Sharon Miller
Holmesville, OH

Makes 7 servings
(Ideal slow-cooker size: 4-quart)

1 1/2 lbs. uncooked boneless skinless chicken breasts, cubed
2 1/2 cups apples, finely chopped
10 3/4-oz. can 98% fat-free cream of mushroom soup, undiluted
4-oz. can mushroom pieces
1 medium-sized onion, chopped
1/2 cup skim milk
2-3 tsp. curry powder, according to your taste preference
1/4 tsp. paprika
1 cup peas, thawed

1. Combine all ingredients except peas in greased slow cooker.
2. Cook on low 5-6 hours.
3. Add peas.
4. Cook an additional hour.
5. Serve over noodles or rice if desired.

Per Serving: 200 calories (35 calories from fat), 4g total fat (1g saturated, 0g trans), 55mg cholesterol, 490mg sodium, 20g total carbohydrate (4g fiber, 11g sugar), 22g protein, 6%DV vitamin A, 4%DV vitamin C, 6%DV calcium, 8%DV iron.

Chicken Curry

Michelle Steffen
Harrisonburg, VA

Makes 6 servings
(Ideal slow-cooker size: 4-quart)

1 large tart cooking apple, unpeeled, cored, and diced
1 large onion, finely chopped
3 ribs celery, thinly sliced
1-2 Tbsp. curry powder, according to your taste preference
1-2 Tbsp. canola oil
1/2 tsp. salt
1/4 tsp. black pepper
2 cups chicken breast, cooked and diced
1-2 cups low-fat, low-sodium chicken broth

1. Sauté apple, onion, celery, and curry powder in skillet in canola oil until tender and glazed.
2. Season with salt and pepper. Combine in slow cooker with chicken and chicken broth.
3. Cover. Cook on high for 30 minutes, and then on low for 90 minutes.
4. Serve over cooked brown rice or sweet potatoes. Top with your choice of raisins, pineapple tidbits, toasted almond slivers, plain yogurt, and toasted coconut.

Per Serving: 220 calories (40 calories from fat), 4g total fat (1g saturated, 0g trans), 35mg cholesterol, 170mg sodium, 28g total carbohydrate (2g fiber, 4g sugar), 17g protein, 0%DV vitamin A, 0%DV vitamin C, 4%DV calcium, 10%DV iron.

Chicken Jambalaya
Martha Ann Auker
Landisburg, PA

Makes 6 servings
(Ideal slow-cooker size: 5-quart)

1 lb. uncooked boneless, skinless chicken
  breast, cubed
3 cups fat-free chicken broth
3/4 cup water
1 1/2 cups uncooked brown rice
4 ozs. reduced-fat, smoked turkey sausage,
  diced
1/2 cup celery with leaves, thinly sliced
1/2 cup onion, chopped
1/2 cup green bell pepper, chopped
2 tsp. Cajun seasoning
2 garlic cloves, minced
1/8 tsp. hot pepper sauce, optional
1 bay leaf
14 1/2-oz. can no-salt diced tomatoes,
  undrained

1. In a large nonstick skillet, sauté chicken
2-3 minutes.
2. Stir together remaining ingredients in
slow cooker.
3. Add sautéed chicken.
4. Cover. Cook on high 6 hours.

Per Serving: 370 calories (60 calories from fat), 7g total fat
(1.5g saturated, 0g trans), 75mg cholesterol, 620mg
sodium, 42g total carbohydrate (4g fiber, 4g sugar), 34g
protein, 4%DV vitamin A, 10%DV vitamin C, 10%DV
calcium, 15%DV iron.

Note: You can substitute 1 cup low-sodium
tomato juice for 3/4 cup water.

Dawn's Low-Fat Chicken Cacciatore
Dawn Day
Westminster, CA

Makes 10 servings
(Ideal slow-cooker size: 3-quart)

2 lbs. uncooked boneless, skinless chicken
  breasts, cubed
1/2 lb. fresh mushrooms
1 bell pepper, chopped
1 medium-sized onion, chopped
12-oz. can low-sodium chopped tomatoes
6-oz. can low-sodium tomato paste
12-oz. can low-sodium tomato sauce
1/2 tsp. dried oregano
1/2 tsp. dried basil
1/2 tsp. garlic powder
1/2 tsp. salt
1/2 tsp. black pepper

1. Combine all ingredients in slow cooker.
2. Cover. Cook on low 8 hours.
3. Serve over rice or whole wheat, or
semolina, pasta.

Per Serving: 200 calories (30 calories from fat), 3.5g total
fat (1g saturated, 0g trans), 75mg cholesterol, 500mg
sodium, 10g total carbohydrate (2g fiber, 4g sugar), 30g
protein, 10%DV vitamin A, 20%DV vitamin C, 6%DV
calcium, 10%DV iron.

Note: You can substitute 2 cups fresh diced
tomatoes for 12-oz. can tomatoes.

  *If you are not concerned about increasing your
sodium intake, you may want to use 1 tsp. salt
instead of 1/2 tsp.*

Cape Breton Chicken

Joanne Kennedy
Plattsburgh, NY

Makes 5 servings
(Ideal slow-cooker size: 4-quart)

4 uncooked boneless, skinless chicken
   breast halves, cubed
1 medium-sized onion, chopped
1 small-medium-sized green bell pepper,
   chopped
1 cup celery, chopped
1 quart low-sodium stewed, or crushed,
   tomatoes
1 cup water
1/2 cup tomato paste
2 Tbsp. Worcestershire sauce
2 Tbsp. brown sugar
1 tsp. black pepper

1. Combine all ingredients in slow cooker.
2. Cover. Cook on low 7 hours.
3. Serve over rice.

Per Serving: 240 calories (25 calories from fat), 2.5g total
fat (0.5g saturated, 0g trans), 60mg cholesterol, 190mg
sodium, 27g total carbohydrate (6g fiber, 16g sugar), 25g
protein, 30%DV vitamin A, 40%DV vitamin C, 10%DV
calcium, 25%DV iron.

Chicken and Bean Torta

Vicki Dinkel, Sharon Springs, KS

Makes 6 servings
(Ideal slow-cooker size: 4- or 5-quart)

1 lb. uncooked boneless, skinless chicken
   breasts
1 medium-sized onion
1/2 tsp. garlic salt
1/4 tsp. black pepper
15-oz. can ranch-style black beans
15-oz. can low-sodium diced tomatoes
   with green chilies
4 tortillas
1 1/2 cups grated low-fat cheddar cheese
salsa
fat-free sour cream
lettuce
tomatoes

1. Cut chicken in small pieces. Brown with
onion in nonstick skillet. Drain well.
2. Season with garlic salt and pepper. Stir in
beans and tomatoes.
3. Place strips of foil on bottom and up
sides of slow cooker forming an X. Spray foil
and cooker lightly with non-fat cooking spray.
4. Place 1 tortilla on bottom of cooker.
Spoon on one-third of chicken mixture and
one-quarter of the cheese.
5. Repeat layers, ending with a tortilla
sprinkled with cheese on top.
6. Cover. Cook on low 4-5 hours.
7. Remove to platter using foil strips as
handles. Gently pull out foil and discard.
8. Serve with salsa, sour cream, lettuce, and
tomatoes.

Per Serving: 510 calories (90 calories from fat), 10g total fat
(3.5g saturated, 0.5g trans), 75mg cholesterol, 1250mg
sodium, 60g total carbohydrate (9g fiber, 11g sugar), 45g
protein, 20%DV vitamin A, 30%DV vitamin C, 45%DV
calcium, 25%DV iron.

*Note: If your diet allows, use mild Rotel tomatoes
in place of the tomatoes with green chilies.*

Italian Chicken Stew

Mary Longenecker
Bethel, PA

Makes 4 servings
(Ideal slow-cooker size: 5- or 6-quart)

2 uncooked boneless, skinless chicken
   breast halves, cut in 1¹/₂″ pieces
19-oz. can cannellini beans, drained and
   rinsed
15¹/₂-oz. can kidney beans, drained and
   rinsed
14¹/₂-oz. can low-sodium diced tomatoes,
   undrained
1 cup celery, chopped
1 cup carrots, sliced
2 small garlic cloves, coarsely chopped
1 cup water
¹/₂ cup dry red wine, or low-fat chicken
   broth
3 Tbsp. tomato paste
1 Tbsp. sugar
1¹/₂ tsp. dried Italian seasoning

1. Combine chicken, cannellini beans,
kidney beans, tomatoes, celery, carrots, and
garlic in slow cooker. Mix well.
2. In medium bowl, combine all remaining
ingredients. Mix well. Pour over chicken and
vegetables. Mix well.
3. Cover. Cook on low 5-6 hours or on high
3 hours.

Per Serving: 340 calories (25 calories from fat), 2.5g total
fat (0.5g saturated, 0g trans), 35mg cholesterol, 1460mg
sodium, 53g total carbohydrate (14g fiber, 12g sugar), 29g
protein, 100%DV vitamin A, 20%DV vitamin C, 20%DV
calcium, 25%DV iron.

Chicken Tortilla Casserole

Jeanne Allen
Rye, CO

Makes 8-10 servings
(Ideal slow-cooker size: 5- or 6-quart)

4 whole boneless, skinless chicken breasts,
   cooked and cut in 1″ pieces (reserve ¹/₄
   cup broth chicken was cooked in)
10 6″ flour tortillas, cut in strips about ¹/₂″
   wide x 2″ long
2 medium-sized onions, chopped
1 tsp. canola oil
10³/₄-oz. can fat-free chicken broth
10³/₄-oz. can 98% fat-free cream of
   mushroom soup
2 4-oz. cans mild green chilies, chopped
1 egg
1 cup low-fat cheddar cheese, grated

1. Pour reserved chicken broth in slow
cooker sprayed with non-fat cooking spray.
2. Scatter half the tortilla strips in bottom of
slow cooker.
3. Mix remaining ingredients together,
except the second half of the tortilla strips and
the cheese.
4. Layer half the chicken mixture into the
cooker, followed by the other half of the
tortillas, followed by the rest of the chicken
mix.
5. Cover. Cook on low 4-6 hours or on high
3-5 hours.
6. Add the cheese to the top of the dish
during the last 20-30 minutes of cooking.
7. Uncover and allow casserole to rest 15
minutes before serving.

Per Serving: 280 calories (70 calories from fat), 7g total fat
(2.5g saturated, 1g trans), 65mg cholesterol, 570mg
sodium, 28g total carbohydrate (2g fiber, 3g sugar), 23g
protein, 2%DV vitamin A, 2%DV vitamin C, 20%DV
calcium, 15%DV iron.

Chicken and Dumplings

Annabelle Unternahrer
Shipshewana, IN

Makes 5-6 servings
(Ideal slow-cooker size: 3- or 4-quart)

1 lb. uncooked boneless, skinless chicken breasts, cut in 1" cubes
1 lb. frozen vegetables of your choice
1 medium-sized onion, diced
2 12-oz. jars fat-free low-sodium chicken broth, divided
1½ cups low-fat buttermilk biscuit mix

1. Combine chicken, vegetables, onion, and chicken broth (reserve ½ cup, plus 1 Tbsp., broth) in slow cooker.
2. Cover. Cook on high 2 hours.
3. Mix biscuit mix with reserved broth until moistened. Drop by tablespoonfuls over hot chicken and vegetables.
4. Cover. Cook on high 10 minutes.
5. Uncover. Cook on high 20 minutes more.

Per Serving: 330 calories (70 calories from fat) (2g saturated, 0g trans), 65mg cholesterol, 600mg sodium, 31g total carbohydrate (5g fiber, 7g sugar), 33g protein, 6%DV vitamin A, 10%DV vitamin C, 10%DV calcium, 20%DV iron.

Note: For a less brothy stew, add another ½ pound vegetables.

Oriental Chicken Ginger

Dianna R. Milhizer
Brighton, MI

Makes 6 servings
(Ideal slow-cooker size: 6-quart)

6 uncooked chicken breast halves, cut-up
1 cup carrots, diced
½ cup minced onion
½ cup low-sodium soy sauce
¼ cup rice vinegar
¼ cup sesame seeds
1 Tbsp. ground ginger,
    or ¼ cup grated gingerroot
¾ tsp. salt
1 tsp. sesame oil
2 cups broccoli florets
1 cup cauliflower florets

1. Combine all ingredients except broccoli and cauliflower in slow cooker.
2. Cover. Cook on low 3-5 hours. Stir in broccoli and cauliflower and cook an additional hour.
3. Serve over brown rice.

Per Serving: 230 calories (60 calories from fat) (1.5g saturated, 0g trans), 75mg cholesterol, 1090mg sodium, 12g total carbohydrate (4g fiber, 4g sugar), 31g protein, 100%DV vitamin A, 30%DV vitamin C, 10%DV calcium, 15%DV iron.

Note: You can use a variety of vegetables that are in season for this recipe—zucchini, celery, Chinese peas, and turnips. Chop or slice them and add during the last hour of cooking.

Chickenetti

Miriam Nolt
New Holland, PA
Ruth Hershey
Paradise, PA

Makes 10 servings
(Ideal slow-cooker size: 6- 7-quart)

1 cup fat-free, low-sodium chicken broth
16-oz. pkg. spaghetti, cooked
4-6 cups cubed and cooked chicken, or
    turkey, breast
10¾-oz. can fat-free, low-sodium cream of
    mushroom soup or cream of celery
    soup
1 cup water
¼ cup green bell peppers, chopped
½ cup diced celery
½ tsp. black pepper
1 medium-sized onion, grated
½ lb. fat-free white or yellow American
    cheese, cubed

1. Put chicken broth into very large slow
cooker. Add spaghetti and chicken.
2. In large bowl, combine soup and water
until smooth. Stir in remaining ingredients;
then pour into slow cooker.
3. Cover. Cook on low 2-3 hours.

Per Serving: 210 calories (25 calories from fat), 3g total fat
(1g saturated, 0g trans), 50mg cholesterol, 630mg sodium,
20g total carbohydrate (1g fiber, 4g sugar), 24g protein,
0%DV vitamin A, 0%DV vitamin C, 20%DV calcium,
6%DV iron.

Note: If your diet allows, you may want to add ½
tsp. salt to Step 2, when stirring together the
diluted soup and chopped vegetables.

Easy Chicken A la King

Jenny R. Unternahrer
Wayland, IA

Makes 6 servings
(Ideal slow-cooker size: 4-quart)

1½ lbs. uncooked boneless, skinless
    chicken breast
10¾-oz. can fat-free, low-sodium cream of
    chicken soup
3 Tbsp. flour
¼ tsp. black pepper
9-oz. pkg. frozen peas and onions, thawed
    and drained
2 Tbsp. chopped pimentos
½ tsp. paprika

1. Cut chicken into bite-sized pieces and
place in slow cooker.
2. Combine soup, flour, and pepper. Pour
over chicken. Do not stir.
3. Cover. Cook on high 2½ hours or low
5-5½ hours.
4. Stir in peas and onions, pimentos, and
paprika.
5. Cover. Cook on high 20-30 minutes.

Per Serving: 280 calories (70 calories from fat), 7g total fat
(2g saturated, 0g trans), 100mg cholesterol, 510mg sodium,
13g total carbohydrate (2g fiber, 0g sugar), 39g protein,
10%DV vitamin A, 10%DV vitamin C, 4%DV calcium,
15%DV iron.

Variation:
Add ¼-½ cup chopped green peppers to Step 2.
Sharon Brubaker
Myerstown, PA

Note: If your diet allows, you may want to add ½
tsp. salt to the mixture in Step 2.

Wanda's Chicken and Rice Casserole
Wanda Roth
Napoleon, OH

Makes 8 servings
(Ideal slow-cooker size: 6-quart)

1 cup long grain rice, uncooked
3 cups water
2 tsp. low-sodium chicken bouillon granules
10¾-oz. can fat-free, low-sodium cream of chicken soup
2 cups chopped, cooked chicken breast
¼ tsp. garlic powder
1 tsp. onion salt
1 cup grated, fat-free cheddar cheese
16-oz. bag frozen broccoli, thawed

1. Combine all ingredients except broccoli in slow cooker.
2. One hour before end of cooking time, stir in broccoli.
3. Cook on high for a total of 3-4 hours or on low for a total of 6-7 hours.

Per Serving: 200 calories (20 calories from fat), 2.5g total fat (0.5g saturated, 0g trans), 30mg cholesterol, 960mg sodium, 25g total carbohydrate (2g fiber, 1g sugar), 18g protein, 15%DV vitamin A, 20%DV vitamin C, 20%DV calcium, 10%DV iron.

Note: If casserole is too runny as the end of the cooking time nears, remove lid from slow cooker for 15 minutes while continuing to cook on high.

Marinated Chinese Chicken Salad
Lee Ann Hazlett
Delavan, WI

Makes 8 servings
(Ideal slow-cooker size: 5- or 6-quart)

Marinade:
3 cloves minced garlic
1 Tbsp. fresh ginger, grated
1 tsp. dried red pepper flakes
2 Tbsp. honey
3 Tbsp. low-sodium soy sauce
6 boneless, skinless chicken breast halves

Dressing:
½ cup rice wine vinegar
1 clove garlic, minced
1 tsp. fresh ginger, grated
1 Tbsp. honey

Salad:
1 large head iceberg lettuce, shredded
2 carrots, julienned
½ cup roasted peanuts, chopped
¼ cup cilantro, chopped
½ package maifun noodles, fried in hot oil

1. Mix marinade ingredients in a small bowl.
2. Place chicken in slow cooker and pour marinade over chicken, coating each piece well.
3. Cover. Cook on low 6 to 8 hours or high 3 to 4 hours.
4. Remove chicken from slow cooker and cool. Reserve juices. Shred chicken into bite-sized pieces.
5. In a small bowl, combine the dressing ingredients with ½ cup of the juice from the slow cooker.
6. In a large serving bowl toss together the shredded chicken, lettuce, carrots, peanuts, cilantro, and noodles.

7. Just before serving, drizzle with the salad dressing. Toss well and serve.

Per Serving: 130 calories (20 calories from fat), 2.5g total fat (0.5g saturated, 0g trans), 55mg cholesterol, 250mg sodium, 6g total carbohydrate (0g fiber, 4g sugar), 21g protein, 8%DV vitamin A, 2%DV vitamin C, 2%DV calcium, 6%DV iron.

Note: You may substitute chow mein noodles for the maifun noodles.

Swedish Meatballs
Connie Slagle
Roann, IN

Makes 4 servings
(Ideal slow-cooker size: 4-quart)

3 slices bread, cubed
1 cup evaporated skim milk, divided
1 Tbsp. low-cal margarine
¼ cup shallots, minced
½ lb. lean ground turkey
1 egg, slightly beaten
½ tsp. salt
¼-½ tsp. black pepper, according to your taste preference
¼ cup, plus 2 Tbsp., flour
1 cup fat-free, low-sodium chicken broth
1 Tbsp. low-sodium Worcestershire sauce

1. In a mixing bowl, toss bread cubes and ½ cup milk. Let stand 5 minutes.
2. In a skillet, melt margarine. Add shallots and cook 2 minutes over medium heat.
3. Add shallots, meat, egg, salt, and pepper to bread and milk mixture.
4. Mix well; then shape into equal-sized balls.
5. Place ¼ cup flour on waxed paper. Roll meatballs in flour, coating evenly.
6. Place meatballs in slow cooker. Add chicken broth and Worcestershire sauce.
7. Cover. Cook on low 4-6 hours.
8. Mix remaining 2 Tbsp. flour with remaining ½ cup milk (and a small amount of water if desired) until smooth. Remove meatballs to warm platter. Stir thickened milk into cooking juices until smooth. Cover and cook on high for 10 minutes, or until juices are thickened.
9. Stir meatballs back into sauce and heat through. Serve over noodles or rice.

Per Serving: 220 calories (70 calories from fat), 8g total fat (2g saturated, 0g trans), 85mg cholesterol, 610mg sodium, 20g total carbohydrate (2g fiber, 8g sugar), 19g protein, 10%DV vitamin A, 0%DV vitamin C, 20%DV calcium, 10%DV iron.

Dawn's Terrific Turkey Breast

Dawn Day
Westminster, CA

Makes 10 servings
(Ideal slow-cooker size: 5-quart)

2 1/2-lb. turkey breast
2 Tbsp. canola oil
2 cups onions, chopped
2 garlic cloves, chopped
1 tsp. black pepper
1 tsp. salt
1 tsp. dried rosemary
1/2 tsp. dried sage
2 cups fat-free, low-sodium chicken broth
1/2 cup white wine, optional
1/4 cup flour, optional

1. Brown turkey breast in oil. Remove from skillet and place in slow cooker.
2. Sauté onions and garlic in reserved drippings. Stir in seasonings, broth, and wine and mix well.
3. Pour seasoned broth over turkey in slow cooker.
4. Cover. Cook on low 6-8 hours.
5. Remove turkey from cooker and allow to rest for 10 minutes on warm platter.
6. Remove 1 cup broth from cooker and place in bowl. Mix 1/4 cup flour into broth in bowl until smooth. Stir back into broth in cooker until smooth. Cover and cook on high for 10 minutes, or until broth is thickened.
7. Meanwhile, slice turkey. Serve with gravy or au jus.

Per Serving: 160 calories (50 calories from fat), 5g total fat (1.5g saturated, 0g trans), 55mg cholesterol, 310mg sodium, 3g total carbohydrate (0.5g fiber, 2g sugar), 22g protein, 0%DV vitamin A, 4%DV vitamin C, 2%DV calcium, 8%DV iron.

Turkey with Mushroom Sauce

Judi Manos
West Islip, NY

Makes 12 servings
(Ideal slow-cooker size: 6-quart)

1 large boneless, skinless turkey breast, halved
2 Tbsp. butter, melted
2 Tbsp. dried parsley
1/2 tsp. dried oregano
1/2 tsp. salt
1/4 tsp. black pepper
1/2 cup white wine
1 cup fresh mushrooms, sliced
2 Tbsp. cornstarch
1/4 cup cold water

1. Place turkey in slow cooker. Brush with butter.
2. Mix together parsley, oregano, salt, pepper, and wine. Pour over turkey.
3. Top with mushrooms.
4. Cover. Cook on low 7-8 hours.
5. Remove turkey and keep warm.
6. Skim any fat from cooking juices.
7. In a saucepan, combine cornstarch and water until smooth. Gradually add cooking juices. Bring to a boil. Cook and stir 2 minutes until thickened.
8. Slice turkey and serve with sauce.

Per Serving: 100 calories (20 calories from fat), 2.5g total fat (1.5g saturated, 0g trans), 45mg cholesterol, 140mg sodium, 2g total carbohydrate (0g fiber, 0g sugar), 16g protein, 2%DV vitamin A, 0%DV vitamin C, 0%DV calcium, 6%DV iron.

Lemony Turkey Breast

Joyce Shackelford
Green Bay, WI
Mrs. Carolyn Baer
Conrath, WI

Makes 12 servings
(Ideal slow-cooker size: 6-quart)

1 5-lb. bone-in turkey breast, cut in half
   and skin removed, partially frozen in
   center
1 medium-sized lemon, halved
1 tsp. lemon-pepper seasoning
1 tsp. garlic salt
4 tsp. cornstarch
1/2 cup fat-free, reduced-sodium chicken
   broth

1. Place turkey, meaty side up, in slow
cooker sprayed with non-fat cooking spray.
2. Squeeze half of lemon over turkey.
Sprinkle with lemon pepper and garlic salt.
3. Place lemon halves under turkey.
4. Cover. Cook on low 5-7 hours.
5. Remove turkey. Discard lemons.
6. Allow turkey to rest 15 minutes before
slicing.

Per Serving: 190 calories (10 calories from fat), 1g total fat
(0g saturated, 0g trans), 110mg cholesterol, 260mg sodium,
1g total carbohydrate (0g fiber, 0g sugar), 40g protein,
0%DV vitamin A, 0%DV vitamin C, 2%DV calcium,
10%DV iron.

*Note: To make gravy, pour cooking liquid into a
cup. Skim the fat. In saucepan, combine
cornstarch and broth until smooth. Gradually stir
in cooking liquid. Bring to a boil. Cook and stir
for 2 minutes. Serve over turkey slices.*

Cranberry-Orange
Turkey Breast

Lee Ann Hazlett
Delavan, WI

Makes 9 servings
(Ideal slow-cooker size: 6-quart)

1/2 cup orange marmalade
16-oz. can whole cranberries in sauce
2 tsp. orange zest, grated
3-lb. turkey breast

1. Combine marmalade, cranberries, and
zest in a bowl.
2. Place the turkey breast in the slow
cooker and pour half the orange-cranberry
mixture over the turkey.
3. Cover. Cook on low 7-8 hours or on high
3 1/2-4 hours, until turkey juices run clear.
4. Add remaining half of orange-cranberry
mixture for the last half hour of cooking.
5. Remove turkey to warm platter and allow
to rest for 15 minutes before slicing.
6. Serve with orange-cranberry sauce.

Per Serving: 270 calories (10 calories from fat), 1g total fat
(0g saturated, 0g trans), 125mg cholesterol, 90mg sodium,
18g total carbohydrate (2g fiber, 16 sugar), 46g protein,
0%DV vitamin A, 4%DV vitamin C, 2%DV calcium,
15%DV iron.

Easy and Delicious Turkey Breast

Gail Bush
Landenberg, PA

Makes 6 servings
(Ideal slow-cooker size: 5- or 6-quart)

1 turkey breast, skin removed
15-oz. can whole-berry cranberry sauce
1 envelope low-sodium dry onion soup
   mix
1/2 cup orange juice
1/2 tsp. salt
1/4 tsp. black pepper

1. Place turkey breast in slow cooker.
2. Combine remaining ingredients. Pour over turkey.
3. Cover. Cook on low 6-8 hours.

Per Serving: 250 calories (5 calories from fat), 1g total fat (0g saturated, 0g trans), 85mg cholesterol, 360mg sodium, 29g total carbohydrate (1g fiber, 19g sugar), 31g protein, 0%DV vitamin A, 0%DV vitamin C, 2%DV calcium, 10%DV iron.

Italian Turkey Sandwiches

Joette Droz
Kalona, IA
Barbara Walker
Sturgis, SD

Makes 10 servings
(Ideal slow-cooker size: 6-quart)

1 bone-in turkey breast (5 1/2 lbs.), skin
   removed
1/2 cup green bell pepper, chopped
1 medium-sized onion, chopped
1/4 cup chili sauce
3 Tbsp. white vinegar
2 Tbsp. dried oregano or Italian seasoning
4 tsp. beef bouillon granules

1. Place turkey breast, green pepper, and onion in slow cooker.
2. Combine chili sauce, vinegar, oregano, and bouillon. Pour over turkey and vegetables.
3. Cover. Cook on low 5-6 hours, or until meat juices run clear and vegetables are tender.
4. Remove turkey, reserving cooking liquid. Shred the turkey with 2 forks.
5. Return to cooking juices.
6. For each serving, spoon approximately 1/2 cup onto a kaiser or hard sandwich roll.

Per Serving: 270 calories (30 calories from fat), 3g total fat (0.5g saturated, 0g trans), 50mg cholesterol, 760mg sodium, 35g total carbohydrate (2g fiber, 5g sugar), 24g protein, 4%DV vitamin A, 10%DV vitamin C, 8%DV calcium, 20%DV iron.

Turkey Enchiladas

Joyce Shackelford
Green Bay, WI

Makes 8 servings
(Ideal slow-cooker size: 3-quart)

10-oz. turkey breast, roasted
10-oz. can low-sodium tomato sauce
4-oz. can chopped green chilies
1 cup onions, chopped
2 Tbsp. Worcestershire sauce
1-2 Tbsp. chili powder
1/4 tsp. garlic powder
8 7″ flour tortillas

1. Remove skin from turkey. Place in slow cooker.
2. Combine tomato sauce, chilies, onions, Worcestershire sauce, chili powder, and garlic powder. Pour over turkey.
3. Cover. Cook on low 6-8 hours.
4. Remove turkey. Shred with a fork and return to cooker.
5. Spoon about 1/2 cup turkey mixture down center of each tortilla. Fold bottom of tortilla over filling and roll up. Add toppings of your choice.

Per Serving: 180 calories (40 calories from fat), 4.5g total fat (1g saturated, 0g trans), 20mg cholesterol, 490mg sodium, 24g total carbohydrate (3g fiber, 3g sugar), 12g protein, 10%DV vitamin A, 10%DV vitamin C, 8%DV calcium, 10%DV iron.

Optional toppings:
green onions, chopped
ripe olives, sliced
tomatoes, chopped
shredded low-fat cheddar cheese
fat-free sour cream
lettuce, shredded

Broccoli Turkey Supreme

Karen Waggoner
Joplin, MO

Makes 8 servings
(Ideal slow-cooker size: 5- or 6-quart)

4 cups cooked turkey breast, cubed
10³/4-oz. can condensed cream of chicken soup
10-oz. pkg. frozen broccoli florets, thawed and drained
6.9-oz. pkg. low-sodium plain rice mix
1 1/2 cups fat-free milk
1 cup fat-free chicken broth
1 cup celery, chopped
8-oz. can sliced water chestnuts, drained
3/4 cup low-fat mayonnaise
1/2 cup onions, chopped

1. Combine all ingredients in slow cooker.
2. Cook uncovered on high for 2-2 1/2 hours, or until rice is tender.

Per Serving: 380 calories (100 calories from fat), 11g total fat (2.5g saturated, 0g trans), 70mg cholesterol, 630mg sodium, 37g total carbohydrate (3g fiber, 9g sugar), 32g protein, 10%DV vitamin A, 20%DV vitamin C, 10%DV calcium, 10%DV iron.

Turkey Meat Loaf

Martha Ann Auker
Landisburg, PA

Makes 8 servings
(Ideal slow-cooker size: 4-quart)

1½ lbs. lean ground turkey
2 egg whites
⅓ cup ketchup
1 Tbsp. Worcestershire sauce
1 tsp. dried basil
½ tsp. salt
½ tsp. black pepper
2 small onions, chopped
2 potatoes, finely shredded
2 small red bell peppers, finely chopped

1. Combine all ingredients in a large bowl.
2. Shape into a loaf to fit in your slow cooker. Place in slow cooker.
3. Cover. Cook on low 6-8 hours.

Per Serving: 200 calories (60 calories from fat), 7g total fat (2g saturated, 0g trans), 65mg cholesterol, 380mg sodium, 16g total carbohydrate (2g fiber, 4g sugar), 17g protein, 20%DV vitamin A, 40%DV vitamin C, 4%DV calcium, 10%DV iron.

Turkey Roast

Donna Lantgen
Rapid City, SD

Makes 10 servings
(Ideal slow-cooker size: 4- or 5-quart)

2 lbs. fat-free ground turkey
2 Tbsp. poultry seasoning
2 slices bread, cubed
1 egg

1. Combine all ingredients. Form into a round or oval loaf (according to the shape of your slow cooker) and place in the cooker.
2. Cook 6-7 hours on low. Remove from cooker and allow to sit for 15 minutes before slicing and serving.

Per Serving: 120 calories (15 calories from fat), 2g total fat (0g saturated, 0g trans), 55mg cholesterol, 85mg sodium, 3g total carbohydrate (0g fiber, 0g sugar), 23g protein, 2%DV vitamin A, 0%DV vitamin C, 2%DV calcium, 10%DV iron.

Notes: Mix in any of the following when combining ingredients to add flavor to the Roast:

1 medium-sized onion, finely chopped
1 green or red bell pepper, finely chopped
6 ozs. fresh mushrooms, sliced
½ cup low-fat, low-sodium barbecue sauce
½ cup ketchup
1 tsp. salt
½ tsp. black pepper
1 can 98% fat-free, low-sodium condensed
   cream of mushroom soup

Southern Barbecue Spaghetti Sauce

Mrs. Carolyn Baer, Conrath, WI
Lavina Hochstedler, Grand Blanc, MI

Makes 12 servings
(Ideal slow-cooker size: 4- or 5-quart)

1 lb. lean ground turkey
2 medium-sized onions, chopped
1½ cups sliced fresh mushrooms
1 medium-sized green bell pepper,
   chopped
2 garlic cloves, minced
14½-oz. can diced tomatoes, undrained
12-oz. can tomato paste
8-oz. can tomato sauce
1 cup ketchup
½ cup fat-free beef broth
2 Tbsp. Worcestershire sauce
2 Tbsp. brown sugar

1 Tbsp. ground cumin
2 tsp. chili powder
12 cups hot cooked spaghetti

1. In a large nonstick skillet, cook the turkey, onions, mushrooms, green pepper, and garlic over medium heat until meat is no longer pink. Drain.

2. Transfer to slow cooker. Stir in tomatoes, tomato paste, tomato sauce, ketchup, broth, Worcestershire sauce, brown sugar, cumin, and chili powder. Mix well.

3. Cook on low 4-5 hours. Serve over spaghetti.

Per Serving: 330 calories (20 calories from fat), 2g total fat (0g saturated, 0g trans), 15mg cholesterol, 530mg sodium, 60g total carbohydrate (6g fiber, 10g sugar), 20g protein, 30%DV vitamin A, 20%DV vitamin C, 6%DV calcium, 20%DV iron.

Saucy Meatballs

Michelle Steffen
Harrisonburg, VA

Makes 6 servings
(Ideal slow-cooker size: 3-quart)

½ lb. lean ground turkey
1 cup oat bran
1 clove garlic, crushed
2 Tbsp. water
1 Tbsp. low-sodium soy sauce
3 egg whites
½ cup onions, diced
½ cup low-sodium chili sauce
½ cup grape jelly
¼ cup Dijon mustard

1. Combine turkey, oat bran, garlic, water, soy sauce, egg whites, and onions. Shape into 24 balls (1 Tbsp. per ball).

2. Place meatballs on baking sheet and bake at 350° for 15-20 minutes until browned. (They can be made ahead and frozen.)

3. Mix together chili sauce, grape jelly, and Dijon mustard.

4. Combine meatballs and sauce in slow cooker.

5. Cover. Cook on low 6-8 hours.

Per Serving: 210 calories (45 calories from fat), 5g total fat (1g saturated, 0g trans), 30mg cholesterol, 650mg sodium, 36g total carbohydrate (3g fiber, 22g sugar), 12g protein, 0%DV vitamin A, 0%DV vitamin C, 4%DV calcium, 10%DV iron.

BBQ Balls

Judy Moore
Pendleton, IN

Makes 5 servings
(Ideal slow-cooker size: 4-quart)

1 lb. 99% fat-free ground turkey
2 eggs
1 cup uncooked minute rice
1 medium-sized onion, chopped
1-lb. can cranberry sauce
14-oz. bottle ketchup
2 Tbsp. Worcestershire sauce
½ tsp. garlic powder

1. Blend ground turkey, eggs, rice, and onion. Form into balls.

2. Bake at 400 ° for 20 minutes or until brown. Drain.

3. Combine cranberry sauce, ketchup, Worcestershire sauce, and garlic powder.

4. Place meatballs in slow cooker. Pour sauce over top. Stir to coat.

5. Cover. Cook on low 2 hours.

Per Serving: 270 calories (30 calories from fat), 3.5g total fat (0.5g saturated, 0g trans), 110mg cholesterol, 1090mg sodium, 37g total carbohydrate (2g fiber, 15g sugar), 27g protein, 10%DV vitamin A, 10%DV vitamin C, 4%DV calcium, 15%DV iron.

Note: You can add a little of the sauce to the meatball mixture for extra flavor.

Sloppy Joes Italia

Nanci Keatley
Salem, OR

Makes 12 servings
(Ideal slow-cooker size: 4- or 5-quart)

1½ lbs. ground turkey, browned in
   nonstick skillet
1 cup onions, chopped
2 cups low-sodium tomato sauce
1 cup fresh mushrooms, sliced
2 Tbsp. Splenda
1-2 Tbsp. Italian seasoning, according to
   your taste preference
12 reduced-calorie hamburger buns
12 slices low-fat mozzarella cheese,
   optional

1. Place ground turkey, onions, tomato
sauce, and mushrooms in slow cooker.
2. Stir in Splenda and Italian seasoning.
3. Cover. Cook on low 3-4 hours.
4. Serve ¼ cup of Sloppy Joe mixture on
each bun, topped with cheese, if desired.

Per Serving: 200 calories (50 calories from fat),
6g total fat (1.5g saturated, 0g trans), 45mg
cholesterol, 680mg sodium, 25g total carbohydrate
(4g fiber, 6g sugar), 15g protein, 8%DV vitamin A,
4%DV vitamin C, 4%DV calcium, 15%DV iron.

Ground Turkey Potato Dinner

Marjorie Yoder Guengerich
Harrisonburg, VA

Makes 6 servings
(Ideal slow-cooker size: 4- or 5-quart)

1 lb. ground turkey
5 cups raw potatoes, sliced
1 onion, sliced
½ tsp. salt
dash of black pepper
14½-oz. can cut green beans, undrained
4-oz. can mushroom pieces, undrained,
   optional
10¾-oz. can cream of chicken soup

1. Crumble uncooked ground turkey in slow
cooker.
2. Add potatoes, onions, salt, and pepper.
3. Add beans and mushrooms. Pour soup
over top.
4. Cover. Cook on high 4 hours or on low 6-
8 hours.

Per Serving: 250 calories (40 calories from fat), 4g total fat
(1g saturated, 0g trans), 35mg cholesterol, 900mg sodium,
31g total carbohydrate (5g fiber, 3g sugar), 24g protein,
2%DV vitamin A, 20%DV vitamin C, 6%DV calcium,
15%DV iron.

Cabbage Joe

Sue Hamilton
Minooka, IL

Makes 6 servings
(Ideal slow-cooker size: 5-quart)

1 lb. lean ground turkey
3 cups cabbage, shredded
2 cups barbecue sauce

1. Brown turkey in a nonstick skillet over medium heat.
2. Combine cabbage, turkey, and sauce in slow cooker.
3. Cover. Cook on low 6-8 hours.

Per Serving: 230 calories (60 calories from fat), 7g total fat (1.5g saturated, 0g trans), 60mg cholesterol, 1210mg sodium, 26g total carbohydrate (2g fiber, 21g sugar), 14g protein, 8%DV vitamin A, 10%DV vitamin C, 4%DV calcium, 10%DV iron.

Note: Use as sandwich filling, if you wish, in rolls.

Turkey Hash

Joy Sutter
Iowa City, IA

Makes 6 servings
(Ideal slow-cooker size: 5-quart)

3/4 lb. lean ground turkey
1 cup onions, sliced
1 cup carrots, cut julienne-style
2 cups canned tomatoes with juice
2 cups low-sodium tomato juice
6 ozs. long grain white rice
2 tsp. chili powder
1/4 tsp. black pepper, freshly ground

1. Brown ground turkey in a nonstick skillet.
2. Combine all ingredients in slow cooker.
3. Cook on high 3 hours.

Per Serving: 250 calories (50 calories from fat), 5g total fat (1.5g saturated, 0g trans), 45mg cholesterol, 130mg sodium, 36g total carbohydrate (4g fiber, 8g sugar), 14g protein, 200%DV vitamin A, 20%DV vitamin C, 6%DV calcium, 20%DV iron.

Stuffed Green Peppers

Jean Moore
Pendleton, IN

Makes 8 servings
(Ideal slow-cooker size: 4- or 6-quart oval, so that the peppers can all sit on the bottom of the cooker)

8 small green peppers, tops removed and seeded
10-oz. pkg. frozen corn
3/4 lb. 99% fat-free ground turkey
3/4 lb. extra-lean ground beef
8-oz. can low-sodium tomato sauce
1/2 tsp. garlic powder
1/4 tsp. black pepper
1 cup shredded low-fat American cheese
1/2 tsp. Worcestershire sauce
1/4 cup onions, chopped
3 Tbsp. water
2 Tbsp. ketchup

1. Wash peppers and drain well. Combine all ingredients except water and ketchup in mixing bowl. Stir well.
2. Stuff peppers 2/3 full.
3. Pour water in slow cooker. Arrange peppers on top.
4. Pour ketchup over peppers.
5. Cover. Cook on high 3-4 hours or on low 7-9 hours.

Per Serving: 200 calories (35 calories from fat), 4g total fat (1.5g saturated, 0g trans), 30mg cholesterol, 530mg sodium, 21g total carbohydrate (4g fiber, 7g sugar), 23g protein, 20%DV vitamin A, 100%DV vitamin C, 20%DV calcium, 10%DV iron.

Note: For a zestier flavor, use 99% fat-free Italian turkey sausage instead of the ground turkey, and use 1 cup salsa instead of the tomato sauce.

Zucchini-Vegetable Pot

Edwina Stoltzfus
Narvon, PA

Makes 6 servings
(Ideal slow-cooker size: 3¹/2- or 4-quart)

¹/2 lb. ground turkey
2 cups zucchini, diced
2 ribs celery, chopped
¹/4 cup green bell peppers, chopped
1 large onion, chopped
2 large tomatoes, chopped
¹/4 cup rice, uncooked
³/4 tsp. salt
¹/4 tsp. garlic salt
¹/8 tsp. nutmeg
¹/4 tsp. black pepper
1 tsp. Worcestershire sauce

1. Brown turkey in nonstick skillet.
2. Meanwhile, place vegetables in slow cooker. Top with rice and ground turkey.
3. Sprinkle seasonings over top.
4. Cover. Cook on high 3-4 hours.

Per Serving: 80 calories (5 calories from fat), 1g total fat (0g saturated, 0g trans), 15mg cholesterol, 380mg sodium, 9g total carbohydrate (2g fiber, 3g sugar), 11g protein, 0%DV vitamin A, 10%DV vitamin C, 2%DV calcium, 6%DV iron.

Slow-Cooker Pizza

Evelyn L. Ward
Greeley, CO
Ann Van Doren
Lady Lake, FL

Makes 8 servings
(Ideal slow-cooker size: 6-quart)

1 Tbsp. olive oil
1¹/2 lbs. 99% fat-free ground turkey
¹/4 cup onions, chopped
28-oz. jar fat-free, low-sodium spaghetti sauce
4¹/2-oz. can sliced mushrooms, drained
1-1¹/2 tsp. Italian seasoning, according to your taste preference
12-oz. pkg. wide egg noodles, slightly under-cooked
2 cups fat-free, shredded mozzarella cheese
2 cups low-fat, low-sodium, shredded cheddar cheese

1. In a large skillet, cook turkey and onions in olive oil until no longer pink. Drain.
2. Stir in spaghetti sauce, mushrooms, and Italian seasoning.
3. Spray slow cooker with non-fat cooking spray. Spread one-quarter of meat sauce in pot.
4. Cover with one-third of noodles. Top with one-third of cheeses.
5. Repeat layers twice.
6. Cover. Cook on low 3 hours. Do not overcook.

Per Serving: 360 calories (70 calories from fat), 8g total fat (2g saturated, 0g trans), 60mg cholesterol, 1290mg sodium, 23g total carbohydrate (3g fiber, 8g sugar), 48g protein, 15%DV vitamin A, 8%DV vitamin C, 100%DV calcium, 15%DV iron.

Note: You may create your own Italian seasoning by combining equal parts of dried basil, oregano, rosemary, marjoram, thyme, and sage. Mix well. Stir in a tightly covered jar in a dry and dark place.

Turkey Macaroni

Jean Moore
Pendleton, IN
Jeanne Allen
Rye, CO

Makes 6 servings
(Ideal slow-cooker size: 5-quart)

1 tsp. vegetable oil
1½ lbs. 99% fat-free ground turkey
2 10¾-oz. cans condensed low-sodium
    tomato soup, undiluted
16-oz. can corn, drained
½ cup onions, chopped
4-oz. can sliced mushrooms, drained
2 Tbsp. ketchup
1 Tbsp. prepared mustard
¼ tsp. black pepper
¼ tsp. garlic powder
2 cups dry macaroni, cooked and drained

1. Heat oil in medium skillet. Brown turkey. Drain.
2. Combine all ingredients except macaroni in slow cooker. Stir to blend. Cover.
3. Cook on high 3-4 hours or on low 4-6 hours. Stir in cooked and drained macaroni 15 minutes before serving.

Per Serving: 300 calories (40 calories from fat), 4.5g total fat (0g saturated, 0g trans), 45mg cholesterol, 420mg sodium, 38g total carbohydrate (3g fiber, 4g sugar), 34g protein, 8%DV vitamin A, 30%DV vitamin C, 2%DV calcium, 20%DV iron.

Sausage Pasta

Rose Hankins
Stevensville, MD

Makes 6 servings
(Ideal slow-cooker size: 5-quart)

1 lb. turkey sausage, cut in 1" chunks
1 cup green and/or red bell peppers,
    chopped
1 cup celery, chopped
1 cup red onions, chopped
1 cup green zucchini, chopped
8-oz. can tomato paste
2 cups water
14-oz. can tomatoes, chopped
¼ cup cooking wine
1 Tbsp. Italian seasoning
1 lb. cooked pasta

1. Combine all ingredients except pasta in slow cooker.
2. Cover. Cook on low 8-10 hours.
3. Add pasta 10 minutes before serving.

Per Serving: 220 calories (60 calories from fat), 7g total fat (2g saturated, 0g trans), 55mg cholesterol, 730mg sodium, 27g total carbohydrate (4g fiber, 5g sugar), 14g protein, 15%DV vitamin A, 20%DV vitamin C, 6%DV calcium, 15%DV iron.

Note: If diets allow, enjoy this served with a thick slice of Italian bread for each person. Sprinkle with olive oil and garlic. Broil 1-2 minutes.

Noodleless Lasagna

Nanci Keatley
Salem, OR

Makes 4 servings
(Ideal slow-cooker size: 4- or 5-quart)

1½ lbs. fat-free ground turkey
1½ cups meat-free, low-sodium spaghetti
   sauce
8 ozs. sliced mushrooms
1½ cups fat-free ricotta cheese
1 egg, beaten
1 cup grated mozzarella cheese
   (part skim), divided
1½ tsp. Italian seasoning
10 slices turkey pepperoni

1. Brown ground turkey in a nonstick
skillet.
2. Add spaghetti sauce and mushrooms and
mix with meat.
3. Pour half of turkey mixture into slow
cooker sprayed with nonfat cooking spray.
4. In a small bowl, mix together the ricotta
cheese, egg, ¼ cup of mozzarella, and the
Italian seasoning. Beat well with a fork.
5. Lay half of pepperoni slices on top of
turkey mixture.
6. Spread half of cheese mixture over
pepperoni.
7. Repeat layers, finishing by sprinkling the
remaining mozzarella on top.
8. Cover. Cook on low 4-4½ hours.

Per Serving: 480 calories (130 calories from fat), 15g total
fat (5g saturated, 0g trans), 190mg cholesterol, 2070mg
sodium, 19g total carbohydrate (2g fiber, 8g sugar), 67g
protein, 10%DV vitamin A, 6%DV vitamin C, 30%DV
calcium, 25%DV iron.

*Note: If you are not concerned about increasing
your sodium intake, you could add ½ tsp. salt
and an additional cup of spaghetti sauce to Step
2.*

Red Rice

Nadine L. Martinitz
Salina, KS

Makes 6-8 servings
(Ideal slow-cooker size: 4-quart)

5 slices turkey bacon
1 large onion, chopped
2 16-oz. cans sodium-free diced tomatoes
1 cup uncooked long grain rice
1 cup low-fat turkey ham, finely chopped
¼ tsp. salt
¼ tsp. black pepper
1½ tsp. garlic powder, optional
2 tsp. dried parsley flakes
1 tsp. dried oregano
1 Tbsp. hot sauce, optional

1. Saute turkey bacon in skillet. Remove
and crumble.
2. Cook onion in drippings until
transparent.
3. Combine bacon, onions, tomatoes, rice,
turkey ham, and seasonings in slow cooker.
4. Cover and cook on low 6-8 hours or on
high 3-4 hours.

Per Serving: 170 calories (35 calories from fat), 4 total fat
(12.5g saturated, 0g trans), 25mg cholesterol, 600mg
sodium, 26g total carbohydrate (2g fiber, 5g sugar), 9g
protein, 10%DV vitamin A, 10%DV vitamin C, 4%DV
calcium, 10%DV iron.

Beef Main Dishes

Swiss Steak with Carrots

Becky Harder
Monument, CO

Makes 6 servings
(Ideal slow-cooker size: 4- or 5-quart)

2 lbs. lean beef round steak, cut 1" thick
1/4 cup flour
1 tsp. salt
1 rib celery, chopped
2 carrots, pared and chopped
1/4 cup onions, chopped
1/2 tsp. Worcestershire sauce
2 cups whole tomatoes
1/2-1 cup low-sodium tomato juice
1/2 cup grated, low-fat, low-sodium
   American cheese, optional

1. Cut steak into six serving pieces. Dredge in flour mixed with salt. Place in slow cooker.
2. Add chopped vegetables and Worcestershire sauce.
3. Pour tomatoes over meat and vegetables.
4. Cover. Cook on low 7-10 hours.
5. Just before serving sprinkle with grated cheese, if desired.

Per Serving: 270 calories (70 calories from fat), 8g total fat (3g saturated, 0g trans), 95mg cholesterol, 690mg sodium, 11g total carbohydrate (2g fiber, 5g sugar), 37g protein, 100%DV vitamin A, 6%DV vitamin C, 15%DV calcium, 30%DV iron.

Nadine & Hazel's Swiss Steak

Nadine Martinitz
Salina, KS
Hazel L. Propst
Oxford, PA

Makes 10 servings
(Ideal slow-cooker size: 5- or 6-quart)

3 lbs. lean round steak
1/3 cup flour
2 tsp. salt
1/2 tsp. black pepper
2 Tbsp. vegetable oil
1 large onion, or more, sliced
1 large bell pepper, or more, sliced
14 1/2-oz. can low-sodium stewed tomatoes,
** or 3-4 fresh tomatoes, chopped**
water

1. Cut meat into 10 pieces. Pound both sides. Mix together flour, salt, and pepper. Dredge each piece of meat on both sides in flavored flour.
2. Saute meat in oil over medium heat on top of stove, until browned. Transfer to slow cooker.
3. Brown onion and pepper in pan drippings. Add tomatoes and bring to boil. Stir pan drippings loose. Pour over steak. Add water to completely cover steak.
4. Cover. Cook on low 6-8 hours.

Per Serving: 190 calories (60 calories from fat), 7g total fat (2g saturated, 0g trans), 70mg cholesterol, 510mg sodium, 7g total carbohydrate (1g fiber, 3g sugar), 23g protein, 0%DV vitamin A, 0%DV vitamin C, 2%DV calcium, 20%DV iron.

Note: To add some flavor, stir your favorite dried herbs into Step 3. Or add fresh herbs in the last hour of cooking.

Fruited Flank Steak

Jean Butzer
Batavia, NY

Makes 5 servings
(Ideal slow-cooker size: 4- or 5-quart)

1 lb. flank steak
1/4 tsp. salt
dash of black pepper
30-oz. can fruit cocktail in light syrup
1 Tbsp. vegetable oil
1 Tbsp. lemon juice
1/4 cup low-sodium teriyaki sauce
1 tsp. red wine vinegar
1 clove garlic, minced

1. Place flank steak in slow cooker. Sprinkle with salt and pepper.
2. Drain fruit cocktail, saving 1/4 cup syrup.
3. Combine 1/4 cup syrup with remaining ingredients, except fruit.
4. Pour syrup over steak.
5. Cover. Cook on low 7-9 hours.
6. Add drained fruit during the last 10 minutes of cooking time.
7. Cut meat into thin slices across the grain to serve.

Per Serving: 250 calories (70 calories from fat), 7g total fat (2g saturated, 0g trans), 55mg cholesterol, 710mg sodium, 28g total carbohydrate (2g fiber, 25g sugar), 19g protein, 8%DV vitamin A, 2%DV vitamin C, 2%DV calcium, 15%DV iron.

Slow-Cooked Coffee Beef Roast

Mrs. Carolyn Baer
Conrath, WI

Makes 12 servings
(Ideal slow-cooker size: 4- or 5-quart)

1 1/2 lbs. boneless beef sirloin tip roast, cut in half
2 tsp. canola oil
1 1/2 cups sliced fresh mushrooms
1/2 cup sliced green onions
2 garlic cloves, minced
1 1/2 cups brewed coffee
1 tsp. liquid smoke, optional
1/2 tsp. salt
1/2 tsp. chili powder
1/4 tsp. black pepper
1/4 cup cornstarch
1/2 cup cold water

1. In a large nonstick skillet, brown roast over medium-high heat on all sides in oil. Transfer roast to slow cooker.
2. In the same skillet, sauté mushrooms, onions, and garlic until tender.
3. Stir the coffee, liquid smoke if desired, salt, chili powder, and pepper into the vegetables. Pour over roast.
4. Cook on low for 8-10 hours or until meat is tender.
5. Remove roast and keep warm.
6. Pour cooking juices into a 2-cup measuring cup; skim fat.
7. Combine cornstarch and water in a saucepan until smooth. Gradually stir in 2 cups of cooking juices.
8. Bring to a boil; cook and stir for 2 minutes or until thickened. Serve with sliced beef.

Per Serving: 100 calories (30 calories from fat), 3.5g total fat (1g saturated, 0g trans), 35mg cholesterol, 120mg sodium, 4g total carbohydrate (0.5g fiber, 1g sugar), 12g protein, 0%DV vitamin A, 2%DV vitamin C, 0%DV calcium, 8%DV iron.

Machaca Beef

Jeanne Allen
Rye, CO

Makes 12 servings
(Ideal slow-cooker size: 4-quart)

1 1/2-lb. lean beef roast
1 large onion, sliced
4-oz. can chopped green chilies
2 low-sodium beef bouillon cubes
1 1/2 tsp. dry mustard
1/2 tsp. garlic powder
3/4 tsp. seasoning salt
1/2 tsp. black pepper
1 cup low-sodium salsa

1. Combine all ingredients except salsa in slow cooker. Add just enough water to cover.
2. Cover cooker and cook on low 10-12 hours, or until beef is tender. Drain and reserve liquid.
3. Shred beef using two forks to pull it apart.
4. Combine beef, salsa, and enough of the reserved liquid to make a desired consistency.
5. Use this filling for burritos, chalupas, quesadillas, or tacos.

Per Serving: 80 calories (20 calories from fat), 2.5g total fat (1g saturated, 0g trans), 30mg cholesterol, 400mg sodium, 3g total carbohydrate (0g fiber, 1g sugar), 10g protein, 0%DV vitamin A, 0%DV vitamin C, 2%DV calcium, 8%DV iron.

After living in New Mexico for the past 30 years, I get homesick for New Mexican cuisine now that I live in Colorado. I keep memories of New Mexico alive by cooking foods that remind me of home.

Old World Sauerbraten

C. J. Slagle
Roann, IN
Angeline Lang
Greeley, CO

Makes 12 servings
(Ideal slow-cooker size: 5-quart)

4-lb. lean beef rump roast
1 cup water
1 cup vinegar
1 lemon, sliced but unpeeled
10 whole cloves
1 large onion, sliced
4 bay leaves
5 whole peppercorns
2 Tbsp. salt
2 Tbsp. sugar
12 low-fat gingersnaps, crumbled

1. Place meat in deep ceramic or glass bowl.
2. Combine water, vinegar, lemon, cloves, onion, bay leaves, peppercorns, salt, and sugar. Pour over meat. Cover and refrigerate 24-36 hours. Turn meat several times while marinating.
3. Place beef in slow cooker. Pour 1 cup marinade over meat.
4. Cover. Cook on low 6-8 hours. Remove meat.
5. Strain meat juices and return to pot. Turn to high. Stir in gingersnaps. Cover and cook on high 10-14 minutes.
6. Allow meat to rest for 15 minutes. Slice. Then pour finished sauce over meat to serve.

Per Serving: 200 calories (60 calories from fat), 6g total fat (2g saturated, 0g trans), 70mg cholesterol, 1250mg sodium, 13g total carbohydrate (1g fiber, 6g sugar), 23g protein, 0%DV vitamin A, 0%DV vitamin C, 2%DV calcium, 20%DV iron.

Pepsi Pot Roast

Mrs. Don Martins
Fairbank, IA

Makes 12 servings
(Ideal slow-cooker size: 5- or 6-quart)

3-lb. pot roast
2 10¾-oz. cans fat-free, low-sodium cream of mushroom soup
1 envelope dry onion soup mix
2 16-oz. bottles diet cola

1. Place meat in slow cooker.
2. In large bowl mix together mushroom soup, dry onion soup mix, and cola. Pour over roast in cooker.
3. Cover. Cook on high 6 hours.

Per Serving: 170 calories (60 calories from fat), 7g total fat (2g saturated, 0.5g trans), 70mg cholesterol, 430mg sodium, 4g total carbohydrate (0g fiber, 0g sugar), 23g protein, 0%DV vitamin A, 0%DV vitamin C, 2%DV calcium, 15%DV iron.

Steak and Gravy

Susan Scheel
West Fargo, ND

Makes 5 servings
(Ideal slow-cooker size: 4-quart)

1 lb. round steak, trimmed of fat
1 Tbsp. vegetable oil
1½ cups water
12-oz. can low-sodium tomato sauce
1 tsp. garlic powder
¼ tsp. black pepper
½ tsp. salt
2 Tbsp. flour
¼ cup cold water

1. Cut steak into bite-sized pieces. Brown in vegetable oil on all sides. Place in slow cooker.
2. Mix together 1½ cups water, tomato sauce, and seasonings and pour over steak.
3. Combine flour and ¼ cup cold water to make paste. Stir into liquid in slow cooker.
4. Cover. Cook on low 8 hours.
5. Serve over rice or potatoes.

Per Serving: 170 calories (70 calories from fat), 7g total fat (2g saturated, 0g trans), 55mg cholesterol, 680mg sodium, 8g total carbohydrate (1g fiber, 3g sugar), 19g protein, 10%DV vitamin A, 8%DV vitamin C, 2%DV calcium, 15%DV iron.

Note: You may wait until 30 minutes before serving to do Step 3.

Pot Roast

Rosemarie Fitzgerald, Gibsonia, PA

Makes 8-10 servings
(Ideal slow-cooker size: 5-quart)

2 beef bouillon cubes
¼ cup boiling water
14½-oz. can low-sodium diced or stewed tomatoes
1 cup dry red wine or burgundy
1.8-oz. box dry leek soup mix
1 Tbsp. Worcestershire sauce
4 cloves garlic, crushed or sliced
1 tsp. dried rosemary
1 tsp. dried thyme
1 tsp. dried marjoram
3 lbs. lean boneless beef pot roast, rolled and tied
2½ cups sliced carrots
½ cup parsnips, peeled, halved crosswise
4 Tbsp. flour
⅓ cup cold water

1. Dissolve bouillon cubes in boiling water. Pour into slow cooker.
2. Stir in tomatoes, wine, dry soup mix, Worcestershire sauce, garlic, and herbs.
3. Add meat. Roll in liquid to coat.
4. Put vegetables around meat.
5. Cover. Cook on low 9-11 hours.
6. Remove meat to plate. Cover to keep warm. Turn slow cooker to high.
7. Whisk flour into ⅓ cup cold water. Stir into liquid and cook, covered, for 10 minutes.
8. Serve meat sliced with vegetables on the side and gravy.

Per Serving: 260 calories (70 calories from fat), 7g total fat (2.5g saturated, 0g trans), 80mg cholesterol, 740mg sodium, 16g total carbohydrate (3g fiber, 5g sugar), 29g protein, 100%DV vitamin A, 10%DV vitamin C, 6%DV calcium, 25%DV iron.

Note: You could add 5 red or white potatoes, quartered, to Step 4.

Italian Pot Roast

Betty Chalker
Dalhart, TX

Makes 8 servings
(Ideal slow-cooker size: 6-quart)

1-lb. boneless round roast
1 medium-sized onion, sliced
¼ tsp. salt
¼ tsp. black pepper
2 8-oz. cans no-salt-added tomato sauce
.7 oz. pkg. dry Italian salad dressing mix

1. Slice roast in quarters for even cooking and to distribute the flavors better. Place in slow cooker.
2. Cover with sliced onions.
3. In small bowl, stir together remaining ingredients and pour over meat and onions.
4. Cook on high 3 hours, or on high 30 minutes and then low for 4 hours, or until meat is tender.
5. Shred meat and serve in sauce over rice or mashed potatoes.

Per Serving: 100 calories (25 calories from fat), 3g total fat (1g saturated, 0g trans), 35mg cholesterol, 720mg sodium, 8g total carbohydrate (1g fiber, 5g sugar), 12g protein, 10%DV vitamin A, 10%DV vitamin C, 2%DV calcium, 10%DV iron.

Dilled Pot Roast

Kathryn Yoder
Minot, ND

Makes 8 servings
(Ideal slow-cooker size: 4- or 5-quart)

2¾-lb. beef pot roast
1 tsp. salt
¼ tsp. black pepper
2 tsp. dried dill weed, divided
¼ cup water
2 Tbsp. wine vinegar
4 Tbsp. flour
½ cup water
2 cups fat-free sour cream

1. Sprinkle both sides of beef with salt, pepper, and 1 tsp. dill weed. Place in slow cooker.
2. Add ¼ cup water and vinegar.
3. Cover. Cook on low 7-9 hours.
4. Remove meat from pot. Turn cooker to high.
5. Stir flour into ½ cup water. Stir into meat drippings.
6. Stir in additional 1 tsp. dill weed if you wish.
7. Cover. Cook on high 5 minutes.
8. Stir in sour cream.
9. Cover. Cook on high another 5 minutes.
10. Slice beef and serve with sour cream sauce.

Per Serving: 270 calories (80 calories from fat), 8g total fat (3g saturated, 0g trans), 100mg cholesterol, 390mg sodium, 13g total carbohydrate (0g fiber, 5g sugar), 34g protein, 0%DV vitamin A, 0%DV vitamin C, 6%DV calcium, 20%DV iron.

Pot Roast

Janie Steele
Moore, OK

Makes 16 servings
(Ideal slow-cooker size: 6-quart)

1 Tbsp. olive oil
2-lb. boneless beef top round roast
2 cups apple juice
16-oz. can tomato sauce
2 small onions, chopped
3 Tbsp. white vinegar
1 Tbsp. salt
3/4 tsp. ground ginger, or 1 Tbsp. fresh
   gingerroot, minced
2-3 tsp. ground cinnamon
1/4 cup cornstarch
1 cup water

1. Brown roast in olive oil on all sides in a skillet. Then place it in your slow cooker.
2. Combine juice, tomato sauce, onions, vinegar, salt, ginger, and cinnamon. Pour over roast.
3. Cook on high 5-7 hours.
4. Mix cornstarch and water until smooth. Remove roast and keep warm on a platter. Stir cornstarch water into juices in cooker.
5. Return roast to cooker and continue cooking 1 hour on high, or until meat is done and gravy thickens.

Per Serving: 150 calories (45 calories from fat), 5g total fat (1.5g saturated, 0g trans), 50mg cholesterol, 640mg sodium, 9g total carbohydrate (less than 1g fiber, 5g sugar), 17g Protein, 6%DV vitamin A, 4%DV vitamin C, 2%DV calcium, 15%DV iron.

Note: This recipe would also work well for a pork roast.

Low-Fat Crock-Pot Roast

Charlotte Shaffer
East Earl, PA

Makes 10 servings
(Ideal slow-cooker size: 6-quart)

3-lb. boneless beef roast
4 carrots, cut into 2" pieces
4 potatoes, cut into quarters
2 onions, quartered
1 cup fat-free, low-sodium beef broth
1 tsp. garlic powder
1/2 tsp. Mrs. Dash seasoning
1/2 tsp. salt
1/2 tsp. black pepper

1. Place roast in slow cooker.
2. Add carrots around edges, pushing them down so they reach the bottom of the cooker.
3. Add potatoes and onions.
4. Mix together broth and seasonings and pour over roast.
5. Cover. Cook on low 10 hours or on high 6 hours.

Per Serving: 260 calories (60 calories from fat), 7 total fat (2g saturated, 0g trans), 80mg cholesterol, 180mg sodium, 20g total carbohydrate (3g fiber, 4g sugar), 30g protein, 80%DV vitamin A, 20%DV vitamin C, 2%DV calcium, 20%DV iron.

Notes: You may brown the roast in a nonstick skillet on all sides before placing in cooker for added flavor.

If you want gravy, and if your diet allows, add a second cup of fat-free beef broth to Step 4. Remove the roast from the cooker at the end of the cooking time and keep warm on a platter. Turn the cooker to high until cooking juices come to a boil. Meanwhile, mix 1/4 cup flour into 1/2 cup cold water until smooth. When cooking juices boil, stir in flour water, stirring constantly until smooth and thickened. Serve with sliced beef.

Succulent Steak

Betty B. Dennison
Grove City, PA

Makes 6 servings
(Ideal slow-cooker size: 4-quart)

1½ lbs. round steak, cut ½"-¾" thick
¼ cup flour
½ tsp. salt
¼ tsp. black pepper
¼ tsp. paprika
2 onions, sliced
4-oz. can sliced mushrooms, drained
½ cup fat-free, low-sodium beef broth
2 tsp. Worcestershire sauce
2 Tbsp. flour
3 Tbsp. water

1. Mix together ¼ cup flour, salt, pepper, and paprika.
2. Cut steak into 6 pieces. Dredge meat in seasoned flour until lightly coated.
3. Layer half of onions, half of steak, and half of mushrooms into slow cooker. Repeat.
4. Combine beef broth and Worcestershire sauce. Pour over mixture in slow cooker.
5. Cover. Cook on low 8-10 hours.
6. Remove steak to serving platter and keep warm. Mix together 2 Tbsp. flour and water. Stir into juices in cooker and cook on high until thickened, about 10 minutes. Pour over steak and serve.

Per Serving: 190 calories (50 calories from fat), 6g total fat (2g saturated, 0g trans), 70mg cholesterol, 340mg sodium, 10g total carbohydrate (1g fiber, 2g sugar), 24g protein, 0%DV vitamin A, 0%DV vitamin C, 0%DV calcium, 20%DV iron.

Beef Burgundy

Joyce Kaut
Rochester, NY

Makes 8 servings
(Ideal slow-cooker size: 4-quart)

2 slices lean turkey bacon, cut in squares
2 lbs. lean sirloin tip or round steak, cubed
¼ cup flour
1 tsp. salt
½ tsp. seasoning salt
¼ tsp. dried marjoram
½ tsp. dried thyme
¼ tsp. black pepper
1 garlic clove, minced
1 low-sodium beef bouillon cube, crushed
1 cup burgundy wine
¼ lb. fresh mushrooms, sliced
2 Tbsp. cornstarch
2 Tbsp. cold water

1. Cook bacon in nonstick skillet until browned. Remove bacon, reserving drippings.
2. Coat beef with flour and brown on all sides in bacon drippings.
3. Combine steak, bacon drippings, bacon, seasonings, garlic, bouillon, and wine in slow cooker.
4. Cover. Cook on low 6-8 hours.
5. Add mushrooms.
6. Dissolve cornstarch in water. Add to slow cooker.
7. Cover. Cook on high 15 minutes.
8. Serve over noodles.

Per Serving: 180 calories (45 calories from fat), 5g total fat (1.5g saturated, 0g trans), 55mg cholesterol, 630mg sodium, 7g total carbohydrate (0g fiber, 1g sugar), 18g protein, 0%DV vitamin A, 0%DV vitamin C, 2%DV calcium, 15%DV iron.

Note: If your diet allows, you may want to increase the salt to 1½ tsp. or the seasoning salt to 1 tsp.

Corned Beef

Elaine Vigoda
Rochester, NY

Makes 12 servings
(Ideal slow-cooker size: 5- or 6-quart)

3 large carrots, cut into chunks
1 cup chopped celery
1 tsp. salt*
1/2 tsp. black pepper*
1 cup water
4-lb. corned beef
1 large onion, cut into pieces
4 potatoes, peeled and chunked
half a small head of cabbage, cut in
  wedges

1. Place carrots, celery, seasonings, and water in slow cooker.
2. Add beef. Cover with onions.
3. Cover. Cook on low 8-10 hours or on high 5-6 hours. (If your schedule allows, this dish has especially good taste and texture if you begin it on high for 1 hour, and then turn it to low for 5-6 hours, before going on to Step 4.)
4. Lift corned beef out of cooker and add potatoes, pushing them to bottom of slow cooker. Return beef to cooker.
5. Cover. Cook on low 1 hour.
6. Lift corned beef out of cooker and add cabbage, pushing the wedges down into the broth. Return beef to cooker.
7. Cover. Cook on low 1 more hour.
8. Remove corned beef. Cool and slice on the diagonal. Serve surrounded by vegetables.

Per Serving: 340 calories (130 calories from fat), 15g total fat (5g saturated, 0.5g trans), 75mg cholesterol, 1110mg sodium, 35g total carbohydrate (7g fiber, 6g sugar), 19g protein, 80%DV vitamin A, 40%DV vitamin C, 8%DV calcium, 20%DV iron.

If the corned beef that you buy includes a spice packet, use either it or the salt and pepper called for in this recipe. Do not use both. (The nutritional analysis for this recipe was based on the 1 tsp. salt and 1/2 tsp. black pepper specified here, and not on a spice packet.)

Note: *Horseradish is a tasty condiment to serve alongside this dish.*

CC Roast
(Company's Coming)

Anne Townsend
Albuquerque, NM

Makes 8 servings
(Ideal slow-cooker size: 4- or 5-quart)

3-lb. boneless pot roast
2 Tbsp. flour
1 Tbsp. prepared mustard
1 Tbsp. chili sauce
1 Tbsp. Worcestershire sauce
1 tsp. red cider vinegar
1 tsp. sugar
4 potatoes, sliced
2 onions, sliced

1. Place pot roast in slow cooker.
2. Make a paste with the flour, mustard, chili sauce, Worcestershire sauce, vinegar, and sugar. Spread over the roast.
3. Top with potatoes and then the onions.
4. Cover. Cook on low 10-12 hours.

Per Serving: 320 calories (70 calories from fat), 8g total fat (3g saturated, 0g trans), 100mg cholesterol, 160mg sodium, 24g total carbohydrate (3g fiber, 3g sugar), 36g protein, 0%DV vitamin A, 20%DV vitamin C, 2%DV calcium, 25%DV iron.

Easy Beef
Evelyn Page
Rapid City, SD

Makes 4 servings
(Ideal slow-cooker size: 4- or 5-quart)

1 lb. lean beef stewing meat, trimmed of
  fat
10½-oz. can French onion soup, undiluted
10¾-oz. can 98% fat-free mushroom soup,
  undiluted

1. Combine meat and soups in slow cooker.
2. Cook on low 4-5 hours.
3. Serve over rice.

Per Serving: 330 calories (80 calories from fat), 9g total fat
(2.5g saturated, 1g trans), 75mg cholesterol, 1110mg
sodium, 34g total carbohydrate (0.5g fiber, 4g sugar), 26g
protein, 0%DV vitamin A, 0%DV vitamin C, 4%DV
calcium, 20%DV iron.

Note: *If your diet allows, you may want to add ½
tsp. salt and ¼ tsp. black pepper to Step 1.*

Easy Company Beef
Joyce B. Suiter
Garysburg, NC

Makes 12 servings
(Ideal slow-cooker size: 4-quart)

3 lbs. lean stewing beef, cubed
10¾-oz. can fat-free, low-sodium cream of
  mushroom soup
7-oz. jar mushrooms, undrained
½ cup red wine
1 envelope dry onion soup mix

1. Combine all ingredients in slow cooker.
2. Cover. Cook on low 10 hours.
3. Serve over noodles, rice, or pasta.

Per Serving: 130 calories (40 calories from fat), 4.5g total
fat (1.5g saturated, 0g trans), 45mg cholesterol, 370mg
sodium, 4g total carbohydrate (0g fiber, 0g sugar), 16g
protein, 0%DV vitamin A, 0%DV vitamin C, 2%DV
calcium, 10%DV iron.

Crock-Pot Stroganoff
Evelyn Page
Rapid City, SD

Makes 10 servings
(Ideal slow-cooker size: 5- or 6-quart)

1½-lb. round steak, trimmed of fat
¼ cup flour
½ tsp. black pepper
½ tsp. salt
1 tsp. garlic, minced
1 small onion, chopped
1 Tbsp. low-sodium soy sauce
1 beef bouillon cube
10¾-oz. can 98% fat-free cream of
  mushroom soup
1 cup water
8-oz. pkg. fat-free cream cheese, cubed

1. Cut steak into strips 1" long and ½"
wide.
2. Mix with flour, pepper, salt, and garlic.
3. Combine with onion, soy sauce, bouillon,
soup, and water in slow cooker.
4. Cook on low 6-7 hours, stirring
occasionally.
5. Add cream cheese cubes last 30 minutes
of cooking.
6. Serve over cooked wide noodles.

Per Serving: 140 calories (40 calories from fat), 4.5g total
fat (1.5g saturated, 0g trans), 45mg cholesterol, 760mg
sodium, 8g total carbohydrate (0g fiber, 1g sugar), 18g
protein, 4%DV vitamin A, 2%DV vitamin C, 6%DV
calcium, 10%DV iron.

Beef Stroganoff

Gloria Julien
Gladstone, MI

Makes 6 servings
(Ideal slow-cooker size: 4-quart)

1½ lbs. lean beef stewing meat, trimmed
   of fat
1 onion, chopped
1 clove garlic, minced
1 tsp. salt
¼ tsp. black pepper
1 lb. fresh mushrooms
10¾-oz. can 98% fat-free cream of
   mushroom soup
1 cup water
1 cup fat-free sour cream

1. Combine all ingredients except sour
cream in slow cooker.
2. Cook on low 6-8 hours.
3. Stir in sour cream.
4. Cook on high for a few minutes to heat
sour cream.

Per Serving: 240 calories (70 calories from fat), 7g total fat
(2.5g saturated, 0.5g trans), 75mg cholesterol, 800mg
sodium, 15g total carbohydrate (1g fiber, 6g sugar), 27g
protein, 6%DV vitamin A, 2%DV vitamin C, 8%DV
calcium, 20%DV iron.

Note: This saucy dish works well served over no-yolk noodles.

Beef-Lite

Rebecca Leichty
Harrisonburg, VA

Makes 5 servings
(Ideal slow-cooker size: 3-quart)

1 lb. extra-lean ground beef
1 pkg. dry onion soup mix
10¾-oz. can 98% fat-free cream of celery
   soup
10¾-oz. can 98% fat-free cream of
   mushroom soup

1. Spray slow cooker with fat-free cooking
spray.
2. Combine all ingredients in slow cooker.
3. Cook on low for 6-8 hours.
4. Serve over hot rice.

Per Serving: 410 calories (110 calories from fat), 12 total
fat (4.5g saturated, 1.5g trans), 40mg cholesterol, 1100mg
sodium, 50g total carbohydrate (1g fiber, 2g sugar), 24g
protein, 2%DV vitamin A, 0%DV vitamin C, 6%DV
calcium, 20%DV iron.

Veal Hawaiian

Dorothy VanDeest
Memphis, TN

Makes 4 servings
(Ideal slow-cooker size: 4-quart)

1½ lbs. boneless veal shoulder, trimmed
 of all fat and cut into 1" cubes
1 cup water
¼ cup sherry
2 Tbsp. low-sodium soy sauce
1 tsp. ground ginger
1 tsp. artificial sweetener

1. Lightly brown veal in a nonstick skillet.
2. Combine remaining ingredients in slow cooker. Stir in veal.
3. Cover. Cook on low 6 hours.

Per Serving: 220 calories (60 calories from fat), 7g total fat
(3g saturated, 0g trans), 130mg cholesterol, 470mg sodium,
1g total carbohydrate (0g fiber, 0g sugar), 32g protein, 0%DV
vitamin A, 0%DV vitamin C, 4%DV calcium, 10%DV iron.

*Notes: You may substitute pork shoulder for the
veal.*
 This is tasty served over rice.

Sauerkraut Chop Suey

Gloria Julien
Gladstone, MI

Makes 10 servings

1 lb. beef stewing meat, trimmed of fat
1 lb. pork roast, cubed and trimmed of fat
2 10¾-oz. cans 98% fat-free cream of
 mushroom soup
1 envelope dry onion soup mix
27-oz. can sauerkraut
2 cups skim milk
12-oz. pkg. kluski (or extra-sturdy) noodles

1. Combine all ingredients except noodles in
slow cooker.
2. Cook on low 8-10 hours.
3. Add uncooked noodles 2 hours before
serving, or cook noodles fully, drain, and stir
into chop suey 15 minutes before serving.

Per Serving: 300 calories (60 calories from fat), 7g total fat
(2.5g saturated, 0.5g trans), 95mg cholesterol, 780mg
sodium, 33g total carbohydrate (2g fiber, 4g sugar), 25g
protein, 2%DV vitamin A, 2%DV vitamin C, 8%DV
calcium, 15%DV iron.

Hamburger Cabbage
Donna Lantgen
Rapid City, SD

Makes 6 servings
(Ideal slow-cooker size: 4- or 5-quart)

1 lb. extra-lean ground beef
1 medium-sized head cabbage, cut in
    bite-sized pieces, or shredded,
    whichever you prefer
1 small onion, diced
1 tsp. salt
1/4 tsp. black pepper
1 cup ketchup

1. Brown beef in nonstick skillet.
2. Place half the cut cabbage in the cooker.
Top with half the onions.
3. Place beef over vegetables and sprinkle
with half the seasonings.
4. Top with remaining cabbage, onions, and
seasonings.
5. Spread ketchup over all.
6. Cook on low 6 hours, or until vegetables
are done to your liking.

Per Serving: 210 calories (70 calories from fat)
(3g saturated, 0g trans), 7g total fat, 30mg cholesterol, 560mg sodium,
20g total carbohydrate (4g fiber, 9g sugar), 18g protein,
10%DV vitamin A, 40%DV vitamin C, 8%DV calcium,
15%DV iron.

Casserole for Skinnies
Betty Moore
Plano, IL

Makes 6 servings
(Ideal slow-cooker size: 5- or 6-quart)

1 small head cabbage, chopped
2 large onions, diced
6-8 ribs celery, chopped
1 1/2-2 lbs. extra-lean ground beef
2 15-oz. cans low-sodium stewed tomatoes
2 14 1/2-oz. cans green beans, drained
1 tsp. dried basil
1 tsp. dried oregano
1/2 tsp. dried thyme
3-4 cups water

1. Combine all ingredients in slow cooker.
2. Cook on low 7-9 hours.

Per Serving: 370 calories (130 calories from fat), 14g total
fat (6g saturated, 0.5g trans), 55mg cholesterol, 530mg
sodium, 26g total carbohydrate (9g fiber, 14g sugar), 36g
protein, 20%DV vitamin A, 60%DV vitamin C, 15%DV
calcium, 40%DV iron.

Notes:
*1. You may substitute 1 1/2-2 lbs. lean stewing meat
instead of ground chuck.*
*2. You may also substitute 1 1/2-2 lbs. ground
turkey instead of the ground beef.*

Hamburg, Cabbage & Potato Dinner

Becky Frey
Lebanon, PA

Makes 6-8 servings
(Ideal slow-cooker size: 5- or 6-quart)

1 lb. extra-lean ground beef
6 medium potatoes, quartered
1 medium-sized head of cabbage, cut in
  chunks
3/4 tsp. salt
1/2 tsp. black pepper
2 cups water

1. Brown ground beef in nonstick skillet.
2. Layer in slow cooker potatoes, cabbage, and hamburger. Sprinkle seasonings over each layer.
3. Pour water over top.
4. Cover. Cook on low 7-8 hours or until vegetables are tender.

Per Serving: 250 calories (50 calories from fat), 6g total fat (2g saturated, 0g trans), 20mg cholesterol, 75mg sodium, 34g total carbohydrate (6g fiber, 4g sugar), 16g protein, 4%DV vitamin A, 80%DV vitamin C, 8%DV calcium, 15%DV iron.

Beef-Vegetable Casserole

Edwina Stoltzfus
Narvon, PA

Makes 8 servings
(Ideal slow-cooker size: 5-quart)

1 lb. extra-lean ground beef or turkey
1 medium-sized onion, chopped
1/2 cup celery, chopped
4 cups cabbage, chopped
2 1/2 cups canned stewed tomatoes, slightly
  mashed
1 Tbsp. flour
1 tsp. salt
1 Tbsp. sugar
1/4-1/2 tsp. black pepper, according to your
  taste preference

1. Sauté meat, onion, and celery in nonstick skillet until meat is browned.
2. Pour into slow cooker.
3. Top with layers of cabbage, tomatoes, flour, salt, sugar, and pepper.
4. Cover. Cook on high 4-5 hours.

Per Serving: 140 calories (50 calories from fat), 5g total fat (2g saturated, 0g trans), 20mg cholesterol, 710mg sodium, 10g total carbohydrate (2g fiber, 6g sugar), 13g protein, 8%DV vitamin A, 20%DV vitamin C, 8%DV calcium, 10%DV iron.

Stuffed Cabbage

Miriam Nolt
New Holland, PA

Makes 8 servings
(Ideal slow-cooker size: 5-quart)

4 cups water
12 large cabbage leaves, cut from head at
  base and washed
1 lb. lean ground beef or lamb
1/2 cup rice, cooked
1/2 tsp. salt
1/4 tsp. black pepper
1/4 tsp. dried thyme
1/4 tsp. nutmeg
1/4 tsp. cinnamon
6-oz. can tomato paste
3/4 cup water

1. Boil 4 cups water in saucepan. Turn off heat. Soak cabbage leaves in water for 5 minutes. Remove. Drain. Cool.
2. Combine ground beef, rice, salt, pepper, thyme, nutmeg, and cinnamon.
3. Place 2 Tbsp. of mixture on each cabbage leaf. Roll firmly. Stack in slow cooker.
4. Combine tomato paste and 3/4 cup water. Pour over stuffed cabbage.
5. Cover. Cook on low 8-10 hours.

Per Serving: 140 calories (50 calories from fat), 5g total fat (2g saturated, 0g trans), 20mg cholesterol, 220mg sodium, 10g total carbohydrate (2g fiber, 2g sugar), 13g protein, 10%DV vitamin A, 20%DV vitamin C, 4%DV calcium, 10%DV iron.

Mexicali Round Steak

Marcia S. Myer
Manheim, PA

Makes 6 servings
(Ideal slow-cooker size: 5-quart)

1 1/2 lbs. round steak, trimmed of fat
1 cup frozen corn, thawed
1/2-1 cup fresh cilantro, chopped, according
  to your taste preference
1/2 cup low-sodium, fat-free beef broth
3 ribs celery, sliced
1 large onion, sliced
20-oz. jar salsa
15-oz. can black beans, or pinto beans,
  rinsed and drained
1 cup fat-free cheddar cheese

1. Cut beef into 6 pieces. Place in slow cooker.
2. Combine remaining ingredients, except cheese, and pour over beef.
3. Cover. Cook on low 8-9 hours.
4. Sprinkle with cheese before serving.

Per Serving: 290 calories (60 calories from fat), 6g total fat (2g saturated, 0g trans), 70mg cholesterol, 900mg sodium, 26g total carbohydrate (7g fiber, 2g sugar), 35g protein, 20%DV vitamin A, 20%DV vitamin C, 25%DV calcium, 25%DV iron.

Beef and Beans

Barbara L. McGinnis
Hobe Sound, FL

Makes 10 servings
(Ideal slow-cooker size: 4-quart)

2½ lbs. beef, trimmed of fat and cut into ¾" pieces
15½-oz. can kidney beans, drained and rinsed
15½-oz. can great northern beans, drained and rinsed
2 14½-oz. cans diced tomatoes with garlic and onions, undrained
1 tsp. salt
½ tsp. black pepper

1. Combine all ingredients in slow cooker.
2. Cover. Cook on low 8-9 hours, or until beef is tender.
3. Serve in soup bowls as soup, or over rice.

Per Serving: 250 calories (50 calories from fat), 6g total fat (2g saturated, 0g trans), 70mg cholesterol, 650mg sodium, 19g total carbohydrate (5g fiber, 4g sugar), 29g protein, 6%DV vitamin A, 6%DV vitamin C, 10%DV calcium, 20%DV iron.

Cowtown Favorite

Jean H. Robinson
Cinnaminson, NJ

Makes 10 servings
(Ideal slow-cooker size: 4-quart)

2½ lbs. boneless beef, cut in 1"-square pieces and trimmed of fat
1 tsp. black pepper
½ tsp. salt
1 Tbsp. flour
1 medium-sized onion, sliced thin
3 large potatoes, peeled and chopped
3 cups carrots, in ½" slices
1 rib celery
2 cups green beans, cut in 1" pieces
2 14-oz. cans low-sodium stewed tomatoes, undrained
10¾-oz. can low-sodium tomato soup
2 Tbsp. tapioca

1. Combine black pepper, salt, and flour in a plastic bag. Add half the beef cubes. Shake to coat. Place beef in slow cooker. Flour the remaining cubes, and then add them to the cooker.
2. Layer onions, potatoes, carrots, celery, and green beans on top of meat.
3. Mix tomatoes, soup, and tapioca together. Pour over meat and vegetables.
4. Cover. Cook on high 5 hours or on low 8-9 hours.

Per Serving: 260 calories (50 calories from fat), 6g total fat (2g saturated, 0g trans), 70mg cholesterol, 190mg sodium, 26g total carbohydrate (5g fiber, 7g sugar), 25g protein, 200%DV vitamin A, 30%DV vitamin C, 6%DV calcium, 25%DV iron.

10-Layer Slow-Cooker Dish
Norma Saltzman
Shickley, NE

Makes 8 servings
(Ideal slow-cooker size: 5-quart)

1½ lbs. lean ground chuck
6 medium-sized potatoes, thinly sliced
1 medium onion, thinly sliced
½ tsp. salt
½ tsp. black pepper
15-oz. can corn, undrained
15-oz. can peas, undrained
¼ cup water
10¾-oz. can fat-free, low-sodium cream of
   mushroom soup

1. Brown ground chuck in nonstick skillet. Then create the following layers in the slow cooker.
2. Layer 1: one-fourth of the potatoes, mixed with one-half the onions, salt, and pepper.
3. Layer 2: half-can of corn.
4. Layer 3: one-fourth of the potatoes.
5. Layer 4: half-can of peas.
6. Layer 5: one-fourth of the potatoes, mixed with one-half the onions, salt, and pepper.
7. Layer 6: remaining corn.
8. Layer 7: remaining potatoes.
9. Layer 8: remaining peas and water.
10. Layer 9: ground chuck.
11. Layer 10: soup.
12. Cover. Cook on high 4 hours.

Per Serving: 370 calories (90 calories from fat), 9g total fat (3.5g saturated, 0.5g trans), 30mg cholesterol, 720mg sodium, 49g total carbohydrate (7g fiber, 6g sugar), 25g protein, 0%DV vitamin A, 30%DV vitamin C, 4%DV calcium, 25%DV iron.

Hungarian Goulash
Pat Bertsche
Flanagan, IL

Makes 10 servings
(Ideal slow-cooker size: 4-quart)

1 lb. extra-lean ground beef
1 large-sized onion, sliced
1 clove garlic, minced
½ cup ketchup
2 Tbsp. Worcestershire sauce
1 Tbsp. brown sugar
1-1½ tsp. salt
2 tsp. paprika
½ tsp. dry mustard
1 cup water
¼ cup flour
¼ cup cold water

1. Place meat in slow cooker. Cover with onions.
2. Combine garlic, ketchup, Worcestershire sauce, sugar, salt, paprika, mustard, and 1 cup water. Pour over meat.
3. Cook on low 5-6 hours.
4. Dissolve flour in ¼ cup cold water. Stir into meat mixture.
5. Cook on high 10-15 minutes, or until slightly thickened.
6. Serve over noodles or rice.

Per Serving: 90 calories (20 calories from fat), 2.5g total fat (1g saturated, 0g trans), 25mg cholesterol, 660mg sodium, 9g total carbohydrate (0.5g fiber, 3g sugar), 10g protein, 8%DV vitamin A, 2%DV vitamin C, 2%DV calcium, 8%DV iron.

Note: To brighten the flavor, you may add ¼ cup pickle cubes or 2 Tbsp. lemon zest when stirring in thickening in Step 4.

Goulash with Vegetables

Mrs. Audrey L. Kneer
Williamsfield, IL

Makes 7 servings
(Ideal slow-cooker size: 4-quart)

1 lb. extra-lean ground beef
1 medium-sized onion, chopped
1 clove garlic, chopped
14½-oz. can low-sodium diced tomatoes
16-oz. can kidney beans, drained
½ cup green bell pepper, chopped
1 cup celery, chopped
1 tsp. salt
1 Tbsp. Worcestershire sauce
½ tsp. paprika
1 Tbsp. sugar
1 bay leaf
¼ tsp. black pepper

1. Brown lean ground beef, onion, and garlic in a nonstick skillet over medium heat.
2. Combine all ingredients in slow cooker.
3. Cover. Cook on low 5-6 hours.
4. Serve over or with mashed potatoes.

Per Serving: 190 calories (60 calories from fat), 6g total fat (2.5g saturated, 0g trans), 25mg cholesterol, 800mg sodium, 17g total carbohydrate (4g fiber, 5g sugar), 18g protein, 2%DV vitamin A, 10%DV vitamin C, 8%DV calcium, 15%DV iron.

Ground Beef Casserole

Lois J. Cassidy
Willow Street, PA

Makes 8 servings
(Ideal slow-cooker size: 6-quart)

1½ lbs. lean ground chuck
6-8 potatoes, sliced
water and ½ tsp. cream of tartar
1 medium-sized onion, sliced
1 clove garlic, minced
½ tsp. salt
½ tsp. dried basil
½ tsp. dried thyme
¼ tsp. black pepper
14½-oz. can cut green beans with juice
10¾-oz. can fat-free, low-sodium cream of mushroom soup

1. Crumble uncooked ground chuck in bottom of slow cooker.
2. Slice potatoes into mixing bowl filled with water mixed with cream of tartar to keep potatoes from turning dark. Stir together; then drain potatoes and discard water.
3. Add potatoes, onion, garlic, salt, basil, thyme, and black pepper to cooker.
4. Pour beans over all. Spread can of mushroom soup over beans.
5. Cover. Cook on low 6-8 hours.

Per Serving: 340 calories (80 calories from fat), 9g total fat (3.5g saturated, 0.5g trans), 30mg cholesterol, 610mg sodium, 43g total carbohydrate (6g fiber, 3g sugar), 23g protein, 0%DV vitamin A, 20%DV vitamin C, 6%DV calcium, 20%DV iron.

Note: If you have time, brown the chuck in a nonstick skillet before putting it in the slow cooker.

For a creamier dish, mix half a soup can of water with the mushroom soup before placing over beans.

Beef Stew

Barbara L. McGinnis
Hobe Sound, FL

Makes 8 servings
(Ideal slow-cooker size: 5-quart)

1½ lbs. boneless, beef chuck roast,
    trimmed of fat
1 envelope dry low-sodium onion soup
    mix
½ tsp. black pepper
6 cups water
2 cups potatoes, peeled and cubed
8 medium-sized carrots, cut into chunks
1 medium-sized onion, chopped
1 cup frozen peas, thawed
1 cup frozen corn, thawed
5 Tbsp. cornstarch
6 Tbsp. cold water

1. Place beef in slow cooker. Sprinkle with soup mix and pepper.
2. Pour water around meat.
3. Cover. Cook on low for 8 hours.
4. Remove roast and let stand for 5 minutes.
5. Add vegetables to slow cooker. Cube beef and return to slow cooker.
6. Cover. Cook on low 1½ hours, or until veggies are tender.
7. Combine cornstarch and cold water until smooth. Stir into stew.
8. Cover. Cook on high 1 more hour.

Per Serving: 240 calories (40 calories from fat), 4.5g total fat (1.5g saturated, 0g trans), 50mg cholesterol, 170mg sodium, 31g total carbohydrate (5g fiber, 7g sugar), 21g protein, 300%DV vitamin A, 20%DV vitamin C, 4%DV calcium, 20%DV iron.

Slow-Cooker Stew

Rhonda L. Burgoon
Collingswood, NJ

Makes 6 servings
(Ideal slow-cooker size: 4- or 5-quart)

1 lb. lean beef, cubed
2 cups low-sodium diced canned tomatoes,
    undrained
1 cup non-fat, low-sodium beef broth
¼ cup red wine
1 Tbsp. Worcestershire sauce
1 bay leaf
1 tsp. dried thyme
1 tsp. dried rosemary
1 tsp. dried marjoram
1 Tbsp. garlic, crushed
½ tsp. black pepper
1 onion, diced
2-3 medium-sized potatoes, diced
1 cup carrots, chopped

1. Combine all ingredients in slow cooker.
2. Cover. Cook on high 4-6 hours.

Per Serving: 170 calories (35 calories from fat), 4g total fat (1.5g saturated, 0g trans), 45mg cholesterol, 300mg sodium, 15g total carbohydrate (3g fiber, 5g sugar), 18g protein, 100%DV vitamin A, 20%DV vitamin C, 8%DV calcium, 15%DV iron.

Note: If your sodium count allows, you may want to add ¼-½ tsp. salt to Step 1.

Beef Barley Stew

Bonita Ensinberger
Albuquerque, NM

Makes 6 servings
(Ideal slow-cooker size: 5-quart)

½ lb. lean round steak, cut in ½" cubes
4 carrots, peeled and cut in ¼" slices
1 cup yellow onions, chopped
½ cup green bell peppers, coarsely
   chopped
1 clove garlic, pressed
½ lb. fresh button mushrooms, quartered
¾ cup dry pearl barley
½ tsp. salt
¼ tsp. ground black pepper
½ tsp. dried thyme
½ tsp. dried sweet basil
1 bay leaf
5 cups fat-free, low-sodium beef broth

1. Combine all ingredients in slow cooker.
2. Cover. Cook on low 9-10 hours.

Per Serving: 220 calories (45 calories from fat), 5g total fat
(1g saturated, 0g trans), 25mg cholesterol, 520mg sodium,
29g total carbohydrate (6g fiber, 5g sugar), 16g protein,
200%DV vitamin A, 20%DV vitamin C, 4%DV calcium,
15%DV iron.

Beef and Beans over Rice

Robin Schrock
Millersburg, OH

Makes 8 servings
(Ideal slow-cooker size: 4-quart)

1½ lbs. boneless, round steak
1 Tbsp. prepared mustard
1 Tbsp. chili powder
½ tsp. salt, optional
¼ tsp. black pepper
1 garlic clove, minced
2 14½-oz. cans low-sodium diced
   tomatoes
1 medium-sized onion, chopped
1 beef bouillon cube, crushed
16-oz. can kidney beans, rinsed and
   drained

1. Cut steak into thin strips.
2. Combine mustard, chili powder, salt (if
desired), pepper, and garlic in a bowl.
3. Add steak. Toss to coat.
4. Transfer to slow cooker. Add tomatoes,
onion, and bouillon.
5. Cover. Cook on low 5-7 hours.
6. Stir in beans. Cook 30 minutes longer.
7. Serve over rice.

Per Serving: 190 calories (40 calories from fat), 4.5g total
fat (1.5g saturated, 0g trans), 50mg cholesterol, 870mg
sodium, 15g total carbohydrate (4g fiber, 4g sugar), 21g
protein, 10%DV vitamin A, 8%DV vitamin C, 0%DV
calcium, 15%DV iron.

Brevard Stew
David R. Britchfield
Melbourne, FL

Makes 10 servings
(Ideal slow-cooker size: 5-quart)

1½ lbs. lean stewing beef, cut in 1" cubes
1 cup onions, chopped
1 Tbsp. olive oil
3 medium-sized potatoes, cut in 1" cubes
28-oz. can low-sodium crushed tomatoes, undrained
16-oz. can cream-style corn, drained and rinsed
16-oz. can low-sodium lima beans, drained and rinsed
16-oz. can low-sodium cut carrots, drained and rinsed
1 Tbsp. Worcestershire sauce
¾ tsp. salt
½ tsp. dried marjoram leaves
4 slices bacon, cooked and crumbled
¼ tsp. red pepper sauce

1. In a large skillet, brown beef and onions in olive oil over medium heat until beef is brown on all sides. Drain.
2. Combine all ingredients except bacon and red pepper sauce in slow cooker sprayed with non-fat cooking spray. Mix well.
3. Cover. Cook on low 8-9 hours.
4. Stir bacon and red pepper sauce into stew just before serving.

Per Serving: 270 calories (60 calories from fat), 7g total fat (2g saturated, 0g trans), 45mg cholesterol, 530mg sodium, 35g total carbohydrate (6g fiber, 5g sugar), 20g protein, 100%DV vitamin A, 20%DV vitamin C, 6%DV calcium, 25%DV iron.

Veggie Beef Stew
Irene Hull
Anderson, IN

Makes 5 servings
(Ideal slow-cooker size: 3- or 4-quart)

¾ lb. lean stewing meat, trimmed of fat and cut into ½" cubes
2 tsp. canola oil
14½-oz. can low-sodium, low-fat beef broth
14½-oz. can low-sodium stewed tomatoes
1½ cups butternut squash, peeled and cubed
1 cup frozen corn
½ cup carrots, chopped
dash of salt
dash of black pepper
dash of dried oregano
2 Tbsp. cornstarch
¼ cup water

1. In a skillet, brown stewing meat in canola oil over medium heat. Transfer to slow cooker.
2. Add beef broth, vegetables, salt, pepper, and oregano.
3. Cover. Cook on high 5-6 hours.
4. Combine cornstarch and water until smooth. Stir into stew.
5. Cover. Cook on high 30 minutes.

Per Serving: 200 calories (50 calories from fat), 5g total fat (1.5g saturated, 0g trans), 40mg cholesterol, 180mg sodium, 22g total carbohydrate (4g fiber, 6g sugar), 17g protein, 150%DV vitamin A, 20%DV vitamin C, 6%DV calcium, 15%DV iron.

Best Everyday Stew

Elizabeth L. Richards
Rapid City SD

Makes 8 servings
(Ideal slow-cooker size: 6-quart)

2¼ lbs. flank steak, 1½" thick
8 red potatoes, small to medium in size
10 baby carrots
1 large clove garlic, diced
1 medium-sized to large onion, chopped
1 cup baby peas
3 ribs celery, cut in 1" pieces
3 cups cabbage, in chunks
2 8-oz. cans low-sodium tomato sauce
1 Tbsp. Worcestershire sauce
2 bay leaves
¼-½ tsp. dried thyme, according to your
 taste preference
¼-½ tsp. dried basil, according to your
 taste preference
¼-½ tsp. dried marjoram, according to
 your taste preference
1 Tbsp. parsley
2 cups water or more, if desired
4 cubes beef or vegetable bouillon

1. Trim flank steak of fat. Cut in 1½" cubes.
Brown slowly in nonstick skillet.
2. Quarter potatoes.
3. Combine all ingredients in large slow
cooker.
4. Cover. Cook on high 1 hour. Turn to low
and cook 9 additional hours.

Per Serving: 260 calories (60 calories from fat), 7g total fat
(2g saturated, 0g trans), 75mg cholesterol, 1330mg sodium,
22g total carbohydrate (4g fiber, 6g sugar), 29g protein,
40%DV vitamin A, 20%DV vitamin C, 6%DV calcium,
25%DV iron.

Let all soups and stews sit overnight in
refrigerator and skim off any fat in the morning.

Gone-All-Day Dinner

Susan Scheel
West Fargo, ND

Makes 8 servings
(Ideal slow-cooker size: 5-quart)

1 cup uncooked wild rice, rinsed and
 drained
1 cup celery, chopped
1 cup carrots, chopped
2 4-oz. cans mushrooms, drained
1 large onion, chopped
½ cup slivered almonds
3 beef bouillon cubes
2½ tsp. seasoned salt
2 lbs. boneless round steak, cut in bite-
 sized pieces
3 cups water

1. Layer ingredients in slow cooker in order
listed. Do not stir.
2. Cover. Cook on low 6-8 hours.
3. Stir before serving.

Per Serving: 300 calories (90 calories from fat), 10g total fat
(2g saturated, 0g trans), 70mg cholesterol, 1110mg sodium,
24g total arbohydrate (4g fiber, 3g sugar), 28g protein,
80%DV vitamin A, 2%DV vitamin C, 4%DV calcium,
20%DV iron.

Hearty Beef Stew

Laurie Sylvester
Ridgely, MD

Makes 8 servings
(Ideal slow-cooker size: 5- or 6-quart)

2 lbs. lean stewing beef, cubed
2 Tbsp. quick-cooking tapioca
2 ribs celery
4 onions, quartered
1 Tbsp. sugar
4 carrots, cut up
4 potatoes, cubed
16-oz. can string beans, undrained
10¾-oz. can low-sodium tomato soup
½ cup water
1 tsp. salt
½ tsp. black pepper
1 Tbsp. fresh parsley

1. Combine all ingredients except parsley in slow cooker.
2. Cover. Cook on high 6-8 hours. Stir in parsley just before serving.

Per Serving: 300 calories (60 calories from fat), 6g total fat (2g saturated, 0g trans), 70mg cholesterol, 440mg sodium, 35g total carbohydrate (5g fiber, 10g sugar), 26g protein, 100%DV vitamin A, 30%DV vitamin C, 6%DV calcium, 25%DV iron.

Lotsa Tomatoes Beef Stew

Bernice A. Esau
North Newton, KS

Makes 6 servings
(Ideal slow-cooker size: 6- or 7-quart)

2 lbs. extra-lean stewing beef cubes,
  trimmed of fat
5-6 carrots, cut in 1″ pieces
1 large onion, cut in chunks
3 ribs celery, sliced
6 medium-sized tomatoes, cut up and
  gently mashed
½ cup quick-cooking tapioca
1 whole clove, or ¼-1/2 tsp. ground cloves
1 tsp. dried basil
½ tsp. dried oregano
2 bay leaves
2 tsp. salt
½ tsp. black pepper
3-4 potatoes, cubed

1. Place all ingredients in slow cooker. Mix together well.
2. Cover. Cook on high 5½-6 hours.

Per Serving: 400 calories (70 calories from fat), 8g total fat (2.5g saturated, 0g trans), 90mg cholesterol, 110mg sodium, 48g total carbohydrate (7g fiber, 10g sugar), 34g protein, 200%DV vitamin A, 50%DV vitamin C, 60%DV calcium, 30%DV iron.

Note: Add 2-3 Tbsp. instant mashed potatoes during the last 30 minutes of cooking if the cooking juices are too thin.

Fruity Vegetable Beef Stew

Esther S. Martin, Ephrata, PA
Mrs. Carolyn Baer, Conrath, WI

Makes 4 servings
(Ideal slow-cooker size: 4-quart)

3/4 lb. lean beef stewing meat, cut into
   1/2" cubes
2 tsp. canola oil
14 1/2-oz. can fat-free beef broth
14 1/2-oz. can stewed tomatoes, cut up
1 1/2 cups butternut squash, peeled and
   cubed
1 cup frozen corn, thawed
6 dried apricot or peach halves, quartered
1/2 cup carrots, chopped
1 tsp. dried oregano
1/4 tsp. salt
1/4 tsp. black pepper
2 Tbsp. cornstarch
1/4 cup water
2 Tbsp. fresh parsley, minced

1. Brown meat in oil in a non-stick skillet over medium heat.

2. Combine meat, broth, tomatoes, squash, corn, apricots, carrots, oregano, salt, and pepper in slow cooker.

3. Cook on high 5-6 hours, or until vegetables and meat are tender.

4. Combine cornstarch and water until smooth. Stir into stew.

5. Cook on high 30 minutes, or until stew is thickened.

6. Add parsley just before serving.

Per Serving: 280 calories (60 calories from fat), 7g total fat (1.5g saturated, 0g trans), 50mg cholesterol, 510mg sodium, 35g total carbohydrate (5g fiber, 13g sugar), 23g protein, 150%DV vitamin A, 20%DV vitamin C, 8%DV calcium, 20%DV iron.

With the sweet flavor from apricots and squash we think this dish has a South American or Cuban flair. The addition of corn makes it even more hearty.

Slow-Cooker Stew

Sharon Wantland
Menomonee Falls, WI

Makes 6 servings
(Ideal slow-cooker size: 4- or 5-quart)

1 1/2 lbs. beef stewing meat
1 medium-sized onion, chopped
4 carrots, peeled and cut in slices
2 ribs celery cut in pieces
4 medium-sized potatoes, peeled and cut
   in cubes
28-oz. can sodium-free whole tomatoes,
   undrained
10 1/2-oz. can fat-free beef broth
1 Tbsp. Worcestershire sauce
2 Tbsp. dried parsley flakes
1 bay leaf
1 tsp. salt
1/4 tsp. black pepper
2 Tbsp. quick-cooking tapioca

1. Brown beef cubes over medium heat in nonstick skillet. Transfer to slow cooker.

2. Add remaining ingredients. Stir to blend.

3. Cook on low 6-8 hours.

Per Serving: 240 calories (40 calories from fat), 4.5g total fat (1.5g saturated, 0g trans), 50mg cholesterol, 520mg sodium, 30g total carbohydrate (5g fiber, 6g sugar), 21g protein, 150%DV vitamin A, 30%DV vitamin C, 6%DV calcium, 20%DV iron.

German Dinner

Sharon Miller
Holmesville, OH

Makes 6 servings
(Ideal slow-cooker size: 4- or 5-quart)

32-oz. bag sauerkraut, drained
1 lb. extra-lean ground beef
1 small green bell pepper, grated
2 11½-oz. cans V8 juice
½ cup chopped celery, optional

1. Combine all ingredients in slow cooker.
2. Cook for 1 hour on high, and then on low 8-10 hours.

Per Serving: 170 calories (60 calories from fat) (3g saturated, 0g trans), 30mg cholesterol, 1160mg sodium, 10g total carbohydrate (4g fiber, 3g sugar), 17g protein, 10%DV vitamin A, 40%DV vitamin C, 6%DV calcium, 25%DV iron.

Tangy Barbecue Sandwiches

Lavina Hochstedler, Grand Blanc, MI
Lois M. Martin, Lititz, PA

Makes 18 sandwiches
(Ideal slow-cooker size: 6-quart)

3 cups chopped celery
1 cup chopped onions
1 cup low-sodium ketchup
1 cup low-sodium barbecue sauce
1 cup water
2 Tbsp. vinegar
2 Tbsp. Worcestershire sauce
2 Tbsp. brown sugar
1 tsp. chili powder
1 tsp. salt
½ tsp. black pepper
½ tsp. garlic powder
4-lb. lean boneless chuck roast

1. Combine all ingredients except roast in slow cooker. When well mixed, add roast.
2. Cover. Cook on low 7-9 hours.
3. Remove roast. Cool and shred meat. Return to sauce. Heat well.
4. Serve on buns.

Per Serving: 300 calories (60 calories from fat), 7g total fat (2g saturated, 0g trans), 60mg cholesterol, 840mg sodium, 36g total carbohydrate (4g fiber, 10g sugar), 24g protein, 0%DV vitamin A, 0%DV vitamin C, 8%DV calcium, 20%DV iron.

Pork and Beef Barbecue

Susan Scheel
West Fargo, ND

Makes 14 servings
(Ideal slow-cooker size: 5- or 6-quart)

8-oz. can tomato sauce
1/2 cup brown sugar, packed
1/4 cup chili powder, or less
1/4 cup cider vinegar
2 tsp. Worcestershire sauce
1 tsp. salt
1 lb. lean beef stewing meat,
   cut into 3/4" cubes
1 lb. lean pork tenderloin,
   cut into 3/4" cubes
3 green bell peppers, chopped
3 large onions, chopped

1. Combine tomato sauce, brown sugar, chili powder, cider vinegar, Worcestershire sauce, and salt in slow cooker.
2. Stir in meats, green peppers, and onions.
3. Cover. Cook on high 6-8 hours.
4. Shred meat with two forks. Stir all ingredients together well.
5. Serve on buns.

Per Serving: 270 calories (50 calories from fat), 6g total fat (1.5g saturated, 0.5g trans), 40mg cholesterol, 480mg sodium, 38g total carbohydrate (3g fiber, 14g sugar), 18g protein, 20%DV vitamin A, 20%DV vitamin C, 8%DV calcium, 20%DV iron.

Beef Sandwiches

Robin Schrock
Millersburg, OH

Makes 12 servings
(Ideal slow-cooker size: 4- or 5-quart)

2-lb. boneless beef roast
3 medium-sized onions, chopped
2 cups red wine vinegar
3 bay leaves
1/2 tsp. salt, optional
1/4 tsp. ground cloves
1/2 tsp. garlic powder

1. Cut roast in half. Place in slow cooker.
2. Combine onions, vinegar, bay leaves, salt, cloves, and garlic powder. Pour over roast.
3. Cover. Cook on low 11-12 hours.
4. Discard bay leaves.
5. Remove meat. Shred with a fork.
6. Serve on hamburger buns.

Per Serving: 230 calories (50 calories from fat), 6g total fat (1.5g saturated, 0g trans), 45mg cholesterol, 330mg sodium, 27g total carbohydrate (4g fiber, 4g sugar), 19g protein, 0%DV vitamin A, 0%DV vitamin C, 0%DV calcium, 15%DV iron.

Note: If you prefer a somewhat sweeter flavoring, and your diet allows, you may want to add 1/4 cup brown sugar, 1/2 cup raisins, or several tablespoons of Splenda to Step 2.

Beef Pitas

Dede Peterson
Rapid City, SD

Makes 2 servings
(Ideal slow-cooker size: 2-quart)

½ lb. beef or pork, cut into small cubes
½ tsp. dried oregano
dash of black pepper
1 cup fresh tomatoes, chopped
2 Tbsp. fresh green bell peppers, diced
¼ cup nonfat sour cream
1 tsp. red wine vinegar
1 tsp. vegetable oil
2 large pita breads, heated and cut in half

1. Place meat in slow cooker. Sprinkle with oregano and black pepper.
2. Cook on low 3-4 hours.
3. In a separate bowl, combine tomatoes, green peppers, sour cream, vinegar, and oil.
4. Fill pitas with meat. Top with vegetable- and sour-cream mixture.

Per Serving: 380 calories (80 calories from fat), 9g total fat (2.5g saturated, 0g trans), 75mg cholesterol, 410mg sodium, 44g total carbohydrate (3g fiber, 6g sugar), 30g protein, 20%DV vitamin A, 20%DV vitamin C, 10%DV calcium, 25%DV iron.

French Dip

Loretta Weisz
Auburn, WA

Makes 12 servings
(Ideal slow-cooker size: 4- or 5-quart)

2-lb. beef top round roast, trimmed
3 cups water
1 cup light soy sauce
1 tsp. dried rosemary
1 tsp. dried thyme
1 tsp. garlic powder
1 bay leaf
3 whole peppercorns

1. Place roast in slow cooker. Add water, soy sauce, and seasonings.
2. Cover. Cook on high 5-6 hours.
3. Remove meat from broth. Thinly slice or shred. Keep warm.
4. Strain broth and skim off fat. Pour broth into small cups for dipping.
5. Serve beef on rolls.

Per Serving: 260 calories (60 calories from fat), 7g total fat (2g saturated, 0g trans), 70mg cholesterol, 630mg sodium, 20g total carbohydrate (1g fiber, 1g sugar), 26g protein, 0%DV vitamin A, 0%DV vitamin C, 4%DV calcium, 20%DV iron.

Slow-Cooked Steak Fajitas

Virginia Graybill, Hershey, PA

Makes 12 servings
(Ideal slow-cooker size: 4-quart)

1½ lbs. beef flank steak
15-oz. can low-sodium diced tomatoes
  with garlic and onion, undrained
1 jalapeno pepper, seeded and chopped*
2 garlic cloves, minced
1 tsp. ground coriander
1 tsp. ground cumin
1 tsp. chili powder
½ tsp. salt
2 medium-sized onions, sliced
2 medium-sized green bell peppers,
  julienned
2 medium-sized sweet red bell peppers,
  julienned
1 Tbsp. fresh parsley, minced
2 tsp. cornstarch
1 Tbsp. water
12 6" flour tortillas, warmed
¾ cup fat-free sour cream
¾ cup low-sodium salsa

1. Slice steak thinly into strips across grain. Place in slow cooker.
2. Add tomatoes, jalapeno, garlic, coriander, cumin, chili powder, and salt.
3. Cover. Cook on low 7 hours.
4. Add onions, peppers, and parsley.
5. Cover. Cook 1-2 hours longer, or until meat is tender.
6. Combine cornstarch and water until smooth. Gradually stir into slow cooker.
7. Cover. Cook on high 30 minutes, or until slightly thickened.
8. Using a slotted spoon, spoon about ½ cup of meat mixture down the center of each tortilla.
9. Add 1 Tbsp. sour cream and 1 Tbsp. salsa to each.
10. Fold bottom of tortilla over filling and roll up.

Per Serving: 250 calories (60 calories from fat), 7g total fat (2g saturated, 0g trans), 35mg cholesterol, 570mg sodium, 31g total carbohydrate (2g fiber, 4g sugar), 16g protein, 30%DV vitamin A, 60%DV vitamin C, 10%DV calcium, 20%DV iron.

When cutting jalapeno peppers, use rubber or plastic gloves to protect your hands. Avoid touching your face.

Slow-Cooker Fajita Stew

Sara Puskar, Abingdon, MD
Nancy Wagner Graves, Manhattan, KS

Makes 8 servings
(Ideal slow-cooker size: 3- or 4-quart)

2½ lbs. boneless beef top round steak
1 onion, chopped
1-oz. envelope dry fajita seasoning mix
  (about 2 Tbsp.)
14-oz. can diced tomatoes, undrained
1 red bell pepper, cut into 1" pieces
¼ cup flour
¼ cup water

1. Trim excess fat from beef and cut into 2" pieces. Combine with onion in slow cooker.
2. Mix together fajita seasoning and undrained tomatoes. Pour over beef.
3. Place cut-up peppers on top.
4. Cover. Cook on low 6-8 hours, or until beef is tender.
5. Combine flour and water in a small bowl. Stir well to mix.
6. Gradually add to slow cooker.
7. Cover. Cook on high 15-20 minutes until thickened, stirring occasionally.

Per Serving: 320 calories (60 calories from fat), 7g total fat (2.5g saturated, 0g trans), 85mg cholesterol, 330mg sodium, 31g total carbohydrate (2g fiber, 3g sugar), 31g protein, 20%DV vitamin A, 20%DV vitamin C, 4%DV calcium, 25%DV iron.

Note: This is delicious served over hot rice.

Slow-Cooker Enchiladas
Robin Schrock
Millersburg, OH

Makes 6 servings
(Ideal slow-cooker size: 4-quart)

1 lb. lean ground beef
1 cup onions, chopped
½ cup green bell pepper, chopped
16-oz. can pinto or kidney beans, rinsed
  and drained
10-oz. can diced tomatoes and green
  chilies
1 cup water
1 tsp. chili powder
16-oz. can black beans, rinsed and drained
½ tsp. ground cumin
½ tsp. salt
¼ tsp. black pepper
dash of dried red pepper flakes and/or
  several drops Tabasco sauce, if you like
1 cup shredded low-fat sharp cheddar
  cheese
1 cup shredded low-fat Monterey Jack
  cheese
6 flour tortillas (6 or 7 inches)

1. In a nonstick skillet, brown beef, onions,
and green pepper.
2. Add remaining ingredients, except
cheeses and tortillas. Bring to a boil.
3. Reduce heat. Cover and simmer for 10
minutes.
4. Combine cheeses in a bowl.
5. In slow cooker, layer about ¾ cup beef
mixture, one tortilla, and about ¼ cup cheese.
Repeat layers until all ingredients are used.
6. Cover. Cook on low 5-7 hours.

Per Serving: 490 calories (110 calories from fat), 12g total
fat (4.5g saturated, 0g trans), 35mg cholesterol, 1480mg
sodium, 51g total carbohydrate (8g fiber, 6g sugar), 43g
protein, 10%DV vitamin A, 20%DV vitamin C, 80%DV
calcium, 30%DV iron.

Low-Fat Slow-Cooker Barbecue
Martha Hershey
Ronks, PA

Makes 12 sandwich servings
(Ideal slow-cooker size: 3-quart)

1 lb. extra-lean ground beef
2 cups celery, chopped fine
1 cup onions, chopped
1 Tbsp. whipped butter
2 Tbsp. red wine vinegar
1 Tbsp. brown sugar
3 Tbsp. Worcestershire sauce
1 tsp. salt
1 tsp. yellow prepared mustard
1 cup ketchup
2 cups water

1. Brown ground beef, celery, and onions in
a nonstick skillet.
2. Combine all ingredients in slow cooker.
3. Cover and cook on high for 4 hours.
4. Serve in sandwich rolls.

Per Serving: 110 calories (45 calories from fat), 5g total fat
(2g saturated, 0g trans), 15mg cholesterol, 540mg sodium,
8g total carbohydrate (0.5g fiber, 3g sugar), 8g protein,
6%DV vitamin A, 6%DV vitamin C, 2%DV calcium,
8%DV iron.

Meat Loaf

Jody Moore
Pendleton, IN

Makes 8 servings
(Ideal slow-cooker size: 3- or 4-quart)

1/2 lb. extra-lean ground beef
1 lb. lean ground turkey
1 medium-sized onion, chopped
2 eggs
2/3 cup dry quick oats
1 envelope dry onion soup mix
1/2-1 tsp. liquid smoke
1 tsp. dry mustard
1 cup ketchup, divided

1. Mix beef, turkey, and chopped onion thoroughly.
2. Combine with eggs, oats, dry soup mix, liquid smoke, mustard, and all but 2 Tbsp. of ketchup.
3. Shape into loaf and place in slow cooker sprayed with non-fat cooking spray. Top with remaining ketchup.
4. Cover. Cook on low 8-10 hours or on high 4-6 hours.

Per Serving: 210 calories (45 calories from fat), 5g total fat (1.5g saturated, 0g trans), 80mg cholesterol, 1040mg sodium, 18g total carbohydrate (2g fiber, 5g sugar), 23g protein, 8%DV vitamin A, 6%DV vitamin C, 4%DV calcium, 10%DV iron.

Meat Loaf and Mushrooms

Rebecca Meyerkorth
Wamego, KS

Makes 6 servings
(Ideal slow-cooker size: 3 1/2- or 4-quart)

2 1-oz. slices whole wheat bread
1/2 lb. extra-lean ground beef
3/4 lb. fat-free ground turkey
1 1/2 cups mushrooms, sliced
1/2 cup minced onions
1 tsp. Italian seasoning
3/4 tsp. salt
2 eggs
1 clove garlic, minced
3 Tbsp. ketchup
1 1/2 tsp. Dijon mustard
1/8 tsp. ground red pepper

1. Fold two strips of tin foil, each long enough to fit from the top of the cooker, down inside and up the other side, plus a 2-inch overhang on each side of the cooker—to function as handles for lifting the finished loaf out of the cooker.
2. Process bread slices in food processor until crumbs measure 1 1/3 cups.
3. Combine bread crumbs, beef, turkey, mushrooms, onions, Italian seasoning, salt, eggs, and garlic in bowl. Shape into loaf to fit in slow cooker.
4. Mix together ketchup, mustard, and pepper. Spread over top of loaf.
5. Cover. Cook on low 5 hours.
6. When finished, pull loaf up gently with foil handles. Place loaf on warm platter. Pull foil handles away. Allow loaf to rest for 10 minutes before slicing.

Per Serving: 230 calories (60 calories from fat), 7g total fat (2g saturated, 0g trans), 100mg cholesterol, 1190mg sodium, 15g total carbohydrate (2g fiber, 4g sugar), 27g protein, 4%DV vitamin A, 0%DV vitamin C, 4%DV calcium, 15%DV iron.

Meat Loaf with a Mexican Touch

Karen Waggoner
Joplin, MO

Makes 6 servings
(Ideal slow-cooker size: 4-quart)

1¼ lbs. extra-lean ground beef
4 cups hash browns, thawed
1 egg, lightly beaten, or egg substitute
2 Tbsp. dry vegetable soup mix
2 Tbsp. low-sodium taco seasoning
2 cups fat-free shredded cheddar cheese, divided

1. Mix together ground beef, hash browns, egg, soup mix, taco seasoning, and 1 cup of cheese. Shape into loaf.
2. Line slow cooker with tin foil, allowing ends of foil to extend out over edges of cooker, enough to grab hold of and to lift the loaf out when it's finished cooking. Spray the foil with nonfat cooking spray.
3. Place loaf in cooker. Cover. Cook on low 4 hours.
4. Sprinkle with remaining cheese and cover until melted.
5. Gently lift loaf out, using tin-foil handles. Allow to rest 10 minutes, then slice and serve.

Per Serving: 350 calories (80 calories from fat), 9g total fat (3.5g saturated, 0g trans), 70mg cholesterol, 1040mg sodium, 32g total carbohydrate (4g fiber, 1g sugar), 34g protein, 15%DV vitamin A, 10%DV vitamin C, 35%DV calcium, 15%DV iron.

Low-Cal Meat Loaf

Jeanette Oberholtzer
Manheim, PA
Charlotte Shaffer
East Earl, PA
Dorothy VanDeest
Memphis, TN

Makes 6 servings
(Ideal slow-cooker size: 3½-quart)

½ lb. extra-lean ground beef
3 cups shredded cabbage
1 green bell pepper, chopped
½ tsp. salt
1 Tbsp. dried onion flakes
½ tsp. caraway seeds, optional

1. Thoroughly combine all ingredients.
2. Shape into a round loaf.
3. Place on rack in slow cooker.
4. Cover. Cook on high 3-4 hours.

Per Serving: 80 calories (30 calories from fat), 3.5g total fat (1.5g saturated, 0g trans), 15mg cholesterol, 230mg sodium, 4g total carbohydrate (2g fiber, 2g sugar), 9g protein, 4%DV vitamin A, 25%DV vitamin C, 2%DV calcium, 6%DV iron.

Notes:
The recipe can be easily doubled if you have a large crowd to feed. Use a 6-quart cooker and cook on high for 4-5 hours or on low 6-7 hours.
To add color and flavor, serve with chili sauce or ketchup.

Porcupine Meatballs
Jennifer Dzialonski
Brishton, MI

Makes 5 servings
(Ideal slow-cooker size: 3½-quart)

¾ lb. extra-lean ground beef or ground
   turkey
1 cup skim milk
½ cup uncooked long grain rice
1 medium-sized onion, chopped
1 cup dry bread crumbs
½ tsp. salt
dash of black pepper
10¾-oz. can low-fat, low-sodium cream of
   mushroom soup
½ cup skim milk

1. Combine meat, 1 cup skim milk, rice,
onion, bread crumbs, salt, and pepper in a
bowl.
2. Shape with an ice cream scoop. Place in
slow cooker.
3. Mix together soup and ½ cup milk. Pour
over meatballs.
4. Cover. Cook on low 5 hours.
5. Serve with mushroom-soup gravy.

Per Serving: 140 calories (80 calories from fat), 9g total fat
(3.5g saturated, 1g trans), 30mg cholesterol, 920mg
sodium, 40g total carbohydrate (1g fiber, 6g sugar), 21g
protein, 0%DV vitamin A, 0%DV vitamin C, 15%DV
calcium, 20%DV iron.

Meatball Stew
Becky Frey
Lebanon, PA

Makes 6 servings
(Ideal slow-cooker size: 3-quart)

1 lb. extra-lean ground beef
1 egg
1 cup bread crumbs
1 medium-sized onion, chopped
¾ tsp. salt
14½-oz. can low-sodium diced tomatoes
10½-oz. can fat-free, low-sodium beef
   broth
¼ tsp. dried thyme
3 carrots, scrubbed and diced
1 medium-sized onion, chopped
1 rib celery, chopped

1. Combine ground beef, egg, bread
crumbs, onion, and salt.
2. Shape into very small meatballs.
3. Brown meatballs in nonstick skillet.
4. Mix remaining ingredients in slow
cooker. Spoon in meatballs and stir together
gently.
5. Cover. Cook on high 3-4 hours.
6. Serve over potatoes or spaghetti.

Per Serving: 240 calories (60 calories from fat), 6g total fat
(2.5g saturated, 0g trans), 45mg cholesterol, 490mg
sodium, 29g total carbohydrate (3g fiber, 5g sugar), 17g
protein, 80%DV vitamin A, 8%DV vitamin C, 6%DV
calcium, 20%DV iron.

Sweet and Sour Meatballs

Alice Miller
Stuarts Draft, VA

Makes 4 servings
(Ideal slow-cooker size: 4-quart)

1 lb. extra-lean ground chuck
1/2 cup dry bread crumbs
1/4 cup fat-free milk
3/4 tsp. salt
1/4 tsp. black pepper
1 egg, beaten
2 Tbsp. finely chopped onions
1/2 tsp. Worcestershire sauce

Sauce:
1/3 cup packed brown sugar
2 Tbsp. cornstarch
13 1/4-oz. can unsweetened pineapple
  chunks, undrained
1/3 cup vinegar
1 Tbsp. soy sauce
1 green bell pepper, chopped
1/3 cup water

1. Combine meatball ingredients. Shape into 3/4-1" balls. Brown in nonstick skillet. Drain. Place in slow cooker.
2. Add brown sugar and cornstarch to skillet. Stir in remaining ingredients. Heat to boiling, stirring constantly. Pour over meatballs.
3. Cover. Cook on low 3-4 hours.

Per Serving: 380 calories (110 calories from fat), 12g total fat (4.5g saturated, 0g trans), 90mg cholesterol, 850mg sodium, 40g total carbohydrate (2g fiber, 28g sugar), 28g protein, 0%DV vitamin A, 20%DV vitamin C, 10%DV calcium, 20%DV iron.

Note: If you like pineapples, use a 20-oz. can of chunks, instead of the 13 1/4-oz. can.

Mexican Corn Bread

Jeanne Heyerly
Chenoa, IL

Makes 6 servings
(Ideal slow-cooker size: 4-quart)

1 lb. extra-lean ground chuck
16-oz. can cream-style corn
1 cup cornmeal
1/2 tsp. baking soda
1 tsp. salt
1/4 cup oil
1 cup fat-free milk
2 eggs, beaten
1/2 cup low-sodium taco sauce
2 cups shredded fat-free cheddar cheese
1 medium-sized onion, chopped
1 garlic clove, minced
4-oz. can diced green chilies

1. Brown ground chuck in nonstick skillet.
2. While meat is browning, combine corn, cornmeal, baking soda, salt, oil, milk, eggs, and taco sauce. Pour half of mixture into slow cooker.
2. Layer cheese, onion, garlic, green chilies, and ground beef on top of cornmeal mixture. Cover with remaining cornmeal mixture.
3. Cover. Cook on high 1 hour and on low 3 1/2-4 hours, or only on low 6 hours.

Per Serving: 360 calories (90 calories from fat), 10g total fat (3g saturated, 0g trans), 60mg cholesterol, 1300mg sodium, 39g total carbohydrate (4g fiber, 6g sugar), 29g protein, 10%DV vitamin A, 0%DV vitamin C, 40%DV calcium, 15%DV iron.

African Beef Curry

Rebecca Leichty
Harrisonburg, VA

Makes 6 small servings
(Ideal slow-cooker size: 3-quart)

1 lb. extra-lean ground beef, browned
1 large onion, thinly sliced
1 green bell pepper, diced
1 tomato, peeled and diced
1 apple, peeled, cored, and diced
1-2 tsp. curry (or more to taste)
4 cups prepared rice

1. Spray slow cooker with fat-free cooking spray.
2. Add all ingredients except rice in slow cooker and mix well.
3. Cover and cook on high 6-8 hours.
4. Serve over hot rice.

Per Serving: 340 calories (70 calories from fat), 7g total fat (3g saturated, 0g trans), 30mg cholesterol, 50mg sodium, 47g total carbohydrate (2g fiber, 6g sugar), 20g protein, 6%DV vitamin A, 20%DV vitamin C, 4%DV calcium, 20%DV iron.

Notes:
1. You can thicken this by stirring in 6-oz. can of tomato paste in Step 2, if you wish.
2. This is interesting served with a spoonful of lowfat or non-fat "lemon-enhanced" vanilla yogurt on top of each individual dish.

Ground Beef 'N' Biscuits

Karen Waggoner
Joplin, MO

Makes 8 servings
(Ideal slow-cooker size: 6-quart oval)

1½ lbs. extra-lean ground beef
½ cup celery, chopped
½ cup onions, chopped
2 Tbsp. flour
1 tsp. salt
¼ tsp. black pepper
½ tsp. dried oregano
2 8-oz. cans tomato sauce
10-oz. pkg. frozen peas, thawed
2 7½-oz. cans refrigerated buttermilk biscuits
2 cups fat-free shredded cheddar cheese

1. Brown ground beef, celery, and onions in nonstick skillet.
2. Stir in flour, salt, pepper, and oregano.
3. Add tomato sauce and peas.
4. Pour into slow cooker. (A large oval cooker allows the biscuits to be arranged over top. You can also divide the mixture between two round slow cookers and accommodate the biscuits in that way.)
5. Arrange biscuits over top and sprinkle with cheese.
6. Cook uncovered on high for 1-1½ hours.

Per Serving: 370 calories (80 calories from fat), 9g total fat (3.5g saturated, 0g trans), 35mg cholesterol, 1470mg sodium, 38g total carbohydrate (3g fiber, 5g sugar), 34g protein, 20%DV vitamin A, 10%DV vitamin C, 30%DV calcium, 25%DV iron.

Hamburger Casserole
Becky Harder
Monument, CO

Makes 6 servings
(Ideal slow-cooker size: 4- or 5-quart)

1½ lbs. extra-lean ground beef
½ tsp. salt
¼ tsp. black pepper
2 large potatoes, sliced
2-3 medium-sized carrots, sliced
2 cups frozen peas
2 medium-sized onions, sliced
2 ribs celery, sliced
10¾-oz. can low-sodium tomato soup
soup can of water

1. Brown ground beef in a nonstick skillet over medium heat. Season with salt and pepper.
2. Layer vegetables into slow cooker in order given.
3. Place ground beef on top of celery.
4. Mix tomato soup with water. Pour into slow cooker.
5. Cover. Cook on low 6-8 hours or on high 3-5 hours.

Per Serving: 320 calories (100 calories from fat), 11g total fat (4g saturated, 0g trans), 40mg cholesterol, 360mg sodium, 28g total carbohydrate (5g fiber, 7g sugar), 28g protein, 100%DV vitamin A, 30%DV vitamin C, 4%DV calcium, 25%DV iron.

Beef and Noodle Casserole
Delores Scheel
West Fargo, N

Makes 10 servings
(Ideal slow-cooker size: 4-quart)

1 lb. extra-lean ground beef
1 medium-sized onion, chopped
1 medium-sized green bell pepper, chopped
17-oz. can whole-kernel corn, drained
4-oz. can mushroom stems and pieces, drained
1 tsp. salt
¼ tsp. black pepper
11-oz. jar salsa
5 cups dry medium egg noodles, cooked
28-oz. can low-sodium diced tomatoes, undrained
1 cup low-fat shredded cheddar cheese

1. Brown ground beef and onion in nonstick skillet over medium heat. Transfer to slow cooker.
2. Top with remaining ingredients in order listed.
3. Cover. Cook on low 4 hours.

Per Serving: 460 calories (100 calories from fat), 11g total fat (4g saturated, 0g trans), 75mg cholesterol, 1300mg sodium, 61g total carbohydrate (7g fiber, 9g sugar), 31g protein, 15%DV vitamin A, 30%DV vitamin C, 25%DV calcium, 30%DV iron.

Beef and Rice Casserole

Colleen Heatwole
Burton, MI

Makes 6 servings
(Ideal slow-cooker size: 5-quart)

1/2 lb. extra-lean ground beef
1 onion, chopped
1 clove garlic, minced
1/2 cup green bell pepper, cut finely
1/2 cup celery, diced
1 tsp. dried basil
1 tsp. dried oregano
10 3/4-oz. can reduced-fat, low-sodium
   cream of mushroom soup
1 cup water
4 cups cooked brown rice

1. Brown ground beef, onion, garlic, green pepper, and celery in a nonstick skillet over medium heat. Season with basil and oregano.
2. Combine soup and water in separate bowl.
3. Spray slow cooker with nonfat cooking spray.
4. Layer 2 cups of cooked rice on bottom of slow cooker. Add half of ground beef and half of soup mixture.
5. Repeat layers.
6. Cover. Cook on low 4 hours.

Per Serving: 250 calories (50 calories from fat), 6g total fat (2g saturated, 0.5g trans), 15mg cholesterol, 380mg sodium, 37g total carbohydrate (3g fiber, 2g sugar), 12g protein, 2%DV vitamin A, 10%DV vitamin C, 4%DV calcium, 10%DV iron.

China Dish

Lois Stoltzfus
Honey Brook, PA

Makes 6 servings
(Ideal slow-cooker size: 4-quart)

1 1/2 lbs. extra-lean ground beef
10 3/4-oz. can cream of chicken soup
10 3/4-oz. can 98% fat-free cream of
   mushroom soup
3 1/2 cups water
2 cups celery, chopped
1 cup onions, chopped
1 cup brown rice, uncooked
3 Tbsp. Worcestershire sauce

1. Brown ground beef in a nonstick skillet.
2. Combine all ingredients in slow cooker.
3. Cover. Cook on low 6-8 hours.

Per Serving: 400 calories (140 calories from fat), 15g total fat (6g saturated, 1g trans), 45mg cholesterol, 950mg sodium, 36g total carbohydrate (2g fiber, 3g sugar), 28g protein, 6%DV vitamin A, 8%DV vitamin C, 8%DV calcium, 20%DV iron.

Stuffed Peppers

Mary E. Wheatley
Mashpee, MA

Makes 4 servings
(Ideal slow-cooker size: 5-quart)

1 lb. extra-lean ground beef
4 large green bell peppers, tops removed,
    cleaned of seeds and cored, but not cut
    in half
8-oz. can tomato sauce, divided
15-oz. can Spanish rice
1 large onion, chopped
1/2 tsp. salt
1/4 tsp. black pepper

1. Combine all ingredients, except 1/2 can of tomato sauce.
2. Stuff green peppers full.
3. Place peppers in slow cooker. Pour remaining tomato sauce over peppers.
4. Cover. Cook on high 4 hours.

Per Serving: 340 calories (110 calories from fat), 12g total
fat (4.5g saturated, 0g trans), 40mg cholesterol, 470mg
sodium, 31g total carbohydrate (5g fiber, 6g sugar), 27g
protein, 30%DV vitamin A, 150%DV vitamin C, 6%DV
calcium, 25%DV iron.

Stuffed Green Peppers

Jean Butzer
Batavia, NY

Makes 6 servings
(Ideal slow-cooker size: 5-quart)

6 green bell peppers
1/2 lb. extra-lean ground beef
1/4 cup finely chopped onions
1 Tbsp. pimento, chopped
3/4 tsp. salt
1/4 tsp. black pepper
12-oz. can low-sodium whole-kernel corn,
    drained
1 Tbsp. Worcestershire sauce
1 tsp. prepared mustard
10¾-oz. can condensed low-sodium cream
    of tomato soup

1. Cut a slice off the top of each pepper. Remove core, seeds, and white membrane.
2. In a small bowl, combine beef, onions, pimento, salt, black pepper, and corn.
3. Spoon into peppers. Stand peppers up in slow cooker.
4. Combine Worcestershire sauce, mustard, and tomato soup. Pour over peppers.
5. Cover. Cook on low 5-6 hours.

Per Serving: 170 calories (40 calories from fat), 4.5g total
fat (2g saturated, 0g trans), 15mg cholesterol, 650mg
sodium, 24g total carbohydrate (4g fiber, 8g sugar), 11g
protein, 25%DV vitamin A, 120%DV vitamin C, 2%DV
calcium, 15%DV iron.

Slow-Cooker Pizza

Wilma J. Haberkamp
Fairbank, IA

Makes 8 servings
(Ideal slow-cooker size: 6-quart)

1 lb. extra-lean ground beef
2 small onions, chopped
14-oz. can fat-free pizza sauce
14-oz. can low-fat, low-sodium spaghetti
  sauce
1 tsp. garlic powder
1¼ tsp. black pepper
1 tsp. dried oregano
¼ tsp. rubbed sage
12 ozs. dry kluski noodles

1. Brown ground beef and onions in nonstick skillet.
2. In skillet, or in a large bowl, mix together browned meat and onions, pizza sauce, spaghetti sauce, and seasonings and herbs.
3. Boil noodles according to directions on package until tender. Drain.
4. Layer half of beef sauce in bottom of cooker. Spoon in noodles. Top with remaining beef sauce.
5. Cook on low 1-1½ hours if ingredients are hot when placed in cooker. If the sauce and noodles are at room temperature or have just been refrigerated, cook on high for 2-2½ hours.

Per Serving: 320 calories (70 calories from fat), 8g total fat (2.5g saturated, 0g trans), 65mg cholesterol, 610mg sodium, 42g total carbohydrate (3g fiber, 6g sugar), 20g protein, 8%DV vitamin A, 10%DV vitamin C, 4%DV calcium, 20%DV iron.

Quick Lasagna

Frances Musser
Newmanstown, PA

Makes 6 servings
(Ideal slow-cooker size: 4-quart)

¼ lb. extra-lean ground beef
8-oz. pkg. broad egg noodles
1 cup fat-free cottage cheese
½ cup shredded low-fat mozzarella cheese
¼ cup grated Parmesan cheese
2½ cups spaghetti sauce

1. Brown ground beef in a nonstick skillet. Set aside.
2. Cook noodles and drain. Toss noodles with both cheeses.
3. Mix together browned beef and spaghetti sauce.
4. Spoon one-third of meat sauce in bottom of slow cooker.
5. Layer in half of noodles. Repeat layers.
6. Cover. Cook on low 5-6 hours.

Per Serving: 300 calories (80 calories from fat), 9 total fat (3.5g saturated, 0g trans), 50mg cholesterol, 590mg sodium, 33g total carbohydrate (3g fiber, 6g sugar), 21g protein, 10%DV vitamin A, 10%DV vitamin C, 20%DV calcium, 15%DV iron.

Note: If you wish, and your diet permits, add 1 Tbsp. Italian seasoning, or 1½ tsp. dried basil and 1½ tsp. dried oregano, to Step 3.

Pork Main Dishes

Ham and Potatoes

Judy Buller
Bluffton, OH

Makes 8 servings
(Ideal slow-cooker size: 6-quart)

2 cups carrots, sliced
6 cups raw potatoes, sliced
1 small onion, sliced thin
2-2½ cups lean ham, cubed
3 Tbsp. margarine
½ cup flour
3 cups skim milk
¼ tsp. black pepper
½ tsp. parsley
2 Tbsp. Dijon mustard
1 cup shredded, reduced-fat cheddar
   cheese

1. Layer carrots, potatoes, onion, and ham in slow cooker.
2. In a skillet, melt margarine. Stir in flour. Gradually add milk. Stir frequently until sauce is smooth and thickened.
3. Add pepper, parsley, mustard, and shredded cheese. Continue heating and stirring until cheese is melted.
4. Pour over vegetables and ham in slow cooker. Push the vegetables down into the sauce, making sure all ingredients are covered as fully as possible.
5. Cover. Cook on low 6 hours, or on high 2 hours and then on low 2 hours.

Per Serving: 380 calories (100 calories from fat), 11g total fat (4g saturated, 1g trans), 30mg cholesterol, 930mg sodium, 46g total carbohydrate (5g fiber, 11g sugar), 26g protein, 200%DV vitamin A, 30%DV vitamin C, 30%DV calcium, 15%DV iron.

Ham and Scalloped Potatoes

Betty Chalker
Dalhart, TX

Makes 8 servings
(Ideal slow-cooker size: 6-quart)

1½ lbs. 98% fat-free ham, cut into
    8 pieces
8-10 medium-sized potatoes, peeled and
    thinly sliced
2 onions, peeled and thinly sliced
½ tsp. salt
¼ tsp. black pepper, or more, according to
    your taste
1 cup fat-free grated cheddar or American
    cheese
10¾-oz. can 98% fat-free cream of celery
    soup
paprika

1. Layer half of ham, potatoes, and onions
in slow cooker. Sprinkle with half the salt and
pepper, and then half the grated cheese.
2. Repeat layers.
3. Spoon undiluted soup over ingredients.
4. Cook on low 8-10 hours or high 4 hours.

Per Serving: 310 calories (30 calories from fat), 3.5g total
fat (1g saturated, 0g trans), 40mg cholesterol, 1130mg
sodium, 46g total carbohydrate (5g fiber, 5g sugar), 23g
protein, 6%DV vitamin A, 30%DV vitamin C, 20%DV
calcium, 10%DV iron.

Broccoli and Ham Dinner

Delores Scheel
West Fargo, ND

Makes 6 servings
(Ideal slow-cooker size: 4-quart)

10¾-oz. can 98% fat-free cream of
    mushroom soup
8-oz. jar low-sodium, fat-free cheese
    spread
1 cup skim milk
1 cup instant rice, uncooked
1 rib celery, chopped
1 small onion, chopped
3 cups cooked ham, cubed
16-oz. pkg. frozen broccoli cuts, thawed
    and drained

1. In a bowl, mix together cream of
mushroom soup, cheese spread, milk, rice,
celery, and onion.
2. Stir in ham.
3. Cover. Cook on low 3-4 hours.
4. One hour before serving time, stir in
broccoli.

Per Serving: 260 calories (70 calories from fat), 8g total fat
(3.5g saturated, 0g trans), 35mg cholesterol, 1180mg
sodium, 19g total carbohydrate (3g fiber, 6g sugar), 29g
protein, 20%DV vitamin A, 30%DV vitamin C, 25%DV
calcium, 10%DV iron.

Ham & Yam Dish
Leona Miller
Millersburg, OH

Makes 8 servings
(Ideal slow-cooker size: 4- or 5-quart)

40-oz. can yams in water, drained
1½ lbs. extra-lean smoked ham, cut into
bite-sized cubes
20-oz. can unsweetened pineapple chunks,
or crushed pineapple, in light juice,
drained
¼ cup dark brown sugar

1. Spray slow cooker with nonfat cooking spray.
2. Stir all ingredients together gently in the slow cooker.
3. Cook on high 1½-2 hours or on low 4-6 hours.

Per Serving: 320 calories (45 calories from fat), 5g total fat (1.5g saturated, 0g trans), 45mg cholesterol, 930mg sodium, 47g total carbohydrate (3g fiber, 36g sugar), 21g protein, 300%DV vitamin A, 10%DV vitamin C, 6%DV calcium, 20%DV iron.

Ham-Yam-Apple
Joan Rosenberger
Stephens City, VA

Makes 4 servings
(Ideal slow-cooker size: 5-quart)

1 slice fully cooked ham (about 1 lb.)
29-oz. can sweet potatoes or yams, drained
2 apples, thinly sliced
¼ cup light brown sugar
2 Tbsp. orange juice

1. Cube ham.
2. Combine all ingredients in slow cooker.
3. Cook on low 4-5 hours, or until apples are tender.

Per Serving: 460 calories (60 calories from fat), 7g total fat (2g saturated, 0g trans), 60mg cholesterol, 1520mg sodium, 73g total carbohydrate (5g fiber, 57g sugar), 28g protein, 200%DV vitamin A, 20%DV vitamin C, 8%DV calcium, 25%DV iron.

Chow Mein
Barbara Walker
Sturgis, SD

Makes 8 servings
(Ideal slow-cooker size: 3- or 4-quart)

5 pork chops, trimmed of fat and cubed
1-1½ lbs. round steak, cubed
6 cups water
1 rib celery, chopped
1 medium-large onion, chopped
1 can bean sprouts, drained
4 Tbsp. low-sodium soy sauce

1. Brown pork and steak in nonstick skillet. Drain.
2. Combine all ingredients in slow cooker.
3. Cover. Cook on high 3-4 hours.
4. Add soy sauce and thicken with 3 Tbsp. cornstarch mixed with ¼ cup cold water, if desired.
5. Serve over rice or chow mein noodles.

Per Serving: 170 calories (60 calories from fat), 7g total fat (2.5g saturated, 0g trans), 70mg cholesterol, 320mg sodium, 2g total carbohydrate (0.5g fiber, 1g sugar), 24g protein, 0%DV vitamin A, 2%DV vitamin C, 2%DV calcium, 10%DV iron.

Note: If your sodium count allows, you may want to add 1 tsp. salt to Step 2.

Verenika Casserole

Ilene Bontrager
Arlington, KS

Makes 8 servings
(Ideal slow-cooker size: 6-quart)

Ham Gravy:
¼ cup onions, chopped
1 Tbsp. butter
1 cup flour
6½ cups skim milk
3-4 cups turkey ham, cubed
½-1 tsp. salt
½ tsp. black pepper
4 ozs. fat-free sour cream

Cheese Filling:
24-oz. tub lowfat cottage cheese
1 egg, beaten

8 10" tortillas, cut in 2" squares or
  diamonds, or 4 cups cooked noodles

1. Sauté chopped onions in butter in large saucepan.
2. Add flour and then milk gradually. Stir until thick and bubbly. Stir in cubed ham.
3. Add salt, pepper and sour cream.
4. In a mixing bowl, stir together cottage cheese and egg.
5. Layer in slow cooker: half the ham gravy, then half the tortilla pieces or cooked noodles, and then half the cheese filling. Repeat layers.
6. Cover. Cook on low 5-6 hours.

Per Serving: 250 calories (50 calories from fat), 6g total fat (3g saturated, 0g trans), 65mg cholesterol, 1220mg sodium, 25g total carbohydrate (0.5g fiber, 12g sugar), 25g protein, 10%DV vitamin A, 4%DV vitamin C, 30%DV calcium, 10%DV iron.

Pork Chop Combo

Doris Perkins
Mashpee, MA

Makes 4 servings
(Ideal slow-cooker size: 5- or 6-quart)

4 pork chops, trimmed of fat
2 8-oz. cans garlic/basil/oregano tomato
  sauce
5 potatoes, cut in chunks
5 carrots, sliced
5 onions, sliced
water needed during cooking time to keep
  chops from sticking

1. Put a trivet on the bottom of your slow cooker to keep the pork from sticking.
2. Add pork chops and tomato sauce.
3. Place steamer on top of chops. Then add potatoes, carrots, and onions.
4. Cook on low 6-8 hours.

Per Serving: 280 calories (70 calories from fat), 8g total fat (3g saturated, 0g trans), 15mg cholesterol, 300mg sodium, 43g total carbohydrate (6g fiber, 5g sugar), 11g protein, 6%DV vitamin A, 40%DV vitamin C, 15%DV calcium, 15%DV iron.

Notes: If you don't have a steamer for your cooker, change the order of the layers: place the potatoes in the bottom of the cooker, followed by the carrots, and then the onions, followed by the chops. Pour tomato sauce over all.

If your diet allows, you may want to lightly sprinkle salt and black pepper over each layer of vegetables.

Barbecued Pork Chops

Loretta Weisz
Aubrun, WA

Makes 6 servings
(Ideal slow-cooker size: 5-quart)

4 loin pork chops, ¾" thick,
  trimmed of fat
1 cup ketchup
1 cup hot water
2 Tbsp. vinegar
1 Tbsp. Worcestershire sauce
2 tsp. brown sugar
½ tsp. black pepper
½ tsp. chili powder
½ tsp. paprika

1. Place pork chops in slow cooker.
2. Combine remaining ingredients. Pour over chops.
3. Cover. Cook on high 5-6 hours.
4. Cut chops in half and serve.

Per Serving: 180 calories (60 calories from fat), 7g total fat (2.5g saturated, 0g trans), 60mg cholesterol, 430mg sodium, 11g total carbohydrate (0.5g fiber, 5g sugar), 20g protein, 8%DV vitamin A, 2%DV vitamin C, 2%DV calcium, 8%DV iron.

Three-Ingredient Sauerkraut Meal

Esther J. Yoder
Hartville, OH

Makes 8 servings
(Ideal slow-cooker size: 5-quart)

2 cups low-sodium barbecue sauce
1 cup water
2 lbs. thinly sliced lean pork chops,
  trimmed of fat
2 lbs. sauerkraut, rinsed

1. Mix together barbecue sauce and water.
2. Combine barbecue sauce, pork chops, and sauerkraut in slow cooker.
3. Cover. Cook on low 8-10 hours

Per Serving: 300 calories (90 calories from fat), 11g total fat (3.5g saturated, 0g trans), 90mg cholesterol, 1450mg sodium, 18g total carbohydrate (3g fiber, 12g sugar), 32g protein, 4%DV vitamin A, 10%DV vitamin C, 6%DV calcium, 20%DV iron.

Fruited Pork Chops

Mrs. Carolyn Baer
Conrath, WI

Makes 6 servings
(Ideal slow-cooker size: 5- or 6-quart)

3 Tbsp. all-purpose flour
1½ tsp. dried oregano
¾ tsp. salt
¼ tsp. garlic powder
¼ tsp. black pepper
6 lean boneless pork loin chops (about 5
   ozs. each)
1 Tbsp. olive or canola oil
20-oz. can unsweetened pineapple chunks
1 cup water
2 Tbsp. brown sugar
2 Tbsp. dried minced onion
2 Tbsp. tomato paste
¼ cup raisins

1. In a large resealable plastic bag, combine flour, oregano, salt, garlic powder, and pepper.

2. Add pork chops one at a time and shake to coat.

3. Brown pork chops on both sides in a nonstick skillet using canola oil. Transfer browned chops to slow cooker.

4. Drain pineapple, reserving juice. Set pineapple aside.

5. In a mixing bowl, combine ¾ cup reserved pineapple juice, water, brown sugar, dried onion, and tomato paste. Pour over chops.

6. Sprinkle raisins over top.

7. Cook on high 3-3½ hours or until meat is tender and a meat thermometer reads 160°. Stir in reserved pineapple chunks. Cook 10 minutes longer or until heated through.

Per Serving: 280 calories (80 calories from fat), 9g total fat (2.5g saturated, 0g trans), 65mg cholesterol, 350mg sodium, 28g total carbohydrate (2g fiber, 22g sugar), 24g protein, 4%DV vitamin A, 20%DV vitamin C, 6%DV calcium, 10%DV iron.

Notes:
1.This is good served over brown rice.
2. If your diet allows, you may want to place 1 tsp. salt (instead of the ¾ tsp.) in coating mixture in Step 1.

Tasty Pork Tenderloin

Janice Yoskovich
Carmichaels, PA

Makes 8 servings
(Ideal slow-cooker size: 4-quart)

1½ lbs. pork tenderloin
12 ozs. chili sauce
16-oz. can jellied cranberry sauce
2 Tbsp. brown sugar
5 cups cooked long grain enriched rice

1. Place pork tenderloin in slow cooker.

2. Mix together chili sauce, cranberry sauce, and brown sugar. Pour over pork.

3. Cover and cook on high 4-5 hours, and then on low 3-4 hours.

4. Serve over rice.

Per Serving: 360 calories (30 calories from fat), 3g total fat (1g saturated, 0g trans), 45mg cholesterol, 510mg sodium, 62g total carbohydrate (1g fiber, 26g sugar), 20g protein, 2%DV vitamin A, 4%DV vitamin C, 2%DV calcium, 10%DV iron.

Pork Stew

Cyndie Marrara
Port Matilda, PA

Makes 6 servings
(Ideal slow-cooker size: 4-quart)

2 sweet potatoes or yams, peeled and cut
   in small pieces
10-oz. pkg. frozen corn
10-oz. pkg. frozen Italian beans
1 medium-sized onion, chopped
1½ lbs. lean pork, cut in small pieces
14½-oz. can low-sodium diced tomatoes,
   undrained
¾ cup water
1 tsp. garlic, chopped
¼ tsp. salt
⅛ tsp. black pepper

1. Combine potatoes, corn, beans, and
onion in slow cooker.
2. Place pork on top.
3. Stir together tomatoes, water, garlic, salt,
and pepper. Pour over pork.
4. Cover. Cook on low 7 hours.

Per Serving: 340 calories (100 calories from fat), 11g total
fat (4g saturated, 0g trans), 105mg cholesterol, 370mg
sodium, 22g total carbohydrate (4g fiber, 10g sugar), 36g
protein, 100%DV vitamin A, 20%DV vitamin C, 0%DV
calcium, 15%DV iron.

Pork with Veggies Dinner

Judy Miles
Centreville, MD

Makes 6 servings
(Ideal slow-cooker size: 3½-quart)

1 lb. pork roast, cut into strips ½" thick
1 large onion, chopped
1 small green bell pepper, sliced
8 ozs. fresh mushrooms, sliced
8-oz. can low-sodium tomato sauce
4 carrots, sliced
1½ Tbsp. vinegar
1 tsp. salt
2 tsp. Worcestershire sauce

1. Brown pork in a skillet over medium
heat in a nonstick skillet.
2. Combine all ingredients in slow cooker.
3. Cover. Cook on low 6-8 hours.
4. Serve over hot rice.

Per Serving: 210 calories (70 calories from fat), 7g total fat
(2.5g saturated, 0g trans), 70mg cholesterol, 700mg
sodium, 12g total carbohydrate (3g fiber, 6g sugar), 25g
protein, 200%DV vitamin A, 20%DV vitamin C, 4%DV
calcium, 10%DV iron.

Dawn's Harvest Pork Roast

Dawn Day
Westminster, CA

Makes 8 servings
(Ideal slow-cooker size: 4-quart)

2 lbs. pork tenderloin, fat trimmed
2 Tbsp. canola oil
3 cups apple juice
3 Granny Smith apples
1 cup fresh cranberries
3/4 tsp. salt
1/2 tsp. black pepper

1. Brown roast on all sides in skillet in canola oil. Place in slow cooker.
2. Add remaining ingredients.
3. Cover. Cook on low 6-8 hours.

Per Serving: 290 calories (80 calories from fat), 9g total fat (2g saturated, 0g trans), 90mg cholesterol, 290mg sodium, 19g total carbohydrate (2g fiber, 16g sugar), 32g protein, 0%DV vitamin A, 0%DV vitamin C, 0%DV calcium, 8%DV iron.

German Pot Roast

Eleanor Larson
Glen Lyon, PA

Makes 12 servings
(Ideal slow-cooker size: 5-quart)

2 lbs. boneless, lean pork roast
1 tsp. garlic salt
1/2 tsp. black pepper
4 large sweet potatoes, peeled and diced
2 medium-sized onions, sliced
1/2 tsp. dried oregano
14 1/2-oz. can low-sodium tomatoes

1. Place pork roast in slow cooker.
2. Sprinkle with garlic salt and pepper.
3. Add remaining ingredients.
4. Cover. Cook on high 4-5 hours or on low 7-8 hours.

Per Serving: 170 calories (45 calories from fat), 5g total fat (2g saturated, 0g trans), 45mg cholesterol, 290mg sodium, 14g total carbohydrate (2g fiber, 4g sugar), 16g protein, 100%DV vitamin A, 4%DV vitamin C, 4%DV calcium, 4%DV iron.

Barbecued Ribs & Sauce

Mary Longenecker
Bethel, PA

Makes 10 servings
(Ideal slow-cooker size: 4-quart)

3 lbs. lean country-style ribs
2 1/2 lbs. sauerkraut, rinsed
2 cups low-sodium barbecue sauce
1 cup water

1. Place ribs on bottom of cooker.
2. Layer sauerkraut over ribs.
3. Mix barbecue sauce and water together. Pour over meat and kraut.
4. Cover. Cook on low 8-10 hours.

Per Serving: 230 calories (80 calories from fat), 9g total fat (3g saturated, 0g trans), 50mg cholesterol, 1470mg sodium, 19g total carbohydrate (3g fiber, 13g sugar), 17g protein, 4%DV vitamin A, 20%DV vitamin C, 6%DV calcium, 15%DV iron.

Pineapple Pork

Anne Townsend
Albuquerque, NM

Makes 4 servings
(Ideal slow-cooker size: 4-quart)

8 country-style pork ribs
black pepper to taste
1/4 tsp. paprika
20-oz. can unsweetened pineapple tidbits
2 Tbsp. Dijon mustard
2 Tbsp. fast-cooking tapioca, optional

1. Slice ribs into 8 sections. Place in slow cooker sprayed with nonfat cooking spray.
2. Combine remaining ingredients. Pour over ribs.
3. Cover. Cook on low 6-8 hours.
4. If you wish, 30 minutes before the end of the cooking time, stir in tapioca in order to thicken the cooking juices.

Per Serving: 130 calories (45 calories from fat), 5g total fat (1.5g saturated, 0g trans), 25mg cholesterol, 210mg sodium, 13g total carbohydrate (1g fiber, 11g sugar), 9g protein, 0%DV vitamin A, 10%DV vitamin C, 4%DV calcium, 8%DV iron.

Note: These ribs are great the next day. Refrigerate them after cooking, and then remove the fat before reheating to serve.

Ribs with Apples and Kraut

Dede Peterson
Rapid City, SD

Makes 7 servings
(Ideal slow-cooker size: 6-quart)

1 1/2 lbs. pork ribs, trimmed of fat
1/2 tsp. salt
1/4-1 1/2 tsp. black pepper, according to your taste
1/2 cup water, apple juice, or white wine, optional
2 16-oz. cans, or 1 2-lb. bag, sauerkraut, undrained
3 medium-sized onions, sliced into rings
2 8-oz. cans mushrooms, drained
3 large apples, cored and cut in wedges
1/3 cup brown sugar
1/2 tsp. celery seed

1. Brown ribs in a nonstick skillet, top and bottom. Season with salt and pepper.
2. Place ribs in slow cooker. Deglaze skillet with 1/2 cup water, apple juice, or white wine, if you wish. Set drippings aside.
3. In large bowl, mix together sauerkraut, onions, mushrooms, apples wedges, brown sugar, and celery seed. Spoon over ribs. Pour any reserved drippings over top.
4. Cook on low 7-9 hours or on high 3-4 hours.

Per Serving: 250 calories (80 calories from fat), 9g total fat (3.5g saturated, 0g trans), 55mg cholesterol, 590mg sodium, 25g total carbohydrate (5g fiber, 18g sugar), 18g protein, 2%DV vitamin A, 25%DV vitamin C, 6%DV calcium, 15%DV iron.

Barbecued Pork

Rhonda L. Burgoon
Collingswood, NJ

Makes 8 servings
(Ideal slow-cooker size: 4- or 5-quart)

2 lbs. boneless pork top loin
1½ cups onions, chopped
1 cup diet soda
1 cup low-sodium barbecue sauce

1. Place pork in slow cooker. Combine all other ingredients in a bowl and then pour over pork.
2. Cover. Cook on high 4-6 hours or until meat is very tender.
3. Slice or shred pork. Stir back into sauce.
4. Serve on wheat or multigrain buns.

Per Serving: 200 calories (50 calories from fat), 6g total fat (2g saturated, 0g trans), 55mg cholesterol, 470mg sodium, 11g total carbohydrate (0.5g fiber, 9g sugar), 23g protein, 2%DV vitamin A, 4%DV vitamin C, 4%DV calcium, 4%DV iron.

Note: If your calorie count allows, you may want to add another 1/2 cup barbecue sauce to Step 1 to create a juicier sandwich filling.

Slow-Cooked Pork Stew

Virginia Graybill
Hershey, PA

Makes 8 servings
(Ideal slow-cooker size: 5-quart)

2 lbs. lean pork loin, cut into 1" cubes
½ lb. baby carrots
3 large potatoes, cut into 1" cubes
2 parsnips, cut into 1" cubes
2 onions, cut into wedges, slices, or chopped coarsely
3 garlic cloves, minced
1-2 tsp. ground black pepper, depending on your taste preferences
1 tsp. dried thyme
1 tsp. salt
2½ cups low-sodium canned vegetable juice
2 Tbsp. brown sugar
1 Tbsp. prepared mustard
4 tsp. tapioca

1. Place pork in slow cooker.
2. Add carrots, potatoes, parsnips, onions, garlic, pepper, thyme, and salt. Mix together well.
3. In a medium bowl, combine vegetable juice, brown sugar, mustard, and tapioca. Pour over meat and vegetables.
4. Cover. Cook on low 6 hours or on high 4 hours.

Per Serving: 300 calories (60 calories from fat), 7g total fat (2.5g saturated, 0g trans), 65mg cholesterol, 490mg sodium, 34g total carbohydrate (5g fiber, 11g sugar), 26g protein, 60%DV vitamin A, 30%DV vitamin C, 8%DV calcium, 15%DV iron.

Sausage-Sweet Potato Bake

Betty K. Drescher
Quakertown, PA

Makes 6 servings
(Ideal slow-cooker size: 4-quart)

1/2 lb. lean sausage, cut in 1/4-1/2" slices
3 medium-sized sweet potatoes, peeled
  and sliced thin
4 medium-sized apples, peeled and cut in
  chunks
1 Tbsp. sugar
2 Tbsp. flour
1/4 tsp. ground cinnamon
1/4 tsp. salt
1/4-1/2 cup water

1. Brown sausage in nonstick skillet. Drain.
2. Layer sweet potatoes, apples, and sausage in slow cooker sprayed with nonfat cooking spray.
3. Combine remaining ingredients. Pour over all.
4. Cover. Cook on low 6-7 hours or on high 3-4 hours.

Per Serving: 230 calories (70 calories from fat), 7g total fat (2.5g saturated, 0g trans), 15mg cholesterol, 260mg sodium, 38g total carbohydrate (5g fiber, 22g sugar), 4g protein, 200%DV vitamin A, 10%DV vitamin C, 2%DV calcium, 6%DV iron.

Note: *To allow for more even cooking of the ingredients, slice the sweet potatoes thin and cut the apples in thicker chunks. The apples cook soft faster than the potatoes.*

Sauerkraut and Kielbasa

Colleen Heatwole
Burton, MI

Makes 4 servings
(Ideal slow-cooker size: 4 1/2- or 5-quart)

1 1/2 lbs. fresh or canned sauerkraut,
  drained and rinsed
1 lb. reduced-fat turkey kielbasa, cut in 1"
  slices

1. Combine sauerkraut and turkey kielbasa in slow cooker.
2. Cover. Cook on low 5-6 hours.
3. Stir before serving.

Per Serving: 190 calories (80 calories from fat), 9g total fat (3g saturated, 0g trans), 75mg cholesterol, 2120mg sodium, 10g total carbohydrate (4g fiber, 3g sugar), 19g protein, 0%DV vitamin A, 20%DV vitamin C, 6%DV calcium, 20%DV iron.

Notes:
1. This is delicious served with mashed potatoes.
2. This is a basic recipe. My family prefers this version over more elaborate ones with onions or apples or caraway seeds!

Cabbage with Kielbasa

Millie Schellenburg
Washington, NJ

Makes 8 servings
(Ideal slow-cooker size: 6-quart)

2 cups water
1 1/2 medium-sized heads of cabbage,
    chopped
3/4 lb. kielbasa, cut into 1/2" slices
8 medium-sized potatoes, cut into chunks
1 onion, sliced

1. Combine all ingredients in slow cooker.
2. Cover. Cook on low 3 hours, or until cabbage and potatoes are done to your liking.

Per Serving: 380 calories (140 calories from fat), 16g total fat (6g saturated, 0g trans), 30mg cholesterol, 390mg sodium, 49g total carbohydrate (9g fiber, 8g sugar), 13g protein, 4%DV vitamin A, 80%DV vitamin C, 8%DV calcium, 15%DV iron.

Economy One-Dish Supper

Betty Drescher
Quakertown, PA

Makes 6 servings
(Ideal slow-cooker size: 5-quart)

1/2 lb. lean sausage
1 1/2 cups potatoes, grated or cubed
1 cup water
1/2 tsp. cream of tartar
1 cup raw carrots, grated or sliced thin
1/4 cup rice, uncooked
1 onion, minced
1/4 tsp. salt
1/4 tsp. black pepper
1/4 tsp. curry powder
3 cups low-sodium tomato juice

1. Brown sausage in nonstick skillet. Cut into 1/4"-thick slices.
2. Mix water and cream of tartar. Toss with potatoes. Drain.
3. Layer sausage, potatoes, carrots, rice, and onion in slow cooker.
4. Combine salt, pepper, curry powder, and tomato juice. Pour over all.
5. Cover. Cook on low 8-10 hours or on high 4-5 hours.

Per Serving: 150 calories (60 calories from fat), 7g total fat (2.5g saturated, 0g trans), 15mg cholesterol, 280mg sodium, 18g total carbohydrate (3g fiber, 7g sugar), 5g protein, 100%DV vitamin A, 20%DV vitamin C, 2%DV calcium, 8%DV iron.

Sausage and Cabbage

Melanie Thrower
McPherson, KS

Makes 6 servings
(Ideal slow-cooker size: 3- or 4-quart)

8 ozs. lite smoked sausage or kielbasa
1 head cabbage, chopped
2 onions, diced
1/2 tsp. salt
1/4 tsp. black pepper
1/4 cup hot water
1 beef bouillon cube

1. Slice sausage into small pieces.
2. Layer cabbage, onions, and sausage in bottom of slow cooker.
3. Add seasonings. Dissolve bouillon cube in water.
4. Cook on high 3-4 hours, or until cabbage is done to your liking.

Per Serving: 130 calories (70 calories from fat), 7g total fat (2.5g saturated, 0g trans), 15mg cholesterol, 330mg sodium, 12g total carbohydrate (4g fiber, 7g sugar), 5g protein, 4%DV vitamin A, 40%DV vitamin C, 8%DV calcium, 6%DV iron.

Sausage Vegetable Stew

Rosann Zeiset
Stevens, PA

Makes 10 servings
(Ideal slow-cooker size: 5- or 6-quart)

1 lb. sausage (regular, turkey, or smoked)
4 cups potatoes, cooked and cubed
4 cups carrots, cooked and sliced
4 cups green beans, cooked
28-oz. can tomato sauce
1 tsp. onion powder
¼ or ½ tsp. black pepper, according to
   your taste

1. Slice sausage into 1½" pieces. Place in slow cooker.
2. Add cooked vegetables. Pour tomato sauce over top.
3. Sprinkle with onion powder and pepper. Stir.
4. Cook on high 3-4 hours or low 8-10 hours.

Per Serving: 230 calories (80 calories from fat), 9g total fat (3g saturated, 0g trans), 15mg cholesterol, 930mg sodium, 32g total carbohydrate (6g fiber, 9g sugar), 8g protein, 200%DV vitamin A, 30%DV vitamin C, 6%DV calcium, 15%DV iron.

Note: If your diet allows, you may want to add ½ tsp. salt to Step 3.

Bratwursts

Dede Peterson
Rapid City, SD

Makes 8 servings
(Ideal slow-cooker size: 4-quart)

8 bratwursts
1 large onion, sliced
12-oz. can of beer
1 cup chili sauce
1 Tbsp. Worcestershire sauce
1 cup ketchup
2 Tbsp. vinegar
½ tsp. salt
2 Tbsp. brown sugar
1 Tbsp. paprika

1. Boil bratwursts in water in skillet for 10 minutes to remove fat.
2. Drain bratwursts and place in slow cooker.
3. Mix together remaining ingredients in bowl and then pour over meat.
4. Cook on low 4-5 hours.

Per Serving: 160 calories (45 calories from fat), 5g total fat (1.5g saturated, 0g trans), 10mg cholesterol, 1000mg sodium, 24g total carbohydrate (0.5g fiber, 17g sugar), 3g protein, 20%DV vitamin A, 10%DV vitamin C, 2%DV calcium, 4%DV iron.

Bratwurst Stew

Lauren M. Eberhard
Senecca, IL

Makes 8 servings
(Ideal slow-cooker size: 5-quart)

2 10³/4-oz. cans fat-free chicken broth
4 medium-sized carrots, sliced
2 ribs of celery, cut in chunks
1 medium-sized onion, chopped
1 tsp. dried basil
1/2 tsp. garlic powder
3 cups chopped cabbage
2 1-lb. cans great northern beans, drained
5 fully cooked bratwurst links, cut into
    1/2" slices

1. Combine all ingredients in slow cooker.
2. Cook on high 3-4 hours, or until veggies are tender.

Per Serving: 120 calories (30 calories from fat), 3.5g total fat (1g saturated, 0g trans), 5mg cholesterol, 320mg sodium, 15g total carbohydrate (5g fiber, 4g sugar), 7g protein, 150%DV vitamin A, 10%DV vitamin C, 6%DV calcium, 10%DV iron.

Note: You can eat this as a stew, or over hot corn bread or rice.

Lamb Stew

Dottie Schmidt
Kansas City, MO

Makes 6 servings
(Ideal slow-cooker size: 6-quart)

2 lbs. lean lamb, cubed
1/2 tsp. sugar
2 Tbsp. canola oil
1 1/2 tsp. salt
1/4 tsp. black pepper
1/4 cup flour
2 cups water
3/4 cup red cooking wine
1/4 tsp. garlic powder
2 tsp. Worcestershire sauce
6-8 carrots, sliced
4 small onions, quartered
4 ribs celery, sliced
3 medium-sized potatoes, diced

1. Sprinkle lamb with sugar. Brown in oil in skillet.
2. Remove lamb and place in cooker, reserving drippings. Stir salt, pepper, and flour into drippings in skillet until smooth. Stir in water and wine until smooth, stirring loose the meat drippings. Continue cooking and stirring occasionally until broth simmers and thickens.
3. Pour into cooker. Add remaining ingredients and stir until well mixed.
4. Cover. Cook on low 8-10 hours.

Per Serving: 440 calories (130 calories from fat), 15g total fat (5g saturated, 0g trans), 90mg cholesterol, 940mg sodium, 39g total carbohydrate (7g fiber, 11g sugar), 32g protein, 400%DV vitamin A, 20%DV vitamin C, 8%DV calcium, 25%DV iron.

Bean and Other Main Dishes

New Mexico Pinto Beans

John D. Allen
Rye, CO

Makes 8 servings
(Ideal slow-cooker size: 4- or 5-quart)

2½ cups dried pinto beans
3 qts. water
½ cup lean ham, diced
2 garlic cloves, crushed
1 medium-sized onion, chopped
1 tsp. crushed red chili peppers, optional
½ tsp. salt
¼ tsp. black pepper
1 tsp. dried oregano, optional
1 tsp. dried thyme, optional

1. Sort beans. Discard pebbles, shriveled beans, and floaters. Wash beans under running water. Place in saucepan, cover with 3 quarts water, and soak overnight.

2. Drain beans and discard soaking water. Pour beans into slow cooker. Cover with fresh water.

3. Add meat, garlic, onions, chili peppers if you wish, salt, and pepper, and other seasonings if you want. Cook on low 6-10 hours, or until beans are soft.

Per Serving: 90 calories (15 calories from fat), 1.5g total fat (0g saturated, 0g trans), 10mg cholesterol, 380mg sodium, 12g total carbohydrate (4g fiber, 1g sugar), 6g protein, 0%DV vitamin A, 0%DV vitamin C, 4%DV calcium, 8%DV iron.

Notes:
If you want to round out the flavor, add a 14½-oz. can stewed or diced tomatoes to Step 3.
If your diet allows, you may want to increase the salt to 1 tsp.

Mexican Pinto Beans

Colleen Heatwole
Burton, MI

Makes 8 servings
(Ideal slow-cooker size: 4- or 5-quart)

1 lb. dried pinto beans, soaked overnight
  in water and drained
4 cups fresh water
1 large onion, chopped
14 1/2-oz. can tomatoes
2 garlic cloves, minced
2 tsp. chili powder
1/4 lb. lean ham, chopped

1. Combine all ingredients in slow cooker.
2. Cover. Cook on high 2 hours. Reduce heat. Cook on low 8 hours.

Per Serving: 230 calories (15 calories from fat), 1.5g total fat (0g saturated, 0g trans), 5mg cholesterol, 320mg sodium, 40g total carbohydrate (15g fiber, 5g sugar), 16g protein, 8%DV vitamin A, 8%DV vitamin C, 10%DV calcium, 20%DV iron.

Notes:

If your diet allows, you may want to add 1/2 tsp. salt to Step 1.

If you prefer some more zip to your beans, you may serve these with salsa.

Scandinavian Beans

Virginia Bender
Dover, DE

Makes 8 servings
(Ideal slow-cooker size: 5-quart)

1 lb. dried pinto beans
6 cups water
12 ozs. lean turkey bacon
1 onion, chopped
2-3 garlic cloves, minced
1/4 tsp. black pepper
1 tsp. salt
1/4 cup molasses
1 cup ketchup
1/4 tsp. Tabasco sauce
1 tsp. Worcestershire sauce
1/2 cup brown sugar
1/2 cup cider vinegar
1/4 tsp. dry mustard

1. Soak beans in 6 cups water in soup pot for 8 hours. Bring beans to boil and cook 1 1/2-2 hours, or until soft. Drain, reserving liquid.
2. Combine all ingredients in slow cooker, using just enough bean liquid to cover everything. Cook on low 5-6 hours.

Per Serving: 270 calories (80 calories from fat), 9g total fat (2.5g saturated, 0g trans), 40mg cholesterol, 1350mg sodium, 40g total carbohydrate (3g fiber, 25g sugar), 10g protein, 0%DV vitamin A, 0%DV vitamin C, 8%DV calcium, 15%DV iron.

Anasazi Beans

Melanie Thrower
McPherson, KS

Makes 4 servings
(Ideal slow-cooker size: 3-quart)

2 cups dry anasazi beans, cleaned
4 cups water
1 Tbsp. minced garlic
1 small onion, diced
1 tsp. salt
½ tsp. baking soda

1. Combine all ingredients in slow cooker.
2. Cook on high 3-4 hours.

Per Serving: 320 calories (10 calories from fat), 1g total fat (0g saturated, 0g trans), 0mg cholesterol, 740mg sodium, 58g total carbohydrate (19g fiber, 2g sugar), 21g protein, 0%DV vitamin A, 0%DV vitamin C, 15%DV calcium, 30%DV iron.

Note: These are a sweet-tasting bean with a texture cooked similar to a pinto bean. You may garnish them with salsa to add spice.

From-Scratch Baked Beans

Wanda Roth
Napoleon, OH

Makes 6 servings
(Ideal slow-cooker size: 3½- or 4-quart)

2½ cups great northern dried beans
4 cups water
1½ cups tomato sauce
½ cup brown sugar
2 tsp. salt
1 small onion, chopped
½ tsp. chili powder

1. Wash and drain dry beans. Combine beans and water in slow cooker. Cook on low 8 hours, or overnight.
2. Stir in remaining ingredients. Cook on low 6 hours. If the beans look too watery as they near the end of their cooking time, you can remove the lid during the last 30-60 minutes.

Per Serving: 350 calories (10 calories from fat), 1g total fat (0g saturated, 0g trans), 0mg cholesterol, 1170mg sodium, 71g total carbohydrate (17g fiber, 26g sugar), 18g protein, 0%DV vitamin A, 4%DV vitamin C, 15%DV calcium, 30%DV iron.

New England Baked Beans

Mary Wheatley
Mashpee, MA
Jean Butzer
Batavia, NY

Makes 8 servings
(Ideal slow-cooker size: 4-quart)

1 lb. dried beans—great northern, pea
   beans, or navy beans
1/4 lb. lean turkey bacon slices, diced
1 qt. water
1 tsp. salt
1/4-1/2 tsp. black pepper, according to taste
2 Tbsp. brown sugar
1/2 cup molasses
1 tsp. dry mustard
1/2 tsp. baking soda
1 onion, coarsely chopped
5 cups water

1. Wash beans and remove any stones or
shriveled beans.
2. Meanwhile, simmer turkey bacon in 1
quart water in saucepan for 10 minutes. Drain.
Do not reserve liquid.
3. Combine all ingredients in slow cooker.
4. Cook on high until contents come to a
boil. Turn to low. Cook 14-16 hours, or until
beans are tender.

Per Serving: 300 calories (35 calories from fat), 3.5g total
fat (1g saturated, 0g trans), 15mg cholesterol, 570mg
sodium, 54g total carbohydrate (12g fiber, 20g sugar), 15g
protein, 0%DV vitamin A, 0%DV vitamin C, 15%DV
calcium, 25%DV iron.

Barbecued Lima Beans

Carol Findling
Princeton, IL

Makes 6 servings
(Ideal slow-cooker size: 3 1/2-quart)

1 1/4 cups dried lima beans
half a medium-sized onion, chopped in
   large pieces
1/2 tsp. salt
1/2 tsp. dry mustard
1 tsp. cider vinegar
2 Tbsp. molasses
1/4 cup chili sauce or medium salsa
several drops Tabasco sauce

1. Place beans in bowl and cover with
water. Let beans soak overnight. Drain,
reserving 1 cup liquid from beans.
2. Combine all ingredients in slow cooker,
including 1 cup bean liquid.
3. Cook on low 8-10 hours.

Per Serving: 180 calories (5 calories from fat), 0.5g total fat
(0g saturated, 0g trans), 0mg cholesterol, 330mg sodium,
35g total carbohydrate (9g fiber, 11g sugar), 9g protein,
0%DV vitamin A, 0%DV vitamin C, 6%DV calcium,
15%DV iron.

*Note: The recipe as noted above has almost no
fat. For added flavor, and if your diet allows, add
1/4 lb. lean ham, smoked, or Cajun turkey, or soy-
bacon during the last hour.*

Brown-Sugar Barbecued Lima Beans

Hazel L. Propst
Oxford, PA

Makes 10 servings
(Ideal slow-cooker size: 5-quart)

1½ lbs. dried lima beans
6 cups water
2¼ cups chopped onions
1 cup brown sugar
1½ cups ketchup
13 drops Tabasco sauce
1 cup dark corn syrup
1 Tbsp. salt
4 slices lean turkey bacon, diced

1. Soak washed beans in large soup pot in water overnight. Do not drain.
2. Add onions. Bring to boil. Simmer 30-60 minutes, or until beans are tender. Drain beans, reserving liquid.
3. Combine all ingredients except bean liquid in slow cooker. Mix well. Pour in enough liquid so that beans are barely covered.
4. Cover. Cook on low 10 hours, or on high 4-6 hours. Stir occasionally.
5. If the beans are too soupy as they near the end of their cooking time, remove the lid for the last hour or so of cooking.

Per Serving: 490 calories (20 calories from fat), 2g total fat (0g saturated, 0g trans), 5mg cholesterol, 1270mg sodium, 108g total carbohydrate (15g fiber, 51g sugar), 16g protein, 0%DV vitamin A, 4%DV vitamin C, 10%DV calcium, 30%DV iron.

New Orleans Red Beans

Cheri Janzen
Houston, TX

Makes 6 servings
(Ideal slow-cooker size: 3½-quart)

2 cups dried kidney beans
5 cups water
¼ lb. lean hot sausage, cut in small pieces
2 onions, chopped
2 cloves garlic, minced
1 tsp. salt

1. Wash beans. Remove any stones or floaters. In saucepan, combine beans and water. Boil 2 minutes. Remove from heat. Soak 1 hour.
2. Brown sausage slowly in nonstick skillet. Add onions, garlic, and salt and sauté until tender.
3. Combine all ingredients, including the bean water, in slow cooker.
4. Cover. Cook on low 8-10 hours. During last 20 minutes of cooking, stir frequently and mash lightly with spoon.
5. Serve over hot cooked white rice.

Per Serving: 200 calories (110 calories from fat), 12g total fat (4.5 saturated, 0g trans), 20mg cholesterol, 870mg sodium, 17g total carbohydrate (4g fiber, 4g sugar), 8g protein, 0%DV vitamin A, 0%DV vitamin C, 4%DV calcium, 8%DV iron.

Note: Offer salsa as a condiment.

No-Meat Baked Beans

Esther Becker
Gordonville, PA

Makes 8-10 servings
(Ideal slow-cooker size: 3½-quart)

1 lb. dried navy beans
6 cups water
1 small onion, chopped
¾ cup ketchup
½ cup brown sugar
¾ cup water
1 tsp. dry mustard
3 Tbsp. dark molasses
1 tsp. salt

1. Soak beans in water overnight in large soup kettle. Cook beans in water until soft, about 1½ hours. Drain, discarding bean water.
2. Stir together all ingredients in slow cooker. Mix well.
3. Cover. Cook on low 5-8 hours, or until beans are well flavored but not breaking down.

Per Serving: 290 calories (10 calories from fat), 1g total fat (0g saturated, 0g trans), 0mg cholesterol, 580mg sodium, 60g total carbohydrate (14g fiber, 25g sugar), 13g protein, 0%DV vitamin A, 0%DV vitamin C, 15%DV calcium, 30%DV iron.

Four Zesty Beans

Ann Van Doren
Lady Lake, FL

Makes 10 servings
(Ideal slow-cooker size: 4- or 5-quart)

2 15½-oz. cans great northern beans, rinsed and drained
2 15-oz. cans black beans, rinsed and drained
15-oz. can butter beans, rinsed and drained
15-oz. can baked beans, undrained
2 cups salsa
½ cup brown sugar

1. In slow cooker combine northern beans, black beans, butter beans, and baked beans.
2. Stir in salsa and brown sugar.
3. Cover. Cook on low 2-2½ hours.

Per Serving: 300 calories (10 calories from fat), 1.5g total fat (0g saturated, 0g trans), 0mg cholesterol, 840mg sodium, 60g total carbohydrate (14g fiber, 16g sugar), 16g protein, 10%DV vitamin A, 8%DV vitamin C, 10%DV calcium, 25%DV iron.

Sweet-Sour Bean Trio
Barbara Walker
Sturgis, SD

Makes 8 servings
(Ideal slow-cooker size: 3½-quart)

4 slices lean bacon
1 onion, chopped
¼ cup brown sugar
1 tsp. prepared mustard
1 clove garlic, crushed
½ tsp. salt
¼ cup vinegar
16-oz. can low-sodium lima beans, drained
16-oz. can low-sodium baked beans, undrained
16-oz. can low-sodium kidney beans, drained

1. Brown bacon in a nonstick skillet. Crumble. Combine bacon, 2 Tbsp. drippings from bacon, onion, brown sugar, mustard, garlic, salt, and vinegar.
2. Mix with beans in slow cooker.
3. Cover. Cook on low 6-8 hours.

Per Serving: 210 calories (20 calories from fat), 2g total fat (0.5g saturated, 0g trans), 5mg cholesterol, 570mg sodium, 40g total carbohydrate (9g fiber, 15g sugar), 11g protein, 4%DV vitamin A, 4%DV vitamin C, 6%DV calcium, 10%DV iron.

Note: These beans are a good side dish or are good served over rice.

Five-Baked Beans
Betty B. Dennison
Grove City, PA

Makes 12 servings
(Ideal slow-cooker size: 4- or 5-quart)

6 slices turkey bacon
1 cup onions, chopped
1 clove garlic, minced
16-oz. can low-sodium lima beans, drained
16-oz. can low-sodium beans with tomato sauce, undrained
15½-oz. can low-sodium red kidney beans, drained
15-oz. can low-sodium butter beans, drained
15-oz. can low-sodium garbanzo beans, drained
¾ cup ketchup
½ cup unsulfured molasses
¼ cup brown sugar
1 Tbsp. prepared mustard
1 Tbsp. Worcestershire sauce
1 onion sliced and cut into rings, optional

1. In a nonstick skillet, cook bacon until browned.
2. Combine chopped onions, bacon, garlic, lima beans, beans with tomato sauce, kidney beans, butter beans, garbanzo beans, ketchup, molasses, brown sugar, mustard, and Worcestershire sauce in slow cooker.
3. Top with onions if desired.
4. Cover. Cook on low 10-12 hours or high 4-5 hours.

Per Serving: 200 calories (20 calories from fat), 2g total fat (0.5g saturated, 0g trans), 5mg cholesterol, 600mg sodium, 40g total carbohydrate (7g fiber, 16g sugar), 8g protein, 4%DV vitamin A, 4%DV vitamin C, 8%DV calcium, 20%DV iron.

Note: If you prefer less sweet beans, leave out the molasses and add the liquid from all the canned beans.

Six-Bean Barbecued Beans

Gladys Longacre
Susquehanna, PA

Makes 15-18 servings
(Ideal slow-cooker size: 5-quart)

1-lb. can kidney beans, drained
1-lb. can pinto beans, drained
1-lb. can great northern beans, drained
1-lb. can butter beans, drained
1-lb. can navy beans, drained
1-lb. can pork and beans, undrained
¼ cup barbecue sauce
¼ cup prepared mustard
⅓ cup ketchup
1 small onion, chopped
1 small bell pepper, chopped
¼ cup sorghum molasses
1 cup brown sugar

1. Mix together all ingredients in slow cooker.
2. Cook on low 4-6 hours.

Per Serving: 330 calories (10 calories from fat), 1.5g total fat (0g saturated, 0g trans), 0mg cholesterol, 740mg sodium, 66g total carbohydrate (13g fiber, 25g sugar), 15g protein, 0%DV vitamin A, 10%DV vitamin C, 15%DV calcium, 25%DV iron.

Pody Scout Beans

Jody Moore, Pendleton, IN

Makes 15 servings
(Ideal slow-cooker size: 5- or 6-quart)

1 lb. ground turkey
1 tsp. garlic
1 medium-sized onion, chopped
1 cup barbecue sauce
½ cup brown sugar
6 1-lb. cans of beans of your choice (pinto, lima, kidney, chili, great northern, and so on), each drained

1. Brown ground turkey in a nonstick skillet over medium heat.
2. Combine all ingredients in slow cooker.
3. Cover. Cook on high 3 hours.

Per Serving: 120 calories (20 calories from fat), 2g total fat (0.5g saturated, 0g trans), 15mg cholesterol, 320mg sodium, 18g total carbohydrate (2g fiber, 12g sugar), 8g protein, 2%DV vitamin A, 2%DV vitamin C, 2%DV calcium, 6%DV iron.

Note: To add more zest, stir in 4-oz. can chopped green chilies and/or ¼ tsp. dried mustard to Step 2.

Nan's Barbecued Beans

Nan Decker, Albuquerque, NM

Makes 10-12 servings
(Ideal slow-cooker size: 3½-quart)

1 lb. lean ground chuck
1 onion, chopped
5 cups canned baked beans
2 Tbsp. cider vinegar
1 Tbsp. Worcestershire sauce
2 Tbsp. brown sugar
½ cup ketchup

1. Brown ground beef and onion in nonstick skillet. Drain.
2. Combine all ingredients in slow cooker.
3. Cover. Cook on low 4-6 hours.

Per Serving: 260 calories (50 calories from fat), 6g total fat (1.5g saturated, 0g trans), 20mg cholesterol, 670mg sodium, 35g total carbohydrate (8g fiber, 13g sugar), 16g protein, 10%DV vitamin A, 0%DV vitamin C, 6%DV calcium, 15%DV iron.

Smoky Maple Baked Beans
Sharon Miller
Holmesville, OH

Makes 10 servings
(Ideal slow-cooker size: 3-quart)

half a medium-sized onion, chopped
5 slices turkey bacon, chopped
4 ozs. extra-lean ground beef
16-oz. can vegetarian beans in tomato sauce, undrained
16-oz. can vegetarian baked beans, undrained
16-oz. can red kidney beans, rinsed and drained
1/2 cup tomato sauce
2 Tbsp. brown sugar
1-2 Tbsp. liquid smoke
1/2 tsp. maple flavoring

1. Sauté onions and bacon in nonstick skillet sprayed with non-stick cooking spray until onions are tender. Place in slow cooker.
2. Brown beef in nonstick skillet. Place in cooker.
3. Combine all ingredients in slow cooker.
4. Cook on high 4-6 hours. Stir before serving.

Per Serving: 200 calories (30 calories from fat), 3 total fat (1g saturated, 0g trans), 10mg cholesterol, 580mg sodium, 32g total carbohydrate (8g fiber, 10g sugar), 11g protein, 4%DV vitamin A, 4%DV vitamin C, 6%DV calcium, 15%DV iron.

"Lean" Cowboy Beans
John D. Allen
Rye, CO

Makes 8 servings
(Ideal slow-cooker size: 4-quart)

1 lb. ground turkey
16-oz. can baked beans, undrained
16-oz. can kidney beans, drained
2 cups onions, chopped
3/4 cup brown sugar
1 cup ketchup
2 Tbsp. dry mustard
1/4 tsp. salt
2 tsp. cider vinegar

1. Brown turkey in nonstick skillet over medium heat.
2. Combine all ingredients in slow cooker sprayed with non-fat cooking spray.
3. Cover. Cook on high 1-2 hours.

Per Serving: 320 calories (50 calories from fat), 5g total fat (1g saturated, 0g trans), 35mg cholesterol, 880mg sodium, 53g total carbohydrate (7g fiber, 30g sugar), 18g protein, 10%DV vitamin A, 8%DV vitamin C, 6%DV calcium, 15%DV iron.

Note: For a milder taste, sauté the chopped onions with the turkey in Step 1. You may also decrease the dry mustard to 1 Tbsp., or according to your taste.

Sweet and Sour Beans

Julette Leaman
Harrisonburg, VA

Makes 6-8 servings
(Ideal slow-cooker size: 3¹/2- or 4-quart)

5 slices lean turkey bacon
4 medium-sized onions, cut in rings
¹/2 cup brown sugar
1 tsp. dry mustard
¹/2 tsp. salt
¹/4 cup cider vinegar
1-lb. can green beans, drained
2 1-lb. cans butter beans, drained
1-lb., 11-oz. can pork and beans,
   undrained

1. Brown bacon in nonstick skillet and crumble. Drain all but 2 Tbsp. bacon drippings. Stir in onions, brown sugar, mustard, salt, and vinegar. Simmer 20 minutes.
2. Combine all ingredients in slow cooker.
3. Cover. Cook on low 3 hours.

Per Serving: 400 calories (35 calories from fat), 4g total fat (1g saturated, 0g trans), 15mg cholesterol, 1640mg sodium, 80g total carbohydrate (12g fiber, 48g sugar), 14g protein, 0%DV vitamin A, 0%DV vitamin C, 15%DV calcium, 25%DV iron.

Mixed Slow-Cooker Beans

Carol Peachey
Lancaster, PA

Makes 6 servings
(Ideal slow-cooker size: 3¹/2- or 4-quart)

16-oz. can kidney beans, drained
15¹/2-oz. can baked beans, undrained
1 pint home-frozen, or 1-lb. pkg. frozen,
   lima beans
1 pint home-frozen green beans, or 1-lb.
   pkg. frozen, green beans
4 slices lean turkey bacon, browned and
   crumbled
¹/2 cup ketchup
¹/3 cup sugar
¹/3 cup brown sugar
2 Tbsp. vinegar
¹/2 tsp. salt

1. Combine beans and bacon in slow cooker.
2. Stir together remaining ingredients. Add to beans and mix well.
3. Cover. Cook on low 4-5 hours.

Per Serving: 360 calories (30 calories from fat), 3.5g total fat (0.5g saturated, 0g trans), 10mg cholesterol, 1100mg sodium, 71g total carbohydrate (12g fiber, 33g sugar), 14g protein, 10%DV vitamin A, 0%DV vitamin C, 10%DV calcium, 20%DV iron.

Barbecued Green Beans

Arlene Wengerd
Millersburg, OH

Makes 4-6 servings
(Ideal slow-cooker size: 3½-quart)

5 slices lean turkey bacon
¼ cup chopped onions
¾ cup ketchup
⅓ cup brown sugar
3 tsp. Worcestershire sauce
½ tsp. salt
4 cups frozen green beans, thawed

1. Brown bacon in skillet until crisp and then break into pieces. Reserve 2 Tbsp. bacon drippings.
2. Sauté onions in bacon drippings.
3. Combine ketchup, brown sugar, Worcestershire sauce, and salt. Stir into bacon and onions.
4. Pour mixture over green beans and mix lightly.
5. Pour into slow cooker and cook on high 3½-4½ hours or on low 7-9 hours.

Per Serving: 130 calories (25 calories from fat), 2.5g total fat (0.5g saturated, 0g trans), 10mg cholesterol, 960mg sodium, 25g total carbohydrate (2g fiber, 17g sugar), 3g protein, 0%DV vitamin A, 0%DV vitamin C, 4%DV calcium, 8%DV iron.

Easy Baked Beans

Alma Weaver
Ephrata, PA

Makes 8 servings
(Ideal slow-cooker size: 2½-quart)

2 16-oz. cans baked beans
¼ cup brown sugar
½ tsp. dried mustard
½ cup ketchup
2 small onions, chopped
1 tsp. Worcestershire sauce

1. Combine all ingredients in slow cooker.
2. Cover. Cook on high 2 hours.

Per Serving: 180 calories (15 calories from fat), 1.5g total fat (0g saturated, 0g trans), 5mg cholesterol, 610mg sodium, 38g total carbohydrate (8g fiber, 17g sugar), 6g protein, 10%DV vitamin A, 2%DV vitamin C, 6%DV calcium, 8%DV iron.

Note: You can reduce the amount of brown sugar without harming the dish, if you prefer a less-sweet outcome.

Mexican Rice & Beans

Jeanne Allen
Rye, CO

Makes 6 servings
(Ideal slow-cooker size: 4-quart)

16-oz. can Mexican-style beans, undrained
16-oz. can crushed tomatoes, undrained
1 1/2 cups converted rice, uncooked
1 large onion, finely chopped
4 1/2-oz. can chopped green chiles,
   undrained
2 cloves garlic, minced
1 1/2 cups shredded reduced-fat cheese,
   divided

  1. Combine all ingredients except 3/4 cup
cheese in slow cooker sprayed with non-fat
cooking spray.
  2. Cover. Cook on low 6-7 hours.
  3. Sprinkle with remaining cheese 1 hour
before serving.

Per Serving: 340 calories (25 calories from fat), 2.5g total
fat (1.5g saturated, 0g trans), 5mg cholesterol, 110mg
sodium, 63g total carbohydrate (8g fiber, 3g sugar), 18g
protein, 10%DV vitamin A, 30%DV vitamin C, 30%DV
calcium, 20%DV iron.

Fruity Baked Bean Casserole

Elaine Unruh
Minneapolis, MN

Makes 6-8 servings
(Ideal slow-cooker size: 4- or 5-quart)

5 slices lean turkey bacon
3 medium-sized onions, chopped
16-oz. can lima beans, drained
16-oz. can kidney beans, drained
2 16-oz. cans baked beans, undrained
15 1/2-oz. can unsweetened pineapple
   chunks, or crushed pineapple,
   undrained
1/4 cup brown sugar
1/4 cup cider vinegar
1/4 cup molasses
1/2 cup ketchup
2 Tbsp. prepared mustard
1/2 tsp. garlic salt
1 green bell pepper, chopped

  1. Cook bacon in skillet. Crumble. Reserve
2 Tbsp. drippings in skillet. Place bacon in
slow cooker.
  2. Add onions to drippings and sauté until
soft. Drain. Add to bacon in slow cooker.
  3. Add beans and pineapple to cooker. Mix
well.
  4. Combine brown sugar, vinegar, molasses,
ketchup, mustard, garlic salt, and green
pepper. Mix well. Stir into mixture in slow
cooker.
  5. Cover. Cook on high 2-3 hours.

Per Serving: 370 calories (35 calories from fat), 3.5g total
fat (0.5g saturated, 0g trans), 10mg cholesterol, 1080mg
sodium, 71g total arbohydrate (14g fiber, 31g sugar), 14g
protein, 10%DV vitamin A, 20%DV vitamin C, 10%DV
calcium, 20%DV iron.

Apple Bean Bake

Barbara A. Yoder
Goshen, IN

Makes 10 servings
(Ideal slow-cooker size: 4-quart)

4 Tbsp. butter
2 large Granny Smith apples, cubed
1/2 cup brown sugar
1/4 cup sugar
1/2 cup ketchup
1 tsp. cinnamon
1 Tbsp. molasses
1 tsp. salt
24-oz. can great northern beans, undrained
24-oz. can pinto beans, undrained

1. Melt butter in skillet. Add apples and cook until tender.
2. Stir in brown sugar and sugar. Cook until they melt. Stir in ketchup, cinnamon, molasses, and salt.
3. Add beans. Mix well. Pour into slow cooker.
4. Cover. Cook on high 2-4 hours.

Per Serving: 220 calories (40 calories from fat), 4.5g total fat (2.5g saturated, 0g trans), 10mg cholesterol, 490mg sodium, 41g total carbohydrate (6g fiber, 19g sugar), 7g protein, 0%DV vitamin A, 0%DV vitamin C, 8%DV calcium, 10%DV iron.

Ann's Boston Baked Beans

Ann Driscoll
Albuquerque, NM

Makes 20 servings
(Ideal slow-cooker size: 4- or 5-quart)

1 cup raisins
2 small onions, diced
2 tart apples, diced
1 cup fat-free, low-sodium chili sauce
1 cup chopped lean ham
2 1-lb., 15-oz. cans baked beans, undrained
3 tsp. dry mustard
1/2 cup sweet pickle relish

1. Mix together all ingredients.
2. Cover. Cook on low 6-8 hours.

Per Serving: 180 calories (15 calories from fat), 2g total fat (0g saturated, 0g trans), 10mg cholesterol, 530mg sodium, 34g total carbohydrate (6g fiber, 18g sugar), 7g protein, 0%DV vitamin A, 0%DV vitamin C, 4%DV calcium, 6%DV iron.

Creole Black Beans

Joyce Kaut
Rochester, NY

Makes 6-8 servings
(Ideal slow-cooker size: 4-quart)

¾ lb. lean smoked sausage, sliced in
   ¼" pieces and browned
3 15-oz. cans black beans, drained
1½ cups chopped onions
1½ cups chopped green bell peppers
1½ cups chopped celery
4 garlic cloves, minced
2 tsp. dried thyme
1½ tsp. dried oregano
1½ tsp. black pepper
1 chicken bouillon cube
3 bay leaves
8-oz. can tomato sauce
1 cup water

1. Combine all ingredients in slow cooker.
2. Cover. Cook on low 8 hours or on high 4 hours.
3. Remove bay leaves before serving.

Per Serving: 250 calories (80 calories from fat), 9g total fat (3g saturated, 0g trans), 15mg cholesterol, 1080mg sodium, 34g total carbohydrate (11g fiber, 6g sugar), 13g protein, 0%DV vitamin A, 30%DV vitamin C, 10%DV calcium, 20%DV iron.

Notes:
   For a different consistency, you may substitute a 14½-oz. can of low-sodium stewed tomatoes for the tomato sauce.
   This is tasty served over steamed rice.

Red Beans and Rice

Lavina Hochstedler
Grand Blanc, MI

Makes 8 servings
(Ideal slow-cooker size: 3½- or 4-quart)

1 medium-sized onion, chopped
½ cup green bell peppers, chopped
2 cloves garlic, minced
2 Tbsp. olive oil or canola oil
⅓ cup fresh cilantro or parsley, minced
3 16-oz. cans red beans, rinsed and
   drained
¾ cup water
½ tsp. salt
1 tsp. ground cumin
¼ tsp. black pepper

1. In a large skillet, sauté onion, green pepper, and garlic in oil until tender. Or wilt the onion, pepper, and garlic in the microwave for 2 minutes on High.
2. Add cilantro. Stir in beans, water, salt, cumin, and pepper. Transfer to slow cooker.
3. Cover. Cook on low 5-6 hours.

Per Serving: 320 calories (40 calories from fat), 4.5g total fat (0.5g saturated, 0g trans), 0mg cholesterol, 150mg sodium, 56g total carbohydrate (16g fiber, 4g sugar), 14g protein, 4%DV vitamin A, 10%DV vitamin C, 2%DV calcium, 6%DV iron.

Notes:
   1. If beans are watery as they near the end of the cooking time, remove the lid for the last hour of cooking.
   2. Serve over hot, cooked rice.
   3. If diets allow, you can serve the dish with grated cheese for each diner to add to his/her individual serving.

Lentil and Rice Pilaf

Andrea Cunningham
Arlington, KS

Makes 8-10 servings
(Ideal slow-cooker size: 4- or 5-quart)

2-5 large onions, depending on your taste
preference
2 Tbsp. olive oil
6 cups water
1¾ cups lentils, sorted, washed, and
drained
2 cups brown rice, washed and drained

1. Slice onions into ½" circles. Place in nonstick skillet with olive oil. Sauté over medium heat until onions are golden brown.
2. Remove about 1-onion's-worth from skillet and place on paper towel to drain.
3. Place remaining onions and drippings in slow cooker. Combine with water, lentils, and brown rice.
4. Cover. Cook on low 6-8 hours.
5. Serve hot or cold. Garnish with crisp brown onions.

Per Serving: 350 calories (30 calories from fat), 3.5g total fat (0.5g saturated, 0g trans), 0mg cholesterol, 15mg sodium, 66g total carbohydrate (16g fiber, 7g sugar), 16g protein, 0%DV vitamin A, 0%DV vitamin C, 4%DV calcium, 25%DV iron.

Notes:
1. This is good to dip into with pita triangles. It is also good served as a main dish with a basic green salad topped with herbal vinaigrette dressing.
2. If your diet allows, you may want to add 1 tsp. salt to Step 3.
3. If you like some bite to lentils and rice, add ¼-½ tsp. freshly ground pepper to Step 3.

Pasta with Lentil Sauce

Joy Sutter
Iowa City, IA

Makes 4-6 servings
(Ideal slow-cooker size: 4- or 5-quart)

½ cup onions, chopped
½ cup carrots, chopped
½ cup celery, chopped
2 cups diced tomatoes in liquid
1 cup tomato sauce
3-4 ozs. dried lentils, rinsed and drained
½ tsp. dried oregano
½ tsp. dried basil
½ tsp. garlic powder
¼ tsp. crushed red pepper flakes
4 cups angel-hair pasta, hot, cooked

1. Mix all ingredients except pasta in slow cooker.
2. Cover. Cook on low 8-10 hours, or on high 3-5 hours.
3. Cook pasta according to package directions.
4. Place cooked pasta in large serving bowl and pour lentil sauce over top. Toss to combine.

Per Serving: 230 calories (10 calories from fat), 1g total fat (0g saturated, 0g trans), 0mg cholesterol, 360mg sodium, 46g total carbohydrate (8g fiber, 8g sugar), 10g protein, 50%DV vitamin A, 15%DV vitamin C, 6%DV calcium, 25%DV iron.

Carrot Lentil Casserole

Pat Bishop
Bedminster, PA

Makes 6 servings
(Ideal slow-cooker size: 4- or 5-quart)

1 large onion, chopped
1 cup carrots, finely chopped
¾ cup dry lentils
¾ cup brown rice, uncooked
¾ cup low-fat cheese
½ cup green bell pepper, chopped
½ tsp. dried thyme
½ tsp. dried basil
½ tsp. dried oregano
¼ tsp. salt
¼ tsp. sage
¼ tsp. garlic powder
1 cup low-sodium canned tomatoes,
   undrained
1 cup low-fat, low-sodium chicken broth

1. Combine all ingredients in slow cooker.
2. Cover. Cook on high 4-5 hours.

Per Serving: 230 calories (20 calories from fat), 2g total fat (1g saturated, 0g trans), 5mg cholesterol, 260mg sodium, 39g total carbohydrate (10g fiber, 6g sugar), 15g protein, 80%DV vitamin A, 20%DV vitamin C, 20%DV calcium, 20%DV iron.

BBQ Veggie Joes

Andrea Cunningham
Arlington, KS

Makes 10 servings
(Ideal slow-cooker size: 3-quart)

1 cup dried lentils, rinsed and sorted
2 cups water
1½ cups celery, chopped
1½ cups carrots, chopped
1 cup onions, chopped
¾ cup ketchup
2 Tbsp. dark brown sugar
2 Tbsp. Worcestershire sauce
2 Tbsp. cider vinegar

1. In a medium saucepan, combine lentils and water. Bring to a boil. Reduce heat. Cover and simmer 10 minutes.
2. Combine celery, carrots, onions, ketchup, brown sugar, Worcestershire sauce, and lentils with water in slow cooker. Mix well.
3. Cover. Cook on low 8-10 hours, or until lentils are soft.
4. Stir in vinegar just before serving.
5. Allow ½ cup filling for each sandwich.

Per Serving: 230 calories (20 calories from fat), 2.5g total fat (0g saturated, 0g trans), 0mg cholesterol, 480mg sodium, 45g total carbohydrate (9g fiber, 10g sugar), 10g protein, 100%DV vitamin A, 0%DV vitamin C, 8%DV calcium, 20%DV iron.

Cottage Cheese Casserole

Melani Guengerich Novinger
Austin, TX

Makes 6 servings
(Ideal slow-cooker size: 3-quart)

2½ tsp. margarine
½ cup fresh mushrooms, chopped
½ cup onions, chopped
½ cup celery, chopped
1 clove garlic, minced
½ tsp. dried marjoram
¾ cup low-sodium tomato paste
4 cups cooked macaroni
1¼ cups water
2 tsp. salt
1 tsp. sugar
¼ cup parsley, chopped
2 cups low-fat, low-sodium cottage cheese
⅓ cup grated Parmesan cheese

1. Sauté mushrooms, onions, celery, and garlic in margarine in a skillet over medium heat.
2. Combine sautéed vegetables, marjoram, tomato paste, macaroni, water, salt, and sugar.
3. Put half of macaroni mixture in slow cooker.
4. Top with 1 cup cottage cheese, half of Parmesan cheese, and parsley.
5. Repeat layers.
6. Cover. Cook on high 4-5 hours.

Per Serving: 270 calories (40 calories from fat), 4.5g total fat (1.5g saturated, 0g trans), 5mg cholesterol, 930mg sodium, 40g total carbohydrate (4g fiber, 6g sugar), 18g protein, 15%DV vitamin A, 20%DV vitamin C, 20%DV calcium, 20%DV iron.

Note: *If you enjoy a tomatoey flavor, and your diet allows, you could add an 8-oz. can of low-sodium tomato sauce to Step 2 and reduce the water to ¾ cup.*

Tastes-Like-Chili-Rellenos

Roseann Wilson
Albuquerque, NM

Makes 6 servings
(Ideal slow-cooker size: 4- or 5-quart)

2 4-oz. cans whole green chilies
½ lb. grated fat-free cheddar cheese
½ lb. grated fat-free Monterey Jack cheese
14½-oz. can low-sodium stewed tomatoes
4 eggs
2 Tbsp. flour
¾ cup fat-free evaporated milk

1. Spray sides and bottom of slow cooker with nonfat cooking spray.
2. Cut chilies into strips. Layer chilies and cheeses in slow cooker. Pour in stewed tomatoes.
3. Combine eggs, flour, and milk. Pour into slow cooker.
4. Cover. Cook on high 2-3 hours.

Per Serving: 230 calories (40 calories from fat), 4.5g total fat (1.5g saturated, 0g trans), 135mg cholesterol, 920mg sodium, 15g total carbohydrate (2g fiber, 9g sugar), 28g protein, 20%DV vitamin A, 10%DV vitamin C, 100%DV calcium, 8%DV iron.

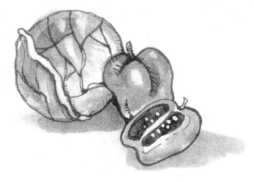

Macaroni and Cheddar Cheese

Elaine Patton
West Middletown, PA

Makes 7 servings
(Ideal slow-cooker size: 3½-quart)

2½ cups fat-free or 2% milk
1 egg, beaten
1 tsp. salt
dash of pepper
3 cups low-fat cheddar cheese, shredded
 or cubed
8-oz. pkg. macaroni, cooked al dente

1. Combine all ingredients except macaroni in slow cooker.
2. Cook on high for 1 hour.
3. Add macaroni. Cook on low 4 more hours.

Per Serving: 170 calories (40 calories from fat), 4.5 total fat (2.5g saturated, 0g trans), 40mg cholesterol, 400mg sodium, 15g total carbohydrate (0g fiber, 6g sugar), 17g protein, 6%DV vitamin A, 0%DV vitamin C, 45%DV calcium, 6%DV iron.

Macaroni and Cheddar/Parmesan Cheese

Sherry L. Lapp
Lancaster, PA

Makes 8 servings
(Ideal slow-cooker size: 4-quart)

8-oz. pkg. elbow macaroni, cooked al dente
13-oz. can fat-free evaporated milk
1 cup fat-free milk
2 large eggs, slightly beaten
4 cups grated fat-free sharp cheddar cheese, divided
¼ tsp. salt
⅛ tsp. white pepper
¼ cup grated fat-free Parmesan cheese

1. Spray inside of cooker with nonfat cooking spray. Then, in cooker, combine lightly cooked macaroni, evaporated milk, milk, eggs, 3 cups cheddar cheese, salt, and pepper.
2. Top with remaining cheddar and Parmesan cheeses.
3. Cover. Cook on low 3 hours.

Per Serving: 190 calories (15 calories from fat), 1.5g total fat (0g saturated, 0g trans), 60mg cholesterol, 740mg sodium, 17g total carbohydrate (0g fiber, 7g sugar), 26g protein, 10%DV vitamin A, 0%DV vitamin C, 70%DV calcium, 2%DV iron.

Macaroni and Velveeta Cheese

Lisa F. Good
Harrisonburg, VA

Makes 6 servings
(Ideal slow-cooker size: 2- or 3-quart)

1½ cups dry macaroni
1 Tbsp. butter
1 tsp. salt
½ lb. Velveeta Light cheese, sliced
1 qt. fat-free milk

1. Combine macaroni, butter, and salt.
2. Layer cheese over top.
3. Pour in milk.
4. Cover. Cook on high 2-3 hours, or until macaroni are soft.

Per Serving: 270 calories (80 calories from fat), 9g total fat (5g saturated, 1.5g trans), 30mg cholesterol, 1070mg sodium, 32g total carbohydrate (0g fiber, 12g sugar), 16g protein, 0%DV vitamin A, 0%DV vitamin C, 35%DV calcium, 2%DV iron.

Lasagna

Rosemarie Fitzgerald
Gibsonia, PA

Makes 8 servings
(Ideal slow-cooker size: 4- or 5-quart)

4½ cups fat-free, low-sodium meatless spaghetti sauce
½ cup water
16-oz. container fat-free ricotta cheese
2 cups shredded part-skim mozzarella cheese, divided
¾ cup grated Parmesan cheese, divided
1 egg
2 tsp. minced garlic
1 tsp. Italian seasoning
8-oz. box no-cook lasagna noodles

1. Mix spaghetti sauce and ½ cup water in a bowl.
2. In a separate bowl, mix ricotta, 1½ cups mozzarella cheese, ½ cup Parmesan cheese, egg, garlic, and seasoning.
3. Spread ¼ of the sauce mixture in bottom of slow cooker. Top with ⅓ of the noodles, breaking if needed to fit.
4. Spread with ⅓ of the cheese mixture, making sure noodles are covered.
5. Repeat layers twice more.
6. Spread with remaining sauce.
7. Cover. Cook on low 5 hours.
8. Sprinkle with remaining cheeses. Cover. Let stand 10 minutes to allow cheeses to melt.

Per Serving: 360 calories (90 calories from fat), 10g total fat (4.5g saturated, 0g trans), 40mg cholesterol, 870mg sodium, 39g total carbohydrate (6g fiber, 10g sugar), 25g protein, 0%DV vitamin A, 0%DV vitamin C, 50%DV calcium, 10%DV iron.

Garden-Fresh Chili Sauce
Dianna Milhizer
Brighton, MI

Makes 4 quarts, or 16 servings
(Ideal slow-cooker size: 6-quart)

1 1/2 cups tomato juice
12 dried red (hot chili) peppers, chopped,
  or enough to make 2 cups-worth
4 quarts fresh tomatoes, peeled and
  chopped
2 cups onions, chopped
2 cups red sweet peppers, chopped
1 tsp. ground ginger
1 tsp. ground nutmeg
1 tsp. whole cloves
1 bay leaf
2 tsp. ground cinnamon
2 tsp. salt
4 cups white vinegar
1 tsp. whole peppercorns

1. Bring 1 1/2 cups tomato juice to a boil.
Place dried peppers in hot juice and allow to
steep and soften for 5 minutes. Cover your
hands with plastic gloves. Remove stems from
dried peppers, and then puree the peppers in
your food processor.
2. Combine all ingredients in large slow
cooker.
3. Cover. Cook on high 4 hours.
4. Remove bay leaf.
5. Freeze or can in pint jars.

Per Serving: 80 calories (5 calories from fat), 1g total fat
(0g saturated, 0g trans), 0mg cholesterol, 310mg sodium,
16g total carbohydrate (3g fiber, 7g sugar), 2g protein,
40%DV vitamin A, 100%DV vitamin C, 2%DV calcium,
6%DV iron.

Notes:
1. If you prefer a smoother sauce you may puree
it in a blender.
2. This is an excellent side dish for Mexican
recipes and can be used as a flavoring when

cooking pork, chicken, or beef. A little bit goes a
long way! You may reduce the amount of chili
peppers but then the sauce isn't as pungent. It
makes a great last-minute, end-of-the-garden-
season use for your tomatoes and peppers.

Marinara Sauce
Dorothy VanDeest
Memphis, TN

Makes 12 servings
(Ideal slow-cooker size: 4-quart)

2 28-oz. cans low-sodium whole tomatoes
1 onion, finely chopped
2 carrots, pared and finely chopped
1 clove garlic, chopped
2 Tbsp. vegetable oil
1 Tbsp. brown sugar
1/2 tsp. salt

1. Puree tomatoes in blender or food
processor.
2. In a skillet, sauté onions, carrots, and
garlic in oil until tender. Do not brown.
3. Combine all ingredients in slow cooker.
Stir well.
4. Cover. Cook on low 6-10 hours.
5. Remove cover. Stir well.
6. Cook on high uncovered for 1 hour for a
thicker marinara sauce.

Per Serving: 50 calories (25 calories from fat), 2.5g total fat
(0g saturated, 0g trans), 0mg cholesterol, 15mg sodium, 8g
total carbohydrate (2g fiber, 4g sugar), 1g protein, 50%DV
vitamin A, 20%DV vitamin C, 4%DV calcium, 4%DV iron.

Note: You can make this in advance of needing it
and then freeze it in handy serving-size containers.

Delicious Spaghetti Sauce

Andrea Cunningham
Arlington, KS

Makes 8 servings
(Ideal slow-cooker size: 4-quart)

2 tsp. olive oil
1 medium-sized onion, finely chopped
6 cloves garlic, minced
56-oz. can low-sodium crushed tomatoes,
    or 7 cups fresh, peeled, diced tomatoes
6-oz. can low-sodium tomato paste
2 tsp. dried basil
1/2 tsp. dried oregano
1 tsp. salt
1/2 tsp. black pepper
1 Tbsp. sugar
2 Tbsp. fresh parsley, chopped

1. Heat oil in a saucepan over medium heat. Add onion and garlic. Sauté until onion becomes very soft (about 10 minutes).
2. Combine all ingredients except parsley in slow cooker.
3. Cover. Cook on low 6-8 hours.
4. Add parsley. Cook an additional 30 minutes.
5. Serve over cooked noodles.

Per Serving: 110 calories (15 calories from fat), 2g total fat (0g saturated, 0g trans), 0mg cholesterol, 570mg sodium, 22g total carbohydrate (5g fiber, 3g sugar), 4g protein, 30%DV vitamin A, 20%DV vitamin C, 10%DV calcium, 20%DV iron.

Slimmed-Down Pasta Sauce

Dolores Kratz
Souderton, PA

Makes 3 1/2 cups sauce, or 4 servings
(Ideal slow-cooker size: 3-quart)

24-oz. can low-sodium tomato juice
6-oz. can tomato paste
1/2 cup carrots, grated
2 large cloves, mashed
1 tsp. dried oregano leaves, crushed
1 tsp. onion salt
1 medium bay leaf
dash of pepper

1. Combine all ingredients in slow cooker.
2. Cover. Cook on low 2-4 hours.
3. Remove bay leaf.
4. Serve over your favorite pasta.

Per Serving: 80 calories (0 calories from fat), 0g total fat (0g saturated, 0g trans), 0mg cholesterol, 510mg sodium, 18g total carbohydrate (4g fiber, 8g sugar), 3g protein, 100%DV vitamin A, 60%DV vitamin C, 4%DV calcium, 10%DV iron.

Lentil Tacos

Judy Buller
Bluffton, OH

Makes 6 servings
(Ideal slow-cooker size: 4-quart)

3/4 cup onions, finely chopped
1/8 tsp. garlic powder
1 tsp. canola oil
1/2 lb. dry lentils, picked clean of stones
  and floaters
1 Tbsp. chili powder
2 tsp. ground cumin
1 tsp. dried oregano
2 cups fat-free, low-sodium chicken broth
1 cup salsa
12 taco shells
shredded lettuce
tomatoes, chopped
shredded, reduced-fat cheddar cheese
fat-free sour cream
taco sauce

1. Sprinkle garlic powder over onions and
sauté in oil in skillet until tender. Add lentils
and spices. Cook and stir for 1 minute.
2. Place lentil mixture and broth in slow
cooker.
3. Cover. Cook on low 3 hours for
somewhat-crunchy lentils, or on low 6 hours
for soft lentils.
4. Add salsa.
5. Spoon about 1/4 cup into each taco shell.
Top with lettuce, tomatoes, cheese, sour
cream, and taco sauce.

Per Serving: 340 calories (100 calories from fat), 11g total
fat (3.5g saturated, 2g trans), 15mg cholesterol, 600mg
sodium, 42g total carbohydrate (5g fiber, 12g sugar), 19g
protein, 40%DV vitamin A, 20%DV vitamin C, 50%DV
calcium, 15%DV iron.

Note: This mixture is also tasty served over rice.

Sloppy Joes

Darla Sathre
Baxter, MN

Makes 8 servings
(Ideal slow-cooker size: 3- or 4-quart)

1 onion
1 green bell pepper
4 cloves garlic
2 carrots
8-oz. pkg. tempeh (we like 5-grain)
2 Tbsp. olive oil
1 envelope dry onion soup mix
1/4 tsp. ground cumin
16-oz. can pinto beans, drained
16-oz. can fat-free refried beans
1/2 cup barbecue sauce

1. Dice the onion, green pepper, garlic,
carrots, and tempeh. Sauté briefly in olive oil
in skillet.
2. Combine with onion soup mix, cumin,
beans, and barbecue sauce in slow cooker. You
may want to slightly mash the pinto beans.
3. Cook on low 8-9 hours.
4. Serve on buns. Open-faced is less sloppy!

Per Serving: 340 calories (70 calories from fat), 8g total fat
(1g saturated, 0g trans), 0mg cholesterol, 890mg sodium,
56g total carbohydrate (12g fiber, 9g sugar), 16g protein,
50%DV vitamin A, 20%DV vitamin C, 10%DV calcium,
25%DV iron.

Note: You may want to increase the cumin to
1/2 tsp., if you prefer more bite.
You may serve this over pasta or rice, or just-
as-is as a side dish.

Pizza Sloppy Joe

Sue Hamilton
Minooka, IL

Makes 6 servings
(Ideal slow-cooker size: 4-quart)

1 cup textured vegetable protein (T.V.P., soy)
7-oz. can mushrooms, undrained
15-oz. can low-sodium tomato sauce
14.5-oz. can low-sodium Italian diced tomatoes with basil, garlic, and oregano
1/2 tsp. fennel seeds
1/2 tsp. crushed red peppers
1 tsp. Italian seasoning
1 tsp. minced roasted garlic
1/2 tsp. salt

1. Combine all ingredients in slow cooker.
2. Cover. Cook on low 6-8 hours.

Per Serving: 90 calories (10 calories from fat), 1g total fat (0g saturated, 0g trans), 0mg cholesterol, 1060mg sodium, 15g total carbohydrate (5g fiber, 7g sugar), 9g protein, 10%DV vitamin A, 10%DV vitamin C, 10%DV calcium, 15%DV iron.

Vegetable-Stuffed Peppers

Shirley Hinh
Wayland, IA

Makes 8 servings
(Ideal slow-cooker size: 6-quart oval, so the peppers can each sit on the bottom of the cooker)

4 large green, red, or yellow bell peppers
1/2 cup quick-cooking rice
1/4 cup minced onions
1/4 cup black olives, sliced
2 tsp. lite soy sauce
1/4 tsp. black pepper
1 clove garlic, minced
28-oz. can low-sodium whole tomatoes
6-oz. can low-sodium tomato paste
15 1/4-oz. can corn or kidney beans, drained

1. Cut tops off peppers (reserve) and remove seeds. Stand peppers up in slow cooker.
2. Mix remaining ingredients in a bowl. Stuff peppers.
3. Place pepper tops back on the peppers. Pour remaining ingredients over the stuffed peppers and work down in between the peppers.
4. Cover. Cook on low 6-8 hours, or until the peppers are done to your liking.
5. If you prefer, you may add 1/2 cup tomato juice if recipe is too dry.
6. Cut peppers in half and serve.

Per Serving: 100 calories (20 calories from fat), 2g total fat (0g saturated, 0g trans), 0mg cholesterol, 420mg sodium, 22g total carbohydrate (3g fiber, 6g sugar), 3g protein, 10%DV vitamin A, 60%DV vitamin C, 4%DV calcium, 8%DV iron.

Fruit and Vegetable Curry

Melani Guengerich Novinger
Austin, TX

Makes 6 servings
(Ideal slow-cooker size: 4-quart)

4 onions, coarsely chopped
2 Tbsp. vegetable oil
2 cloves garlic, minced
1 tsp. gingerroot, grated
1½ Tbsp. ground cumin
½ tsp. cayenne pepper
1½ Tbsp. ground coriander
¼ tsp. ground cardamom
¼ tsp. ground cloves
1 tsp. ground turmeric
2 medium-sized zucchini,
    quartered lengthwise and sliced
¾ cup water
1 cup green beans, cut
2 firm, tart apples, cored and cubed
half a red bell pepper, chopped
1 cup dried apricots, chopped
½ cup currants or raisins
½ cup apricot conserve (or smashed
    halves and juice)

1. Sauté the onions in oil for 10 minutes. Stir in garlic, gingerroot, and spices. Continue to sauté, stirring constantly for about 3 minutes.
2. Transfer to slow cooker. Add zucchini, water, green beans, apples, red bell pepper, and dried apricots.
3. Cover. Cook on high 5-6 hours or on low 10-12 hours.
4. Stir in raisins and apricot conserve just before serving.

Per Serving: 300 calories (50 calories from fat) (1g saturated, 0g trans), 0mg cholesterol, 20mg sodium, 63g total carbohydrate (7g fiber, 48g sugar), 4g protein, 20%DV vitamin A, 30%DV vitamin C, 8%DV calcium, 15%DV iron.

Note: This is tasty served over brown rice and topped with peanuts and chopped or sliced bananas.

Surprise Stuffed Peppers

Dorothy VanDeest
Memphis, TN

Makes 4 servings
(Ideal slow-cooker size: 5-quart, or large enough that
each pepper can sit on the floor of the cooker)

2 cups low-sodium tomato juice
6-oz. can tomato paste
2 7-oz. cans chunk-style tuna, drained and
    rinsed
2 Tbsp. dried onion flakes
2 Tbsp. dried veggie flakes
¼ tsp. garlic powder
4 medium-sized green bell peppers, tops
    removed and seeded

1. Mix tomato juice and tomato paste, reserving 1 cup.
2. Mix remaining tomato-juice mixture with tuna, onion flakes, veggie flakes, and garlic powder.
3. Fill peppers equally with mixture. Place upright in slow cooker.
4. Pour the reserved 1 cup tomato-juice mixture over peppers.
5. Cover. Cook on low 8-9 hours, or until peppers are done to your liking.

Per Serving: 220 calories (5 calories from fat), 0.5g total fat (0g saturated, 0g trans), 60mg cholesterol, 460mg sodium, 23g total carbohydrate (5g fiber, 9g sugar), 30g protein, 20%DV vitamin A, 200%DV vitamin C, 4%DV calcium, 10%DV iron.

Seafood Main Dishes

Tex-Mex Luau

Dorothy VanDeest
Memphis, TN

Makes 6 servings
(Ideal slow-cooker size: 3- or 4-quart)

1½ lbs. frozen firm-textured fish fillets,
   thawed
2 onions, thinly sliced
2 lemons, divided
2 Tbsp. butter, melted
2 tsp. salt
1 bay leaf
4 whole peppercorns
1 cup water

1. Cut fillets into serving portions.
2. Combine onion slices and 1 sliced lemon
in butter, along with salt, bay leaf, and
peppercorns. Pour into slow cooker.
3. Place fillets on top of onion and lemon
slices. Add water.
4. Cover. Cook on high 3-4 hours.
5. Before serving, carefully remove fish
fillets with slotted spoon. Place on heatproof
plate.

6. Sprinkle with juice of half of the second
lemon. Garnish with remaining lemon slices.
7. Serve hot with Avocado Sauce (see
below), if desired. Or chill and serve cold, also
with Avocado Sauce, if you wish.

Per Serving: 160 calories (50 calories from fat), 5g total fat
(2.5g saturated, 0g trans), 65mg cholesterol, 870mg
sodium, 7g total carbohydrate (2g fiber, 3g sugar), 22g
protein, 4%DV vitamin A, 20%DV vitamin C, 6%DV
calcium, 4%DV iron.

Avocado Sauce

7½ ozs. frozen low-fat avocado dip,
   thawed
½ cup fat-free sour cream
2 Tbsp. lemon juice
half a small onion, finely chopped

Combine all ingredients. Mix well.

Herbed Flounder

Dorothy VanDeest
Memphis, TX

Makes 6 servings
(Ideal slow-cooker size: 6-quart oval)

2 lbs. flounder fillets (fresh or frozen)
1/2 tsp. salt
3/4 cup chicken broth
2 Tbsp. lemon juice
2 Tbsp. dried chives
2 Tbsp. dried minced onion
1/2-1 tsp. leaf marjoram
4 Tbsp. fresh parsley, chopped

1. Wipe fish as dry as possible. Cut fish into portions to fit slow cooker.
2. Sprinkle with salt.
3. Combine broth and lemon juice. Stir in remaining ingredients.
4. Place a meat rack in the slow cooker. Lay fish on rack. Pour liquid mixture over each portion.
5. Cover. Cook on high 3-4 hours.

Per Serving: 160 calories (20 calories from fat), 2.5g total fat (0.5 saturated, 0g trans), 75mg cholesterol, 2590mg sodium, 5g total carbohydrate (0.5g fiber, 2g sugar), 29g protein, 8%DV vitamin A, 10%DV vitamin C, 6%DV calcium, 4%DV iron.

Fish Feast

Anne Townsend
Albuquerque, NM

Makes 8 servings
(Ideal slow-cooker size: 6-quart oval)

3 lbs. red snapper fillets
1 Tbsp. garlic, minced
1 large onion, sliced
1 green bell pepper, cut in 1" pieces
2 unpeeled zucchini, sliced
14-oz. can low-sodium diced tomatoes
1/2 tsp. dried basil
1/2 tsp. dried oregano
1/4 tsp. salt
1/4 tsp. black pepper
1/4 cup dry white wine or white grape juice

1. Rinse snapper and pat dry. Place in slow cooker sprayed with non-fat cooking spray.
2. Mix remaining ingredients together and pour over fish.
3. Cover. Cook on high 2-3 hours, being careful not to overcook the fish.

Per Serving: 200 calories (25 calories from fat), 2.5g total fat (0.5g saturated, 0g trans), 65mg cholesterol, 260mg sodium, 7g total carbohydrate (2g fiber, 3g sugar), 36g protein, 4%DV vitamin A, 20%DV vitamin C, 8%DV calcium, 6%DV iron.

Notes:

1. Red snapper can be pricey. You may substitute a sturdy white fish.

2. Serve in a bowl; the Feast is juicy. Or serve as a topping for rice.

Crockpot Oyster Stew

Judy Miles
Centreville, MD

Makes 8 servings:
(Ideal slow-cooker size: 3-quart)

2 qts. 2% milk
3 Tbsp. butter
2 pints fresh oysters
1 1/2 tsp. salt
2 tsp. Worcestershire sauce

1. Heat milk on high in covered slow cooker 1 1/2 hours.
2. In a saucepan, melt butter. Add oysters with liquid. Simmer on low until edges of oysters curl.

3. Add salt and Worcestershire sauce to oysters. Combine with hot milk in slow cooker.

4. Cover. Cook on low 2-3 hours, stirring occasionally.

Per Serving: 240 calories (110 calories from fat), 12g total fat (7g saturated, 0g trans), 95mg cholesterol, 830mg sodium, 17g total carbohydrate (0g fiber, 12g sugar), 17g protein, 10%DV vitamin A, 0%DV vitamin C, 35%DV calcium, 45%DV iron.

Dawn's Spaghetti Sauce with Crab
Dawn Day
Westminster, CA

Makes 4-6 servings
(Ideal slow-cooker size: 2- or 3-quart)

1 medium-sized onion, chopped
1/2 lb. fresh mushrooms, sliced
2 12-oz. cans low-sodium tomato sauce, or
    1 12-oz. can low-sodium tomato sauce and
    1 12-oz. can low-sodium chopped tomatoes
6-oz. can tomato paste
1/2 tsp. garlic powder
1/2 tsp. dried basil
1/2 tsp. dried oregano
1/2 tsp. salt
1 lb. crabmeat
16 ozs. angel-hair pasta, cooked

1. Sauté onions and mushrooms in non-stick skillet over low heat. When wilted, place in slow cooker.

2. Add tomato sauce, tomato paste, and seasonings. Stir in crab.

3. Cover. Cook on low 4-6 hours.

4. Serve over angel-hair pasta.

Per Serving: 550 calories (45 calories from fat), 5g total fat (0g saturated, 0g trans), 80mg cholesterol, 1710mg sodium, 88g total carbohydrate (9g fiber, 12g sugar), 42g protein, 20%DV vitamin A, 30%DV vitamin C, 15%DV calcium, 35%DV iron.

Crockpot Shrimp Marinara
Judy Miles
Centreville, MD

Makes 6 servings
(Ideal slow-cooker size: 3 1/2-quart)

16-oz. can low-sodium tomatoes, cut up
2 Tbsp. minced parsley
1 clove garlic, minced
1/2 tsp. dried basil
1/2 tsp. salt
1/4 tsp. black pepper
1 tsp. dried oregano
6-oz. can tomato paste
1/2 tsp. seasoned salt
1 lb. shrimp, cooked and shelled
3 cups spaghetti
grated Parmesan cheese

1. Combine tomatoes, parsley, garlic, basil, salt, pepper, oregano, tomato paste, and seasoned salt in slow cooker.

2. Cover. Cook on low 6-7 hours.

3. Stir shrimp into sauce.

4. Cover. Cook on high 10-15 minutes.

5. Serve over cooked spaghetti. Top with Parmesan cheese.

Per Serving: 210 calories (15 calories from fat), 1.5g total fat (0g saturated, 0g trans), 145mg cholesterol, 720mg sodium, 29g total carbohydrate (4g fiber, 4g sugar), 21g protein, 10%DV vitamin A, 10%DV vitamin C, 10%DV calcium, 25%DV iron.

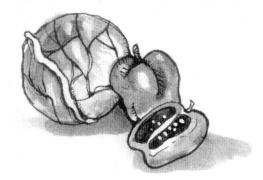

Company Casserole

Vera Schmucker
Goshen, IN

Makes 6 servings
(Ideal slow-cooker size: 4- or 5-quart)

1¼ cups uncooked rice
2 Tbsp. butter, melted
3 cups fat-free, low-sodium chicken broth
1 cup water
3 cups cut-up, cooked skinless chicken
   breast
2 4-oz. cans sliced mushrooms, drained
⅓ cup light soy sauce
12-oz. pkg. shelled frozen shrimp
8 green onions, chopped, 2 Tbsp. reserved
⅔ cup slivered almonds

1. Combine rice and butter in slow cooker. Stir to coat rice well.
2. Add remaining ingredients except almonds and 2 Tbsp. green onions.
3. Cover. Cook on low 6-8 hours or on high 3-4 hours, until rice is tender.
4. Sprinkle almonds and green onions over top before serving.

Per Serving: 410 calories (130 calories from fat), 15g total fat (3.5g saturated, 0g trans), 150mg cholesterol, 850mg sodium, 26g total carbohydrate (5g fiber, 10g sugar), 42g protein, 0%DV vitamin A, 10%DV vitamin C, 15%DV calcium, 25%DV iron.

Note: If your diet allows, add ½ tsp. salt to Step 2.

Shrimp Jambalaya

Karen Ashworth
Duenweg, MO

Makes 8 servings
(Ideal slow-cooker size: 5-quart)

2 Tbsp. margarine
2 medium-sized onions, chopped
2 green bell peppers, chopped
3 ribs celery, chopped
1 cup chopped, cooked lean ham
2 garlic cloves, chopped
1½ cups uncooked minute rice
1½ cups fat-free low sodium beef broth
28-oz. can low-sodium chopped tomatoes
2 Tbsp. chopped parsley, fresh or dried
1 tsp. dried basil
½ tsp. dried thyme
¼ tsp. black pepper
⅛ tsp. cayenne pepper
1 lb. shelled, deveined, medium-sized
   shrimp
1 Tbsp. chopped parsley for garnish

1. One-half hour before assembling recipe, melt margarine in slow cooker set on high. Add onions, peppers, celery, ham, and garlic. Cook 30 minutes.
2. Add rice. Cover and cook 15 minutes.
3. Add broth, tomatoes, 2 Tbsp. parsley, and remaining seasonings. Cover and cook on high 1 hour.
4. Add shrimp. Cook on high 30 minutes, or until liquid is absorbed.
5. Garnish with 1 Tbsp. parsley.

Per Serving: 160 calories (35 calories from fat), 4g total fat (1g saturated, 0g trans), 15mg cholesterol, 350mg sodium, 23g total carbohydrate (3g fiber, 5g sugar), 9g protein, 10%DV vitamin A, 30%DV vitamin C, 8%DV calcium, 6%DV iron.

Note: If you wish, and your diet allows, you may want to add ½ tsp. salt to Step 3.

Salmon Cheese Casserole
Wanda S. Curtin
Bradenton, FL

Makes 6 servings
(Ideal slow-cooker size: 2-quart)

14³/4-oz. can salmon with liquid
4-oz. can mushrooms, drained
1¹/2 cups bread crumbs
¹/3 cup eggbeaters
1 cup grated fat-free cheese
1 Tbsp. lemon juice
1 Tbsp. minced onion

1. Flake fish in bowl, removing bones. Stir in remaining ingredients. Pour into lightly greased slow cooker.
2. Cover. Cook on low 2¹/2-3¹/2 hours.

Per Serving: 150 calories (40 calories from fat), 4g total fat (1g saturated, 0g trans), 70mg cholesterol, 650mg sodium, 9g total carbohydrate (1g fiber, 1g sugar), 19g protein, 0%DV vitamin A, 0%DV vitamin C, 20%DV calcium, 6%DV iron.

Simple Tuna Delight
Karen Waggoner
Joplin, MO

Makes 3 servings
(Ideal slow-cooker size: 2-quart)

1³/4 cups frozen vegetables
12-oz. can water-packed tuna, drained
10³/4-oz. can low-sodium condensed cream of chicken or celery soup

1. Combine all ingredients in slow cooker.
2. Cover. Cook on high 1¹/2 hours, stirring occasionally.

3. Serve over hot cooked rice or noodles.

Per Serving: 290 calories (60 calories from fat), 7g total fat (2g saturated, 0g trans), 40mg cholesterol, 1220mg sodium, 21g total carbohydrate (5g fiber, 4g sugar), 35g protein, 80%DV vitamin A, 6%DV vitamin C, 6%DV calcium, 15%DV iron.

Tuna Casserole
Dorothy VanDeest
Memphis, TN

Makes 6 servings
(Ideal slow-cooker size: 3-quart)

2 6-oz. cans tuna, water-packed, rinsed and drained
1¹/2 cups cooked macaroni
¹/2 cup onions, finely chopped
¹/4 cup green bell peppers, finely chopped
4-oz. can sliced mushrooms, drained
10-oz. pkg. frozen cauliflower, partially thawed
¹/2 cup low sodium, fat-free chicken broth

1. Combine all ingredients in slow cooker. Stir well.
2. Cover. Cook on low 4-6 hours or on high 2-3 hours.

Per Serving: 210 calories (20 calories from fat), 2.5g total fat (0.5g saturated, 0g trans), 35mg cholesterol, 1940mg sodium, 16g total carbohydrate (3g fiber, 4g sugar), 32g protein, 4%DV vitamin A, 20%DV vitamin C, 4%DV calcium, 15%DV iron.

Note: If you like some zest, and your diet allows, you may want to add ¹/2-1 tsp. seasoning salt to Step 1.

Tuna Noodle Casserole

Kathryn Yoder
Minot, ND

Makes 8 servings
(Ideal slow-cooker size: 5-quart)

2 cups nonfat powdered milk
4 Tbsp. cornstarch
2 Tbsp. onion flakes
4 Tbsp. low-sodium chicken bouillon
   granules
1/2 tsp. dried thyme
1 Tbsp. dried parsley
1/4 tsp. black pepper
4 cups cold water
2 6-oz. cans water-packed tuna, drained
4-oz. can sliced mushrooms, drained
6-oz. can sliced water chestnuts, drained
16-oz. pkg. frozen mixed vegetables,
   thawed
8-oz. pkg. wide noodles, cooked al dente
   and drained
1/2 cup toasted sliced almonds

1. Mix powdered milk, cornstarch, onion flakes, bouillon, dried herbs, and pepper in a large saucepan.
2. Add water. Cook over medium heat until thickened.
3. Add tuna, mushrooms, water chestnuts, vegetables, and noodles. Pour into slow cooker sprayed with non-fat cooking spray.
4. Sprinkle almonds over casserole.
5. Cover. Cook on low 3-4 hours.

Per Serving: 470 calories (50 calories from fat), 6g total fat (1g saturated, 0g trans), 50mg cholesterol, 1110mg sodium, 67g total carbohydrate (5g fiber, 32g sugar), 39g protein, 40%DV vitamin A, 10%DV vitamin C, 80%DV calcium, 15%DV iron.

Tuna Oriental

Lizzie Ann Yoder
Hartville, OH

Makes 3 servings
(Ideal slow-cooker size: 2-quart)

half a green bell pepper, cut in 1/4" strips
1 small onion, thinly sliced
2 tsp. olive oil
1/3 cup unsweetened pineapple juice
1 1/2 tsp. cornstarch
2/3 cup canned unsweetened pineapple
   chunks, drained
1 Tbsp. sugar (scant)
1 Tbsp. vinegar
6-oz. can solid, water-packed tuna, drained
   and flaked
1/8 tsp. black pepper
dash of Tabasco sauce

1. Cook green pepper and onion with oil in a skillet over medium heat, leaving the vegetables slightly crisp.
2. Mix pineapple juice with cornstarch. Add to green pepper mixture.
3. Cook, stirring gently until thickened.
4. Add remaining ingredients. Pour into slow cooker.
5. Cover. Cook on low 1 hour.

Per Serving: 170 calories (35 calories from fat), 3.5g total fat (0.5g saturated, 0g trans), 20mg cholesterol, 210mg sodium, 18g total carbohydrate (2g fiber, 15g sugar), 17g protein, 0%DV vitamin A, 20%DV vitamin C, 2%DV calcium, 8%DV iron.

Note: This is tasty served over brown rice.

Soups

Vegetable Beef Soup

Judi Manos
West Islip, NY

Makes 6-8 servings
(Ideal slow-cooker size: 4-quart)

1 lb. boneless round steak, well trimmed
  of fat and cut into ½" cubes
14½-oz. can diced tomatoes, undrained
3 cups water
2 medium-sized potatoes, peeled and
  cubed
2 medium-sized onions, diced
3 ribs celery, sliced
2 carrots, sliced
3 beef bouillon cubes
½ tsp. dried basil
½ tsp. dried oregano
½ tsp. salt
¼ tsp. black pepper
1½ cups frozen mixed vegetables

1. Combine all ingredients, except mixed
vegetables, in slow cooker.
2. Cover. Cook on high 6 hours.
3. Add vegetables.
4. Cover. Cook on high 2 hours.

Per Serving: 220 calories (35 calories from fat), 4g total fat
(1.5g saturated, 0g trans), 45mg cholesterol, 770mg
sodium, 28g total Carbohydrate (6g fiber, 8g sugar), 19g
protein, 100%DV vitamin A, 20%DV vitamin C, 10%DV
calcium, 20%DV iron.

Dawn's Sirloin No-Bean Chili
Dawn Day
Westminster, CA

Makes 10 servings
(Ideal slow-cooker size: 3-quart)

1 lb. sirloin steak, trimmed of all fat
2 Tbsp. canola oil
2 large onions, chopped
16-oz. can low-sodium chopped tomatoes
8-oz. can low-sodium tomato paste
1 1/2 cups low-sodium, low-fat beef broth
1/2 tsp. salt
1/4 tsp. black pepper

1. Cube steak into 1" pieces. Brown pieces in a skillet in oil.
2. Combine all ingredients in slow cooker.
3. Cover. Cook on low 8 hours.

Per Serving: 120 calories (45 calories from fat), 5g total fat (1g saturated, 0g trans), 30mg cholesterol, 290mg sodium, 8g total carbohydrate (2g fiber, 3g sugar), 11g protein, 15%DV vitamin A, 10%DV vitamin C, 4%DV calcium, 10%DV iron.

Notes:
1. If you want a zestier dish, and if your diet allows, you may want to add 2 tsp. chili powder and/or 1 tsp. ground cumin to Step 2.
2. This works well served over rice and topped with low-fat cheddar cheese.

Hearty Vegetable Soup
Betty B. Dennison
Grove City, PA

Makes 8 servings
(Ideal slow-cooker size: 5-quart)

1-1 1/2 lbs. beef chuck, well trimmed of fat and cut in 1/2" cubes
2 Tbsp. shortening
1 tsp. salt
1/4 tsp. black pepper
3 cups potatoes, cubed
2 cups carrots, sliced
2 cups low-sodium stewed tomatoes
1/2 cup celery, chopped
1/2 cup onions, diced
1/2 cup frozen corn
1/2 cup frozen cut green beans
1/2 cup frozen peas

1. Brown meat in shortening in skillet. Add salt and pepper.
2. Place meat, potatoes, carrots, stewed tomatoes, celery, onions, corn, and green beans in slow cooker (everything but the peas).
3. Add enough water to cover all ingredients.
4. Cover. Simmer for 20 minutes.
5. Cook on high for 6 1/2 to 7 hours.
6. One-half hour before the end of the cooking time, stir in peas.

Per Serving: 210 calories (60 calories from fat), 7g total fat (2g saturated, 1g trans), 35mg cholesterol, 350mg sodium, 22g total carbohydrate (5g fiber, 7g sugar), 15g protein, 100%DV vitamin A, 20%DV vitamin C, 4%DV calcium, 15%DV iron.

Note: For a thicker soup, and if your diet allows, coat cubed meat with 2 Tbsp. flour before browning.

Vegetable Beef Barley Soup

Mary Rogers
Waseca, MN

Makes 12 servings
(Ideal slow-cooker size: 5- or 6-quart)

1 lb. lean stewing meat, cut into bite-sized pieces
1/2 cup onions, chopped
1/2 cup cut green beans, fresh or frozen
1/2 cup corn, fresh or frozen
4 cups fat-free, low-sodium beef broth
2 14 1/2-oz. cans low-sodium stewed tomatoes
12-oz. can low-sodium V8 juice
2/3 cup pearl barley, uncooked
1 cup water

1. Combine all ingredients in slow cooker.
2. Cover. Cook on high 5-7 hours, until vegetables are cooked to your liking.

Per Serving: 130 calories (20 calories from fat), 2g total fat (0.5g saturated, 0g trans), 25mg cholesterol, 65mg sodium, 15g total carbohydrate (4g fiber, 5g sugar), 12g protein, 4%DV vitamin A, 10%DV vitamin C, 4%DV calcium, 10%DV iron.

Vegetable Beef Soup

Doris Perkins
Mashpee, MA

Makes 8 servings
(Ideal slow-cooker size: 4-quart)

1 lb. extra-lean ground beef
14 1/2-oz. can low-sodium, stewed tomatoes
10 3/4-oz. can low-sodium tomato soup
1 onion, chopped
2 cups water
15 1/2-oz. can garbanzos, drained
15 1/4-oz. can corn, drained
14 1/2-oz. can sliced carrots, drained
1 cup potatoes, diced
1 cup celery, chopped
1/2 tsp. salt
1/4 tsp. black pepper
chopped garlic to taste, optional

1. Sauté ground beef in nonstick skillet.
2. Combine all ingredients in slow cooker.
3. Cook on low 4-6 hours.

Per Serving: 220 calories (50 calories from fat), 6g total fat (2g saturated, 0g trans), 20mg cholesterol, 590mg sodium, 28g total carbohydrate (5g fiber, 7g sugar), 15g protein, 100%DV vitamin A, 20%DV vitamin C, 8%DV calcium, 15%DV iron.

Notes:
1. You may use green beans and turnips, or any other combination of vegetables you wish.
2. If your diet allows, you may want to top individual servings with a spoonful of low-fat grated cheddar cheese.

Beef Barley Lentil Soup

Janie Steele
Moore, OK

Makes 10 servings
(Ideal slow-cooker size: 5- or 6-quart)

1 lb. extra-lean ground beef
1 medium-sized onion, chopped
2 cups potatoes, cubed
1 cup celery, chopped
1 cup carrots, diced
1 cup dry lentils, rinsed
1/2 cup medium-sized pearl barley
8 cups water
2 tsp. beef bouillon granules
1/2 tsp. salt
1/2 tsp. lemon pepper seasoning
2 14 1/2-oz. cans low-sodium stewed
    tomatoes, undrained

   1. Brown ground beef with onions in a
skillet. Drain.
   2. Combine all ingredients except tomatoes
in slow cooker.
   3. Cook on low 6 hours, or until tender.
   4. Add tomatoes. Cook on low 2 more
hours.

Per Serving: 250 calories (40 calories from fat), 4.5g total
fat (1.5g saturated, 0g trans), 15mg cholesterol, 680mg
sodium, 35g total carbohydrate (9g fiber, 7g sugar), 17g
protein, 60%DV vitamin A, 40%DV vitamin C, 6%DV
calcium, 25%DV iron.

*Note: For added zest, you may want to increase
the lemon pepper seasoning to 1 tsp. You may also
want to add 1/2 tsp. dried basil and 1/2 tsp. dried
thyme to Step 2.*

Hamburger Soup

Betty Moore
Plano, IL

Makes 6 servings
(Ideal slow-cooker size: 4-quart)

1 lb. extra-lean ground beef
1/4 tsp. black pepper
1/4 tsp. dried oregano
1/4 tsp. seasoned salt
1 envelope dry onion soup mix
3 cups hot water
8-oz. can tomato sauce
1 Tbsp. low-sodium soy sauce
1 cup carrots, sliced
1 cup celery, sliced
1 cup macaroni, cooked
1/4 cup grated Parmesan cheese

   1. Combine all ingredients except macaroni
and Parmesan cheese in slow cooker.
   2. Cook on low 6-8 hours.
   3. Turn to high. Add macaroni and
Parmesan cheese.
   4. Cook for another 15-20 minutes.

Per Serving: 160 calories (60 calories from fat), 6g total fat
(2.5g saturated, 0g trans), 25mg cholesterol, 440mg
sodium, 12g total carbohydrate (2g fiber, 4g sugar), 15g
protein, 120%DV vitamin A, 10%DV vitamin C, 6%DV
calcium, 10%DV iron.

Beef Goulash Vegetable Soup

Betty Moore
Plano, IL

Makes 6 servings
(Ideal slow-cooker size: 4-quart)

1 lb. extra-lean ground beef
1 large onion, diced
2 ribs of celery, chopped
8-oz. can no-salt added tomato sauce
3 14½-oz. cans fat-free beef broth
10-oz. pkg. frozen green beans
1½ tsp. chili powder
1 tsp. paprika
½ tsp. black pepper
1½ cups flat wide noodles, cooked

1. Sauté ground chuck, onions, and celery in nonstick skillet until meat is browned and vegetables are crisp-tender. Transfer to slow cooker.
2. Add tomato sauce, broth, green beans, chili powder, paprika, and black pepper. Mix together.
3. Cook on low 6-8 hours.
4. Add noodles 30 minutes before serving.

Per Serving: 240 calories (70 calories from fat), 8g total fat (3g saturated, 0g trans), 40mg cholesterol, 270mg sodium, 19g total carbohydrate (3g fiber, 5g sugar), 23g protein, 15%DV vitamin A, 10%DV vitamin C, 4%DV calcium, 20%DV iron.

Note: To eliminate a step, add 1 cup uncooked noodles to cooker 1 hour before serving.

Beef Vegetable Soup

Sheridy Steele
Ardmore, OK

Makes 8 servings
(Ideal slow-cooker size: 4-quart)

1 lb. extra-lean ground beef
1 medium-sized onion, chopped
½ tsp. salt
¼ tsp. black pepper
3 cups water
3 medium-sized potatoes, cubed
14½-oz. can low-sodium Italian diced tomatoes, undrained
11½-oz. can low-sodium vegetable juice
1 cup celery, sliced
1 cup carrots, sliced
2 Tbsp. sugar
1 Tbsp. dried parsley flakes
2 tsp. dried basil
1 bay leaf

1. Brown ground beef and onion in nonstick skillet.
2. Combine all ingredients in slow cooker.
3. Cook on low 8-10 hours, or until vegetables are done to your liking.
4. Remove bay leaf before serving.

Per Serving: 200 calories (50 calories from fat), 5g total fat (2g saturated, 0g trans), 20mg cholesterol, 460mg sodium, 25g total carbohydrate (4g fiber, 8g sugar), 14g protein, 80%DV vitamin A, 30%DV vitamin C, 8%DV calcium, 15%DV iron.

Note: You may substitute cubed boneless round chuck, well trimmed of fat, in place of the ground beef. You may brown it in a nonstick skillet, also, before placing it in the slow cooker.

Vegetable Beef Soup

Annabelle Unternahrer
Shipshewana, IN

Makes 8 servings
(Ideal slow-cooker size: 4-quart)

1 lb. extra-lean ground beef
4 cups water
1 lb. potatoes, pared and chopped
1 medium-sized onion, chopped
2 4-oz. cans mushroom pieces, drained
1 envelope dry low-sodium onion soup
　mix
16-oz. jar low-sodium chunky salsa
2 medium-sized carrots, chopped

1. Brown ground beef in nonstick skillet.
2. Combine all ingredients in slow cooker.
3. Cover. Cook on low 8 hours or on high 4 hours.

Per Serving: 200 calories (50 calories from fat), 5g total fat (2g saturated, 0g trans), 20mg cholesterol, 1230mg sodium, 22g total carbohydrate (3g fiber, 5g sugar), 14g protein, 80%DV vitamin A, 10%DV vitamin C, 4%DV calcium, 10%DV iron.

Taco Soup

Marla Folkerts
Holland, OH

Makes 6 servings
(Ideal slow-cooker size: 3¹/₂- or 4-quart)

Soup:
1 lb. extra-lean ground beef or ground
　turkey
1 medium-sized onion, chopped
1 medium-sized green bell pepper,
　chopped
1 envelope dry reduced-sodium taco
　seasoning
¹/₂ cup water
4 cups reduced-sodium vegetable juice
1 cup chunky salsa

Toppings:
³/₄ cup shredded lettuce
6 Tbsp. fresh tomato, chopped
6 Tbsp. reduced-fat cheddar cheese,
　shredded
¹/₄ cup green onions or chives, chopped
¹/₄ cup fat-free sour cream or fat-free plain
　yogurt
baked tortilla or corn chips

1. Brown meat with onion in nonstick skillet. Drain.
2. Combine all soup ingredients in slow cooker.
3. Cover. Cook on low 6-8 hours.
4. Serve with your choice of toppings.

Per Serving: 260 calories (60 calories from fat), 7g total fat (2.5g saturated, 0g trans), 30mg cholesterol, 2190mg sodium, 29g total carbohydrate (2g fiber, 9g sugar), 17g protein, 50%DV vitamin A, 50%DV vitamin C, 4%DV calcium, 15%DV iron.

Barbara Jean's Burger Soup

Barbara Jean Fabel
Wausau, WI

Makes 8 servings
(Ideal slow-cooker size: 4- or 5-quart)

2 lbs. extra-lean ground beef
5 cups water
1 medium-sized onion, chopped
14½-oz. can diced tomatoes
½ cup celery, chopped
3 Yukon gold potatoes, cubed
½ cup carrots, chopped
½ cup frozen corn, thawed
¼ tsp. salt
¼ tsp. freshly ground pepper
½ tsp. dried basil
½ cup frozen peas, thawed

1. Brown beef in nonstick skillet.
2. Combine all ingredients in slow cooker, except peas.
3. Cover. Cook on low 6-8 hours.
4. One-half hour before serving, stir in peas.

Per Serving: 290 calories (90 calories from fat), 11g total fat (4g saturated, 0g trans), 40mg cholesterol, 190mg sodium, 22g total carbohydrate (4g fiber, 4g sugar), 26g protein, 40%DV vitamin A, 30%DV vitamin C, 4%DV calcium, 20%DV iron.

Note: If your diet permits, you may want to increase the salt to 1 tsp.

Turkey Rosemary Veggie Soup

Willard E. Roth
Elkhart, IN

Makes 8 servings
(Ideal slow-cooker size: 6-quart)

1 lb. 99% fat-free ground turkey
3 parsley stalks with leaves, sliced
3 scallions, chopped
3 medium carrots, unpeeled, sliced
3 medium potatoes, unpeeled, sliced
3 celery ribs with leaves
3 small onions, sliced
1-lb. can whole-kernel corn with juice
1-lb. can green beans with juice
1-lb. can low-sodium diced Italian-style tomatoes
3 cans water
3 packets dry Herb-Ox vegetable broth
1 Tbsp. crushed rosemary, fresh or dry

1. Brown turkey with parsley and scallions in iron skillet. Drain. Pour into slow cooker sprayed with non-fat cooking spray.
2. Add vegetables, water, dry vegetable broth, and rosemary.
3. Cover. Cook on low 8 hours.

Per Serving: 200 calories (15 calories from fat), 1.5g total fat (0g saturated, 0g trans), 25mg cholesterol, 510mg sodium, 31g total carbohydrate (6g fiber, 9g sugar), 18g protein, 100%DV vitamin A, 20%DV vitamin C, 6%DV calcium, 15%DV iron.

Note: This is tasty served topped with a dollop of non-fat yogurt and corn bread on the side.

Ground Turkey Soup

Betty K. Drescher
Quakertown, PA

Makes 12 servings
(Ideal slow-cooker size: 5- or 6-quart)

1 lb. 99% fat-free ground turkey
1 cup onions, chopped
1 clove garlic, minced
15-oz. can kidney beans, drained
1 cup carrots, sliced
1 cup celery, sliced
1/4 cup rice, uncooked
1 quart low-sodium diced Italian tomatoes
2 cups green beans
1 tsp. parsley flakes
half a green bell pepper
1 tsp. salt
1/8 tsp. black pepper
1 Tbsp. Worcestershire sauce
1 bay leaf
3 cups water

   1. Brown turkey in a large skillet.
   2. Combine with remaining ingredients in slow cooker.
   3. Cover. Cook on low 8-9 hours.

Per Serving: 120 calories (5 calories from fat), 1g total fat (0g saturated, 0g trans), 15mg cholesterol, 710mg sodium, 16g total carbohydrate (4g fiber, 5g sugar), 13g protein, 60%DV vitamin A, 10%DV vitamin C, 8%DV calcium, 10%DV iron.

Stew in a Snap

Janice Yoskovich
Carmichaels, PA

Makes 6 servings
(Ideal slow-cooker size: 4-quart)

2 cups water
2 potatoes, diced
1 envelope dry onion soup mix
16-oz. pkg. mixed frozen vegetables
1 lb. ground turkey
4 slices bacon, diced and browned to a crisp
1/4 tsp. black pepper
2 cloves garlic, minced
1 Tbsp. sugar
1 Tbsp. flour
28-oz. can chopped stewed tomatoes

   1. Combine all ingredients in slow cooker.
   2. Cook on high 5-6 hours; then turn to low for 2-3 hours.

Per Serving: 280 calories (70 calories from fat), 7g total fat (2g saturated, 0g trans), 45mg cholesterol, 280mg sodium, 34g total carbohydrate (7g fiber, 8g sugar), 21g protein, 50%DV vitamin A, 30%DV vitamin C, 8%DV calcium, 25%DV iron.

Meatball Mushroom Soup

Nanci Keatley
Salem, OR

Makes 8 servings
(Ideal slow-cooker size: 3¹/₂-quart)

¹/₂ lb. ground turkey
¹/₂ tsp. garlic powder
¹/₂ tsp. onion powder
¹/₄ tsp. black pepper
1 large egg
1 Tbsp. olive oil
1 cup carrots, sliced
2 cloves garlic, crushed
2 cups fresh mushrooms, sliced
10³/₄-oz. can low-fat, or fat-free,
   low-sodium beef broth
10³/₄-oz. can 98% fat-free cream of
   mushroom soup
2 Tbsp. tomato paste
Parmesan cheese for garnish
fresh parsley for garnish

1. In a small bowl mix together ground turkey and seasonings. Add egg, stirring until well blended. Form into small meatballs.
2. Heat olive oil in skillet. Brown meatballs. Drain well.
3. Transfer meatballs to slow cooker. Add remaining ingredients, except Parmesan cheese and parsley.
4. Cover. Cook on low 6-8 hours or on high 3-4 hours.

Per Serving: 100 calories (45 calories from fat), 5g total fat (1g saturated, 0g trans), 25mg cholesterol, 290mg sodium, 7g total carbohydrate (0.5g fiber, 2g sugar), 8g protein, 80%DV vitamin A, 4%DV vitamin C, 2%DV calcium, 4%DV iron.

Cheeseburger Soup

Nanci Keatley
Salem, OR

Makes 6 servings
(Ideal slow-cooker size: 4-quart)

1 lb. ground turkey
1 cup onions, chopped
¹/₂ cup green bell peppers, chopped
2 ribs celery, chopped
20-oz. can beef broth
1 cup non-fat milk
2 cups water
2 Tbsp. flour
8 ozs. low-fat cheddar cheese, grated

1. Brown turkey in nonstick skillet. Spoon into slow cooker.
2. Add vegetables to slow cooker.
3. Heat broth, milk, and water in skillet. Sprinkle flour over liquid. Stir until smooth and let boil for 3 minutes.
4. Pour into slow cooker.
5. Cover. Cook on low 6 hours. Then add cheese and cook another 2-3 hours.

Per Serving: 240 calories (100 calories from fat), 11g total fat (3.5g saturated, 0g trans), 70mg cholesterol, 140mg sodium, 8g total carbohydrate (1g fiber, 5g sugar), 26g protein, 6%DV vitamin A, 10%DV vitamin C, 35%DV calcium, 8%DV iron.

Turkey-Zucchini Soup

Wilma J. Haberkamp
Fairbank, IA

Makes 8 servings
(Ideal slow-cooker size: 4-quart)

8- or 10-oz. pkg. frozen green beans
2 cups zucchini, thinly sliced
2 cups turkey, cooked and chopped
8-oz. can tomato sauce
1/2 cup onions, chopped
1 Tbsp. instant chicken bouillon granules
1 tsp. Worcestershire sauce
1/4 tsp. salt
1/2 tsp. dried savory, crushed
dash of black pepper
4 cups water
3 ozs. light cream cheese, softened

1. Thaw green beans. If you're in a hurry, place them in a strainer and run hot water over them.
2. Combine beans, zucchini, turkey, tomato sauce, onions, bouillon, Worcestershire sauce, salt, savory, black pepper, and water in slow cooker.
3. Cook on high 2-3 hours.
4. Blend 1 cup hot soup with cream cheese. Return to slow cooker and stir well. Cook until hot.

Per Serving: 110calories (35 calories from fat), 3.5g total fat (2g saturated, 0g trans), 30mg cholesterol, 470mg sodium, 7g total carbohydrate (2g fiber, 4g sugar), 13g protein, 10%DV vitamin A, 10%DV vitamin C, 4%DV calcium, 8%DV iron.

Turkey Soup

Mary Rogers
Waseca, MN

Makes 12 servings
(Ideal slow-cooker size: 5-quart)

1 cup macaroni, uncooked
4 cups water
4 10³/4-oz. cans fat-free, low-sodium chicken broth
2 ribs celery, sliced
2 large carrots, sliced
1 cup onions, chopped
2 cloves garlic, mashed
1 tsp. salt
1/2 tsp. black pepper
4 cups cooked turkey, chopped

1. Combine all ingredients except turkey in slow cooker.
2. Cover. Cook on low 8 hours. Add turkey 1 hour before end of cooking time.

Per Serving: 140 calories (25 calories from fat), 2.5g total fat (1g saturated, 0g trans), 35mg cholesterol, 310mg sodium, 9g total carbohydrate (0.5g fiber, 2g sugar), 18g protein, 40%DV vitamin A, 0%DV vitamin C, 4%DV calcium, 10%DV iron.

Note: Experiment by adding more vegetables, such as zucchini, corn, and chopped tomatoes, to Step 1, or halfway through the cooking process so that they don't cook too soft.

Chicken Vegetable Soup

Barbara Walker
Sturgis, SD
Sheridy Steele
Ardmore, OK

Makes 6 servings
(Ideal slow-cooker size: 4-quart)

28-oz. can low-sodium diced tomatoes, undrained
2 cups low-sodium, reduced-fat chicken broth
1 cup frozen corn
2 ribs celery, chopped
6-oz. can tomato paste
¼ cup dry lentils, rinsed
1 Tbsp. sugar
1 Tbsp. Worcestershire sauce
2 tsp. dried parsley flakes
1 tsp. dried marjoram
2 cups cooked chicken breast, cubed

1. Combine all ingredients in slow cooker except chicken.
2. Cover. Cook on low 6-8 hours. Stir in chicken one hour before the end of the cooking time.

Per Serving: 190 calories (20 calories from fat) (0g saturated, 0g trans), 35mg cholesterol, 520mg sodium, 24g total carbohydrate (6g fiber, 7g sugar), 21g protein, 20%DV vitamin A, 20%DV vitamin C, 10%DV calcium, 20%DV iron.

Chicken Stew

Carol Eberly
Harrisonburg, VA

Makes 5 servings
(Ideal slow-cooker size: 4 quart)

1 lb. uncooked boneless, skinless chicken breasts, cubed
14½ oz.-can low-sodium Italian diced tomatoes, undrained
2 potatoes, peeled and cubed
5 carrots, chopped
3 celery ribs, chopped
1 onion, chopped
2 4-oz. cans mushroom stems and pieces, drained
3 chicken bouillon cubes
2 tsp. sugar
½ tsp. dried basil
½ tsp. dill weed
1 tsp. chili powder
¼ tsp. black pepper
1 Tbsp. cornstarch
1 cup water

1. Combine all ingredients except cornstarch and water in slow cooker.
2. Combine water and cornstarch. Stir into slow cooker.
3. Cover. Cook on low 8-10 hours until vegetables are tender.

Per Serving: 300 calories (35 calories from fat) (1g saturated, 0g trans), 75mg cholesterol, 840mg sodium, 33g total carbohydrate (6g fiber, 10g sugar), 33g protein, 200%DV vitamin A, 30%DV vitamin C, 8%DV calcium, 15%DV iron.

Weney's Chicken & Vegetable Stew

Becky Frey
Lebanon, PA

Makes 8 servings
(Ideal slow-cooker size: 4-quart)

4 chicken legs or thighs, skinned
2 carrots, diced
4-6 medium-sized potatoes, diced
2-3 garlic cloves, minced
half a medium-sized head of cabbage, cut
  in chunks
1 green bell pepper, coarsely chopped
1 medium-sized onion, coarsely chopped
14½-oz. can low-sodium diced tomatoes
  (or fresh tomatoes in season)
1 tsp. ground coriander
1 tsp. ground annatto
½ tsp. salt
¼ tsp. black pepper

The day before serving the Stew:
  1. Place chicken in slow cooker, sprinkle
lightly with salt, and cover with water.
  2. Cover. Cook on low 6-8 hours, or until
tender.
  3. Remove chicken from bones and reserve.
  4. Strain and chill broth.

On the next day:
  1. Remove fat from broth.
  2. Place broth, deboned chicken, vegetables,
and seasonings into slow cooker.
  3. Cover. Cook on low 7-8 hours or until
vegetables are tender.

Per Serving: 430 calories (130 calories from fat), 14g total
fat (4g saturated, 0g trans), 90mg cholesterol, 310mg
sodium, 50g total carbohydrate (9g fiber, 8g sugar), 27g
protein, 100%DV vitamin A, 100%DV vitamin C, 15%DV
calcium, 20%DV iron.

*Our dear friend Weney (from Puerto Rico) worked
on our farm for many years. On cool fall evenings*

*he would share this delicious stew with us. He
didn't use a recipe so this is my best effort to
recreate his stew.*

Chicken Borscht

Jeanne Heyerly
Chenoa, IL

Makes 8 servings
(Ideal slow-cooker size: 5- or 6-quart)

1 quart low-fat, low-sodium chicken broth
3 medium-sized potatoes, cubed
3 carrots, sliced
2 ribs celery, sliced
half a medium-sized head of cabbage,
  chopped
2 cups frozen corn
2 cups green beans
1 medium-sized onion, chopped
1 clove garlic, minced
2 cups low-sodium tomato juice
2 cups skinless chicken, cooked and diced
  or shredded
½ tsp. salt
¼ tsp. black pepper

  1. Combine chicken broth, potatoes, carrots,
celery, cabbage, corn, green beans, onions,
garlic, and tomato juice in slow cooker.
  2. Cover. Cook on low 8-10 hours.
  3. Add chicken, salt, and pepper ½-1 hour
before serving.

Per Serving: 230 calories (15 calories from fat), 2g total fat
(0g saturated, 0g trans), 25mg cholesterol, 300mg sodium,
37g total carbohydrate (7g fiber, 10g sugar), 19g protein,
100%DV vitamin A, 80%DV vitamin C, 10%DV calcium,
20%DV iron.

Chicken Noodle Soup with Vegetables

Bernice A. Esau
North Newton, KS

Makes 6 servings
(Ideal slow-cooker size: 4- or 5-quart)

2 onions, chopped
2 cups carrots, sliced
2 cups celery, sliced
10-oz. pkg. frozen peas, optional
2 tsp. salt, optional
1/4 tsp. black pepper
1/2 tsp. dried basil
1/4 tsp. dried thyme
3 Tbsp. dry parsley flakes
4 cups water
2 1/2-3-lb. chicken, cut-up
1 cup uncooked thin noodles

1. Place all ingredients in slow cooker, except chicken and noodles.
2. Remove skin and any fat from chicken pieces. Then place chicken in cooker, on top of the rest of the ingredients.
3. Cover. Cook on high 4-6 hours.
4. One hour before serving, remove chicken. Cool slightly. Cut meat from bones.
5. Return meat to cooker. Add noodles.
6. Cover. Cook on high 1 hour.

Per Serving: 440 calories (70 calories from fat), 8g total fat (2g saturated, 0g trans), 175mg cholesterol, 1030mg sodium, 25g total carbohydrate (6g fiber, 8g sugar), 64g protein, 200%DV vitamin A, 20%DV vitamin C, 8%DV calcium, 25%DV iron.

Optional directions:
1. Place chicken in cooker. Cover 2/3 of it with water and cook for 4 hours on high.
2. Remove chicken. Cool. Cut meat from bone.
3. Add some ice cubes to cooker broth. When cooled, remove fat.
4. Add all ingredients, except noodles.
5. Cover. Cook on high 2-3 hours.

6. Add noodles 1 hour before serving or place cooked noodles in individual bowls and serve chicken soup over noodles.

Roasted Chicken Noodle Soup

Janie Steele
Moore, OK

Makes 8 servings
(Ideal slow-cooker size: 5-quart)

1 cup onions, chopped
1 cup carrots, chopped
1 cup celery, chopped
1 clove garlic, minced
2 tsp. olive or canola oil
1/4 tsp. flour
1/2 tsp. dried oregano
1/2 tsp. dried thyme
1/4 tsp. poultry seasoning
6 cups fat-free chicken broth
4 cups diced potatoes
1 tsp. salt
2 cups skinless roasted chicken, diced
2 cups uncooked wide noodles
1 cup fat-free evaporated milk

1. Brown onions, carrots, celery, and garlic in oil in skillet.
2. Stir in flour, oregano, thyme, and poultry seasoning and blend well. Pour into slow cooker.
3. Mix in broth, potatoes, and salt.
4. Cook on low 5-6 hours, or until potatoes are soft.
5. Add chicken, noodles, and milk. Cook until noodles are tender. Do not bring to a boil after milk is added.

Per Serving: 280 calories (35 calories from fat), 4g total fat (1g saturated, 0g trans), 65mg cholesterol, 520mg sodium, 31g total carbohydrate (3g fiber, 7g sugar), 28g protein, 60%DV vitamin A, 20%DV vitamin C, 15%DV calcium, 20%DV iron.

Chicken Soup in a Pot
Robin Schrock
Millersburg, OH

Makes 4 servings
(Ideal slow-cooker size: 3¹/₂-quart)

4 cups fat-free, low-sodium chicken broth
3 medium-sized carrots, diced
2 celery ribs, diced
1 chicken breast, cooked and cubed
¹/₂ cup uncooked noodles

1. Pour chicken broth into slow cooker. Add carrots and celery.
2. Cover. Cook on low 2 hours.
3. Add chicken and noodles.
4. Cover. Cook on low 1 hour.

Per Serving: 100 calories (10 calories from fat), 1g total fat (0g saturated, 0g trans), 20mg cholesterol, 220mg sodium, 8g total carbohydrate (2g fiber, 3g sugar), 14g pr0tein, 200%DV vitamin A, 0%DV vitamin C, 4%DV calcium, 15%DV iron.

Chicken Chowder Recipe
Sara Puskar
Abingdon, MD

Makes 4 servings
(Ideal slow-cooker size: 3¹/₂-quarts)

¹/₂ cup shredded carrots
1 cup skim milk
¹/₂ cup low-sodium chicken broth
¹/₄ tsp. black pepper
1 cup onions, chopped
1 potato, peeled and cut into ¹/₂" chunks
¹/₂ lb. uncooked boneless, skinless chicken breast cut into 1" cubes
2 15-oz. cans cream-style corn
¹/₂ cup dried potato flakes
¹/₂ cup shredded low-fat cheddar cheese

1. Combine all ingredients except potato flakes and cheese in slow cooker.
2. Cover. Cook on low for 5-7 hours, or until potatoes are tender and chicken is thoroughly cooked.
3. Add potato flakes and stir well to combine.
4. Cook on high, uncovered, for 5-10 minutes, or until chowder has thickened and dried potato flakes have dissolved.
5. Top each serving with cheese.

Per Serving: 380 calories (40 calories from fat), 4g total fat (1.5g saturated, 0g trans), 50mg cholesterol, 720mg sodium, 61g total carbohydrate (5g fiber, 14g sugar), 30g protein, 80%DV vitamin A, 20%DV vitamin C, 20%DV calcium, 15%DV iron.

Note: For more zest, and if your diet allows, you may want to add ¹/₂ tsp. salt to Step 1. You may also want to add ¹/₂ tsp. dried thyme to Step 1.

Chicken Mushroom Stew

Bernice A. Esau
North Newton, KS
Carol Sherwood
Batavia, NY

Makes 6 servings
(Ideal slow-cooker size: 3½- or 4-quart)

6 boneless, skinless chicken breast halves
  (about 1½ lbs.), uncooked
2 Tbsp. cooking oil, divided
8 ozs. sliced fresh mushrooms
1 medium-sized onion, diced
3 cups diced zucchini
1 cup diced green bell peppers
4 garlic cloves, diced
3 medium-sized tomatoes, diced
6-oz. can tomato paste
¾ cup water
2 tsp. salt, optional
1 tsp. dried thyme
1 tsp. dried oregano
1 tsp. dried marjoram
1 tsp. dried basil

1. Cut chicken into 1-inch cubes. Brown in 1 Tbsp. oil in a large skillet. Transfer to slow cooker, reserving drippings.

2. In same skillet, sauté mushrooms, onions, zucchini, green peppers, and garlic in drippings, and remaining 1 Tbsp. oil if needed, until crisp-tender. Place in slow cooker.

3. Add tomatoes, tomato paste, water, and seasonings.

4. Cover. Cook on low 4 hours, or until vegetables are tender.

Per Serving: 260 calories (80 calories from fat), 8g total fat (1.5g saturated, 0g trans), 75mg cholesterol, 880mg sodium, 18g total carbohydrate (5g fiber, 5g sugar), 31g protein, 30%DV vitamin A, 40%DV vitamin C, 6%DV calcium, 20%DV iron.

Note: This is also good served over rice.

Spicy Chicken Rice Soup

Karen Waggoner
Joplin, MO

Makes 6 servings
(Ideal slow-cooker size: 3½- or 4-quart)

4 cups low-fat, low-sodium chicken broth
2 cups chicken, cooked and cubed
2 celery ribs, chopped
2 medium-sized carrots, chopped
1 medium-sized green bell pepper,
  chopped
1 medium-sized onion, chopped
¾ cup long grain rice, uncooked
¼ cup fresh parley or cilantro, minced
½ tsp. salt
½ tsp. black pepper
½ tsp. dried oregano
¼ tsp. ground cumin
¼ tsp. crushed red pepper flakes, optional

1. Combine all ingredients in slow cooker.

2. Cover. Cook on high until boiling point, about 2 hours.

3. Turn down to low for 1½ hours, or just until rice and vegetables are tender.

Per Serving: 160 calories (15 calories from fat), 2g total fat (0g saturated, 0g trans), 35mg cholesterol, 360mg sodium, 14g total carbohydrate (2g fiber, 3g sugar), 19g protein, 100%DV vitamin A, 20%DV vitamin C, 4%DV calcium, 15%DV iron.

Chicken Rice Soup

Michelle Steffen
Harrisonburg, VA

Makes 14 servings
(Ideal slow-cooker size: 6-quart)

3 quarts hot water
1 medium onion, finely chopped
2-3 celery ribs, finely chopped
2 sprigs fresh parsley, finely chopped
1 clove garlic, crushed
2 tsp. salt
1/2 cup carrots, thinly sliced
4 large skinless chicken legs and thighs
1/2 cup fresh parsley, chopped
3 cups hot cooked rice

1. Combine water, onion, celery, 2 sprigs parsley, garlic, salt, carrots, and chicken in slow cooker.
2. Cover. Cook on high 4-5 hours.
3. Remove chicken when tender and debone.
4. Stir cut-up chicken back into soup. Add 1/2 cup fresh chopped parsley
5. To serve, ladle soup into bowls. Add a rounded tablespoonful of hot cooked rice to each bowl.

Per Serving: 80 calories (5 calories from fat), 1g total fat (0g saturated, 0g trans), 15mg cholesterol, 530mg sodium, 11g total carbohydrate (0.5g fiber, 1g sugar), 7g protein, 20%DV vitamin A, 0%DV vitamin C, 2%DV calcium, 4%DV iron.

Note: If you want to eliminate washing another pan, add 1 cup raw long grain rice to the slow-cooker mixture after the chicken has cooked 3-4 hours. Cook on high another hour. When chicken and rice are tender, remove chicken and debone. Continue with Step 5.

Colorful Chicken Stew

Sharon Miller
Holmesville, OH

Makes 10 servings
(Ideal slow-cooker size: 5- or 6-quart)

1 lb. boneless, skinless chicken breasts, uncooked and cubed
14 1/2-oz. can diced Italian tomatoes, undrained
2 medium-sized potatoes, peeled and cubed into 1/2" pieces
4 large carrots, diced
3 celery ribs, diced
1 large onion, chopped
1 medium-sized green bell pepper, chopped
8-oz. can mushroom pieces, drained
2 tsp. chicken bouillon granules
1 pkg. Splenda
1 tsp. chili powder
1/4 tsp. black pepper
1 Tbsp. cornstarch
2 cups cold water

1. Combine first 12 ingredients (through the black pepper) in a large slow cooker.
2. Mix together cornstarch and cold water. Add to slow cooker.
3. Cook on low 8-10 hours, or until vegetables are tender.

Per Serving: 120 calories (15 calories from fat), 1.5g total fat (0g saturated, 0g trans), 25mg cholesterol, 330mg sodium, 16g total carbohydrate (3g fiber, 4g sugar), 11g protein, 100%DV vitamin A, 25%DV vitamin C, 6%DV calcium, 6%DV iron.

San-Antonio Style Tortilla Soup

Rashell Harris
Wichita, KS

Makes 9-10 servings
(Ideal slow-cooker size: 5-quart)

1 Tbsp. olive oil
1 onion, chopped
2 garlic cloves, minced
2 tsp. ground cumin
2 14½-oz. cans fat-free chicken broth
2 15-oz. cans stewed tomatoes
1 Tbsp. jalapeno pepper, minced (remove seeds to reduce heat)
¼ tsp. black pepper
2 cups (about 1½ lbs.) boneless, skinless chicken breast, uncooked and cubed
2 cups water

1. Combine all ingredients in slow cooker.
2. Cover. Cook on low 6-8 hours or on high 4-6 hours.

Per Serving: 320 calories (50 calories from fat), 6g total fat (2g saturated, 0g trans), 30mg cholesterol, 390mg sodium, 44g total carbohydrate (5g fiber, 7g sugar), 22g protein, 10%DV vitamin A, 10%DV vitamin C, 30%DV calcium, 15%DV iron.

Notes:

1. If you like, and your diet permits, you may want to add a 17-oz. can of whole-kernel corn, drained, to Step 1, for an additional Southwest touch to your dish.

2. Use the following garnishes if you wish, and if your diet allows:
2 cups shredded low-fat cheese
fat-free sour cream
cilantro
1 bag baked tortilla chips, crushed

Barley and Chicken Soup

Millie Schellenburg
Washington, NJ

Makes 5 servings
(Ideal slow-cooker size: 5- or 6-quart oval)

½ lb. dry barley
1 small soup chicken
fresh celery, as desired
parsley, as desired
basil, as desired
carrots as desired

1. Combine all ingredients in slow cooker. Cover with water.
2. Cover. Cook on low 4-6 hours.
3. Remove chicken from bones. Discard skin. Return chicken to soup. Continue cooking until barley is soft.

Per Serving: 310 calories (50 calories from fat), 6g total fat (1.5g saturated, 0g trans), 55mg cholesterol, 95mg sodium, 41g total carbohydrate (11g fiber, 4g sugar), 26g protein, 200%DV vitamin A, 10%DV vitamin C, 15%DV calcium, 30%DV iron.

Chicken and Dumplings

Colleen Heatwole
Burton, MI

Makes 8 servings
(Ideal slow-cooker size: 4-quart)

Soup:
4 cups cubed cooked chicken
6 cups fat-free, low-sodium chicken broth
1 Tbsp. fresh parsley, or 1½ tsp. dry
**   parsley flakes**
1 cup onions, chopped
1 cup celery, chopped
6 cups diced potatoes
1 cup green beans
1 cup carrots
1 cup peas, optional

Dumplings: (optional)
2 cups flour (half white and half whole
**   wheat)**
1 tsp. salt
4 tsp. baking powder
1 egg, beaten
2 Tbsp. olive oil
⅔ cup skim milk

1. Combine all soup ingredients, except peas.

2. Cover. Cook on low 4-6 hours.

3. Transfer to large soup kettle with lid. Add peas, if desired. Bring to a boil. Reduce to simmer.

4. To make Dumplings, combine flour, salt, and baking powder in a large bowl.

5. In a separate bowl, combine egg, olive oil, and milk until smooth. Add to flour mixture.

6. Drop by large tablespoonsful on top of simmering broth until the dumplings cover the surface of the soup.

7. Cover. Simmer without lifting the lid for 18 minutes.

Per Serving: 400 calories (60 calories from fat), 7g total fat (1.5g saturated, 0g trans), 80mg cholesterol, 510mg sodium, 51g total carbohydrate (5g fiber, 5g sugar), 32g protein, 50%DV vitamin A, 20%DV vitamin C, 20%DV calcium, 30%DV iron.

Note: I use this recipe a lot. I adapted it from a potpie recipe which needs to be baked in the oven. I like to make this because the soup can cook in the slow cooker while we're at church. When I get home, I transfer it to a soup kettle and make the dumplings while others set the table. The dish is good served with applesauce or fruit salad.

Chicken Clam Chowder

Irene Klaeger
Inverness, FL

Makes 10 servings
(Ideal slow-cooker size: 4-quart)

6 slices lean turkey bacon, diced
¼ lb. lean ham, cubed
2 cups chopped onions
2 cups diced celery
½ tsp. salt
¼ tsp. black pepper
2 cups diced potatoes
2 cups cooked, diced, lean chicken
4 cups fat-free, low-sodium clam juice, or
**   2 cans clams with juice**
1-lb. can whole-kernel corn with liquid
¾ cup flour
4 cups fat-free milk
4 cups shredded fat-free cheddar, or Jack,
**   cheese**
½ cup fat-free evaporated milk
2 Tbsp. fresh parsley

1. Sauté bacon, ham, onions, and celery in nonstick skillet until bacon is crisp and onions and celery are limp. Add salt and pepper.

2. Combine all ingredients in slow cooker except flour, milk, cheese, evaporated milk, and parsley.

3. Cover. Cook on low 6-8 hours or on high 3-4 hours.

4. Whisk flour into milk. Stir into soup, along with cheese, evaporated milk, and parsley. Cook one more hour on high.

Per Serving: 250 calories (35 calories from fat), 3.5g total fat (1g saturated, 0g trans), 45mg cholesterol, 880mg sodium, 23g total carbohydrate (3g fiber, 9g sugar), 31g protein, 10%DV vitamin A, 10%DV vitamin C, 50%DV calcium, 10%DV iron.

Cheesy Menudo

Eileen Eash
Carlsbad, NM

Makes 8 servings
(Ideal slow-cooker size: 3½-quart)

3 16-oz. cans white or yellow hominy, undrained
4-oz. can chopped green chilies
½ lb. Velveeta Light cheese, diced
1 tsp. garlic salt
½ tsp. black pepper
fresh cilantro or parsley, chopped
2 cups cooked chicken or lean beef, chopped

1. Combine all ingredients in slow cooker. Stir well.

2. Cover. Cook on low 4 hours.

Per Serving: 240 calories (50 calories from fat), 6g total fat (2.5g saturated, 1g trans), 40mg cholesterol, 1000mg sodium, 28g total carbohydrate (5g fiber, 3g sugar), 18g protein, 6%DV vitamin A, 2%DV vitamin C, 20%DV calcium, 8%DV iron.

Wild Rice Soup

Joyce Shackelford
Green Bay, WI

Makes 8 servings
(Ideal slow-cooker size: 4-quart)

2 Tbsp. butter
½ cup dry wild rice
6 cups fat-free, low-sodium chicken stock
½ cup onions, minced
½ cup celery, minced
½ lb. winter squash, peeled, seeded, cut in ½" cubes
2 cups chicken, chopped and cooked
½ cup browned, slivered almonds

1. Melt butter in small skillet. Add rice and sauté for 10 minutes over low heat. Transfer to slow cooker.

2. Add all remaining ingredients except chicken and almonds.

3. Cover. Cook on low 4-6 hours. One hour before serving stir in chicken.

4. Top with browned slivered almonds just before serving.

Per Serving: 310 calories (70 calories from fat), 8g total fat (4g saturated, 0g trans), 70mg cholesterol, 320mg sodium, 25g total carbohydrate (3g fiber, 3g sugar), 33g protein, 2%DV vitamin A, 2%DV vitamin C, 8%DV calcium, 25%DV iron.

Wild Rice and Lentil Soup

Maryann Markano
Wilmington, DE

Makes 8-10 servings
(Ideal slow-cooker size: 3¹/2- or 4-quart)

¹/2 cup dried lentils, sorted, rinsed and
  drained
3 cups water
6-oz. pkg. long grain and wild rice blend,
  with spice packet
14-oz. can vegetable broth
10-oz. pkg. frozen mixed vegetables
1 cup skim milk
¹/2 cup reduced-fat mild cheddar cheese,
  shredded

1. Cover lentils with water and soak
overnight or for 6-8 hours. Drain and discard
soaking water.
2. Put all ingredients into slow cooker,
including the 3 cups fresh water. Mix well.
3. Cook on low 5-8 hours, or until the
vegetables are done to your liking.

Per Serving: 240 calories (25 calories from fat), 2.5g total
fat (1.5g saturated, 0g trans), 5mg cholesterol, 280mg
sodium, 42g total carbohydrate (7g fiber, 5g sugar), 13g
protein, 30%DV vitamin A, 10%DV vitamin C, 15%DV
calcium, 15%DV iron.

*Note: It may be necessary to add more water if
the soup seems too thick.*

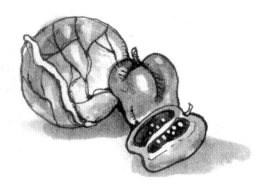

Hearty Split Pea Soup

Beatrice Orgish
Richardson, TX

Makes 9 servings
(Ideal slow-cooker size: 4-quart)

1-lb. pkg. dried split peas
2 cups fully cooked lean ham, diced
1 cup diced carrots
1 medium-sized onion, chopped
2 cloves garlic, minced
2 bay leaves
¹/2 tsp. salt
¹/2 tsp. black pepper
5 cups boiling water
1 cup hot skim milk

1. Layer the first 9 ingredients in slow
cooker in order listed.
2. Cover. Cook on high 4-5 hours.
3. Stir in milk.
4. Discard bay leaves before serving.

Per Serving: 230 calories (30 calories from fat), 3.5g total
fat (1g saturated, 0g trans), 30mg cholesterol, 470mg
sodium, 30g total carbohydrate (11g fiber, 7g sugar), 20g
protein, 50%DV vitamin A, 0%DV vitamin C, 6%DV
calcium, 10%DV iron.

*Note: If you prefer a thinner soup, you may want
to increase the milk to 1¹/2-2 cups.*

Ham and Split Pea Soup

Mary C. Casey
Scranton, PA

Makes 6-8 servings
(Ideal slow-cooker size: 5-quart)

2 cups cooked ham, diced
1 bay leaf
16-oz. pkg. dried split peas
2 ribs celery, sliced
1 small onion, chopped
1/4-1/2 tsp. black pepper, according to your
    taste preference
1/2 tsp. salt
1/4-1/2 tsp. dried marjoram, according to
    your taste preference
1/2 cup carrots, shredded
2 10¾-oz. cans reduced-sodium, low-fat
    chicken broth
5 cups water
1 cup potatoes, cooked and diced, optional

1. Combine all ingredients in slow cooker.
2. Cover. Cook on high 6-8 hours, or until peas are tender.
3. To thicken, remove 4 cups of soup after potatoes have been added and puree in blender.
4. Return to soup. Stir.

Per Serving: 330 calories (30 calories from fat), 3.5g total fat (1g saturated, 0g trans), 25mg cholesterol, 850mg sodium, 48g total carbohydrate (17g fiber, 8g sugar), 29g protein, 50%DV vitamin A, 10%DV vitamin C, 6%DV calcium, 25%DV iron.

Split Pea Soup

Wendy McPhillips
Wichita, KS

Makes 6 servings
(Ideal slow-cooker size: 6-quart)

1½ cups ham, diced
1-lb. pkg. dried split peas
4 medium-sized potatoes
6 carrots, peeled and sliced
2 cups shredded cabbage
water to cover
1 tsp. salt
1/2 tsp. pepper

1. Combine all ingredients in slow cooker.
2. Cover. Cook on low 6-8 hours.

Per Serving: 380 calories (35 calories from fat), 4g total fat (1.5g saturated, 0g trans), 30mg cholesterol, 780mg sodium, 62g total carbohydrate (17g fiber, 10g sugar), 25g protein, 300%DV vitamin A, 30%DV vitamin C, 6%DV calcium, 20%DV iron.

Note: If you like some zing to your soup, you may want to add any or all of the following as garnishes:

2 chipotle peppers in adobe sauce,
    cut up
1/4 tsp. crushed red pepper
shredded, spicy low-fat pepper-Jack
    cheese

Green Bean Soup

Carla Koslowsky
Hillsboro, KS

Makes 4 servings
(Ideal slow-cooker size: 4-quart)

1 ham hock, cooked, cooled, deboned, and
  fat removed—with cooking broth
  reserved and skimmed of fat
2 potatoes, peeled and cubed
½ cup onions, chopped
1 sprig of dill weed
16-oz. can green beans, drained
ham broth and water to equal 6 cups
½ tsp. salt
¼ tsp. black pepper
½ cup milk

1. Combine all ingredients except milk in
slow cooker.
2. Cover. Cook on low 4-5 hours.
3. Add milk just before serving.

Per Serving: 160 calories (30 calories from fat), 3g total fat
(1g saturated, 0g trans), 15mg cholesterol, 660mg sodium,
26g total carbohydrate (5g fiber, 5g sugar), 8g protein,
0%DV vitamin A, 30%DV vitamin C, 8%DV calcium,
10%DV iron.

*Note: You may precook the ham hock in the slow
cooker by covering it with water and then cooking
it on low for 5 hours, or until meat is tender and
falling off the bone.*

Creamy Pork Stew

Betty Moore
Plano, IL

Makes 8 servings
(Ideal slow-cooker size: 5-quart)

2 lbs. ground pork
2 10¾-oz. cans 98% fat-free cream of
  mushroom soup
2 14½-oz. cans green beans with liquid
4 potatoes, diced
4 carrots, chopped
2 small onions, diced
2 10¾-oz. cans condensed vegetarian
  vegetable soup
2 soup cans of water
3 ribs celery, chopped
½ tsp. salt
¼ tsp. black pepper
¼ tsp. garlic powder
½ tsp. dried marjoram

1. Brown ground pork in a non-stick skillet.
2. Combine all ingredients in slow cooker.
3. Cook on low 8-10 hours.

Per Serving: 490 calories (170 calories from fat), 19g total
fat (7g saturated, 1g trans), 80mg cholesterol, 1910mg
sodium, 48g total carbohydrate (9g fiber, 12g sugar), 28g
protein, 200%DV vitamin A, 20%DV vitamin C, 10%DV
calcium, 25%DV iron.

Notes:
  *1. Add a can of diced tomatoes to Step 2 if you
wish.*
  2. This recipe goes well with homemade bread.

Oriental Pork Soup

Kristi See
Weskan, KS

Makes 6 servings
(Ideal slow-cooker size: 3- or 4-quart)

1 lb. lean uncooked pork or chicken, cut in 1/2" cubes
2 medium-sized carrots, cut in julienne strips
4 medium-sized green onions, chopped
1 clove garlic, finely chopped
3-4 Tbsp. low-sodium soy sauce, according to your taste preference
1/2 tsp. finely chopped gingerroot
1/8 tsp. black pepper
10 3/4-oz. can fat-free, reduced-sodium beef broth
1 cup fresh mushrooms, sliced
1 cup bean sprouts

1. Cook meat in large nonstick skillet over medium heat for 8-10 minutes. Stir occasionally.
2. Mix meat and remaining ingredients except mushrooms and bean sprouts in slow cooker.
3. Cover. Cook on low 7-9 hours or on high 3-4 hours.
4. Stir in mushrooms and bean sprouts.
5. Cover. Cook on low 1 hour.

Per Serving: 230 calories (70 calories from fat), 8g total fat (2.5g saturated, 0g trans), 70mg cholesterol, 430mg sodium, 12g total carbohydrate (3g fiber, 7g sugar), 28g protein, 80%DV vitamin A, 10%DV vitamin C, 4%DV calcium, 10%DV iron.

Ham 'n Cheese Soup

Janie Steele
Moore, OK

Makes 7 servings
(Ideal slow-cooker size: 3 1/2- or 4-quart)

2 cups potatoes, cubed (you decide whether to peel or not)
1 1/2 cups water
1 1/2 cups cooked ham, cubed
1 large onion, chopped
3 Tbsp. butter or margarine
3 Tbsp. flour
1/4 tsp. black pepper
3 cups fat-free milk
6 ozs. low-fat shredded cheese
1 cup frozen broccoli, thawed and chopped

1. Combine all ingredients except cheese and broccoli in slow cooker.
2. Cook on low 6-8 hours.
3. Add cheese and broccoli. Stir well. Cook an additional 15 minutes, or until cheese is melted and broccoli is warm.

Per Serving: 250 calories (80 calories from fat) (5g saturated, 0g trans), 35mg cholesterol, 650mg sodium, 22g total carbohydrate (3g fiber, 7g sugar), 19g protein, 10%DV vitamin A, 20%DV vitamin C, 25%DV calcium, 8%DV iron.

Note: You may wilt the onion in the microwave, or sauté it in a nonstick skillet, so that it is soft and its flavor well blended when the soup is served. You may also cook the broccoli lightly in the microwave if you want to make sure it is softened when served.

Irish Stew

Rebecca Leichty
Harrisonburg, VA

Makes 8 servings
(Ideal slow-cooker size: 4- or 5-quart)

2 lbs. boneless lamb, cubed
1½ tsp. salt
¼ tsp. black pepper
2 medium-sized carrots, sliced
1 large onion, diced
3 medium-sized potatoes, diced
1 bay leaf
2 cups water
¼ cup dry small pearl tapioca
1 can small, tender peas

1. Grease slow cooker with fat-free cooking spray.
2. Place cubed lamb in the bottom of slow cooker. Season with salt and pepper.
3. Add carrots, onion, potatoes, and bay leaf, in layers.
4. Stir in water and tapioca.
5. Cover and cook on high for 90 minutes. Turn down to low and cook for 8 hours.
6. Add peas for last hour of cooking.
7. Remove bay leaf before serving.

Per Serving: 280 calories (70 calories from fat) 8g total fat (3g saturated, 1g trans), 65mg cholesterol, 580mg sodium, 27g total carbohydrate (6g fiber, 5g sugar), 25g protein, 80%DV vitamin A, 20%DV vitamin C, 4%DV calcium, 20%DV iron.

Note: *For increased flavor, you may want to divide ½ tsp. Mrs. Dash seasoning among the layers of vegetables in Step 3.*

Shrimp Chowder

Kristi See, Weskan, KS
Karen Waggoner, Joplin, MO

Makes 8 servings
(Ideal slow-cooker size: 5- or 6-quart)

1 lb. red potatoescubed
2½ cups fat-free, reduced-sodium chicken broth
3 celery ribs, chopped
8 green onions, chopped
1½ lbs. medium-sized shrimp, uncooked, peeled, and deveined
½ cup sweet red bell peppers, chopped
1½ cups fat-free milk
¼ cup all-purpose flour
½ cup fat-free evaporated milk
2 Tbsp. fresh parsley, minced
½ tsp. paprika
½ tsp. Worcestershire sauce
⅛ tsp. cayenne pepper
⅛ tsp. black pepper

1. Combine potatoes, broth, celery, onions, shrimp, and red bell peppers in slow cooker.
2. Cover. Cook on low 2 hours, or until vegetables are done to your liking.
3. Stir in 1½ cups milk and gently mash vegetables with potato masher. Leave some small chunks of potato.
4. Combine flour and evaporated milk. Mix until smooth. Gradually stir into soup mixture.
5. Cook and stir uncovered on high until thickened.

Per Serving: 230 calories (15 calories from fat) (0g saturated, 0g trans), 130mg cholesterol, 240mg sodium, 28g total carbohydrate (4g fiber, 12g sugar), 25g protein, 15%DV vitamin A, 30%DV vitamin C, 20%DV calcium, 20%DV iron.

Note: *This chowder is even better the next day after the flavors have melded overnight.*

Corn and Shrimp Chowder

Naomi E. Fast
Hesston, KS

Makes 6 servings
(Ideal slow-cooker size: 3¹/2-quart)

3 slices lean turkey bacon, diced
1 cup chopped onions
2 cups diced, unpeeled red potatoes
2 10-oz. pkgs. frozen corn
1 tsp. Worcestershire sauce
¹/2 tsp. paprika
¹/2 tsp. salt
¹/8 tsp. black pepper
2 6-oz. cans shrimp, drained
2 cups water
2 Tbsp. butter
12-oz. can fat-free evaporated milk
chopped chives

1. Brown bacon in nonstick skillet until lightly crisp. Add onions to drippings and sauté until transparent. Using slotted spoon, transfer bacon and onions to slow cooker.
2. Add remaining ingredients to cooker except milk and chives.
3. Cover. Cook on low 3-4 hours, adding milk and chives 30 minutes before end of cooking time.

Per Serving: 310 calories (70 calories from fat) (3g saturated, 0g trans), 115mg cholesterol, 480mg sodium, 41g total carbohydrate (4g fiber, 11g sugar), 23g protein, 10%DV vitamin A, 20%DV vitamin C, 25%DV calcium, 15%DV iron.

Note: I learned to make this recipe in a 7th-grade home economics class. It made an impression on my father who liked seafood very much. The recipe calls only for canned shrimp, but I often increase its taste appeal with extra cooked shrimp.

Hot & Sour Soup

Judy Govotsos
Frederick, MD

Makes 4 servings
(Ideal slow-cooker size: 3¹/2-quart)

4 cups fat-free, low-sodium chicken broth
8-oz. can sliced bamboo shoots, drained
1 carrot, julienned
8-oz. can water chestnuts, drained and sliced
3 Tbsp. quick-cooking tapioca
6-oz. can sliced mushrooms, drained
1 Tbsp. vinegar, or rice wine vinegar
1 Tbsp. light soy sauce
1 tsp. sugar
¹/4 tsp. black pepper
¹/4-¹/2 tsp. red pepper flakes, according to your taste preference
8-oz. pkg. frozen, peeled, and deveined shrimp, optional
4 ozs. firm tofu, drained and cubed
1 egg, beaten

1. Combine all ingredients, except shrimp, tofu, and egg in slow cooker.
2. Cover. Cook on low 9-11 hours or on high 3-4 hours.
3. Add shrimp and tofu.
4. Cover. Cook 45-60 minutes.
5. Pour egg into the soup in a thin stream. Stir the soup gently until the egg forms fine shreds instead of clumps.

Per Serving: 240 calories (45 calories from fat) (1g saturated, 0g trans), 135mg cholesterol, 600mg sodium, 24g total carbohydrate (4g fiber, 4g sugar), 26g protein, 80%DV vitamin A, 0%DV vitamin C, 25%DV calcium, 30%DV iron.

Note: You may want to stir in ¹/2 tsp. garlic salt, if your diet permits, in Step 1.

Creamy Salmon Chowder

Diane Shetler
Hyde Park, MA

Makes 5 servings
(Ideal slow-cooker size: 3¹/2-quart)

2 cups fat-free chicken broth
2 cups water
10-oz. pkg. frozen corn
1 cup celery, chopped
¹/2 cup onions, chopped
³/4 cup wheat berries
8-oz. pkg. fat-free cream cheese, cut into
 cubes
16-oz. can salmon, drained, skin and
 bones removed, and coarsely flaked
1 Tbsp. dill weed

1. Combine chicken broth, water, corn, celery, onions, and wheat berries in slow cooker.
2. Cover. Cook on low 8-10 hours or on high 3¹/2-4 hours.
3. Turn cooker to high. Add cheese, stirring until melted.
4. Stir in salmon and dill.
5. Cover. Cook 10 minutes longer.

Per Serving: 350 calories (60 calories from fat), 7g total fat (2g saturated, 0g trans), 40mg cholesterol, 790mg sodium, 42g total carbohydrate (6g fiber, 3g sugar), 34g protein, 10%DV vitamin A, 10%DV vitamin C, 35%DV calcium, 15%DV iron.

Vegetable Salmon Chowder

Esther J. Yoder
Hartville, OH

Makes 8 servings
(Ideal slow-cooker size: 3¹/2-quart)

1¹/2 cups potatoes, cubed
1 cup celery, diced
¹/2 cup onions, diced
2 Tbsp. fresh parsley,
 or 1 Tbsp. dried parsley
¹/2 tsp. salt
¹/4 tsp. black pepper
water to cover
16-oz. can pink salmon
4 cups skim milk
2 tsp. lemon juice
2 Tbsp. red bell peppers, finely cut
2 Tbsp. carrots, finely shredded
¹/2 cup instant potatoes

1. Combine cubed potatoes, celery, onions, parsley, salt, pepper, and water to cover in slow cooker.
2. Cook on high for 3 hours, or until soft. Add a bit more water if needed.
3. Add salmon, milk, lemon juice, red peppers, carrots, and instant potatoes.
4. Heat 1 hour more until very hot.

Per Serving: 140 calories (20 calories from fat), 2g total fat (0g saturated, 0g trans), 30mg cholesterol, 115mg sodium, 15g total carbohydrate (1g fiber, 7g sugar), 16g protein, 10%DV vitamin A, 10%DV vitamin C, 15%DV calcium, 4%DV iron.

Notes:
 1. If you enjoy garlic, add a tablespoon or two of it, minced, to Step 1.
 2. If you like a thicker chowder, and your diet allows, increase the instant potatoes in Step 3 to ³/4-1 cup.

Tasty Clam Chowder

Jean H. Robinson
Cinnaminson, NJ

Makes 8 servings
(Ideal slow-cooker size: 5-quart)

2 1-lb. cans low-fat, low-sodium chicken
  broth
3 large potatoes, peeled and diced finely
2 large onions, chopped finely
1-lb. can creamed corn
1 carrot, chopped finely
1 dozen littleneck clams, or 3 6-oz. cans
  minced clams
2 cups low-fat milk
1/4 tsp. black pepper
1/4 tsp. salt
2 Tbsp. fresh parsley, chopped
6 slices bacon, well cooked, drained and
  crumbled, optional

1. Pour broth into slow cooker.
2. Add potatoes, onions, creamed corn, and
carrot.
3. Cover. Cook on high 1 hour. Stir. Cook on
high another hour.
4. Using a potato masher, mash potatoes
coarsely to thicken soup.
4. Add clams, milk, salt, black pepper, salt,
and parsley.
5. Cover. Cook on high 20 minutes.
6. Garnish with crumbled bacon, if desired.

Per Serving: 210 calories (30 calories from fat), 3.5g total
fat (1.5g saturated, 0g trans), 15mg cholesterol, 660mg
sodium, 33g total carbohydrate (3g fiber, 8g sugar), 14g
protein, 40%DV vitamin A, 20%DV vitamin C, 10%DV
calcium, 15%DV iron.

*Note: If your diet permits, you may want to
increase the salt to 1/2 tsp.*

Manhattan Clam Chowder

Joyce Slaymaker
Strasburg, PA
Louise Stackhouse
Benton, PA

Makes 8 servings
(Ideal slow-cooker size: 3 1/2-quart)

1/4 lb. lean turkey bacon, diced and
  browned
1 large onion, chopped
2 carrots, thinly sliced
3 ribs celery, sliced
1 Tbsp. dried parsley flakes
1-lb. 12-oz. can low-sodium tomatoes
1/2 tsp. salt
3 8-oz. cans clams with liquid
2 whole peppercorns
1 bay leaf
1 1/2 tsp. dried crushed thyme
3 medium-sized potatoes, cubed

1. Combine all ingredients in slow cooker.
2. Cover. Cook on low 8-10 hours, or until
vegetables are done to your liking.

Per Serving: 260 calories (45 calories from fat), 5g total fat
(1g saturated, 0g trans), 70mg cholesterol, 710mg sodium,
27g total carbohydrate (4g fiber, 5g sugar), 27g protein,
80%DV vitamin A, 40%DV vitamin C, 20%DV calcium,
100%DV iron.

Lidia's Egg Drop Soup

Shirley Unternahrer Hinh
Wayland, IA

Makes 8 servings
(Ideal slow-cooker size: 3¹/2-quart)

2 14¹/2-oz. cans fat-free, low-sodium
   chicken broth
1 qt. water
2 Tbsp. fish sauce
¹/4 tsp. salt
4 Tbsp. cornstarch
1 cup cold water
2 eggs, beaten
1 chopped green onion
¹/4 tsp. black pepper

1. Combine broth and water in large saucepan.
2. Add fish sauce and salt. Bring to boil.
3. Mix cornstarch into cold water until smooth. Add to soup. Bring to boil while stirring. Remove from heat.
4. Pour beaten eggs into thickened broth, but do not stir. Instead, pull fork through soup with 2 strokes.
5. Transfer to slow cooker. Add green onions and pepper.
6. Cover. Cook on low 1 hour. Keep warm in cooker.
7. Eat plain or with rice.

Per Serving: 50 calories (10 calories from fat), 1g total fat (0g saturated, 0g trans), 45mg cholesterol, 510mg sodium, 5g total carbohydrate (0g fiber, 1g sugar), 4g protein, 0%DV vitamin A, 0%DV vitamin C, 0%DV calcium, 6%DV iron.

Note: One day when the kids were sledding I surprised them with something other than hot cocoa when they came in. "Mmmmm," was all I heard, and, "This tastes great!" "You're the best, Mom!" They finished all the egg drop soup and wondered if I'd make more.

Greek Lentil Soup

Andrea Cunningham
Arlington, KS

Makes 8 servings
(Ideal slow-cooker size: 3¹/2-quart)

1¹/2 cups dried lentils
1¹/2 qts. water
1 medium-sized onion, chopped
1 carrot, peeled and grated
1 rib celery, chopped
3 Tbsp. olive oil
1 bay leaf
2 cloves garlic, minced
1 tsp. salt
¹/2 tsp. dried oregano
1 cube low-sodium beef bouillon
¹/2 cup tomato sauce
3 Tbsp. red wine vinegar

1. Place lentils and water in slow cooker.
2. In a large frying pan, sauté onion, carrot, and celery in oil until limp and glazed. Add to slow cooker.
3. Add bay leaf, garlic, salt, oregano, and bouillon cube to cooker.
4. Cover. Cook on low 6-8 hours.
5. Add tomato sauce and vinegar. Stir well.
6. Cover. Cook on high 30 minutes to blend flavors. Remove bay leaf before serving.

Per Serving: 180 calories (50 calories from fat), 6g total fat (1g saturated, 0g trans), 0mg cholesterol, 470mg sodium, 25g total carbohydrate (9g fiber, 4g sugar), 10g protein, 20%DV vitamin A, 0%DV vitamin C, 4%DV calcium, 20%DV iron.

Note: If you prefer a little more zing, you may want to increase the dried oregano to 1 tsp. and add ¹/2-1 tsp. ground cumin in Step 3.

Crockpot Lentil Soup with Ham

Rhonda L. Burgoon
Collingswood, NJ

Makes 8 servings
(Ideal slow-cooker size: 4-quart)

1 cup onions, chopped
3 cloves garlic, minced
5 cups fat-free, low-sodium chicken broth
1 cup dried lentils
1/2 cup carrots, chopped
2 bay leaves
3 cups Swiss chard, chopped
1 1/2 cups potatoes, chopped
1 cup ham, chopped
14 1/2-oz. can low-sodium diced tomatoes
1 tsp. dried basil
1/2 tsp. dried thyme
1/2 tsp. black pepper
3 Tbsp. fresh parsley, chopped

1. Combine all ingredients except fresh parsley in slow cooker.
2. Cover. Cook on low 7-9 hours.
3. Stir in fresh parsley and serve.

Per Serving: 200 calories (30 calories from fat), 3.5g total fat (1g saturated, 0g trans), 15mg cholesterol, 290mg sodium, 25g total carbohydrate (10g fiber, 5g sugar), 17g protein, 50%DV vitamin A, 20%DV vitamin C, 8%DV calcium, 25%DV iron.

Lentil-Tomato Stew

Marci Baum
Annville, PA

Makes 8 servings
(Ideal slow-cooker size: 6-quart)

3 cups water
28-oz. can low-sodium peeled Italian tomatoes, undrained
6-oz. can low-sodium tomato paste
1/2 cup dry red wine
3/4 tsp. dried basil
3/4 tsp. dried thyme
1/2 tsp. crushed red pepper
1 lb. dried lentils, rinsed and drained with any stones removed
1 large onion, chopped
4 medium-sized carrots, cut in 1/2" rounds
4 medium-sized celery ribs, cut into 1/2" slices
3 garlic cloves, minced
1 tsp. salt
fresh basil or parsley, chopped, for garnish

1. Combine water, tomatoes with juice, tomato paste, red wine, basil, thyme, and crushed red pepper in slow cooker.
2. Break-up tomatoes with a wooden spoon and stir to blend them and the paste into the mixture.
3. Add lentils, onion, carrots, celery, and garlic.
4. Cover. Cook on low 10-12 hours or on high 4-5 hours.
5. Stir in the salt.
6. Serve in bowls, sprinkled with chopped basil or parsley.

Per Serving: 250 calories (10 calories from fat), 1g total fat (0g saturated, 0g trans), 0mg cholesterol, 530mg sodium, 44g total carbohydrate (16g fiber, 7g sugar), 17g protein, 20%DV vitamin A, 20%DV vitamin C, 8%DV calcium, 40%DV iron.

Sweet Potato Lentil Stew

Mrs. Carolyn Baer
Conrath, WI

Makes 6 servings
(Ideal slow-cooker size: 4-quart)

4 cups fat-free vegetable broth
3 cups (about 1¼ lbs.) sweet potatoes,
  peeled and cubed
1½ cups lentils, rinsed
3 medium-sized carrots, cut into 1" pieces
1 medium-sized onion, chopped
4 garlic cloves, minced
½ tsp. ground cumin
¼ tsp. ground ginger
¼ tsp. cayenne pepper
¼ cup minced fresh cilantro or parsley
¼ tsp. salt

1. Combine first nine ingredients in slow cooker.
2. Cook on low 5-6 hours or just until vegetables are tender.
3. Stir in cilantro and salt just before serving.

Per Serving: 280 calories (5 calories from fat), 1g total fat (0g saturated, 0g trans), 0mg cholesterol, 580mg sodium, 54g total carbohydrate (19g fiber, 12g sugar), 16g protein, 300%DV vitamin A, 25%DV vitamin C, 8%DV calcium, 30%DV iron.

Note: *For added flavor, you may want to increase the cumin to 3/4-1 tsp. and the ginger to 1/2 tsp. And if your diet allows, you may also stir in 1/3 cup raisins, 1/4 cup chopped nuts, and 1/4 cup grated coconut just before serving.*

"Mom's Favorite" Vegetable Soup

Wendy McPhillips
Wichita, KS

Makes 5 servings
(Ideal slow-cooker size: 4-quart)

½ cup dry pearl barley
14½-oz. can low-sodium diced tomatoes
1 cup frozen corn
1 cup frozen peas
4 carrots, peeled and sliced
1 cup frozen green beans
water to cover
5 cubes low-sodium beef bouillon
5 cubes low-sodium chicken bouillon
½ tsp. salt
½ tsp. black pepper
½ tsp. dried basil
1 tsp. fresh thyme
½ tsp. fresh dill
1 tsp. fresh parsley

1. Combine all ingredients in slow cooker, except fresh herbs.
2. Cover. Cook on low 6-8 hours.
3. Just before serving, stir in fresh thyme, dill, and parsley.

Per Serving: 190 calories (10 calories from fat), 1.5g total fat (0g saturated, 0g trans), 0mg cholesterol, 2340mg sodium, 40g total carbohydrate (9g fiber, 10g sugar), 7g protein, 200%DV vitamin A, 20%DV vitamin C, 10%DV calcium, 10%DV iron.

Vegetable Minestrone

Marcia S. Myer
Manheim, PA

Makes 12 servings
(Ideal slow-cooker size: 5-quart)

4 cups low-fat, low-sodium chicken broth
4 cups low-sodium tomato juice
1 Tbsp. dried basil
1 tsp. salt
1/2 tsp. dried oregano
1/4 tsp. black pepper
2 medium-sized carrots, sliced
2 ribs celery, chopped
1 medium-sized onion, chopped
1 cup fresh mushrooms, sliced
2 cloves garlic, crushed
28-oz. can low-sodium diced tomatoes
1 1/2 cups uncooked rotini pasta

1. Combine all ingredients except pasta in slow cooker.
2. Cover. Cook on low 7-8 hours.
3. Add pasta.
4. Cover. Cook on high 15-20 minutes.

Per Serving: 70 calories (0 calories from fat), 0g total fat (0g saturated, 0g trans), 0mg cholesterol, 520mg sodium, 13g total carbohydrate (3g fiber, 6g sugar), 5g protein, 50%DV vitamin A, 20%DV vitamin C, 8%DV calcium, 10%DV iron.

Notes:

1. Sprinkle each serving with fat-free Parmesan cheese if you like.

2. If your diet allows, you may want to increase the salt to 2 tsp.

Adirondack Soup

Joanne Kennedy
Plattsburgh, NY

Makes 12 servings
(Ideal slow-cooker size: 6-quart)

2 qts. low-sodium stewed tomatoes
3 1-lb. cans low-sodium vegetable broth
3 cups water
5 large carrots, chopped
1 large onion, chopped
4 celery ribs, chopped
2 tsp. dried basil
1 tsp. dried parsley
1 tsp. black pepper
2 dashes Tabasco sauce
3 cups frozen mixed vegetables, thawed

1. Combine all ingredients except frozen vegetables in slow cooker.
2. Cover. Cook 6 hours on low.
3. Add vegetables.
4. Cover. Cook 1 hour more on low.

Per Serving: 110 calories (0 calories from fat), 0g total fat (0g saturated, 0g trans), 0mg cholesterol, 450mg sodium, 24g total carbohydrate (7g fiber, 13g sugar), 4g protein, 150%DV vitamin A, 20%DV vitamin C, 10%DV calcium, 15%DV iron.

Tomato Green Bean Soup

Colleen Heatwole
Burton, MI

Makes 8 servings
(Ideal slow-cooker size: 4-quart)

1 cup onions, chopped
1 cup carrots, chopped
6 cups low-fat, reduced-sodium chicken broth
1 lb. fresh green beans, cut in 1" pieces
1 clove garlic, minced
3 cups fresh tomatoes, diced
1 tsp. dried basil
1/2 tsp. salt
1/4 tsp. black pepper

1. Combine all ingredients in slow cooker.
2. Cover. Cook on low 6-8 hours.

Per Serving: 70 calories (0 calories from fat), 0g total fat (0g saturated, 0g trans), 0mg cholesterol, 290mg sodium, 10g total carbohydrate (4g fiber, 6g sugar), 6g protein, 80%DV vitamin A, 10%DV vitamin C, 6%DV calcium, 10%DV iron.

Note: This recipe is best with fresh green beans and tomatoes, but if they are not in season you may use canned tomatoes and canned or frozen green beans—or corn. Remember, of course, that canned vegetables are likely to include salt.

Quick-to-Mix Vegetable Soup

Cyndie Marrara
Port Matilda, PA

Makes 4 servings
(Ideal slow-cooker size: 2-quart)

2 cups frozen vegetables
3/4 cup fat-free, low-sodium beef gravy
16-oz. can diced tomatoes
1/4 cup dry red wine
1/2 cup diced onions
1 tsp. garlic, crushed
1/4 tsp. black pepper
1/2 cup water

1. Combine all ingredients in slow cooker.
2. Cover. Cook on high 5 hours or on low 7 hours.

Per Serving: 130 calories (5 calories from fat), 0.5g total fat (0g saturated, 0g trans), 5mg cholesterol, 600mg sodium, 26g total carbohydrate (6g fiber, 4g sugar), 5g protein, 80%DV vitamin A, 10%DV vitamin C, 10%DV calcium, 8%DV iron.

Note: If your diet permits, you may want to add 1/4-1/2 tsp. salt to Step 1.

Dawn's Quick & Healthy Vegetable Soup

Dawn Day
Westminster, CA

Makes 8 servings
(Ideal slow-cooker size: 4-quart)

4 cups vegetable or chicken broth
1 cup frozen corn
1/2 cup carrots, chopped
1/2 cup green beans
1 cup zucchini, cubed
12-oz. can chopped tomatoes
1/2 cup onions, chopped
2 cloves garlic, minced
1/2 tsp. dried thyme
1/2 tsp. dried basil
1/4 tsp. lemon pepper
1 cup broccoli, chopped
1/2 cup frozen peas

1. Combine all ingredients except broccoli and peas in slow cooker.
2. Cover. Cook on low 7 hours or on high 3 1/2 hours.
3. Stir in broccoli. Cook an additional 45 minutes on high.
4. Stir in peas. Cook an additional 15 minutes on high.

Per Serving: 70 calories (0 calories from fat), 0g total fat (0g saturated, 0g trans), 0mg cholesterol, 470mg sodium, 14g total carbohydrate (3g fiber, 6g sugar), 3g protein, 80%DV vitamin A, 20%DV vitamin C, 6%DV calcium, 6%DV iron.

Fresh Tomato Soup

Rebecca Leichty
Harrisonburg, VA

Makes 6 servings
(Ideal slow-cooker size: 3 1/2- or 4-quart)

5 cups ripe tomatoes, diced (your choice about whether or not to peel them)
1 Tbsp. tomato paste
4 cups salt-free chicken broth
1 carrot, grated
1 onion, minced
1 Tbsp. garlic, minced
1 tsp. dried basil
pepper to taste
2 Tbsp. lemon juice
1 bay leaf

1. Combine all ingredients in a slow cooker.
2. Cook on low for 6-8 hours. Stir once while cooking.
3. Remove bay leaf before serving.

Per Serving: 80 calories (5 calories from fat), 0.5g total fat (0g saturated, 0g trans), 0mg cholesterol, 135mg sodium, 14g total carbohydrate (3g fiber, 7g sugar), 6g protein, 40%DV vitamin A, 40%DV vitamin C, 4%DV calcium, 15%DV iron.

Note: To thicken the soup slightly, and if your diet allows, you may want to add a full 6-oz. can of tomato paste instead of just 1 Tbsp.

Mexican Tomato-Corn Soup

Jeanne Heyerly
Chenoa, IL

Makes 8 servings
(Ideal slow-cooker size: 4-quart)

1 medium-sized onion, diced
1 medium-sized green bell pepper, diced
1 clove garlic, minced
1 cup carrots, diced
14 1/2-oz. can low-sodium diced Italian
   tomatoes
2 1/2 cups low-sodium tomato juice
1 qt. low-fat, low-sodium chicken broth
3 cups corn, frozen or canned
4-oz. can chopped chilies, undrained
1 tsp. chili powder
1 1/2 tsp. ground cumin
dash cayenne powder

1. Combine all ingredients in slow cooker.
2. Cover. Cook on low 6-8 hours.

Per Serving: 100 calories (10 calories from fat), 1g total fat
(0g saturated, 0g trans), 0mg cholesterol, 115mg sodium,
20g total carbohydrate (4g fiber, 9g sugar), 6g protein,
50%DV vitamin A, 30%DV vitamin C, 4%DV calcium,
10%DV iron.

*Note: Garnish individual servings with cilantro
leaves, corn or tortilla chips, and/or low-fat
shredded sharp cheddar cheese, if your diet
permits.*

Fresh Corn Chowder

Janie Steele
Moore, OK

Makes 7 servings
(Ideal slow-cooker size: 3 1/2- or 4-quart)

4 large ears of corn, cut off cob, or 1-lb.
   bag frozen whole-kernel corn
1 large onion, chopped
1 celery rib, chopped
1 Tbsp. butter or margarine
1 1/2 cups potatoes, cubed
1 cup water
2 tsp. chicken bouillon granules
1/4 tsp. dried thyme
1/4 tsp. pepper
6 Tbsp. flour
3 cups fat-free milk

1. Combine all ingredients except flour and
milk.
2. Cook on low 8-9 hours, or until potatoes
are tender.
3. Mix flour and milk until smooth. Stir into
corn chowder slowly until thickened.

Per Serving: 180 calories (25 calories from fat), 2.5g total
fat (1.5g saturated, 0g trans), 5mg cholesterol, 190mg
sodium, 34g total carbohydrate (3g fiber, 10g sugar), 8g
protein, 8%DV vitamin A, 10%DV vitamin C, 15%DV
calcium, 6%DV iron.

*Note: If your diet permits, you may want to add
1/2 tsp. salt to Step 1.*

Corn Chowder

Mary Rogers
Waseca, MN

Makes 12 servings
(Ideal slow-cooker size: 4-quart)

½ lb. lean turkey bacon
4 cups diced potatoes
2 cups chopped onions
2 cups fat-free sour cream
1½ cups fat-free milk
2 10¾-oz. cans fat-free, low-sodium cream of chicken soup
2 15¼-oz. cans fat-free, low-sodium whole-kernel corn, undrained

1. Cut bacon into 1" pieces. Cook for 5 minutes in large nonstick skillet, doing it in two batches so all the pieces brown.
2. Add potatoes and onions and a bit of water. Cook 15-20 minutes, until vegetables are tender, stirring occasionally. Drain. Transfer to slow cooker.
3. Combine sour cream, milk, chicken soup, and corn. Place in slow cooker.
4. Cover. Cook on low for 2 hours.

Per Serving: 260 calories (70 calories from fat), 8 total fat (2.5g saturated, 0g trans), 25mg cholesterol, 840mg sodium, 37g total carbohydrate (3g fiber, 10g sugar), 11g protein, 2%DV vitamin A, 20%DV vitamin C, 15%DV calcium, 10%DV iron.

Note: If you'll be gone for most of the day, you may want to use a different procedure from the one above. After Step 1, place bacon, potatoes, onions, 2 inches of water, the 2 cans of soup and the 2 cans of corn into the slow cooker. Cook on low 8-10 hours, or until the vegetables are done to your liking. Thirty minutes before serving, stir in sour cream and milk and continue cooking on low. Serve when soup is heated through and steaming.

Double Corn and Cheddar Chowder

Maryann Markano
Wilmington, DE

Makes 6 servings
(Ideal slow-cooker size: 4-quart)

1 Tbsp. butter or margarine
1 cup onions, chopped
2 Tbsp. all-purpose flour
2½ cups fat-free, reduced-sodium chicken broth
16-oz. can creamed corn
1 cup frozen corn
½ cup red bell peppers, finely chopped
½ tsp. hot pepper sauce
¾ cup shredded, reduced-fat, sharp cheddar cheese
freshly ground pepper to taste (optional)

1. In saucepan on tope of stove, melt butter or margarine. Stir in onions and sauté until wilted. Stir in flour. When well mixed, whisk in chicken broth. Stir frequently over medium heat until broth is thickened.
2. Pour into slow cooker. Mix in remaining ingredients except cheese.
3. Cook on low 4½ hours. About an hour before the end of the cooking time, stir in cheese until melted and well blended.

Per Serving: 200 calories (60 calories from fat), 7g total fat (4g saturated, 0g trans), 20mg cholesterol, 530mg sodium, 25g total carbohydrate (2g fiber, 5g sugar), 12g protein, 20%DV vitamin A, 20%DV vitamin C, 20%DV calcium, 8%DV iron.

Note: You may also add a cup of cooked white or brown rice during the last hour if you like.

Potato Cheddar-Cheese Soup

Marla Folkerts
Holland, OH

Makes 4 servings
(Ideal slow-cooker size: 4-quart)

6-10 potatoes, peeled and cubed
1/2 cup fat-free, low-sodium vegetable
    broth
1 cup water
1 large onion, finely chopped
1/2 tsp. garlic powder
1/8 tsp. white pepper
2 cups fat-free milk, heated
1 cup shredded fat-free sharp, or extra
    sharp, cheddar cheese
paprika

1. Place potatoes, broth, water, onions, and garlic powder in slow cooker.
2. Cover. Cook on low 7-9 hours, or on high 4-6 hours.
3. Mash potatoes, leaving them a bit lumpy. Stir in pepper and milk a little at a time. Add cheese. Cook until cheese has melted, about 5 minutes. Add more milk if you'd like a thinner or creamier soup.
4. Garnish each serving with paprika.

Per Serving: 510 calories (5 calories from fat), 0.5g total fat (0g saturated, 0g trans), 5mg cholesterol, 450mg sodium, 104g total carbohydrate (12g fiber, 12g sugar), 24g protein, 10%DV vitamin A, 60%DV vitamin C, 50%DV calcium, 25%DV iron.

Cream Cheese Potato Soup

Jean H. Robinson
Cinnaminson, NJ

Makes 6 servings
(Ideal slow-cooker size: 3 1/2-quart)

3 cups water
1 cup ham, diced
5 medium-sized potatoes, diced fine
8-oz. pkg. fat-free cream cheese, cubed
half an onion, chopped
1 tsp. garlic salt
1/2 tsp. black pepper
1/2 tsp. dill weed

1. Combine all ingredients in slow cooker.
2. Cover. Cook on high 4 hours, stirring occasionally.
3. Turn to low until ready to serve.

Per Serving: 220 calories (25 calories from fat), 3g total fat (1g saturated, 0g trans), 25mg cholesterol, 400mg sodium, 34g total carbohydrate (4g fiber, 2g sugar), 16g protein, 0%DV vitamin A, 30%DV vitamin C, 10%DV calcium, 10%DV iron.

Cream of Potato Soup

Dale Peterson
Rapid City, SD

Makes 8 servings
(Ideal slow-cooker size: 6- or 7-quart)

4 cups water
1 cup flour
6 large potatoes, peeled and cubed
1 large onion, chopped
2 large carrots, chopped
1/2 cup celery, diced
2 leeks, chopped
4 Tbsp. butter

4 chicken bouillon cubes
1 Tbsp. fresh or dried parsley
1 Tbsp. fresh or dried chives
1 tsp. garlic powder
1 tsp. lemon pepper seasoning
13-oz. can evaporated skim milk
4 ozs. fat-free sour cream
8 ozs. low-fat, low-sodium cheese spread

1. Mix flour and water together in slow cooker.
2. Stir in all remaining ingredients except evaporated milk, sour cream, and cheese spread.
3. Cook on low 8-10 hours.
4. Add evaporated milk, sour cream, and cheese spread during last hour.
5. When cheese is melted, soup is ready to eat.

Per Serving: 360 calories (80 calories from fat), 9g total fat (5g saturated, 0g trans), 30mg cholesterol, 810mg sodium, 56g total carbohydrate (5g fiber, 12g sugar), 17g protein, 80%DV vitamin A, 30%DV vitamin C, 40%DV calcium, 15%DV iron.

Potato Soup
Colleen Heatwole
Burton, MI

Makes 6 servings
(Ideal slow-cooker size: 3½-quart)

6 potatoes, peeled and cubed
2 onions, chopped
1 medium-sized carrot, sliced
1 rib celery, sliced
4 cubes low-sodium chicken or vegetable bouillon
4 cups water
1 Tbsp. parsley flakes
¼ tsp. black pepper
½ tsp. salt, optional
13-oz. can fat-free evaporated milk

1. Combine all ingredients, except evaporated milk in slow cooker.
2. Cover. Cook on high 3-4 hours or low 10-12 hours.
3. Stir in evaporated milk during last hour.

Per Serving: 240 calories (5 calories from fat), 0.5g total fat (0g saturated, 0g trans), 5mg cholesterol, 1090mg sodium, 50g total Carbohydrate (6g fiber, 12g sugar), 10g protein, 50%DV vitamin A, 40%DV vitamin C, 20%DV calcium, 10%DV iron.

Swiss Cheese and Veggie Soup
Sharon Miller
Holmesville, OH

Makes 4 servings
(Ideal slow-cooker size: 3½-quart)

2¼ cups frozen California-blend vegetables (broccoli, carrots, and cauliflower)
½ cup onions, chopped
½ cup water
½ tsp. chicken bouillon granules
1 cup skim milk
3 ozs. shredded fat-free Swiss cheese

1. Combine vegetables, onions, water, and bouillon in slow cooker.
2. Cook on low 6-8 hours, or until vegetables are tender.
3. Pour all ingredients into blender or food processor. Add milk. Process until smooth, or chunky smooth, whichever you prefer.
4. Serve, topped with shredded cheese.

Per Serving: 100 calories (0 calories from fat), 0g total fat (0g saturated, 0g trans), 5mg cholesterol, 290mg sodium, 11g total carbohydrate (3g fiber, 8g sugar), 11g protein, 40%DV vitamin A, 30%DV vitamin C, 40%DV calcium, 4%DV iron.

Note: If you want, and your diet permits, you may like to add ½ tsp. salt to Step 1.

Broccoli Soup

Betty B. Dennison, Grove City, PA

Makes 5 servings
(Ideal slow-cooker size: 4-quart)

2-3 lbs. fresh broccoli
1 Tbsp. margarine
water to cover
2 cups skim milk
1/2 cup Velveeta Light cheese, cut into small
cubes

1. Chop broccoli. Remove any tough stalks and discard.
2. Place chopped broccoli, margarine, and water to cover in slow cooker.
3. Cover. Cook on high 1-2 hours.
4. Add skim milk. Cook for an additional 15 minutes.
5. Stir in 1/2 cup Velveeta Light cheese and continue cooking until cheese is melted into soup.

Per Serving: 160 calories (35 calories from fat), 4g total fat (2g saturated, 1g trans), 10mg cholesterol, 490mg sodium, 22g total carbohydrate (8g fiber, 12g sugar), 16g protein, 100%DV vitamin A, 200%DV vitamin C, 40%DV calcium, 15%DV iron.

Cream of Broccoli and Mushroom Soup

Leona Miller, Millersburg, OH

Makes 12 servings
(Ideal slow-cooker size: 5- or 6-quart)

8 ozs. fresh mushrooms, sliced
2 lbs. fresh broccoli
3 10 3/4-oz. cans 98% fat-free cream of
broccoli soup

1/2 tsp. dried thyme leaves, crushed,
optional
3 bay leaves, optinoal
1 pint fat-free half-and-half
4 ozs. extra-lean smoked ham, chopped
1/4 tsp. black pepper

1. Combine all ingredients in slow cooker.
2. Cook on low 6-8 hours or on high 3 1/2-4 hours.
3. Remove bay leaves before serving.

Per Serving: 110 calories (25 calories from fat), 2.5g total fat (1g saturated, 0g trans), 10mg cholesterol, 580mg sodium, 16g total carbohydrate (3g fiber, 6g sugar), 7g protein, 30%DV vitamin A, 40%DV vitamin C, 10%DV calcium, 6%DV iron.

Cream of Broccoli Soup

Barb Yoder
Angola, IN

Makes 6-8 servings
(Ideal slow-cooker size: 3 1/2- or 4-quart)

1 small onion, chopped
1 Tbsp. oil
20-oz. pkg. frozen broccoli
2 10 3/4-oz. cans fat-free, low-sodium cream
of celery soup
10 3/4-oz. can fat-free, low-sodium cream of
mushroom soup
1 cup grated low-fat American cheese
2 soup cans fat-free milk

1. Sauté onion in oil in skillet until soft. Drain. Place onion in slow cooker.
2. Combine all ingredients in slow cooker.
3. Cover. Cook on low 3-4 hours.

Per Serving: 170 calories (45 calories from fat), 5g total fat (2g saturated, 1g trans), 15mg cholesterol, 1100mg sodium, 19g total carbohydrate (3g fiber, 8g sugar), 13g protein, 20%DV vitamin A, 30%DV vitamin C, 35%DV calcium, 4%DV iron.

Broccoli, Potato, and Cheese Soup

Ruth Shank
Gridley, IL

Makes 6 servings
(Ideal slow-cooker size: 3-quart)

2 cups cubed or diced potatoes
3 Tbsp. chopped onions
10-oz. pkg. frozen broccoli cuts, thawed
2 Tbsp. butter, melted
1 Tbsp. flour
1 cup cubed Velveeta Light cheese
½ tsp. salt
¼ tsp. black pepper
5½ cups fat-free milk

1. Cook potatoes and onions in boiling water in saucepan until potatoes are crisp-tender. Drain. Place in slow cooker.
2. Add remaining ingredients. Stir together.
3. Cover. Cook on low 4 hours.

Per Serving: 230 calories (70 calories from fat), 7g total fat (4.5g saturated, 1g trans), 25mg cholesterol, 780mg sodium, 27g total carbohydrate (3g fiber, 15g sugar), 16g protein, 10%DV vitamin A, 25%DV vitamin C, 40%DV calcium, 6%DV iron.

Note: If you prefer a thicker soup, and your diet allows, you may want to increase the flour to 3 Tbsp.

Elijah's Cucumber Soup

Shirley Unternahrer Hinh
Wayland, IA

Makes 8 servings
(Ideal slow-cooker size: 4-quart)

1 lb. lean ground pork
2 Tbsp. fish sauce
¼ tsp. black pepper
4 large cucumbers, peeled
2 qts. boiling water
2 green onions, chopped
⅛ tsp. black pepper
4 Tbsp. fish sauce
½ tsp. salt

1. Combine pork, 2 Tbsp. fish sauce, and ¼ tsp. black pepper in mixing bowl.
2. Cut peeled cucumbers in half lengthwise and scoop out seeds, creating a channel in each cuke. Stuff pork mixture into cucumbers.
3. Form remaing meat into 1" balls. Drop balls into 2 qts. boiling water in saucepan on top of the stove. Boil until a layer of foam develops on the water. Skim off foam and discard.
4. Drop stuffed cucumbers into boiling water. Simmer for 15 minutes. Transfer cucumbers and pork balls into slow cooker. Add hot liquid from stockpot.
5. Add green onions, ⅛ tsp. black pepper, and 4 Tbsp. fish sauce.
6. Cover. Cook on high 1½-2 hours.
7. Serve over rice in bowl, along with lemon juice and chili sauce.

Per Serving: 200 calories (110 calories from fat), 12g total fat (4.5g saturated, 0g trans), 55mg cholesterol, 1240mg sodium, 6g total carbohydrate (2g fiber, 2g sugar), 16g protein, 0%DV vitamin A, 0%DV vitamin C, 4%DV calcium, 6%DV iron.

Barley-Mushroom Soup

Janie Steele
Moore, OK

Makes 8 servings
(Ideal slow-cooker size: 5-quart)

6 cups fresh mushrooms, sliced
2 large onions, chopped
3 cloves garlic, minced
1 cup celery, chopped
1 cup carrots, chopped
5 cups water (divided)
4 cups dry quick-cooking pearl barley
4 cups low-sodium beef broth
4 tsp. Worcestershire sauce
1-1 1/2 tsp. salt, optional
1 1/2 tsp. dried basil
1 1/2 tsp. dried parsley flakes
1 tsp. dill weed
1 1/2 tsp. dried oregano
1/2 tsp. salt-free seasoning blend
1/2 tsp. dried thyme
1/2 tsp. garlic powder

1. Combine all ingredients in slow cooker.
2. Cook on low 7-8 hours, or until vegetables are done to your liking.

Per Serving: 320 calories (10 calories from fat), 1g total fat (0g saturated, 0g trans), 0mg cholesterol, 310mg sodium, 69g total carbohydrate (14g fiber, 5g sugar), 12g protein, 30%DV vitamin A, 2%DV vitamin C, 6%DV calcium, 20%DV iron.

Barley Cabbage Soup

Betty K. Drescher
Quakertown, PA

Makes 8 servings
(Ideal slow-cooker size: 3 1/2- or 4-quart)

1/4 cup dry pearl barley
6 cups fat-free, low-sodium meat or vegetable broth
1 cup onions, chopped
3-4 cups green cabbage, finely chopped
1/4 cup fresh parsley, chopped
1/2 tsp. celery salt
1/2 tsp. salt
1/8 tsp. black pepper
1 Tbsp. minute tapioca

1. Combine all ingredients in slow cooker.
2. Cover. Cook on low 10-12 hours or on high 5-6 hours.

Per Serving: 60 calories (0 calories from fat), 0g total fat (0g saturated, 0g trans), 0mg cholesterol, 300mg sodium, 10g total carbohydrate (2g fiber, 2g sugar), 5g protein, 0%DV vitamin A, 10%DV vitamin C, 2%DV calcium, 4%DV iron

Cabbage Sausage Soup

Karen Waggoner
Joplin, MO

Makes 8 servings
(Ideal slow-cooker size: 5-quart)

4 cups low-fat, low-sodium chicken broth
1 medium-sized head of cabbage, chopped
2 medium-sized onions, chopped
1/2 lb. fully cooked smoked turkey sausage,
  halved lengthwise and sliced
1/2 cup all-purpose flour
1/4 tsp. black pepper
1 cup skim milk

1. Combine chicken broth, cabbage, onions, and sausage in slow cooker.
2. Cover. Cook on high 5-6 hours, or until cabbage is tender.
3. Mix flour and black pepper in a bowl.
4. Gradually add milk, stirring until smooth.
5. Gradually stir into hot soup.
6. Cook, stirring occasionally for about 15 minutes, until soup is thickened. Serve.

Per Serving: 210 calories (100 calories from fat), 11g total fat (4g saturated, 0g trans), 20mg cholesterol, 790mg sodium, 17g total carbohydrate (3g fiber, 7g sugar), 11g protein, 4%DV vitamin A, 30%DV vitamin C, 10%DV calcium, 15%DV iron.

Cabbage Veggie Soup

Judy Govotsos
Frederick, MD

Makes 8 servings
(Ideal slow-cooker size: 5-quart)

1 cup carrots, sliced
1 cup onions, diced
4 garlic cloves, chopped
6 cups fat-free low-sodium chicken broth
3-4 cups shredded cabbage (or cole slow
  mix ready-cut)
1 cup green beans, fresh, canned, or frozen
2 Tbsp. tomato paste
1-1 1/2 tsp. dried basil
1/4-1/2 tsp. dried oregano
1/2 tsp. salt
1 very small zucchini, diced
1 very small yellow squash, diced

1. Combine all ingredients in slow cooker, except zucchini and squash.
2. Cover. Cook on low 5-6 hours or on high 2-3 hours.
3. Add zucchini and squash.
4. Cover. Cook on low 45 minutes to 1 hour.

Per Serving: 60 calories (0 calories from fat), 0g total fat (0g saturated, 0g trans), 0mg cholesterol, 290mg sodium, 8g total carbohydrate (3g fiber, 4g sugar), 6g protein, 80%DV vitamin A, 20%DV vitamin C, 6%DV calcium, 10%DV iron.

Soup to Get Thin On

Jean H. Robinson
Cinnaminson, NJ

*Makes 20+ servings
(Ideal slow-cooker size: 7-quart,
or 2 4-quart cookers)*

3 48-oz. cans low-fat, low-sodium chicken
    broth
2 medium-sized onions, chopped
5 celery ribs, chopped
5 parsnips, chopped
1 head (8 cups) cabbage, shredded
4 bell peppers (red or green), chopped
8 ozs. mushrooms, chopped
10-oz. pkg. spinach, chopped
10-oz. pkg. frozen broccoli florets
10-oz. pkg. cauliflower
2-3 pieces chopped gingerroot
14½-oz. can crushed tomatoes
1 Tbsp. black pepper
1 Tbsp. salt

1. Combine all ingredients in slow cooker.
2. Cover. Cook on low 6-8 hours.

Per Serving: 90 calories (0 calories from fat), 0g total fat
(0g saturated, 0g trans), 0mg cholesterol, 660mg sodium,
16g total carbohydrate (15g fiber, 5g sugar), 7g protein,
20%DV vitamin A, 40%DV vitamin C, 8%DV calcium,
15%DV iron.

Low-Calorie Soup

Cindy Kiestynick
Glen Lyon, PA

*Makes 14 servings
(Ideal slow-cooker size: 4- or 5-quart)*

2 cups carrots, thinly sliced
2 cups celery, thinly sliced
2 cups cabbage, chopped
8-oz. pkg. frozen green beans
1 onion, chopped
28-oz. can diced tomatoes
3 envelopes dry low-sodium beef-flavored
    soup mix
3 Tbsp. Worcestershire sauce
½ tsp. salt
¼ tsp. black pepper
water to cover

1. Combine all ingredients in slow cooker.
2. Cover. Cook on high 5 hours.

Per Serving: 80 calories (0 calories from fat), 0g total fat
(0g saturated, 0g trans), 0mg cholesterol, 630mg sodium,
17g total carbohydrate (4g fiber, 5g sugar), 2g protein,
100%DV vitamin A, 10%DV vitamin C, 8%DV calcium,
6%DV iron.

*Note: If you like, stir in a handful or two of baby
spinach just before serving.*

Survival Soup

Betty B. Dennison
Grove City, PA

Makes 10 servings
(Ideal slow-cooker size: 5-quart)

3 cups cabbage, cut up
1 cup carrots, cut up
½ cup celery, cut up
1 large onion, diced
1-lb. can French-style green beans, drained
4 cups water
2 beef bouillon cubes
12-oz. can low-sodium tomato juice
½ tsp. salt
¼-½ tsp. black pepper, according to your taste preference

1. Combine cabbage, carrots, celery, onion, and green beans in slow cooker.
2. Heat the water to boiling in a saucepan. Stir in bouillon cubes. When dissolved, pour over vegetables.
3. Add the tomato juice, salt, and pepper.
4. Cover. Cook on low 8-10 hours.

Per Serving: 30 calories (0 calories from fat), 0g total fat (0g saturated, 0g trans), 0mg cholesterol, 410mg sodium, 7g total carbohydrate (2g fiber, 4g sugar), 1g protein, 60%DV vitamin A, 20%DV vitamin C, 4%DV calcium, 4%DV iron.

"Diet" Soup or Cabbage Soup

Colleen Heatwole
Burton, MI

Makes 10 servings
(Ideal slow-cooker size: 5- or 6-quart)

1 head cabbage, sliced thin
3 onions, chopped
2 lbs. tomatoes, chopped
1 medium-sized carrot, thinly sliced
1 red or yellow bell pepper, chopped
2 cubes low-sodium chicken bouillon
1 pkg. dry onion soup mix

1. Combine all ingredients in slow cooker.
2. Cover. Cook on high 4 hours or low 6-8 hours.

Per Serving: 60 calories (5 calories from fat), 0.5g total fat (0g saturated, 0g trans), 0mg cholesterol, 330mg sodium, 14g total carbohydrate (4g fiber, 8g sugar), 3g protein, 50%DV vitamin A, 80%DV vitamin C, 6%DV calcium, 6%DV iron.

Pumpkin Soup

Jane Meiser
Harrisonburg, VA

Makes 6 servings
(Ideal slow-cooker size: 3¹/2-quart)

¼ cup green bell pepper, chopped
1 small onion, finely chopped
2 cups low-sodium chicken stock or broth, fat removed
2 cups pumpkin puree
2 cups skim milk
⅛ tsp. dried thyme
¼ tsp. ground nutmeg
½ tsp. salt
2 Tbsp. cornstarch
¼ cup cold water
1 tsp. fresh parsley, chopped

1. Combine all ingredients except cornstarch, cold water, and fresh parsley in slow cooker. Mix well.
2. Cover. Cook on low 5-6 hours.
3. During the last hour add cornstarch mixed with water and stir until soup thickens.
4. Just before serving, stir in fresh parsley.

Per Serving: 70 calories (0 calories from fat), 0g total fat (0g saturated, 0g trans), 0mg cholesterol, 300mg sodium, 12g total carbohydrate (1g fiber, 8g sugar), 6g protein, 15%DV vitamin A, 10%DV vitamin C, 10%DV calcium, 6%DV iron.

Onion Soup

Rosemarie Fitzgerald
Gibsonia, PA

Makes 8 servings
(Ideal slow-cooker size: 3¹/2-quart)

3 medium-sized onions, thinly sliced
2 Tbsp. butter
2 Tbsp. vegetable oil
1 tsp. salt
1 Tbsp. sugar
2 Tbsp. flour
1 qt. fat-free, low-sodium vegetable broth
½ cup dry white wine
slices of French bread
½ cup grated fat-free Swiss, or Parmesan, cheese

1. Sauté onions in butter and oil in covered skillet until soft. Uncover. Add salt and sugar. Cook 15 minutes. Stir in flour. Cook 3 more minutes.
2. Combine onions, broth, and wine in slow cooker.
3. Cover. Cook on low 6-8 hours.
4. Toast bread. Sprinkle with grated cheese and then broil.
5. Dish soup into individual bowls; then float a slice of broiled bread on top of each serving of soup.

Per Serving: 360 calories (50 calories from fat), 6g total fat (2.5g saturated, 0.5g trans), 10mg cholesterol, 1320mg sodium, 61g total carbohydrate (4g fiber, 7g sugar), 11g protein, 0%DV vitamin A, 0%DV vitamin C, 15%DV calcium, 15%DV iron.

Pizza in a Bowl

Laurie Sylvester
Ridgely, MD

Makes 6 servings
(Ideal slow-cooker size: 3¹/₂-quart)

**26-oz. jar fat-free, low-sodium marinara
  sauce**
14¹/₂-oz. can low-sodium diced tomatoes
4 ozs. low-fat pepperoni, diced or sliced
1¹/₂ cups fresh mushrooms, sliced
1 large bell pepper, diced
1 large red onion, chopped
1 cup water
1 Tbsp. Italian seasoning
1 cup dry macaroni
low-fat shredded mozzarella cheese

1. Combine all ingredients, except cheese in
cooker.
2. Cover. Cook on low 5-6 hours.
3. Ladle into soup bowls. Sprinkle with
cheese.

Per Serving: 280 calories (100 calories from fat), 12g total
fat (3.5g saturated, 0g trans), 15mg cholesterol, 1270mg
sodium, 34g total carbohydrate (5g fiber, 12g sugar), 11g
protein, 10%DV vitamin A, 30%DV vitamin C, 10%DV
calcium, 15%DV iron.

Chicken Stock for Soup
(or other uses)

Stacy Schmucker Stoltzfus
Enola, PA

Makes 3+ quarts
(Ideal slow-cooker size: 6-quart)

**3 lbs. chicken backs and necks, or whole
  chicken**
3 quarts cold water
4 ribs celery, chopped coarsely
6 carrots, unpeeled, sliced thick
2 onions, peeled and quartered
8 peppercorns

1. Rinse chicken. Place in slow cooker. Add
water and vegetables.
2. Cover. Cook on high 4-6 hours.
3. Remove chicken and vegetables from
broth.
4. When broth has cooled slightly, place in
refrigerator to cool completely. Remove fat and
any foam when chilled.
5. The stock is ready for soup. Freeze it in
1-cup containers.
6. Use the cooked chicken and vegetables
for soup or stews.

Per Serving: 220 calories (45 calories from fat), 5g total fat
(1g saturated, 0g trans), 110mg cholesterol, 170mg sodium,
8g total carbohydrate (2g fiber, 5g sugar), 36g protein,
200%DV vitamin A, 10%DV vitamin C, 6%DV calcium,
10%DV iron.

*A note from the recipe's tester: I made a chicken
noodle soup with a portion of the stock just to see
how it turned out. It was probably the best
chicken noodle soup I've ever made! I did discover
that the flavor of the stock was enhanced by
adding salt.*

Veggie Stock

Char Hagner
Montague, MI

Makes 6 cups
(Ideal slow-cooker size: 4-quart)

2 tomatoes, chopped
2 onions, cut up
4 carrots, cut up
1 stalk celery, cut up
1 potato, cut up
6 garlic cloves
dash of salt
1/2 tsp. dried thyme
1 bay leaf
6 cups water

1. Combine tomatoes, onions, carrots, celery, potato, garlic, salt, thyme, bay leaf, and water.
2. Cover. Cook on low 8-10 hours or on high 4-5 hours.
3. Strain stock through large sieve. Discard the solids.
4. Freeze until needed (up to 3 months). Use for soups or stews.

Per Serving: 70 calories (0 calories from fat), 0g total fat (0g saturated, 0g trans), 0mg cholesterol, 75mg sodium, 15g total carbohydrate (3g fiber, 5g sugar), 2g protein, 100%DV vitamin A, 10%DV vitamin C, 4%DV calcium, 6%DV iron.

6-Can Soup

Mrs. Audrey L. Kneer
Williamsfield, IL

Makes 8 servings
(Ideal slow-cooker size: 3 1/2- or 4-quart)

10 3/4-oz. can low-sodium tomato soup
15-oz. can whole-kernel corn, drained
15-oz. can mixed vegetables, drained
15-oz. can chili beans, undrained
14 1/2-oz. can low-sodium diced tomatoes, undrained
14 1/2-oz. can low-sodium, reduced-fat chicken broth

1. Combine all ingredients in slow cooker.
2. Cover. Cook on low 3-4 hours.

Per Serving: 140 calories (15 calories from fat), 1.5g total fat (0g saturated, 0g trans), 0mg cholesterol, 610mg sodium, 27g total carbohydrate (6g fiber, 3g sugar), 7g protein, 50%DV vitamin A, 20%DV vitamin C, 6%DV calcium, 10%DV iron.

15-Bean Soup

Eileen Eash
Carlsbad, NM

Makes 10 servings
(Ideal slow-cooker size: 6-quart)

1 lb. dry 15-bean mixture
2 qts. water
2 cups lean ham, chopped
1 cup onions, chopped
2 cups canned, low-sodium diced tomatoes
1 tsp. chili powder
2 Tbsp. lemon juice
2 cloves garlic, chopped finely
1 tsp. salt
1/2 tsp. black pepper

1. Soak beans in water overnight. Drain.
2. Mix beans, fresh 2 quarts of water, and ham in slow cooker.
3. Cover. Cook on low 8-10 hours.
4. Add remaining ingredients.
5. Cook on high another 1 hour or on low another 2 hours.

Per Serving: 210 calories (20 calories from fat), 2.5g total fat (0.5g saturated, 0g trans), 10mg cholesterol, 1740mg sodium, 33g total carbohydrate (9g fiber, 7g sugar), 14g protein, 10%DV vitamin A, 10%DV vitamin C, 5%DV calcium, 20%DV iron.

Carl's Steak Chili

Jenny R. Unternahrer
Wayland, IA

Makes 4 servings
(Ideal slow-cooker size: 3 1/2-quart)

16-oz. can kidney beans, drained
14 1/2-oz. can low-sodium diced tomatoes
1 lb. lean top round steak, trimmed of fat and cubed
half a medium-sized onion, diced
one-third of a green bell pepper, diced
1 clove garlic, minced
1/2 Tbsp. chili powder
1/4 tsp. black pepper
1/2 tsp. salt
15-oz. can low-sodium tomato sauce
several drops of Tabasco sauce, optional

1. Combine all ingredients in slow cooker. Stir.
2. Cover. Cook on low 8 hours.

Per Serving: 300 calories (60 calories from fat), 6g total fat (2g saturated, 0g trans), 70mg cholesterol, 1660mg sodium, 32g total carbohydrate (8g fiber, 9g sugar), 31g protein, 20%DV vitamin A, 30%DV vitamin C, 10%DV calcium, 30%DV iron.

Note: If you'd like some more zip, add a 4-oz. can of chopped green chilies, undrained, to Step 1.

Slow-Cooked Chili

Bernice A. Esau
North Newton, KS
Carol Sherwood
Batavia, NY

Makes 10 servings
(Ideal slow-cooker size: 5-quart)

2 lbs. extra-lean ground beef
2 16-oz. cans kidney beans, rinsed and
  drained
2 14½-oz. cans low-sodium diced
  tomatoes, undrained
8-oz. can low-sodium tomato sauce
2 medium-sized onions, chopped
1 green bell pepper, chopped
2 garlic cloves, minced
2 Tbsp. chili powder
2 tsp. salt, optional
1 tsp. black pepper
shredded low-fat cheddar cheese, optional

1. Brown beef in nonstick skillet (or
microwave strainer).
2. Place in slow cooker.
3. Add all ingredients, except cheese.
4. Cover. Cook on high 4 hours or on low 8-
10 hours.
5. Garnish individual servings with cheese
if desired.

Per Serving: 270 calories (80 calories from fat), 9g total fat
(3.5g saturated, 0g trans), 35mg cholesterol, 1220mg
sodium, 22g total carbohydrate (6g fiber, 6g sugar), 25g
protein, 25%DV vitamin A, 20%DV vitamin C, 10%DV
calcium, 20%DV iron.

*Note: Serve as a soup, or as a topping for rice or
potatoes.*

Brown-Sugar Chili

Alma Weaver
Ephrata, PA

Makes 8 servings
(Ideal slow-cooker size: 3½-quart)

1 lb. extra-lean ground beef
½ cup brown sugar
2 Tbsp. prepared mustard
1 medium-sized onion, chopped
2 14-oz. cans kidney beans, drained
1 pint low-sodium tomato juice
½ tsp. salt
¼ tsp. black pepper
1 tsp. chili powder

1. Brown lean ground beef and onion in a
nonstick skillet over medium heat. Stir brown
sugar and mustard into meat.
2. Combine all ingredients in slow cooker.
3. Cover. Cook on high 2 hours. If it's
convenient, stir several times during cooking.

Per Serving: 240 calories (50 calories from fat), 6g total fat
(2g saturated, 0g trans), 20mg cholesterol, 590mg sodium,
32g total carbohydrate (4g fiber, 18g sugar), 17g protein,
6%DV vitamin A, 10%DV vitamin C, 6%DV calcium,
20%DV iron.

Classic Beef Chili

Esther S. Martin
Ephrata, PA

Makes 6 servings
(Ideal slow-cooker size: 4-quart)

1 lb. extra-lean ground beef
2 cloves garlic, chopped fine
2 Tbsp. chili powder
1 tsp. ground cumin
28-oz. can crushed tomatoes
15-oz. can red kidney beans, rinsed and
   drained
1 onion, chopped
4-oz. can diced chilies, undrained
2 Tbsp. tomato paste
fresh oregano sprigs for garnish

1. In a large non-stick skillet, brown beef
and garlic over medium heat. Stir to break up
meat. Add chili powder and cumin. Stir to
combine.
2. Mix together tomatoes, beans, onion,
chilies, and tomato paste in slow cooker. Add
beef mixture and mix thoroughly.
3. Cook on high 4-5 hours, or until flavors
are well blended.
4. Garnish with oregano to serve.

Per Serving: 280 calories (70 calories from fat), 8g total fat
(3g saturated, 0g trans), 30mg cholesterol, 300mg sodium,
30g total carbohydrate (11g fiber, 3g sugar), 24g protein,
40%DV vitamin A, 20%DV vitamin C, 8%DV calcium,
20%DV iron.

Chili Bake

Michele Rubola
Selden, NY

Makes 6 servings
(Ideal slow-cooker size: 4-quart)

3 turkey bacon slices
1/2 lb. extra-lean ground round
15 1/2-oz. can lima beans, undrained
15-oz. can pork and beans, undrained
15-oz. can red kidney beans, drained
1/2 cup ketchup
1/2 cup barbecue sauce
1/4 cup firmly packed brown sugar
1 tsp. dry mustard

1. Brown bacon until crisp in nonstick
skillet. Crumble and set aside.
2. Cook beef in nonstick skillet over
medium heat until beef is brown, stirring to
crumble beef.
3. Combine all ingredients in slow cooker.
Stir well.
4. Cover and cook on high for 1 hour; then
reduce to low and cook for 3-4 hours.

Per Serving: 380 calories (60 calories from fat), 7g total fat
(2g saturated, 0g trans), 25mg cholesterol, 1200mg sodium,
59g total carbohydrate (11g fiber, 24g sugar), 22g protein,
10%DV vitamin A, 10%DV vitamin C, 10%DV calcium,
25%DV iron.

Mexican Casserole

Janie Steele
Moore, OK

Makes 8 servings
(Ideal slow-cooker size: 4- or 5-quart)

1 lb. extra-lean ground beef
1 medium-sized onion, chopped
1 small green bell pepper, chopped
16-oz. can kidney beans, rinsed and
   drained
14½ oz.-can diced tomatoes, undrained
8-oz. can tomato sauce
¼ cup water
1 envelope reduced-sodium taco seasoning
1 Tbsp. chili powder
1⅓ cups instant rice, uncooked
1 cup low-fat cheddar cheese

   1. Brown ground beef and onion in nonstick skillet.
   2. Combine all ingredients in slow cooker except rice and cheese.
   3. Cook on low 8-9 hours.
   4. Stir in rice, cover, and cook until tender.
   5. Sprinkle with cheese. Cover and cook until cheese is melted. Serve.

Per Serving: 270 calories (60 calories from fat), 7g total fat (3g saturated, 0g trans), 25mg cholesterol, 820mg sodium, 32g total carbohydrate (5g fiber, 3g sugar), 21g protein, 25%DV vitamin A, 20%DV vitamin C, 15%DV calcium, 20%DV iron.

Many-Beans Chili

Rosann Zeiset
Stevens, PA

Makes 12 servings
(Ideal slow-cooker size: 4-quart)

½ lb. lean hamburger or ground turkey
½ lb. sausage
1 onion, chopped
15-oz. can kidney beans or chili beans,
   undrained
15-oz. can ranch-style beans, undrained
15-oz. can pinto beans, undrained
14½-oz. can stewed tomatoes, undrained
15-oz. can tomato sauce
1 envelope dry chili seasoning mix
3 Tbsp. brown sugar
3 Tbsp. chili powder

   1. Brown hamburger, sausage, and onion together in nonstick skillet.
   2. Combine all ingredients in large slow cooker. Mix well.
   3. Cook on low 8-10 hours.

Per Serving: 240 calories (60 calories from fat), 7g total fat (2g saturated, 0g trans), 15mg cholesterol, 1570mg sodium, 34g total carbohydrate (8g fiber, 11g sugar), 14g protein, 35%DV vitamin A, 10%DV vitamin C, 8%DV calcium, 25%DV iron.

Dawn's 4-Bean Turkey Chili
Dawn Day
Westminster, CA

Makes 10 servings
(Ideal slow-cooker size: 4-quart)

1 lb. ground turkey, browned in nonstick skillet and drained
1 large onion, chopped
6-oz. can low-sodium tomato paste
2 Tbsp. chili powder
12-oz. can chili beans, undrained
12-oz. can kidney beans, undrained
12-oz. can black beans, undrained
12-oz. can pinto beans, undrained
12-oz. can low-sodium tomatoes with juice

1. Combine browned ground turkey, onion, and tomato paste in slow cooker.
2. Add chili powder, beans, and tomatoes. Mix well.
3. Cover. Cook on low 6-7 hours.
4. Serve with grated low-fat cheddar cheese.
5. Sprinkle individual servings with fresh parsley, if you wish.

Per Serving: 190 calories (15 calories from fat), 2g total fat (0g saturated, 0g trans), 20mg cholesterol, 610mg sodium, 27g total carbohydrate (8g fiber, 3g sugar), 19g protein, 20%DV vitamin A, 10%DV vitamin C, 8%DV calcium, 15%DV iron.

Hot Chili
Kristen Allen
Houston, TX

Makes 8 servings
(Ideal slow-cooker size: 5-quart)

2 lbs. 99% fat-free ground turkey
2 medium-sized onions, diced
2 garlic cloves, minced
1 green bell pepper, diced
2/3 Tbsp. chili powder
1 tsp. salt
1 tsp. black pepper
1 tsp. ground cumin
16-oz. can low-sodium stewed or diced tomatoes
2 12-oz. cans low-sodium tomato sauce
2 16-oz. cans Mexican chili beans

1. Brown turkey with onions, garlic, and green pepper in a nonstick skillet. Drain.
2. Combine all ingredients in slow cooker.
3. Cover. Cook on low 6-8 hours.

Per Serving: 320 calories (40 calories from fat), 4.5g total fat (1g saturated, 0g trans), 45mg cholesterol, 1400mg sodium, 36g total carbohydrate (12g fiber, 8g sugar), 37g protein, 80%DV vitamin A, 30%DV vitamin C, 8%DV calcium, 30%DV iron.

Chilly-Chili
Alix Nancy Botsford
Seminole, OK

Makes 6 servings
(Ideal slow-cooker size: 4½- or 5-quart)

2 cups assorted dried beans
1 tsp. salt
1 lb. fat-free ground turkey
1 large onion, chopped
2 tsp. minced garlic
2 Tbsp. olive oil
2 celery ribs, chopped
1 green bell pepper, diced
1 tsp. salt
10-oz. can tomatoes and green chilies, undrained
28-oz. can diced tomatoes, undrained

1. A day—or a week—before you want to serve and eat Chilly-Chili, sort, wash, and cover beans with water for 4-6 hours. Drain.

2. Place in plastic resealable bag. Place in freezer and freeze until solid.

3. On the day you want to serve the chili, place frozen beans in slow cooker. Cover with fresh water. Add 1 tsp. salt (this will keep the beans firm).

4. Cover. Cook on high 2-3 hours, or until you can crush a bean with a fork.

5. Drain, reserving 1-2 cups liquid.

6. In a skillet, brown turkey, onion, and garlic in oil.

7. Add celery, green pepper, and 1 tsp. salt. Continue cooking until vegetables begin to soften. Add both kinds of tomatoes and pour into slow cooker.

8. Add as much bean liquid as you can fit in your slow cooker.

9. Cover. Cook on low 1-8 hours.

Per Serving: 380 calories (60 calories from fat), 6g total fat (1g saturated, 0g trans), 30mg cholesterol, 1390mg sodium, 50g total carbohydrate (18g fiber, 10g sugar), 34g protein, 10%DV vitamin A, 30%DV vitamin C, 20%DV calcium, 35%DV iron.

Garden Chili
Stacy Schmucker Stoltzfus
Enola, PA

Makes 10 servings
(Ideal slow-cooker size: 3½- or 4-quart)

¾ lb. onions, chopped
1 tsp. garlic, minced
1 Tbsp. olive oil
¾ cup celery, chopped
1 large carrot, peeled and thinly sliced
1 large green bell pepper, chopped
1 small zucchini, sliced
¼ lb. fresh mushrooms, sliced
1¼ cups water
14-oz. can kidney beans, drained
14-oz. can low-sodium diced tomatoes with juice
1 tsp. lemon juice
⅛ tsp. dried oregano
1 tsp. ground cumin
1 tsp. chili powder
1 tsp. salt
1 tsp. black pepper

1. Sauté onions and garlic in olive oil in a large skillet over medium heat until tender.

2. Add remaining fresh veggies. Sauté 2-3 minutes. Transfer to slow cooker.

3. Add remaining ingredients.

4. Cover. Cook on low 6-8 hours.

Per Serving: 80 calories (15 calories from fat), 2g total fat (0g saturated, 0g trans), 0mg cholesterol, 500mg sodium, 14g total carbohydrate (4g fiber, 5g sugar), 4g protein, 30%DV vitamin A, 20%DV vitamin C, 6%DV calcium, 6%DV iron.

Note: This is good served over rice.

Vegetarian Chili with Mushrooms

Leona Yoder
Hartville, OH

Makes 8 servings
(Ideal slow-cooker size: 4-quart)

1 cup dried pinto or kidney beans
3 cups water
1 Tbsp. vegetable oil
2 cups onions, chopped
1 green bell pepper, seeded and chopped
2 heaping cups fresh mushrooms, sliced
   (about 10 ozs.)
1 cup carrots, thinly sliced
2 cups fresh or canned unsalted tomatoes,
   chopped
6-oz. can unsalted tomato paste
3/4 cup water
2 Tbsp. chili powder
1 large dried bay leaf
1 Tbsp. vinegar
1-2 tsp. garlic, finely minced

1. Place beans and 3 cups water in a saucepan. Bring to a boil and cook 2 minutes. Do not drain. Let sit 1 hour.
2. Pour beans into slow cooker. If water does not cover beans, add additional water to cover them.
3. Cover cooker. Cook on high 2 hours.
4. Heat oil in skillet. Add onion and green pepper. Cook until onions are transparent. Drain. Add to slow cooker.
5. Add remaining ingredients.
6. Cover. Cook on low 4-6 hours.
7. Remove bay leaf before serving.
8. Serve over brown rice or potatoes.

Per Serving: 100 calories (25 calories from fat), 2.5g total fat (0g saturated, 0g trans), 0mg cholesterol, 170mg sodium, 19g total carbohydrate (5g fiber, 6g sugar), 4g protein, 180%DV vitamin A, 20%DV vitamin C, 4%DV calcium, 10%DV iron.

Notes:
1. Add the onions and green peppers to the cooker without cooking them in the skillet if you like.
2. If your diet allows, you may want to add 1 tsp. salt to Step 5. You can also increase the amount of chili powder and add 1/4-1/2 tsp. black pepper.

Vegetable Chili

Janie Steele
Moore, OK

Makes 7 servings
(Ideal slow-cooker size: 4-quart)

1 1/2 cups chopped onions
3/4 cup chopped red bell pepper
3/4 cup chopped green bell pepper
14 1/2-oz. can fat-free, low-sodium vegetable
   broth
2 10-oz. cans diced tomatoes and green
   chilies, undrained
1/2 cup salsa
1 Tbsp. chili powder
1 tsp. ground cumin
3/4 tsp. garlic powder
15-oz can pinto beans, rinsed and drained
1 cup fresh or frozen corn
1 cup fat-free shredded cheddar cheese

1. Turn slow cooker on high.
2. Combine all ingredients except cheese in slow cooker.
3. Cover. Turn cooker to low and cook for 6-8 hours.
4. Garnish with cheese when serving.

Per Serving: 160 calories (10 calories from fat), 1g total fat (0g saturated, 0g trans), 5mg cholesterol, 850mg sodium, 28g total carbohydrate (7g fiber, 8g sugar), 11g protein, 40%DV vitamin A, 40%DV vitamin C, 25%DV calcium, 10%DV iron.

Hearty Veggie Chili

Nanci Keatley, Salem, OR

Makes 6 servings
(Ideal slow-cooker size: 4- or 5-quart)

1 Tbsp. olive oil
1 onion, chopped
1 carrot, thinly sliced
1 green bell pepper, chopped
8 ozs. fresh or canned mushrooms, sliced
1 small zucchini, sliced or cubed
12 black olives, optional
4 large garlic cloves, minced
28-oz. can low-sodium tomatoes, undrained
2 cups nonfat low-sodium tomato sauce
4-oz. can chopped green chilies
4 cups cooked kidney beans
2-3 Tbsp. chili powder, depending on your taste preference
1 Tbsp. dried oregano
2 tsp. ground cumin
2 tsp. paprika
1 Tbsp. white wine vinegar

1. Sauté onion in olive oil in a skillet.
2. Place in slow cooker.
3. Add remaining ingredients. Mix well.
4. Cover. Cook on low 6-8 hours.

Per Serving: 270 calories (40 calories from fat), 4g total fat (0.5g saturated, 0g trans), 0mg cholesterol, 1570mg sodium, 48g total carbohydrate (13g fiber, 12g sugar), 14g protein, 100%DV vitamin A, 30%DV vitamin C, 20%DV calcium, 30%DV iron.

Norma's Vegetarian Chili

Kathy Hertzler
Lancaster, PA

Makes 8-10 servings
(Ideal slow-cooker size: 5-quart)

2 Tbsp. oil
2 cups minced celery
1 1/2 cups chopped green bell peppers
1 cup minced onions
4 garlic cloves, minced
5 1/2 cups low-sodium stewed tomatoes
2 1-lb. cans kidney beans, undrained
1 1/2-2 cups raisins
1/4 cup wine vinegar
1 Tbsp. chopped parsley
2 tsp. salt
1 1/2 tsp. dried oregano
1 1/2 tsp. ground cumin
1/4 tsp. black pepper
1/4 tsp. Tabasco sauce
1 bay leaf
3/4 cup raw cashews
1 cup grated fat-free cheese

1. Combine all ingredients except cashews and cheese in slow cooker.
2. Cover. Simmer on low for 8 hours. Add cashews and simmer 30 minutes.
3. Garnish individual servings with grated cheese.

Per Serving: 340 calories (80 calories from fat), 9g total fat (1.5g saturated, 0g trans), 0mg cholesterol, 1080mg sodium, 55g total carbohydrate (8g fiber, 28g sugar), 12g protein, 0%DV vitamin A, 30%DV vitamin C, 10%DV calcium, 25%DV iron.

Soups

Vegetarian Chili Soup
Rosemarie Fitzgerald
Gibsonia, PA

Makes 8 servings
(Ideal slow-cooker size: 5-quart)

1 large onion, chopped
1 Tbsp. margarine
1 clove garlic, finely chopped
2 tsp. chili powder
½ tsp. dried oregano, crumbled
2 14½-oz. cans vegetable broth
14½-oz. can no-salt-added stewed, or diced, tomatoes
5 cups water
½ tsp. salt
¼ tsp. black pepper
¾ lb. fresh kale
⅓ cup white long grain rice
19-oz. can cannellini beans, drained and rinsed

1. Sauté onion in skillet with margarine until tender.
2. Add garlic, chili powder, and oregano. Cook for 30 seconds. Pour into slow cooker.
3. Add remaining ingredients except kale, rice, and beans.
4. Cover. Cook on low 7 hours or on high 3-4 hours.
5. Cut kale stalks into small pieces and chop leaves coarsely.
6. Add to soup with rice and beans.
7. Cover. Cook on high 1-2½ hours more, or until rice is tender and kale is done to your liking.

Per Serving: 120 calories (15 calories from fat), 1.5g total fat (0g saturated, 0g trans), 0mg cholesterol, 790mg sodium, 24g total carbohydrate (6g fiber, 6g sugar), 6g protein, 80%DV vitamin A, 20%DV vitamin C, 10%DV calcium, 15%DV iron.

Wintertime-Vegetables Chili
Maricarol Magill
Freehold, NJ

Makes 6 servings
(Ideal slow-cooker size: 6-quart)

1 medium-sized butternut squash, peeled and cubed
2 medium-sized carrots, peeled and diced
1 medium-sized onion, diced
1-4 Tbsp. chili powder, depending upon how hot you like your chili
2 14-oz. cans diced low-sodium tomatoes
4-oz. can chopped mild green chilies
½ tsp. salt
1 cup fat-free, low-sodium vegetable broth
2 16-oz. cans black beans, drained and rinsed
⅓ cup fat-free sour cream

1. In slow cooker, layer all ingredients in order given—except sour cream.
2. Cover. Cook on low 6-8 hours, or until vegetables are tender.
3. Stir before serving.
4. Top individual servings with dollops of sour cream.

Per Serving: 200 calories (10 calories from fat), 1g total fat (0g saturated, 0g trans), 0mg cholesterol, 1310mg sodium, 40g total carbohydrate (13g fiber, 9g sugar), 11g protein, 100%DV vitamin A, 20%DV vitamin C, 20%DV calcium, 15%DV iron.

183

Vegetarian Chili with Corn

Jennifer Dzialowski
Brunton, MI

Makes 8-10 servings
(Ideal slow-cooker size: 6-quart)

2 15-oz. cans diced tomatoes, undrained
2 15-oz. cans kidney beans, drained
15-oz. can garbanzo beans, drained
15-oz. can corn, drained
1 bell pepper, chopped
½ cup, or more, onions, chopped
6 cups low-sodium tomato juice
2 Tbsp. minced garlic
½ tsp. ground cumin
½ tsp. dried oregano
¼-½ tsp. black pepper, according to taste
1-3 tsp. chili powder, according to your
    taste preference
1 cup Textured Vegetarian Protein (T.V.P.)

1. Place tomatoes, kidney beans, garbanzo beans, corn, bell pepper, and onions in slow cooker.
2. Add tomato juice, garlic, cumin, oregano, black pepper, and chili powder. Top with Textured Vegetable Protein.
3. Cover. Cook on low 7-8 hours or on high 4 hours.

Per Serving: 270 calories (15 calories from fat), 2g total fat (0g saturated, 0g trans), 0mg cholesterol, 900mg sodium, 52g total carbohydrate (12g fiber, 15g sugar), 17g protein, 30%DV vitamin A, 80%DV vitamin C, 15%DV calcium, 30%DV iron.

Note: *If your sodium intake allows, you may want to add 1 tsp. salt to Step 2.*

4-Bean Vegetarian Chili

Elaine Patton
West Middletown, PA

Makes 8 servings
(Ideal slow-cooker size: 5-quart)

16-oz. can vegetarian baked beans
19-oz. can black bean soup
15-oz. can kidney beans, drained
15-oz. can garbanzo beans
2 14½-oz. cans stewed or diced tomatoes
2 ribs celery, chopped
1 green bell pepper, chopped
1 onion, chopped
1 Tbsp. dried basil
1 Tbsp. chili powder
1 Tbsp. dried oregano
1 Tbsp. parsley flakes

1. Combine all ingredients in slow cooker.
2. Cook on high 3 hours.

Per Serving: 250 calories (20 calories from fat), 2g total fat (0g saturated, 0g trans), 0mg cholesterol, 1250mg sodium, 49g total carbohydrate (14g fiber, 12g sugar), 12g protein, 25%DV vitamin A, 25%DV vitamin C, 15%DV calcium, 20%DV iron.

Note: *If you would like to be sure the raw vegetables are soft, sauté them in a nonstick skillet before mixing them into the Chili.*

Chili-Chili Bang-Bang
Vera Schmucker
Goshen, IN

Makes 8 servings
(Ideal slow-cooker size: 5-quart)

1¼ cups onions, coarsely chopped
1 cup red bell peppers, chopped
1 cup green bell peppes, chopped
¾ cup celery, chopped
¾ cup carrots, chopped
3 cloves garlic, minced
1 Tbsp. chili powder
1½ cups quartered fresh mushrooms
1 cup zucchini, cubed
28-oz. can low-sodium diced tomatoes
28-oz. can black beans, drained and rinsed
15-oz. can chickpeas, drained and rinsed
11-oz. can kernel corn, undrained
1 Tbsp. ground cumin
1½ tsp. dried oregano
1½ tsp. dried basil
½ tsp. cayenne pepper

1. Combine all ingredients in slow cooker.
2. Cover. Cook on high 4 hours, stirring occasionally.

Per Serving: 230 calories (20 calories from fat), 2g total fat (0g saturated, 0g trans), 0mg cholesterol, 890mg sodium, 48g total carbohydrate (13g fiber, 10g sugar), 12g protein, 100%DV vitamin A, 60%DV vitamin C, 15%DV calcium, 20%DV iron.

Hearty Bean and Vegetable Stew
Jeanette Oberholtzer
Manheim, PA

Makes 12 servings
(Ideal slow-cooker size: 5-quart)

1 lb. dry beans, assorted
2 cups fat-free vegetable broth
½ cup white wine
⅓ cup soy sauce
⅓ cup apple or pineapple juice, unsweetened
vegetable stock or water
½ cup celery, diced
½ cup parsnips, diced
½ cup carrots, diced
½ cup mushrooms, sliced
1 onion, sliced
1 tsp. dried basil
1 tsp. parsley flakes
1 bay leaf
3 cloves garlic, minced
1 tsp. black pepper
1 cup rice or pasta, cooked

1. Sort and rinse beans and soak overnight in water. Drain. Place in slow cooker.
2. Add vegetable juice, wine, soy sauce, and apple or pineapple juice.
3. Cover with vegetable stock or water.
4. Cover. Cook on high 2 hours.
5. Add vegetables, herbs, and spices.
6. Cover cooker. Cook on low 5-6 hours, or until carrots and parsnips are tender.
7. Add cooked rice or pasta.
8. Cover. Cook 1 hour more.

Per Serving: 180 calories (5 calories from fat), 0.5g total fat (0g saturated, 0g trans), 0mg cholesterol, 370mg sodium, 34g total carbohydrate (9g fiber, 6g sugar), 10g protein, 35%DV vitamin A, 10%DV vitamin C, 6%DV calcium, 20%DV iron.

Note: Use 3 or 4 kinds of beans such as black, kidney, pinto, baby lima, lentils, or split peas.

Mexican Rice and Bean Soup

Esther J. Mast
East Petersburg, PA

Makes 6 servings
(Ideal slow-cooker size: 4-quart)

1/2 cup chopped onions
1/3 cup chopped green bell peppers
1 garlic clove, minced
1 Tbsp. oil
4-oz. pkg. sliced or chipped dried beef
18-oz. can low-sodium tomato juice
15 1/2-oz. can red kidney beans, undrained
1 1/2 cups water
1/2 cup long grain rice, uncooked
1 tsp. paprika
1/2-1 tsp. chili powder
1/2 tsp. salt
dash of black pepper

1. Cook onions, green peppers, and garlic in oil in skillet until vegetables are tender but not brown. Transfer to slow cooker.
2. Tear beef into small pieces and add to slow cooker.
3. Add remaining ingredients. Mix well.
4. Cover. Cook on low 6 hours. Stir before serving.

Per Serving: 190 calories (30 calories from fat), 3.5g total fat (0.5g saturated, 0g trans), 10mg cholesterol, 1110mg sodium, 30g total carbohydrate (6g fiber, 5g sugar), 11g protein, 10%DV vitamin A, 20%DV vitamin C, 4%DV calcium, 20%DV iron.

This is a recipe I fixed often when our sons were growing up. We have all enjoyed it in any season of the year.

Beef 'n Black Bean Soup

Deborah Santiago
Lancaster, PA

Makes 10 servings (2 1/2 quarts)
(Ideal slow-cooker size: 4- or 5-quart)

1 lb. extra-lean ground beef
2 14 1/2-oz. cans fat-free, low-sodium chicken broth
14 1/2-oz. can low-sodium, diced tomatoes, undrained
8 green onions, thinly sliced
3 medium carrots, thinly sliced
2 celery ribs, thinly sliced
2 garlic cloves, minced
1 Tbsp. sugar
1 1/2 tsp. dried basil
1/2 tsp. salt
1/2 tsp. dried oregano
1/2 tsp. ground cumin
1/2 tsp. chili powder
2 15-oz. cans black beans, rinsed and drained
1 1/2 cups cooked rice

1. In a nonstick skillet over medium heat, cook beef until no longer pink. Drain.
2. Place beef in slow cooker.
3. Add remaining ingredients except black beans and rice.
4. Cover. Cook on high 1 hour.
5. Reduce to low. Cook 4-5 hours, or until vegetables are tender.
6. Add beans and rice.
7. Cook 1 hour longer on low, or until heated through.

Per Serving: 200 calories (40 calories from fat), 4.5g total fat (1.5g saturated, 0g trans), 15mg cholesterol, 640mg sodium, 23g total carbohydrate (6g fiber, 4g sugar), 17g protein, 6%DV vitamin A, 10%DV vitamin C, 8%DV calcium, 20%DV iron.

Note: If you enjoy tomatoes, you can brighten the flavor by adding a second 14 1/2-oz. can of diced tomatoes, undrained.

Caribbean-Style Black Bean Soup

Sheryl Shenk
Harrisonburg, VA

Makes 8 servings
(Ideal slow-cooker size: 4-quart)

1 lb. dried black beans, washed and stones removed
3 onions, chopped
1 green bell pepper, chopped
4 cloves garlic, minced
1 lean ham hock,
   or ¾ cup lean cubed ham
1 Tbsp. oil
1 Tbsp. ground cumin
1-2 tsp. dried oregano, according to your taste preference
¼-1 tsp. dried thyme, depending upon how much you like thyme
1 tsp. salt
½ tsp. black pepper
3 cups water
2 Tbsp. vinegar
½ cup fat-free sour cream
fresh chopped cilantro

1. Soak beans overnight in 4 quarts water. Drain.
2. Combine soaked beans, onions, green pepper, garlic, ham or ham hock, oil, cumin, oregano, thyme, salt, pepper, and 3 cups fresh water. Stir well.
3. Cover. Cook on low 8-10 hours, or on high 4-5 hours.
4. For a thick soup, remove half of cooked bean mixture and puree until smooth in blender or mash with potato masher. Return to cooker. If you like a soup-ier soup, leave as is.
5. Add vinegar and stir well. If you used a ham hock, debone the ham, cut into bite-sized pieces, and return to soup.

6. Serve soup in bowls with a dollop of sour cream in the middle of each individual serving, topped with fresh cilantro.

Per Serving: 100 calories (30 calories from fat), 3g total fat (0.5g saturated, 0g trans), 5mg cholesterol, 880mg sodium, 14g total carbohydrate (4g fiber, 4g sugar), 5g protein, 0%DV vitamin A, 10%DV vitamin C, 6%DV calcium, 8%DV iron.

Black Bean and Corn Soup

Joy Sutter
Iowa City, IA

Makes 6-8 servings
(Ideal slow-cooker size: 3½- or 4-quart)

2 15-oz. cans black beans, drained and rinsed
14½-oz. can low-sodium Mexican stewed tomatoes, undrained
14½-oz. can diced low-sodium tomatoes, undrained
11-oz. can whole-kernel corn, drained
4 green onions, sliced
2-3 Tbsp. chili powder
1 tsp. ground cumin
½ tsp. dried minced garlic

1. Combine all ingredients in slow cooker.
2. Cover. Cook on high 5-6 hours.

Per Serving: 170 calories (10 calories from fat), 1.5g total fat (0g saturated, 0g trans), 0mg cholesterol, 790mg sodium, 35g total carbohydrate (10g fiber, 9g sugar), 9g protein, 10%DV vitamin A, 10%DV vitamin C, 10%DV calcium, 15%DV iron.

Notes:
1. For a varied taste, use 2 cloves fresh garlic, minced, instead of dried garlic.
2. To include more vegetables, add 1 large rib celery, sliced thin, and 1 small green bell pepper, chopped.

Mexican Black Bean Soup

Becky Harder
Monument, CO

Makes 8 servings
(Ideal slow-cooker size: 4-quart)

28-oz. can fat-free low-sodium chicken
   broth
1 cup onions, chopped
2 tsp. minced garlic
3 cups fat-free black beans
2 tsp. chili powder
¾ tsp. ground cumin
28-oz. can Mexican tomatoes with green
   chilies or jalapenos
¾ tsp. lemon juice
1 bunch green onions
fat-free sour cream

   1. Combine all ingredients except green
onions and sour cream in slow cooker.
   2. Cover. Cook on low 6-8 hours.
   3. Top each individual serving with sliced
green onions sprinkled over a spoonful of sour
cream.

Per Serving: 130 calories (10 calories from fat), 1g total fat
(0g saturated, 0g trans), 0mg cholesterol, 830mg sodium,
24g total carbohydrate (7g fiber, 4g sugar), 10g protein,
10%DV vitamin A, 4%DV vitamin C, 10%DV calcium,
15%DV iron.

Slow-Cooker Black Bean Chili

Mary Seielstad
Sparks, NV

Makes 8 servings
(Ideal slow-cooker size: 3½- or 4-quart)

1 lb. lean pork tenderloin, cut into
   1" chunks
16-oz. jar low-sodium, thick, chunky salsa
3 15-oz. cans black beans, rinsed and
   drained
½ cup fat-free, low-sodium chicken broth
1 medium-sized red bell pepper, chopped
1 medium-sized onion, chopped
1 tsp. ground cumin
2-3 tsp. chili powder
1-1½ tsp. dried oregano
¼ cup fat-free sour cream

   1. Combine all ingredients except sour
cream in slow cooker.
   2. Cover. Cook on low 6-8 hours, or until
pork is tender.
   3. Garnish individual servings with sour
cream.

Per Serving: 250 calories (30 calories from fat), 3.5g total
fat (1g saturated, 0g trans), 40mg cholesterol, 1050mg
sodium, 34g total carbohydrate (10g fiber, 7g sugar), 24g
protein, 10%DV vitamin A, 20%DV vitamin C, 8%DV
calcium, 20%DV iron.

Note: This is good served over brown rice.

Sausage and Black Bean Stew

John D. Allen
Rye, CO

Makes 6 servings
(Ideal slow-cooker size: 6-quart)

3 15-oz. cans black beans, drained and
    rinsed
14½-oz. can fat-free, reduced-sodium
    chicken broth
1 cup celery, sliced
2 4-oz. cans green chilies, chopped
3 cloves garlic, minced
1½ tsp. dried oregano
¾ tsp. coriander, ground
½ tsp. ground cumin
¼ tsp. ground red pepper (not cayenne)
1 lb. link turkey sausage, thinly sliced and
    cooked

1. Combine all ingredients in slow cooker
except sausage.
2. Cover. Cook on low 5-7 hours.
3. Remove 1½ cups of the bean mixture
and puree in blender. Return to slow cooker.
4. Add sliced sausage.
5. Cover. Cook on low 30 minutes.

Per Serving: 310 calories (80 calories from fat), 9g total fat
(2g saturated, 0g trans), 55mg cholesterol, 1580mg sodium,
36g total carbohydrate (13g fiber, 2g sugar), 28g protein,
2%DV vitamin A, 2%DV vitamin C, 15%DV calcium,
25%DV iron.

Note: If your diet permits, you may want to add
¾ tsp. salt to Step 1.

Turkey Chili with Black Beans

Susan Tjon
Austin, TX

Makes 5 servings
(Ideal slow-cooker size: 4- or 5-quart)

1 lb. uncooked ground turkey breast
1 large onion, finely chopped
1 green bell pepper, chopped
14-oz. can fat-free, reduced-sodium
    chicken broth
2 tsp. chili powder, or more, according to
    your preference
½ tsp. ground all-spice
¼ tsp. ground cinnamon
¼ tsp. paprika
15-oz. can black beans, rinsed and drained
14-oz. can tomato puree
2 tsp. cider vinegar

1. Spray skillet with fat-free cooking spray.
Brown turkey with onion and green pepper,
breaking up the turkey and cooking until the
meat is no longer pink.
2. Combine all ingredients in slow cooker.
3. Cook on low 4-5 hours.

Per Serving: 280 calories (80 calories from fat), 9g total fat
(2g saturated, 0g trans), 70mg cholesterol, 560mg sodium,
25g total carbohydrate (8g fiber, 8g sugar), 25g protein,
20%DV vitamin A, 60%DV vitamin C, 8%DV calcium,
25%DV iron.

Note: I brown my turkey the night before so I
only need to combine the ingredients in my slow
cooker in the morning.

Black Bean Chili

Rashell Harris
Wichita, KS

Makes 6 servings
(Ideal slow-cooker size: 6-quart)

2 cups black beans, dried
6 cups water
1 bunch cilantro, chopped
1-2 Tbsp. ground cumin
1 Tbsp. dried oregano
1 tsp. paprika
1/2 tsp. cayenne pepper
2 tsp. olive oil
1 large onion, chopped
1 bell pepper, diced
2 cloves garlic, minced
1 pkg. dry Herb-Ox vegetable broth
1 1/2 cups tomatoes, chopped
1/2 tsp. salt
1/4 cup green onions, chopped
additional cilantro

1. Rinse and soak beans overnight. Drain and rinse before mixing with ingredients and placing in slow cooker.
2. Place all ingredients (including 6 cups fresh water) except tomatoes, salt, and green onions in slow cooker.
3. Cover. Cook on low 8-10 hours or high for 6-8 hours.
4. Add tomatoes and salt. Place in bowls. Garnish with onions and additional cilantro.

Per Serving: 270 calories (30 calories from fat), 3g total fat (0g saturated, 0g trans), 0mg cholesterol, 180mg sodium, 48g total carbohydrate (12g fiber, 12g sugar), 15g protein, 10%DV vitamin A, 25%DV vitamin C, 10%DV calcium, 25%DV iron.

Notes:
1. Serve with corn bread if desired.
2. If diets allow, you may top individual servings with a dollop of lowfat sour cream and a spoonful of grated low-fat cheddar cheese.

Cabbage Bean Soup

Joy Sutter
Iowa City, IA

Makes 24 servings
(Ideal slow-cooker size: 2 6-quart cookers)

16-oz. can kidney beans, drained
15-oz. can black beans, drained
1 cup onions, chopped
4 cups fat-free beef broth
4 cups crushed canned tomatoes
2-3 cups carrots, chopped
1 cup celery, chopped
1 cup tomato sauce
11 cups cabbage, shredded
4 cups frozen mixed vegetables
1/4 cup fresh parsley, chopped
1 1/2 tsp. dried basil
4 cups water (or more)

1. Combine all ingredients in slow cooker.
2. Cook on high 3-5 hours or low 8-10 hours.

Per Serving: 160 calories (5 calories from fat), 1g total fat (0g saturated, 0g trans), 0mg cholesterol, 510mg sodium, 32g total carbohydrate (10g fiber, 9g sugar), 10g protein, 200%DV vitamin A, 30%DV vitamin C, 10%DV calcium, 15%DV iron.

Football Bean Serve

Dianna R. Milhizer
Brighton, MI

Makes 12 servings
(Ideal slow-cooker size: 4-quart)

1 lb. ground turkey
1 cup minced onions
2 cups diced celery
2 cups diced carrots
2 15-oz. cans kidney beans, drained and rinsed
2 15-oz. cans pinto beans, drained and rinsed
2 15-oz. cans diced tomatoes
2 cups water
1 Tbsp. garlic powder
1 Tbsp. parsley flakes
1 Tbsp. dried oregano
1 Tbsp. cumin powder
1 Tbsp. salt

1. Brown turkey with onions in a nonstick skillet over medium heat. Add celery and carrots and cook until just wilted. Place in slow cooker.
2. Add remaining ingredients. Stir to combine.
3. Cover. Cook on low 6-8 hours.
4. Serve over brown rice. If you wish, sprinkle baked tortilla chips over top.

Per Serving: 200 calories (15 calories from fat), 1.5g total fat (0g saturated, 0g trans), 15mg cholesterol, 1280mg sodium, 29g total carbohydrate (8g fiber, 6g sugar), 18g protein, 100%DV vitamin A, 10%DV vitamin C, 10%DV calcium, 20%DV iron.

Notes:
1. This is a perfect dish to serve after an afternoon of football games.
2. This is a high-fiber meal. I usually cook dried beans from scratch the night before making the soup. You can adjust the spices, adding more or less to suit your taste.

3. If you start with dried beans, you can cook them whenever it's convenient for you and keep them in the freezer until you need them. You can then use them for soups or stews or puree them for tacos or sandwiches.

Mexican Bean Soup

Andrea Cunningham
Arlington, KS

Makes 8 servings
(Ideal slow-cooker size: 4- or 5-quart)

3/4 cup dried pinto beans, rinsed
3/4 cup dried kidney beans, rinsed
2 Tbsp. dried onion flakes
2 Tbsp. dried parsley flakes
1 Tbsp. chili powder
2 tsp. ground cumin
1 tsp. dried oregano
6 chicken bouillon cubes
1/2 cup brown rice, uncooked
8 cups water
1 cup uncooked small-cut pasta

1. Combine all ingredients except pasta in slow cooker.
2. Cover. Cook on low 8-10 hours.
3. Add pasta.
4. Cover. Cook on high 30 minutes.

Per Serving: 120 calories (10 calories from fat), 1g total fat (0g saturated, 0g trans), 0mg cholesterol, 1070mg sodium, 24g total carbohydrate (3g fiber, 2g sugar), 5g protein, 0%DV vitamin A, 0%DV vitamin C, 4%DV calcium, 8%DV iron.

This makes a good gift. Put dried beans into a 1-quart jar with lid. Put flavor packet ingredients in a sandwich-size plastic bag. Seal bag with tie or ribbon. Do the same with the pasta. Place in the jar with the beans. Attach the cooking directions to the outside of the jar. You're ready to give a healthy, nutritious gift.

Minestrone Soup

Kathy Moyer
Ottsville, PA

Makes 12 servings
(Ideal slow-cooker size: 4-quart)

1 lb. extra-lean ground beef
1 large onion, chopped
1 clove garlic, minced
2 15½-oz. cans low-sodium stewed
   tomatoes
15-oz. can kidney beans, drained
10-oz. pkg. frozen corn
2 ribs celery, sliced
2 small zucchini, sliced
1 cup uncooked macaroni
2½ cups hot water
2 beef bouillon cubes
½ tsp. salt
2 tsp. Italian seasoning

1. Brown ground beef in nonstick skillet.
2. Combine browned ground beef, onion, garlic, stewed tomatoes, kidney beans, corn, celery, zucchini, and macaroni in slow cooker.
3. Dissolve bouillon cubes in hot water. Combine with salt and Italian seasoning. Add to slow cooker.
4. Cover. Cook on low 6 hours.

Per Serving: 180 calories (35 calories from fat), 4g total fat (1.5g saturated, 0g trans), 15mg cholesterol, 430mg sodium, 24g total carbohydrate (4g fiber, 6g sugar), 13g protein, 4%DV vitamin A, 10%DV vitamin C, 4%DV calcium, 15%DV iron.

Taco Soup

Sara Kinsinger
Stuarts Draft, VA

Makes 6 servings
(Ideal slow-cooker size: 6-quart)

1 large onion, chopped
1 lb. extra-lean ground beef
1 envelope dry taco seasoning
16-oz. can kidney beans, drained
16-oz. can corn, drained
2 qts. tomato juice
¼ cup sugar
½ tsp. salt
¼-½ tsp. black pepper, according to taste
7 ozs. baked corn chips, optional
reduced fat grated cheese, optional
fat-free sour cream, optional

1. Brown the hamburger and chopped onion in a nonstick skillet. Drain.
2. Combine ground beef, onions, taco seasoning, kidney beans, corn, tomato juice, sugar, salt, and pepper in slow cooker.
3. Cook on low 4 hours or until heated through.

Per Serving: 650 calories (210 calories from fat), 23g total fat (7g saturated, 0g trans), 40mg cholesterol, 2200mg sodium, 81g total carbohydrate (9g fiber, 25g sugar), 32g protein, 40%DV vitamin A, 40%DV vitamin C, 30%DV calcium, 30%DV iron.

Note: If you prefer a less juicy stew, remove the lid during the last hour of cooking.

A word from the tester of this recipe: "Our son, Quincy, who would prefer to live on bread and chocolate alone, initially turned up his nose in disgust at the Soup. I explained that I wanted him to try this recipe and give his opinion because that's why I had made the Soup. So. . . 3 good-sized servings later. . . we determined it was a rave review."

Taco Soup

Cheri Jantzen
Houston, TX

Makes 8 servings
(Ideal slow-cooker size: 4-quart)

1 lb. ground venison
1 small onion, chopped
4-oz. can chopped green chilies, undrained
1/2 tsp. salt
1 envelope dry low-sodium taco seasoning
   mix
1 envelope dry low-sodium Ranch-style
   dressing mix
3 14 1/2-oz. cans low-sodium stewed
   tomatoes, undrained
16-oz. can kidney beans, undrained
15-oz. can pinto beans, undrained
1 1/2 cups water

1. Mix all ingredients together in large slow cooker.
2. Cover. Cook on low 8-10 hours.

Per Serving: 290 calories (30 calories from fat), 3.5g total fat (1g saturated, 0g trans), 65mg cholesterol, 1970mg sodium, 40g total carbohydrate (8g fiber, 9g sugar), 24g protein, 20%DV vitamin A, 20%DV vitamin C, 10%DV calcium, 30%DV iron.

Serve with corn bread, crackers, or biscuits.

Taco Twist Soup

Janie Steele
Moore, OK

Makes 6-8 servings
(Ideal slow-cooker size: 3- or 4-quart)

1 medium-sized onion, chopped
2 garlic cloves, minced
2 Tbsp. canola or olive oil
3 cups reduced-sodium beef broth or
   vegetable broth
15-oz. can black beans, rinsed and drained
14 1/2-oz. can diced tomatoes, undrained
1 1/2 cups picante sauce
1 cup spiral pasta, uncooked
1 small green bell pepper, chopped
2 tsp. chili powder
1 tsp. ground cumin
1/2 cup shredded reduced-fat cheese
fat-free sour cream (optional)

1. Sauté onions and garlic in oil in skillet.
2. Combine all ingredients except cheese and sour cream.
3. Cook on low 4-6 hours, or just until pasta is tender.
4. Add cheese and sour cream as desired when serving.

Per Serving: 220 calories (60 calories from fat), 6g total fat (1g saturated, 0g trans), 0mg cholesterol, 1060mg sodium, 31g total carbohydrate (6g fiber, 6g sugar), 11g protein, 10%DV vitamin A, 20%DV vitamin C, 10%DV calcium, 10%DV iron.

Note: An alternative method is to cook the pasta in 3 cups broth on the top of the stove in a saucepan, and then add it (along with the broth in which it cooked) during the last 15 minutes of the Soup's cooking time. That would allow the Soup to cook longer without risking mushy noodles, if that better fits your schedule.

Pasta and Bean Stew

Dale Peterson
Rapid City, SD

Makes 6 servings
(Ideal slow-cooker size: 3¹/2-quart)

1 cup tomatoes, chopped
3/4 cup macaroni shells, uncooked
1/4 cup onions, chopped
1/4 cup green bell peppers, chopped
1 tsp. dried basil leaves
1 tsp. Worcestershire sauce
1 clove garlic, chopped
15-oz. can kidney beans, drained
8-oz. can garbanzo beans, drained
14¹/2-oz. can fat-free chicken broth

1. Combine all ingredients in slow cooker.
2. Cook on low 5-6 hours.

Per Serving: 200 calories (10 calories from fat), 1g total fat (0g saturated, 0g trans), 0mg cholesterol, 510mg sodium, 37g total carbohydrate (6g fiber, 5g sugar), 11g protein, 6%DV vitamin A, 15%DV vitamin C, 6%DV calcium, 20%DV iron.

Note: *To add some zing, stir in 1/3 cup salsa during last 15 minutes of cooking time.*

Oh! Good! Soup!

Alix Nancy Botsford
Seminole, OK

Makes 10 servings
(Ideal slow-cooker size: 5-quart)

2 cups mixed, dried beans
2¹/2 qts. water
1 large onion, chopped
1 garlic clove, minced
28-oz. can low-sodium diced tomatoes
1/2 cup red bell pepper, chopped
1/2 cup celery, chopped
juice of 1 lemon
1 tsp. salt
1 tsp. black pepper
several drops of Tabasco sauce, according to your taste preference
1 cup brown rice, uncooked
1 cup assorted small pasta, cooked

1. Sort and wash beans. Cover with water. Soak 2-6 hours. Drain.
2. Place beans in slow cooker. Add 2¹/2 quarts fresh water.
3. Cover. Cook on high 2 hours.
4. Add all remaining ingredients except pasta.
5. Add enough water so all ingredients are covered.
6. Cover. Cook on high 4-6 hours or on low 8-10 hours.
7. Add pasta just before serving.

Per Serving: 210 calories (10 calories from fat), 1g total fat (0g saturated, 0g trans), 5mg cholesterol, 470mg sodium, 41g total carbohydrate (11g fiber, 6g sugar), 11g protein, 10%DV vitamin A, 20%DV vitamin C, 10%DV calcium, 20%DV iron.

When using pasta for other dishes, always reserve a small handful in a reclosable bag. That way you will have a variety of shapes for this soup.

Vegetarian Soup

Jane Meiser
Harrisonburg, VA

Makes 6 servings
(Ideal slow-cooker size: 3¹/2-quart)

16-oz. can low-sodium diced tomatoes
2 15-oz. cans kidney or pinto beans,
　drained, divided
1 cup onions, chopped
1 clove garlic, minced
8³/4-oz. can whole-kernel corn, drained
¹/2 cup low-sodium picante sauce
¹/2 cup water
¹/2 tsp. salt
1 tsp. ground cumin
1 tsp. dried oregano
1 green bell pepper, diced
reduced-fat shredded cheddar cheese,
　optional

1. Drain tomatoes, reserving juice.
2. Combine juice and 1 can beans in food processor bowl. Process until fairly smooth.
3. Combine all ingredients except green peppers and cheese in slow cooker.
4. Cover. Cook on high 4-5 hours.
5. During last half hour add green peppers.
6. Ladle into bowls to serve. Top with cheese, if desired.

Per Serving: 180 calories (10 calories from fat), 1g total fat (0g saturated, 0g trans), 0mg cholesterol, 990mg sodium, 36g total carbohydrate (8g fiber, 9g sugar), 9g protein, 6%DV vitamin A, 30%DV vitamin C, 8%DV calcium, 15%DV iron.

Navy Bean Vegetable Soup

Lavina Hochstedler
Grand Blanc, MI

Makes 12 servings
(Ideal slow-cooker size: 6-quart)

4 medium-sized carrots, thinly sliced
2 celery ribs, chopped
1 medium-sized onion, chopped
2 cups fully cooked ham cubes, trimmed
　of fat
1¹/2 cups dried navy beans
1.68-oz. pkg. dry vegetable soup mix
1 envelope dry onion soup mix
1 bay leaf
¹/2 tsp. black pepper
8 cups water
1 tsp. salt, optional

1. Combine all ingredients in slow cooker.
2. Cover. Cook on low 9-10 hours.
3. Discard bay leaf before serving.

Per Serving: 160 calories (20 calories from fat), 2.5g total fat (1g saturated, 0g trans), 20mg cholesterol, 520mg sodium, 22g total carbohydrate (8g fiber, 4g sugar), 14g protein, 100%DV vitamin A, 0%DV vitamin C, 6%DV calcium, 15%DV iron.

Note: If you like the taste, and your diet allows, you may want to substitute smoked turkey sausage or kielbasa in place of the ham.

Gourmet White Chili

Rashell Harris
Wichita, KS

Makes 8 servings
(Ideal slow-cooker size: 5-quart)

1 lb. dried great northern white beans
1 Tbsp. olive oil
2 medium-sized onions, chopped
4 cloves garlic, minced
8-oz. can chopped green chilies
2 tsp. ground cumin
2 tsp. dried oregano
1/4 tsp. ground cloves
1/4 tsp cayenne pepper
2 lbs. boneless, skinless, uncooked chicken breasts, cubed
6 cups low-fat, low-sodium chicken broth
2 cups grated low-fat, or fat-free, cheese, divided
1 tsp. salt
1/2 tsp. black pepper

Garnishes:
1 cup fat-free sour cream
1 cup salsa
1/2 cup cilantro

1. Cover beans with water and soak overnight. Drain, discarding soaking water.
2. Sauté onions in olive oil until clear. Add garlic, green chilies, cumin, oregano, cloves, and cayenne. Sauté for 2 minutes more. (This step may be skipped if you are pressed for time.)
3. Place all ingredients in slow cooker except cheese and garnishes.
4. Cover. Cook on low 8-10 hours or on high 4-6 hours.
5. Add 1 cup of cheese. Stir until melted.
6. Serve in bowls topped with garnishes and remaining cheese.

Per Serving: 510 calories (70 calories from fat), 8g total fat (3g saturated, 0g trans), 95mg cholesterol, 770mg sodium, 46g total carbohydrate (11g fiber, 11g sugar), 60g protein, 10%DV vitamin A, 10%DV vitamin C, 50%DV calcium, 50%DV iron.

White Chicken Chili

Virginia Graybill
Hershey, PA

Makes 6 servings
(Ideal slow-cooker size: 3- or 4-quart)

1 Tbsp. olive oil
3/4 lb. uncooked boneless, skinless chicken breast, cubed
1 large onion, chopped
2 garlic cloves, minced
1 cup fat-free chicken broth
2 15 1/2-oz. cans navy beans, rinsed and drained
1 tsp. dry mustard
1 tsp. ground cumin
1/2 tsp. salt
1/4 tsp. black pepper
4 cups (4 ozs.) baked tortilla chips
1/2 cup (2 ozs.) shredded reduced-fat extra-sharp cheddar cheese
fat-free sour cream or fat-free yogurt

1. Warm oil in a large skillet over medium-high heat.
2. Add chicken and cook 10 minutes, or until chicken is no longer pink. Stir frequently. Remove chicken and set aside.
3. Add onion and garlic to skillet. Cook 5 minutes or until tender.
4. Spoon chicken, onion, and garlic into slow cooker.
5. Add broth, beans, mustard powder, cumin, salt, and pepper.
6. Cover. Cook on low 5-6 hours.
7. Serve over tortilla chips and sprinkle with cheese.
8. Place a dab of fat-free sour cream or fat-free yogurt on each serving.

Per Serving: 830 calories (90 calories from fat), 10g total fat (1.5g saturated, 0g trans), 35mg cholesterol, 1830mg sodium, 154g total carbohydrate (17g fiber, 4g sugar), 35g protein, 2%DV vitamin A, 0%DV vitamin C, 35%DV calcium, 30%DV iron.

Chicken Chili with Pesto

Marilyn Mowry
Irving, TX

Makes 4 servings
(Ideal slow-cooker size: 5-quart)

³/₄ lb. boneless, skinless chicken breast, cut into bite-sized pieces
2 tsp. vegetable oil, optional
³/₄ cup onion, finely chopped
1¹/₂ cups carrots, finely chopped
³/₄ cup red bell pepper, finely chopped
³/₄ cup celery, sliced thin
¹/₄ cup canned chopped green chilies
³/₄ tsp. dried oregano
¹/₂ tsp. ground cumin
¹/₄ tsp. salt
¹/₈ tsp. black pepper
16-oz. can cannellini beans or other white beans, rinsed and drained
14¹/₂-oz. can fat-free, low-sodium chicken broth
3 Tbsp. classic pesto sauce (recipe below)

1. Sauté chicken in a nonstick skillet, or in a traditional skillet with oil.
2. Combine all ingredients except pesto sauce in slow cooker.
3. Cook on low 6-8 hours.
4. Stir in pesto just before serving.

Per Serving: 370 calories (110 calories from fat), 12 total fat (2.5g saturated, 0g trans), 50mg cholesterol, 820mg sodium, 36g total carbohydrate (9g fiber, 10g sugar), 29g protein, 200%DV vitamin A, 40%DV vitamin C, 15%DV calcium, 20%DV iron.

Pesto

Makes ³/₄ cup

2 Tbsp. walnuts or pine nuts, coarsely chopped
2 garlic cloves, peeled
3 Tbsp. extra-virgin olive oil
4 cups fresh basil leaves (about 4 ozs.)
¹/₂ cup grated Parmesan cheese
¹/₄ tsp. salt

1. Mince nuts and garlic in food processor.
2. Add oil, and pulse 3 times.
3. Add basil, cheese, and salt. Process until finely minced, scraping sides of bowl.

Dawn's Healthy Chicken Chili

Dawn Day
Westminster, CA

Makes 10 servings
(Ideal slow-cooker size: 6-quart)

3 cups chicken, cooked and cubed
1 large onion, chopped
12-oz. can low-sodium chopped tomatoes
6-oz. can low-sodium tomato paste
3 12-oz. cans low-sodium chili beans, undrained
3 Tbsp. chili powder
1 cup frozen corn

1. Combine all ingredients in slow cooker. Stir well.
2. Cover. Cook on low 8 hours.
3. Serve with low-fat grated cheese.

Per Serving: 250 calories (35 calories from fat), 4g total fat (1g saturated, 0g trans), 60mg cholesterol, 560mg sodium, 26g total carbohydrate (7g fiber, 2g sugar), 28g protein, 30%DV vitamin A, 10%DV vitamin C, 6%DV calcium, 15%DV iron.

Taco Chicken Soup

Colleen Heatwole
Burton, MI
Janie Steele
Moore, OK

Makes 4-6 servings
(Ideal slow-cooker size: 4- or 5-quart)

1 envelope dry reduced-sodium taco seasoning
32-oz. can low-sodium V8 juice
16-oz. jar salsa
15-oz. can black beans
1 cup frozen corn
1 cup frozen peas
2 whole chicken breasts, cooked and shredded

1. Combine all ingredients except corn, peas, and chicken in slow cooker.
2. Cover. Cook on low 4-6 hours. Add remaining vegetables and chicken 1 hour before serving.

Per Serving: 210 calories (15 calories from fat), 2g total fat (0g saturated, 0g trans), 25mg cholesterol, 970mg sodium, 35g total carbohydrate (8g fiber, 9g sugar), 17g protein, 40%DV vitamin A, 40%DV vitamin C, 8%DV calcium, 20%DV iron.

Note: Garnish individual servings with chopped fresh cilantro, and, if diets allow, with chunks of avocado.

Chicken Tortilla Soup

Becky Harder
Monument, CO

Makes 8 servings
(Ideal slow-cooker size: 4- or 5-quart)

4 uncooked boneless, skinless chicken breast halves
2 15-oz. cans black beans, undrained
2 15-oz. cans low-sodium Mexican stewed tomatoes, or Rotel tomatoes
1 cup low-sodium salsa (mild, medium, or hot, whichever you prefer)
4-oz. can chopped green chilies, undrained
14½-oz. can low-sodium tomato sauce
baked tortilla chips
2 cups grated fat-free cheese

1. Combine all ingredients except chips and cheese in large slow cooker.
2. Cover. Cook on low 8 hours.
3. Just before serving, remove chicken breasts and slice into bite-sized pieces. Stir into soup.
4. To serve, put a handful of chips in each individual soup bowl. Ladle soup over chips. Top with cheese.

Per Serving: 330 calories (20 calories from fat), 2.5g total fat (0g saturated, 0g trans), 35mg cholesterol, 1760mg sodium, 55g total carbohydrate (10g fiber, 15g sugar), 28g protein, 10%DV vitamin A, 15%DV vitamin C, 10%DV calcium, 15%DV iron.

Tortilla Soup

Janie Steele
Moore, OK

Makes 7 servings
(Ideal slow-cooker size: 3½- or 4-quart)

16-oz. can fat-free refried beans
15-oz. can black beans, rinsed and drained
14-oz. can fat-free chicken broth
1½ cups frozen corn
¾ cup chunky salsa
¾ cup boneless skinless cooked chicken, cubed
¼ cup water
2 cups reduced-fat shredded cheese (divided)
1 bag baked tortilla chips

1. Combine all ingredients except cheese and chips.
2. Cook on low 3-4 hours, or until heated through.
3. Add half of cheese. Stir until melted
4. Crush chips in bowls. Add soup. Top with sour cream and more crushed chips.

Per Serving: 370 calories (40 calories from fat), 4.5g total fat (1.5g saturated, 0g trans), 20mg cholesterol, 1130mg sodium, 60g total carbohydrate (10g fiber, 3g sugar), 25g protein, 4%DV vitamin A, 4%DV vitamin C, 25%DV calcium, 20%DV iron.

Southwest Corn Soup

Susan Tjon
Austin, TX

Makes 6 servings
(Ideal slow-cooker size: 5-quart)

2 4-oz. cans chopped green chilies,
  undrained
2 small zucchini, cut into bite-sized pieces
1 medium-sized onion, thinly sliced
3 cloves garlic, minced
1 tsp. ground cumin
3 14½-oz. cans fat-free, sodium-reduced
  chicken broth
1½-2 cups shredded, cooked turkey
15-oz. can chickpeas or black beans,
  rinsed and drained
10-oz. pkg. frozen corn
1 tsp. dried oregano
½ cup chopped cilantro

1. Combine all ingredients in slow cooker.
2. Cook on low 4 hours.

Per Serving: 240 calories (40 calories from fat), 4.5g total
fat (1g saturated, 0g trans), 25mg cholesterol, 520mg
sodium, 31g total carbohydrate (7g fiber, 5g sugar), 21g
protein, 6%DV vitamin A, 20%DV vitamin C, 10%DV
calcium, 20%DV iron.

Note: *For a twist on the soup's flavor and
consistency, substitute 1 14½-oz. can low-sodium
diced tomatoes for one of the cans of chicken
broth.*

Salsa Soup

Esther J. Yoder
Hartville, OH

Makes 10 servings
(Ideal slow-cooker size: 4-quart)

1 lb. mild sausage, sliced
1 qt. white navy beans, undrained
2 cups mild or medium salsa
4 cups fat-free chicken broth

1. Brown sausage in skillet and drain well.
2. Combine all ingredients in slow cooker.
3. Cook on low 8-10 hours or high 4-6
hours.

Per Serving: 240 calories (80 calories from fat), 9g total fat
(3g saturated, 0g trans), 15mg cholesterol, 480mg sodium,
27g total carbohydrate (6g fiber, 5g sugar), 14g protein,
6%DV vitamin A, 6%DV vitamin C, 10%DV calcium,
25%DV iron.

Notes:

*If you like a thickened soup, mix ¼ cup
cornstarch with ¼ cup water. Remove 1 cup hot
soup broth from cooker about 15 minutes before
end of cooking time. Whisk together with
cornstarch mixture. When smooth, stir back into
soup in cooker and stir until thickened.*

*This can be served over rice, in addition to
serving it as a soup.*

Taco Bean Soup

Karen Waggoner
Joplin, MO

Makes 12 servings
(Ideal slow-cooker size: 6-quart)

³⁄₄ lb. lean pork sausage
1 lb. extra-lean ground beef
1 envelope dry low-sodium taco seasoning
4 cups water
2 16-oz. cans kidney beans, rinsed and drained
2 14¹⁄₂-oz. cans low-sodium stewed tomatoes
2 14¹⁄₂-oz. cans diced Mexican tomatoes with juice
16-oz. jar chunky salsa

1. Cook sausage and beef in a nonstick skillet over medium heat until no longer pink. Spoon into slow cooker.
2. Add taco seasoning and mix well.
3. Stir in water, beans, tomatoes, and salsa.
4. Cover. Cook on high 1 hour.
5. Uncover. Cook another 30 minutes. Stir occasionally. Serve.

Per Serving: 320 calories (130 calories from fat), 14g total fat (5g saturated, 0g trans), 40mg cholesterol, 1830mg sodium, 27g total carbohydrate (7g fiber, 8g sugar), 20g protein, 20%DV vitamin A, 10%DV vitamin C, 10%DV calcium, 20%DV iron.

Note: If your diet allows, you may want to garnish individual servings with low-fat sour cream, shredded low-fat cheddar cheese, and a sprinkling of sliced ripe olives.

Bean and Ham Soup

Dolores Kratz, Souderton, PA

Makes 10 servings
(Ideal slow-cooker size: 7-quart, or 2 4-quart cookers)

1 lb. mixed dry beans
ham bone from half a ham butt
1¹⁄₂ cups ham, cubed
1 large onion, chopped
³⁄₄ cup celery, chopped
³⁄₄ cup carrots, sliced or chopped
15-oz. can low-sodium diced tomatoes
2 Tbsp. parsley, chopped
1 cup low-sodium tomato juice
5 cups water
2 Tbsp. Worcestershire sauce
1 bay leaf
1 tsp. prepared mustard
¹⁄₂ tsp. chili powder
juice of 1 lemon
1 tsp. salt
¹⁄₂ tsp. black pepper

1. Place beans in saucepan. Cover with water and soak overnight. Drain.
2. Cover beans with fresh water and cook in saucepan 30 minutes uncovered. Drain again. Discard water.
3. Combine beans with remaining ingredients in slow cooker.
4. Cover. Cook on low 9-11 hours.
5. Remove bay leaf and ham bone before serving.

Per Serving: 220 calories (30 calories from fat), 3g total fat (0.5g saturated, 0g trans), 20mg cholesterol, 200mg sodium, 34g total carbohydrate (11g fiber, 7g sugar), 17g protein, 50%DV vitamin A, 10%DV vitamin C, 10%DV calcium, 25%DV iron.

Note: I chop the vegetables and mix the other ingredients together in the evening and then refrigerate them overnight. I have less work in the morning. A wonderful aroma greets the family as they come home for the evening meal. And it's healthy, too!

Italian Soup with Pasta and Beans

Millie Schellenburg, Washington, NJ

Makes 4 servings
(Ideal slow-cooker size: 4-quart)

1 smoked ham hock
1/2 lb. dry cannellini beans
6-oz. can tomato paste
10 cloves garlic, minced
1/2 tsp. hot red pepper flakes, if desired
1/2 lb. pasta, cooked

1. Combine ham hock, beans, tomato paste, garlic, and hot pepper flakes in slow cooker. Cover with water.
2. Cover. Cook on high 4 hours or low 6-8 hours, until ham falls off the bone and the beans are tender.
3. Debone ham. Stir bite-sized chunks of meat back into cooker.
4. Serve over hot pasta.

Per Serving: 210 calories (35 calories from fat), 4g total fat (1g saturated, 0g trans), 35mg cholesterol, 170mg sodium, 33g total carbohydrate (5g fiber, 2g sugar), 11g protein, 15%DV vitamin A, 20%DV vitamin C, 6%DV calcium, 15%DV iron.

Pinto Beans and Ham

Barbara Walker
Sturgis, SD

Makes 10 servings
(Ideal slow-cooker size: 5-quart)

1 lb. dried pinto beans
5 1/2 cups water
1/4 lb. cooked ham, chopped
1 clove garlic, minced
1 Tbsp. chili powder
1 tsp. salt
1 tsp. black pepper
1/4 tsp. dried oregano
1/4 tsp. ground cumin

1. Cover bean with water and soak overnight, or 6-8 hours.
1. In the morning, drain and rinse beans, discard soaking water, and put beans in slow cooker.
2. Add remaining ingredients, including 5 1/2 cups fresh water.
3. Cover. Cook on low 10 hours.
4. Stir once or twice if possible during cooking time.

Per Serving: 60 calories (10 calories from fat), 1g total fat (0g saturated, 0g trans), 5mg cholesterol, 520mg sodium, 8g total carbohydrate (2g fiber, 1g sugar), 4g protein, 6%DV vitamin A, 2%DV vitamin C, 2%DV calcium, 6%DV iron

Navy Bean and Bacon Chowder

Ruth A. Feister
Narvon, PA

Makes 6 servings
(Ideal slow-cooker size: 4-quart)

1½ cups dried navy beans
2 cups cold water
5 slices lean turkey bacon, cooked and crumbled
2 medium-sized carrots, sliced
1 rib celery, sliced
1 medium onion, chopped
1 tsp. dried Italian seasoning
⅛ tsp. black pepper
2 or 3 bay leaves, optional
46-oz. can fat-free, low-sodium chicken broth
1 cup fat-free milk

1. Soak beans in 2 cups cold water for 8 hours.
2. After beans have soaked, drain, if necessary, and place in slow cooker.
3. Add all remaining ingredients, except milk, to slow cooker.
4. Cover. Cook on low 7-9 hours, or until beans are crisp-tender.
5. Place 2 cups cooked bean mixture into blender. Process until smooth. Return to slow cooker.
6. Add milk. Cover and heat on high 10 minutes.

Per Serving: 260 calories (30 calories from fat), 3g total fat (1g saturated, 0g trans), 10mg cholesterol, 400mg sodium, 38g total carbohydrate (14g fiber, 8g sugar), 21g protein, 80%DV vitamin A, 0%DV vitamin C, 15%DV calcium, 30%DV iron.

Note: If you like a zippier soup, you may want to add 1 tsp. ground cumin to Step 3.

Cassoulet Chowder

Miriam Friesen
Staunton, VA

Makes 8 servings
(Ideal slow-cooker size: 3½- or 4-quart)

1¼ cups dry pinto beans
4 cups water
½ lb. lean sausage, cut in ¼" slices, cooked and drained
2 cups cubed cooked lean chicken
2 cups cubed cooked lean ham
1½ cups sliced carrots
8-oz. can low-sodium tomato sauce
¾ cup dry red wine
½ cup chopped onions
½ tsp. garlic powder
1 bay leaf

1. Combine beans and water in large saucepan. Bring to boil. Reduce heat and simmer 1½ hours. Refrigerate beans and liquid 4-8 hours.
2. Combine all ingredients in slow cooker.
3. Cover. Cook on low 8-10 hours or on high 4 hours. If the chowder seems too thin, remove lid during last 30 minutes of cooking time to allow it to thicken.
4. Remove bay leaf before serving.

Per Serving: 200 calories (70 calories from fat), 8g total fat (2.5g saturated, 0g trans), 55mg cholesterol, 360mg sodium, 10g total carbohydrate (2g fiber, 3g sugar), 20g protein, 80%DV vitamin A, 0%DV vitamin C, 4%DV calcium, 8%DV iron.

Black-Eyed Peas

Wendy McPhillips
Wichita, KS

Makes 4-5 servings
(Ideal slow-cooker size: 5-quart)

1-lb. pkg. dried black-eyed peas
1 1/2 cups ham, diced
6 cups water
1/2 tsp. salt
1/4 tsp. black pepper

1. Combine all ingredients in slow cooker.
2. Cover. Cook on low 6-8 hours.
3. Serve with corn bread.

Per Serving: 160 calories (40 calories from fat), 4g total fat (1.5g saturated, 0g trans), 40mg cholesterol, 270mg sodium, 14g total carbohydrate (3g fiber, 0g sugar), 17g protein, 0%DV vitamin A, 0%DV vitamin C, 2%DV calcium, 10%DV iron.

Note: If you want a zestier dish, and if your diet allows, consider adding 2 4-oz. cans diced green chilies, a pinch of red pepper flakes, or several drops Tabasco sauce to Step 1.

Beans with Kielbasa

Colleen Heatwole
Burton, MI

Makes 8 servings
(Ideal slow-cooker size: 4-quart)

1 medium-sized green bell pepper, chopped
15 1/2-oz. can great northern beans
15 1/2-oz. can pinto beans
14 1/2-oz. can low-sodium stewed tomatoes, or diced tomatoes with green chilies
8-oz. can low-sodium tomato sauce
1 large onion, chopped
1 lb. reduced-fat smoked turkey kielbasa, cut in 1" pieces
1 clove garlic, minced
1/4 tsp. black pepper

1. Combine all ingredients in slow cooker.
2. Cover. Cook on low 6-8 hours.

Per Serving: 210 calories (45 calories from fat), 5g total fat (1.5g saturated, 0g trans), 35mg cholesterol, 1010mg sodium, 25g total carbohydrate (7g fiber, 6g sugar), 15g protein, 10%DV vitamin A, 20%DV vitamin C, 8%DV calcium, 15%DV iron.

Note: This is juicy enough to serve over rice, mashed potatoes, or your favorite pasta.

Turkey Sausage Stew

Sheridy Steele
Ardmore, OK

Makes 6 servings
(Ideal slow-cooker size: 3 1/2-4-quart)

1/2 lb. turkey sausage, removed from casing
1 large onion, chopped
2 garlic cloves, minced
3/4 cup carrots, chopped
1 fennel bulb, chopped
1/2 cup celery, chopped
10 3/4-oz. can fat-free, reduced-sodium chicken broth
3 medium tomatoes, peeled, seeded, and chopped
1 tsp. dried basil
1 tsp. dried oregano
1/4 tsp. salt
1 cup uncooked shell pasta
15-oz. can navy beans, drained and rinsed
1/2 cup lowfat Parmesan cheese

1. In nonstick skillet, brown turkey sausage, onion, and garlic. Drain well.
2. Combine all ingredients except cheese in slow cooker.
3. Cook on low 8-9 hours.
4. Sprinkle with cheese to serve.

Per Serving: 280 calories (60 calories from fat), 7 total fat (2.5g saturated, 0g trans), 35mg cholesterol, 930mg sodium, 36g total carbohydrate (7g fiber, 6g sugar), 20g protein, 80%DV vitamin A, 20%DV vitamin C, 20%DV calcium, 20%DV iron.

White Bean Fennel Soup

Janie Steele
Moore, OK

Makes 6 servings
(Ideal slow-cooker size: 5-quart)

1 Tbsp. olive or canola oil
1 large onion, chopped
1 small fennel bulb, sliced thin
5 cups fat-free chicken broth
15-oz. can white kidney, or cannellini, beans, rinsed and drained
14 1/2-oz. can diced tomatoes, undrained
1 tsp. dried thyme
1/4 tsp. black pepper
1 bay leaf
3 cups chopped fresh spinach

1. Sauté onions and fennel in oil in skillet until brown.
2. Combine onions, fennel, broth, beans, tomatoes, thyme, pepper, and bay leaf.
3. Cook on low for several hours, or on high for 1 hour, until fennel and onions are tender.
4. Remove bay leaf.
5. Add spinach about 10 minutes before serving.

Per Serving: 160 calories (25 calories from fat), 3g total fat (0g saturated, 0g trans), 0mg cholesterol, 690mg sodium, 22g total carbohydrate (8g fiber, 4g sugar), 13g protein, 100%DV vitamin A, 40%DV vitamin C, 20%DV calcium, 35%DV iron.

White Bean and Barley Soup

Sharon Miller
Holmesville, OH

Makes 12 servings
(Ideal slow-cooker size: 6-quart)

1 large onion, chopped
2 garlic cloves, minced
1 Tbsp. olive or canola oil
2 24-oz. cans great northern beans (or
   equal amount prepared from dried
   beans), undrained
4 cups no-fat, low-sodium chicken broth
4 cups water
2 large carrots, chunked
2 medium-sized green or red bell peppers,
   chunked
2 celery ribs, chunked
1/2 cup quick-cooking barley
1/4 cup fresh parsley, chopped
2 bay leaves
1/2 tsp. dried thyme
1/4 tsp. black pepper
28-oz. can diced tomatoes, undrained

   1. Sauté onion and garlic in oil in skillet
until just wilted.
   2. Combine all ingredients in slow cooker.
   3. Cook on low 8-10 hours.
   4. Discard bay leaves before serving.

Per Serving: 210 calories (15 calories from fat), 2g total fat
(0g saturated, 0g trans),0mg cholesterol, 260mg sodium,
36g total carbohydrate (9g fiber, 6g sugar), 12g protein,
50%DV vitamin A, 20%DV vitamin C, 15%DV calcium,
20%DV iron.

Notes:
   *1. If you wish, use pearl barley instead of
quick-cooking, but cook it on the stove and add it
halfway through the cooking cycle.*
   *2. If you want, and your diet allows, you may
want to add 1/2-3/4 tsp. salt in Step 2.*

BBB Soup
(Baby Butter Bean Soup)

Dorothy VanDeest
Memphis, TN

Makes 4 servings
(Ideal slow-cooker size: 3-quart)

10-oz. pkg. frozen baby butter beans
2 chicken bouillon cubes
1 1/2 cups boiling water
1/2 to 3/4 cup carrots, very thinly sliced
1/4 cup chopped onions
1/4 cup chopped celery
1/4 cup chopped green bell peppers
dash of dried basil
dash of dried thyme
black pepper to taste

   1. Cook baby butter beans as directed on
package. Drain.
   2. Dissolve bouillon cubes in boiling water.
Cool.
   3. Combine butter beans and chicken broth
in blender. Blend until smooth
   4. Pour into slow cooker. Add remaining
ingredients.
   5. Cover and cook on low 6-10 hours or on
high 2-3 hours.

Per Serving: 110 calories (5 calories from fat), 0.5g total fat
(0g saturated, 0g trans), 0mg cholesterol, 650mg sodium,
22g total carbohydrate (5g fiber, 5g sugar), 6g protein,
30%DV vitamin A, 10%DV vitamin C, 4%DV calcium,
10%DV iron

Vegetables

Vegetable Medley

Deborah Santiago
Lancaster, PA
Judi Manos
West Islip, NY

Makes 8 servings
(Ideal slow-cooker size—4-quart)

4 cups potatoes, diced and peeled
1½ cups frozen whole-kernel corn
4 medium-sized tomatoes, seeded and diced
1 cup carrots, sliced
½ cup onions, chopped
¾ tsp. salt
½ tsp. sugar
¾ tsp. dill weed
¼ tsp. black pepper
½ tsp. dried basil
¼ tsp. dried rosemary

1. Combine all ingredients in slow cooker.
2. Cover. Cook on low 5-6 hours, or until vegetables are tender.

Per Serving: 120 calories (5 calories from fat), 0.5g total fat (0g saturated, 0g trans), 0mg cholesterol, 240mg sodium, 27g total carbohydrate (4g fiber, 5g sugar), 4g protein, 80%DV vitamin A, 20%DV vitamin C, 2%DV calcium, 6%DV iron.

Vegetables with Pasta

Donna Lantgen
Rapid City, SD

Makes 6 servings
(Ideal slow-cooker size: 3½- or 4-quart)

2 cups chopped zucchini
½ cup cherry tomatoes, cut in half
half green or red bell pepper, sliced
half medium-sized onion, sliced
½ cup fresh mushrooms, sliced
4 cloves garlic, minced
1 Tbsp. olive oil
1 Tbsp. Italian seasoning
8-oz. can tomato sauce

1. Combine all ingredients in slow cooker.
2. Cook on low 6 hours or until vegetables are tender.

Per Serving: 80 calories (25 calories from fat), 3g total fat (0g saturated, 0g trans), 0mg cholesterol, 580mg sodium, 12g total carbohydrate (2g fiber, 6g sugar), 4g protein, 20%DV vitamin A, 30%DV vitamin C, 2%DV calcium, 6%DV iron.

Note: Serve with your favorite cooked pasta and top with grated low-fat Parmesan or mozzarella cheese.

Vegetable Rice Casserole

Esther Martin
Ephrata, PA

Makes 8 servings
(Ideal slow-cooker size: 6-quart)

¼ cup uncooked rice
1 lb. zucchini, sliced
1 lb. yellow summer squash, sliced
1 large onion, sliced
1 Tbsp. dried basil, divided
1 medium-sized green bell pepper,
    julienned
4 celery ribs with leaves, chopped
2 large tomatoes, sliced
¼ cup packed brown sugar
½ tsp. salt
¼ tsp. black pepper
2 Tbsp. olive oil

1. Spread rice in slow cooker that has been coated with fat-free cooking spray.
2. Layer in zucchini, yellow squash, onion, and half the basil.
3. Top with green pepper, celery, and tomatoes.
4. Combine brown sugar, salt, and pepper. Sprinkle over vegetables. Drizzle with oil.
5. Cover. Cook on high 3-4 hours, or until the vegetables reach the degree of "doneness" that you prefer.
6. Sprinkle with remaining basil when finished.

Per Serving: 100 calories (35 calories from fat), 4g total fat (0.5g saturated, 0g trans), 0mg cholesterol, 170mg sodium, 16g total carbohydrate (3g fiber, 11g sugar), 2g protein, 10%DV vitamin A, 30%DV vitamin C, 4%DV calcium, 6%DV iron.

Notes:
1. If your diet allows, and if you prefer a less juicy dish, increase the amount of rice to ½ cup.
2. If you want to use fresh basil instead of dried, stir in 3 Tbsp. just before serving the dish.

Vegetable Casserole

Eileen Eash
Carlsbad, NM

Makes 12 servings
(Ideal slow-cooker size: 5- or 6-quart)

2 cups low-sodium stewed tomatoes with
    juice
2 cups carrots, sliced
2 cups onions, diced
2 cups celery, chopped
¾ cup green bell pepper, chopped
2 Tbsp. minute tapioca
2 tsp. seasoned salt
1 cup cabbage, shredded
½ tsp. black pepper
2 cups fresh green beans

1. Combine all ingredients except beans in slightly greased slow cooker.
2. Cover. Cook on low 4-5 hours.
3. Add beans.
4. Cook an additional 2 hours.

Per Serving: 50 calories (0 calories from fat), 0g total fat (0g saturated, 0g trans), 0mg cholesterol, 290mg sodium, 11g total carbohydrate (3g fiber, 6g sugar), 2g protein, 80%DV vitamin A, 20%DV vitamin C, 4%DV calcium, 6%DV iron.

"Stir-Fry" Veggies

Shari and Dale Mast
Harrisonburg, VA

Makes 8 servings
(Ideal slow-cooker size: 6-quart)

16-oz. bag baby carrots
4 ribs celery, chunked
1 medium-sized onion, diced
14¹/₂-oz. can low-sodium Italian-style
    stewed tomatoes
¹/₂ tsp. dried basil
¹/₂ tsp. dried oregano
¹/₂ tsp. salt
1 large red or yellow bell pepper, diced
1 small head cabbage, cut up
1 lb. raw broccoli, cut up

1. Combine carrots, celery, onion, tomatoes, basil, oregano, and salt in slow cooker.
2. Cover. Cook on high 3-4 hours or on low 6-8 hours, stirring occasionally.
3. Stir in pepper, cabbage, and broccoli.
4. Cook 1 hour more on high, or 2 hours more on low, stirring occasionally. You may need to add a little water if there is not liquid left on the veggies.

Per Serving: 90 calories (10 calories from fat), 1g total fat (0g saturated, 0g trans), 0mg cholesterol, 220mg sodium, 19g total carbohydrate (7g fiber, 10g sugar), 4g protein, 200%DV vitamin A, 100%DV vitamin C, 10%DV calcium, 15%DV iron.

Note: *Serve this as a side dish, or as a main dish over hot cooked rice, garnished with Parmesan cheese.*

Tofu and Vegetables

Donna Lantgen
Rapid City, SD

Makes 6 servings
(Ideal slow-cooker size: 4- or 5-quart)

16 ozs. firm tofu, drained and crumbled
¹/₂ cup onion, chopped
¹/₂ cup celery, chopped
2 cups bok choy, chopped
2 cups napa cabbage, chopped
¹/₂ cup pea pods, cut in half

1. Combine all ingredients in slow cooker.
2. Cook on low 6 hours.

Per Serving: 60 calories (25 calories from fat), 3g total fat (0g saturated, 0g trans), 0mg cholesterol, 25mg sodium, 4g total carbohydrate (1g fiber, 2g sugar), 6g protein, 10%DV vitamin A, 10%DV vitamin C, 10%DV calcium, 8%DV iron.

I like to serve this with soy sauce on a bed of rice.

Chinese Vegetables

Rebecca Leichty, Harrisonburg, VA

Makes 6 servings
(Ideal slow-cooker size: 5- or 6-quart)

1 bunch celery, sliced on the diagonal
1 large onion, sliced
1-lb. can bean sprouts, drained
12-oz. pkg. chop-suey vegetables
8-oz. can water chestnuts, drained
2 4-oz. cans sliced mushrooms, drained
1 Tbsp. sugar
3 Tbsp. low-sodium soy sauce
3/4 cup water
1/4 tsp. black pepper, or to taste

1. Spray slow cooker with fat-free cooking spray.
2. Combine all ingredients in slow cooker.
3. Cover. Cook on low 3-6 hours, depending upon how soft or crunchy you like your vegetables.

Per Serving: 120 calories (0 calories from fat), 0g total fat (0g saturated, 0g trans), 0mg cholesterol, 135mg sodium, 28g total carbohydrate (5g fiber, 5g sugar), 4g protein, 4%DV vitamin A, 40%DV vitamin C, 8%DV calcium, 8%DV iron.

Lemon Red Potatoes

Joyce Shackelford, Green Bay, WI

Makes 6 servings
(Ideal slow-cooker size: 4-quart)

1 1/2 lbs. medium-sized red potatoes
1/4 cup water
2 Tbsp. butter, melted
1 Tbsp. lemon juice
3 Tbsp. fresh chives, snipped
chopped fresh parsley
1 tsp. salt
1/2 tsp. black pepper

1. Cut a strip of peel from around the middle of each potato. Place potatoes and water in slow cooker.
2. Cover. Cook on high 2 1/2-3 hours.
3. Drain.
4. Combine butter, lemon juice, chives, and parsley. Pour over potatoes. Toss to coat.
5. Season with salt and pepper.

Per Serving: 120 calories (35 calories from fat), 4g total fat (2.5g saturated, 0g trans), 10mg cholesterol, 400mg sodium, 18g total carbohydrate (2g fiber, 1g sugar), 2g protein, 0%DV vitamin A, 20%DV vitamin C, 2%DV calcium, 6%DV iron.

Rustic Potatoes au Gratin

Nancy Savage
Factoryville, PA

Makes 6 servings
(Ideal slow-cooker size: 5-quart)

1/2 cup skim milk
10 3/4-oz. can light condensed cheddar cheese soup
8-oz. pkg. fat-free cream cheese, softened
1 clove garlic, minced
1/4 tsp. ground nutmeg
1/4 tsp. black pepper
2 lbs. baking potatoes (about 7) cut into 1/4"-thick slices
1 small onion, thinly sliced
paprika

1. Heat milk in small saucepan over medium heat until small bubbles form around edge of pan. Remove from heat.
2. Add soup, cream cheese, garlic, nutmeg, and pepper to pan. Stir until smooth.
3. Spray inside of slow cooker with nonfat cooking spray. Layer one-quarter of potatoes and onions on bottom of slow cooker.
4. Top with one-quarter of soup mixture. Repeat layers 3 times.

5. Cover. Cook on low 6-8 hours, or until potatoes are tender and most of liquid is absorbed.

6. Sprinkle with paprika before serving.

Per Serving: 210 calories (35 calories from fat), 4g total fat (1.5g saturated, 1g trans), 10mg cholesterol, 620mg sodium, 36g total carbohydrate (4g fiber, 4g sugar), 11g protein, 10%DV vitamin A, 20%DV vitamin C, 10%DV calcium, 8%DV iron.

Saucy Scalloped Potatoes
Sue Pennington
Bridgewater, VA

Makes 6 servings
(Ideal slow-cooker size: 3½- or 4-quart)

4 cups peeled, thinly sliced potatoes
10¾-oz. can fat-free, low-sodium cream of celery, or mushroom, soup
12-oz. can fat-free evaporated milk
1 large onion, sliced
½ tsp. salt
¼ tsp. black pepper
1½ cups chopped fully cooked, lean ham

1. Combine potatoes, soup, evaporated milk, onion, salt, and pepper in slow cooker. Mix well.

2. Cover. Cook on high 1 hour. Stir in ham. Reduce to low. Cook 6-8 hours, or until potatoes are tender. Stir well before serving.

Per Serving: 230 calories (40 calories from fat), 4.5g total fat (1.5g saturated, 0g trans), 35mg cholesterol, 630mg sodium, 29g total carbohydrate (3g fiber, 9g sugar), 17g protein, 0%DV vitamin A, 10%DV vitamin C, 20%DV calcium, 8%DV iron.

Cheesy Scalloped Potatoes
Jean Moore
Pendleton, IN

Makes 7 servings
(Ideal slow-cooker size: 4- or 5-quart)

2 lbs. potatoes, peeled and thinly sliced
1 cup water
½ tsp. cream of tartar
1 small onion, thinly sliced
¼ cup flour
¼ tsp. garlic powder
¼ tsp. black pepper
2 Tbsp. low-sodium butter
10¾-oz. can 98% fat-free cream of mushroom soup
4 slices reduced-sodium American cheese

1. Toss potato slices in water and cream of tartar. Drain.

2. Lay half of potatoes in bottom of slow cooker sprayed with non-fat cooking spray.

3. Top with half of the onion slices, flour, garlic powder, and pepper.

4. Add remaining potatoes and onions. Sprinkle with remaining flour, garlic powder, and pepper.

5. Add butter and undiluted soup.

6. Cover. Cook on high 3-4 hours or on low 7-9 hours.

7. Garnish with cheese just before serving.

Per Serving: 200 calories (45 calories from fat), 5g total fat (2.5g saturated, 0g trans), 15mg cholesterol, 420mg sodium, 32g total carbohydrate (3g fiber, 3g sugar), 7g protein, 0%DV vitamin A, 20%DV vitamin C, 10%DV calcium, 8%DV iron.

Garlicky Potatoes

Donna Lantgen
Rapid City, SD

Makes 6 servings
(Ideal slow-cooker size: 3¹/2-quart)

6 potatoes, peeled and cubed
6 garlic cloves, minced
¹/4 cup dried onion, or one medium onion,
chopped
2 Tbsp. olive oil

1. Combine all ingredients in slow cooker.
2. Cook on low 5-6 hours, or until potatoes are soft but not turning brown.

Per Serving: 220 calories (40 calories from fat), 4.5 total fat (0.5g saturated, 0g trans), 0mg cholesterol, 15mg sodium, 40g total carbohydrate (5g fiber, 3g sugar), 5g protein, 0%DV vitamin A, 30%DV vitamin C, 4%DV calcium, 10%DV iron.

Note: For added flavor, stir in ¹/4 tsp. dill weed and/or ¹/4 tsp. dried basil as part of Step 1.

Mustard Potatoes

Frances Musser
Newmanstown, PA

Makes 6 servings
(Ideal slow-cooker size: 4-quart)

¹/2 cup onions, chopped
1 Tbsp. butter
1¹/2 tsp. prepared mustard
1 tsp. salt
¹/4 tsp. black pepper
¹/2 cup fat-free or 2% milk
¹/4 lb. low-fat cheese
6 medium potatoes, cooked and grated

1. Sauté onion in butter in skillet. Add mustard, salt, pepper, milk, and cheese.
2. Place potatoes in slow cooker. Do not press down.
3. Pour mixture over potatoes.
4. Cover. Cook on low 3-4 hours.
5. Toss potatoes with a large spoon when ready to serve.

Per Serving: 230 calories (30 calories from fat), 3.5g total fat (2g saturated, 0g trans), 10mg cholesterol, 430mg sodium, 40g total carbohydrate (5g fiber, 4g sugar), 10g protein, 4%DV vitamin A, 30%DV vitamin C, 20%DV calcium, 10%DV iron.

Note: If you like an unmistakable mustardy taste, and your diet allows, you can double the amount of mustard.

Mashed Potatoes

Elsie Schlabach
Millersburg, OH
Nadine L. Martinitz
Salina, KS

*Makes 12 servings
(Ideal slow-cooker size: 5- or 6-quart)*

**9 large potatoes (5 lbs.), peeled
2 3-oz. pkgs. fat-free cream cheese
1 cup fat-free dairy sour cream
1 tsp. salt
pinch garlic salt
1/2 tsp. paprika
pinch black pepper
1/4 cup chives, optional
2 Tbsp. butter, softened**

1. Cook potatoes in boiling water in saucepan until tender. Drain.
2. Mash potatoes until smooth.
3. Add remaining ingredients. Beat until light and fluffy. Cool.
4. Cover. Place in refrigerator.
5. Pour potatoes into greased slow cooker.
6. Cover. Cook on low 2-3 hours.

Per Serving: 170 calories (25 calories from fat), 2.5g total fat (1.5g saturated, 0g trans), 10mg cholesterol, 310mg sodium, 32g total carbohydrate (4g fiber, 3g sugar), 6g protein, 0%DV vitamin A, 20%DV vitamin C, 8%DV calcium, 8%DV iron.

Great for Sunday dinner.

Do-Ahead Mashed Potatoes

Shari and Dale Mast
Harrisonburg, VA

*Makes 8 servings
(Ideal slow-cooker size: 6-quart)*

**12 medium-sized potatoes, washed, peeled, and quartered
1 small or medium-sized onion, chopped
4 ozs. Neufchatel or fat-free cream cheese
1 tsp. salt
1/4 tsp. black pepper
1 cup skim milk**

1. In a saucepan, cover potatoes and onion with water. Bring to a boil, and then simmer over medium-low heat for 30 minutes or so, until fully softened. Drain.
2. Mash potatoes and onion with a potato masher to remove chunks.
3. In a large mixing bowl, combine partially mashed potatoes, cream cheese, salt, pepper, and milk. Whip together on high for 3 minutes.
4. Transfer potatoes into slow cooker. Cover and refrigerate overnight.
5. Cook on low 3-4 hours.

Per Serving: 280 calories (5 calories from fat), 0.5g total fat (0g saturated, 0g trans), 0mg cholesterol, 400mg sodium, 59g total carbohydrate (7g fiber, 5g sugar), 10g protein, 0%DV vitamin A, 60%DV vitamin C, 10%DV calcium, 15%DV iron.

Note: If your diet allows, you may want to increase the salt to 1 1/4 or 1 1/2 tsp. in Step 3.

Potato Filling

Miriam Nolt
New Holland, PA

Makes 20 servings
(Ideal slow-cooker size: 2 5-quart cookers)

1 cup celery, chopped fine
1 medium-sized onion, minced
1/2 cup butter
2 15-oz. pkgs. low-fat bread cubes
6 eggs, beaten
1 qt. fat-free milk
1 qt. mashed potatoes
3 tsp. salt
2 pinches saffron
1 cup boiling water
1 tsp. black pepper

1. Sauté celery and onion in butter in skillet until transparent.
2. Combine sautéed mixture with bread cubes. Stir in remaining ingredients. Add more milk if mixture isn't very moist.
3. Pour into large, or several medium-sized, slow cookers. Cook on high 3 hours, stirring up from bottom every hour or so to make sure the filling isn't sticking.

Per Serving: 260 calories (45 calories from fat), 5g total fat (2.5g saturated, 0g trans), 65mg cholesterol, 510mg sodium, 70g total carbohydrate (4g fiber, 4g sugar), 10g protein, 0%DV vitamin A, 10%DV vitamin C, 10%DV calcium, 20%DV iron.

Note: This recipe can be cut in half successfully.

Slow Cooker Stuffing with Poultry

Pat Unternahrer
Wayland, IA

Makes 18 servings
(Ideal slow-cooker size: 6- or 7-quart,
or 2 4-quart cookers)

1 large loaf dried low-fat bread, cubed
2 cups chopped, cooked turkey or chicken, skin removed
1 large onion, chopped
3 ribs celery with leaves, chopped
1/4 cup butter, melted
4 cups fat-free chicken broth
1 Tbsp. poultry seasoning
1 tsp. salt
4 eggs, beaten
1/2 tsp. black pepper

1. Mix together all ingredients. Pour into slow cooker.
2. Cover and cook on high 1 hour, then reduce to low 6-8 hours.

Per Serving: 110 calories (40 calories from fat), 4.5g total fat (1.5g saturated, 0g trans), 60mg cholesterol, 270mg sodium, 12g total carbohydrate (4g fiber, 1g sugar), 10g protein, 0%DV vitamin A, 0%DV vitamin C, 6%DV calcium, 10%DV iron.

Fresh Herb Stuffing

Barbara J. Fabel
Wausau, WI

Makes 8 servings
(Ideal slow-cooker size: 6-quart)

3 Tbsp. butter
3 onions, chopped
4 celery ribs, chopped
1/2 cup chopped fresh parsley
1 Tbsp. chopped fresh rosemary
1 Tbsp. chopped fresh thyme
1 Tbsp. chopped fresh marjoram
1 Tbsp. chopped fresh sage
1 tsp. salt
1/2 tsp. freshly-ground black pepper
1 loaf stale low-fat sourdough bread, cut
   in 1-inch cubes
2 cups fat-free chicken broth

1. Sauté onions and celery in butter in skillet until transparent. Remove from heat and stir in fresh herbs and seasonings.
2. Place bread cubes in large bowl. Add onion/herb mixture. Add enough broth to moisten. Mix well but gently. Turn into greased slow cooker.
3. Cover. Cook on high 1 hour. Reduce heat to low and continue cooking 3-4 hours.

Per Serving: 100 calories (45 calories from fat), 5g total fat (3g saturated, 0g trans), 10mg cholesterol, 420mg sodium, 11g total carbohydrate (2g fiber, 3g sugar), 3g protein, 6%DV vitamin A, 6%DV vitamin C, 4%DV calcium, 8%DV iron.

Irish Mashed Potatoes

Esther J. Yoder
Hartville, OH

Makes 9 servings
(Ideal slow-cooker size: 5-quart)

3 lbs. peeled Yukon gold or red potatoes,
   cubed
2 1/2 cups chopped cabbage
3-6 garlic cloves, peeled, according to your
   taste preference
2 cups fat-free low-sodium chicken broth
1/2 cup (4 ozs.) low-fat cream cheese
1/3 cup fat-free or low-fat sour cream
1/4 cup skim or 2% milk
1/2 tsp. kosher salt
1/4 tsp. black pepper

1. Combine potatoes, cabbage, garlic cloves, and chicken broth in slow cooker.
2. Cook on high 2 1/2-4 hours, or until vegetables are soft.
3. Drain. Add remaining ingredients and mash.
4. The potatoes are now ready to serve, or you may pour them back into the slow cooker and set the cooker on low until you're ready to serve.

Per Serving: 160 calories (5 calories from fat) (0g saturated, 0g trans), 0mg cholesterol, 260mg sodium, 31g total carbohydrate (4g fiber, 3g sugar), 7g protein, 4%DV vitamin A, 30%DV vitamin C, 8%DV calcium, 10%DV iron.

Notes:
1. If you prefer more seasoning, and your diet allows, you may want to increase the kosher salt to 1 tsp.
2. If you put the mashed potatoes back into the cooker to keep them warm, stir them up from the bottom and away from the sides before serving.

Potato Stuffed Cabbage

Jeanette Oberholtzer
Manheim, PA

Makes 10 servings
(Ideal slow-cooker size: 6-quart)

half a large head cabbage, sliced thin
2¹/₂ lbs. potatoes (6 or 7 medium-sized),
  peeled and grated
1 onion, sliced
¹/₄ cup rice, uncooked
1 apple, peeled and sliced
¹/₂-1 tsp. dried dill, according to your taste
  preference
¹/₄-¹/₂ tsp. black pepper, according to your
  taste preference
¹/₄ tsp. ground ginger
1 egg white
14¹/₄-oz. can tomatoes

1. Spray inside of cooker with nonfat
cooking spray. Then begin layering vegetables
into cooker. Place one-third of the cabbage,
one-third of the potatoes, one-third of the
onion, one-third of the rice, one-third of the
apple, and one-third of the spices and
seasonings into the cooker.

2. Repeat twice.

3. Beat egg white until frothy. Fold into
tomatoes. Spoon over top of vegetables.

4. Cover. Cook on low 4-6 hours, or until
vegetables jag tender.

Per Serving: 120 calories (0 calories from fat), 0g total fat
(0g saturated, 0g trans), 0mg cholesterol, 135mg sodium,
28g total carbohydrate (5g fiber, 5g sugar), 4g protein,
4%DV vitamin A, 40%DV vitamin C, 8%DV calcium,
8%DV iron.

Pizza Potatoes

Dorothy VanDeest
Memphis, TN

Makes 6 servings
(Ideal slow-cooker size: 3¹/₂-quart)

6 medium-sized potatoes, peeled and
  thinly sliced
1 large onion, thinly sliced
1 Tbsp. olive oil
1 oz. sliced pepperoni
¹/₄ lb. grated low-fat mozzarella cheese
8-oz. can fat-free pizza sauce

1. In a large skillet, sauté potato and onion
slices in oil until onion becomes transparent.
Stir constantly to prevent browning or sticking.
Drain well.

2. Combine potatoes and onions with
pepperoni and cheese in slow cooker.

3. Pour pizza sauce over top.

4. Cover and cook on low for 6-10 hours.

Per Serving: 280 calories (70 calories from fat), 8g total fat
(3g saturated, 0g trans), 15mg cholesterol, 300mg sodium,
43g total carbohydrate (6g fiber, 5g sugar), 11g protein,
6%DV vitamin A, 40%DV vitamin C, 15%DV calcium,
15%DV iron.

*Note: If your diet allows, you may want to add
¹/₂ tsp. salt and ¹/₄ tsp. black pepper to Step 2.*

Baked Potatoes

Mary Jane Musser
Manheim, PA

Makes 6 servings
(Ideal slow-cooker size: 4- or 5-quart)

6 medium-sized baking potatoes
non-fat cooking spray

1. Prick potatoes with a fork.
2. Coat each potato with cooking spray. Place them in slow cooker.
3. Cover. Cook on low 6-8 hours or on high 3-4 hours, or until potatoes jag tender and are not browned.

Per Serving: 160 calories (0 calories from fat), 0g total fat (0g saturated, 0g trans), 0mg cholesterol, 15mg sodium, 37g total carbohydrate (5g fiber, 2g sugar), 4g protein, 0%DV vitamin A, 30%DV vitamin C, 2%DV calcium, 10%DV iron.

Hot German Potato Salad

Char Hagner
Montague, MI
Penny Blosser
Beavercreek, OH

Makes 8 servings
(Ideal slow-cooker size: 3½- or 4-quart)

6-7 cups potatoes, sliced
1 cup onions, chopped
1 cup celery, chopped
1 cup water
⅓ cup vinegar
¼ cup sugar
2 Tbsp. quick-cooking tapioca
1 tsp. salt
1 tsp. celery seed
¼ tsp. black pepper
6 slices lean turkey bacon, cooked and crumbled
¼ cup fresh parsley

1. Combine potatoes, onions, and celery in slow cooker.
2. In a bowl, combine water, vinegar, sugar, tapioca, salt, celery seed, and black pepper.
3. Pour over potatoes. Mix together gently.
4. Cover. Cook on low 6-8 hours or on high 3-4 hours.
5. Stir in bacon and parsley just before serving.

Per Serving: 170 calories (20 calories from fat), 2.5g total fat (0.5g saturated, 0g trans), 10mg cholesterol, 440mg sodium, 32g total carbohydrate (3g fiber, 8g sugar), 4g protein, 0%DV vitamin A, 25%DV vitamin C, 4%DV calcium, 8%DV iron.

German Potato Salad

Lauren Eberhard
Seneca, IL

Makes 8 servings
(Ideal slow-cooker size: 4-quart)

3 slices lean, turkey bacon
3/4 cup chopped onions
103/4-oz. can fat-free, low-sodium cream of
   chicken soup
1/4 cup water
2 Tbsp. cider vinegar
1/2 tsp. sugar
black pepper to taste
4 cups parboiled, cubed potatoes
fresh parsley, chopped

1. Brown bacon in skillet and then crumble. Reserve 2 Tbsp. bacon drippings. Sauté onions in drippings.
2. Blend together soup, water, vinegar, sugar, and pepper. Add bacon and onions. Mix well.
3. Add potatoes and parsley. Mix well. Pour into slow cooker.
4. Cover. Cook on low 2-4 hours, or until potatoes are soft but still holding their shape and heated through.
5. Serve warm or at room temperature.

Per Serving: 110 calories (30 calories from fat), 3.5g total fat (1g saturated, 0g trans), 10mg cholesterol, 370mg sodium, 18g total carbohydrate (2g fiber, 2g sugar), 4g protein, 0%DV vitamin A, 10%DV vitamin C, 2%DV calcium, 6%DV iron.

Note: If your diet permits, you may want to add 1/2 tsp. salt when you mix the soup, water, vinegar, sugar, and pepper together.

Candied Sweet Potatoes

Julie Weaver
Reinholds, PA

Makes 8 servings
(Ideal slow-cooker size: 31/2-quart)

8 medium-sized sweet potatoes
1/2 tsp. salt
20-oz. can unsweetened, crushed
   pineapples, undrained
2 Tbsp. brown sugar
1 tsp. ground nutmeg
1 tsp. ground cinnamon

1. Cook sweet potatoes until soft. Peel. Slice and place in slow cooker.
2. Combine remaining ingredients. Pour over sweet potatoes.
3. Cover. Cook on high 4 hours.

Per Serving: 130 calories (0 calories from fat), 0g total fat (0g saturated, 0g trans), 0mg cholesterol, 160mg sodium, 32g total carbohydrate (4g fiber, 25g sugar), 2g protein, 200%DV vitamin A, 20%DV vitamin C, 4%DV calcium, 10%DV iron.

Pineapple Sweet Potatoes

Annabelle Unternahrer
Shipshewana, IN

Makes 10 servings
(Ideal slow-cooker size: 4-quart)

10-oz. can unsweetened crushed pineapple,
   drained
2 Tbsp. dark brown sugar
40-oz. can unsweetened yams, drained

1. Mix crushed pineapples with brown sugar.
2. Combine with yams in slow cooker sprayed with cooking spray.

3. Cover. Cook on low 2-4 hours, or until heated through.

Per Serving: 130 calories (0 calories from fat), 0g total fat (0g saturated, 0g trans), 0mg cholesterol, 85mg sodium, 31g total carbohydrate (2g fiber, 23g sugar), 2g protein, 300%DV vitamin A, 10%DV vitamin C, 4%DV calcium, 10%DV iron.

Note: This recipe can be doubled easily. Just remember to allow extra time for it to heat; perhaps an additional hour.

Sweet Potato Casserole

Jean Butzer
Batavia, NY

Makes 8 servings
(Ideal slow-cooker size: 3¹/2-quart)

2 29-oz. cans sweet potatoes, drained and mashed
2 Tbsp. brown sugar
1 Tbsp. orange juice
2 eggs, beaten
¹/2 cup fat-free milk
¹/3 cup chopped pecans
¹/3 cup brown sugar
2 Tbsp. flour
2 tsp. butter, melted

1. Combine sweet potatoes and 2 Tbsp. brown sugar.
2. Stir in orange juice, eggs, and milk. Transfer to greased slow cooker.
3. Combine pecans, ¹/3 cup brown sugar, flour, and butter. Spread over sweet potatoes.
4. Cover. Cook on high 3-4 hours.

Per Serving: 330 calories (50 calories from fat), 6g total fat (1.5g saturated, 0g trans), 50mg cholesterol, 180mg sodium, 63g total carbohydrate (4g fiber, 46g sugar), 7g protein, 500%DV vitamin A, 0%DV vitamin C, 10%DV calcium, 20%DV iron.

Rosy Sweet Potatoes

Evelyn L. Ward
Greeley, CO

Makes 8 servings
(Ideal slow-cooker size: 3¹/2- or 4-quart)

40-oz. can unsweetened sweet potato chunks, drained
21-oz. can lite apple pie filling
¹/3 cup brown sugar
¹/3 cup red hots
1 tsp. ground cinnamon

1. Combine all ingredients in a large bowl. Pour into slow cooker sprayed with non-fat cooking spray.
2. Cover. Cook on low 3-4 hours.

Per Serving: 280 calories (25 calories from fat), 3g total fat (1g saturated, 0g trans), 5mg cholesterol, 220mg sodium, 62g total carbohydrate (3g fiber, 46g sugar), 4g protein, 400%DV vitamin A, 2%DV vitamin C, 6%DV calcium, 15%DV iron.

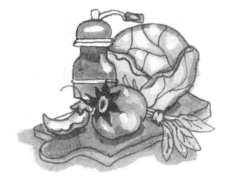

Sweet Potato, Fruit Compote

Ilene Bontrager
Arlington, KS

Makes 8 servings
(Ideal slow-cooker size: 3½-quart)

4 cups sweet potatoes, peeled and cubed
3 tart cooking apples, peeled and diced
20-oz. can unsweetened pineapple chunks,
   undrained
¼ cup brown sugar
1 cup miniature marshmallows, divided

1. Cook sweet potatoes in a small amount of water in a saucepan until almost soft. Drain.
2. Combine sweet potatoes, apples, and pineapples in slow cooker.
3. Sprinkle with brown sugar and ⅔ cup marshmallows.
4. Cover. Cook on low 5-6 hours.
5. Thirty minutes before serving, top potatoes and fruit with remaining ⅓ cup marshmallows. Cover and continue cooking.

Per Serving: 200 calories (0 calories from fat), 0g total fat (0g saturated, 0g trans), 0mg cholesterol, 15mg sodium, 49g total carbohydrate (4g fiber, 31g sugar), 2g protein, 400%DV vitamin A, 20%DV vitamin C, 4%DV calcium, 6%DV iron.

Green Bean Supper

Beverly Flatt-Getz
Warriors Mark, PA

Makes 24-28 servings
(Ideal slow-cooker size: 6- or 7-quart)

2 lbs. new potatoes, or 5 white potatoes
   halved and scrubbed
6 lb. 5-oz. can green beans, drained
15-oz. can whole corn, drained
1 large onion (or 2 medium), diced
5-oz. can lean chunk ham in water
10¾-oz. can fat-free, low-sodium chicken
   broth
½ tsp. garlic powder
½ tsp. onion powder
1 chicken bouillon cube

1. Place potatoes in slow cooker.
2. Add remainder of ingredients.
3. Fill pot half full of water.
4. Cook 6-8 hours, or until the vegetables are done to your liking.

Per Serving: 70 calories (0 calories from fat), 0g total fat (0g saturated, 0g trans), 0mg cholesterol, 510mg sodium, 14g total carbohydrate (3g fiber, 3g sugar), 3g protein, 6%DV vitamin A, 10%DV vitamin C, 2%DV calcium, 6%DV iron.

Note: You can use fresh green beans in place of the canned ones.

Green Beans with Dill

Rebecca Leichty
Harrisonburg, VA

Makes 8 servings
(Ideal slow-cooker size: 3½- or 4-quart)

2 qts. cut green beans, or 4 14½-oz. cans
  cut green beans
2 tsp. beef bouillon granules
½ tsp dill seed
¼ cup water

1. Spray slow cooker with fat-free cooking spray.
2. Add all ingredients and mix well.
3. Cook on high 3-4 hours.

Per Serving: 35 calories (0 calories from fat), 0g total fat
(0g saturated, 0g trans), 0mg cholesterol, 310mg sodium,
8g total carbohydrate (4g fiber, 3g sugar), 2g protein,
15%DV vitamin A, 20%DV vitamin C, 4%DV calcium,
6%DV iron.

Notes:
1. If you like, add 2 Tbsp. minced onions to Step 2.
2. If your sodium counter allows, you may want to add 1 tsp. garlic salt to Step 2.

Slow-Cooker Ratatouille

Nanci Keatley
Salem, OR

Makes 6 servings
(Ideal slow-cooker size: 5- or 6-quart)

1 Tbsp. olive oil
1 large onion, chopped
6 large garlic cloves, minced
1 green bell pepper, cut into strips
1 red bell pepper, cut into strips
1 medium-sized eggplant, cubed
2 cups mushrooms, thickly sliced
4 tomatoes, cubed
1 cup low-sodium tomato puree
¼ cup dry red wine, or wine vinegar
1 Tbsp. lemon juice
2 tsp. dried thyme
1 tsp. dried oregano
1 tsp. ground cumin
½-1 tsp. salt
¼-½ tsp. black pepper
4 Tbsp. minced fresh basil
¼ cup fresh parsley, chopped

1. Turn slow cooker on high for 2 minutes.
2. Pour oil into slow cooker and add remaining ingredients except parsley and fresh basil.
3. Cover. Cook on high 2 hours, then on low 4-5 hours.
4. Stir in fresh basil. Sprinkle with parsley. Serve.

Per Serving: 120 calories (30 calories from fat), 3g total fat
(0g saturated, 0g trans), 0mg cholesterol, 30mg sodium,
20g total carbohydrate (6g fiber, 10g sugar), 4g protein,
30%DV vitamin A, 50%DV vitamin C, 6%DV calcium,
15%DV iron.

Notes:
1. This is delicious over whole wheat pasta or brown rice! It also makes great pizza topping.
2. You may substitute 1 rounded Tbsp. dried basil for the fresh basil. If you do that, then add the basil to Step 2.

Mediterranean Eggplant

Willard E. Roth
Elkhart, IN

Makes 8 servings
(Ideal slow-cooker size: 5-quart)

1 medium-sized red onion, chopped
2 cloves garlic, crushed
1 cup fresh mushrooms, sliced
2 Tbsp. olive oil
1 eggplant, unpeeled, cubed
2 green bell peppers, coarsely chopped
28-oz. can crushed tomatoes
28-oz. can garbanzos, drained and rinsed
2 Tbsp. fresh rosemary
1 cup fresh parsley, chopped
1/2 cup kalamata olives, pitted and sliced

1. Sauté onion, garlic, and mushrooms in olive oil in a skillet over medium heat. Transfer to slow cooker coated with non-fat cooking spray.
2. Add eggplant, peppers, tomatoes, garbanzos, rosemary, and parsley.
3. Cover. Cook on low 5-6 hours.
4. Stir in olives just before serving.
5. Serve with couscous or polenta.

Per Serving: 250 calories (70 calories from fat), 8g total fat (1g saturated, 0g trans), 0mg cholesterol, 370mg sodium, 38g total carbohydrate (9g fiber, 8g sugar), 11g protein, 10%DV vitamin A, 40%DV vitamin C, 15%DV calcium, 30%DV iron.

Caponata

Katrine Rose
Woodbridge, VA

Makes 10 servings
(Ideal slow-cooker size: 4-quart)

1 medium-sized eggplant, peeled and cut into 1/2" cubes
14-oz. can low-sodium diced tomatoes
1 medium-sized onion, chopped
1 red bell pepper, cut into 1/2" pieces
3/4 cup low-sodium salsa
1/4 cup olive oil
2 Tbsp. capers, drained
3 Tbsp. balsamic vinegar
3 garlic cloves, minced
1 1/4 tsp. dried oregano
1/3 cup chopped fresh basil

1. Combine all ingredients except basil and bread in slow cooker.
2. Cover. Cook on low 7-8 hours, or until vegetables are tender.
3. Stir in basil. Serve over slices of toasted French bread.

Per Serving: 340 calories (70 calories from fat), 8g total fat (1.5g saturated, 0.5g trans), 0mg cholesterol, 830mg sodium, 58g total carbohydrate (5g fiber, 5g sugar), 10g protein, 2%DV vitamin A, 10%DV vitamin C, 10%DV calcium, 15%DV iron.

Eggplant Italian

Melanie Thrower
McPherson, KS

Makes 6-8 servings
(Ideal slow-cooker size: 4- or 5-quart;
an oval cooker works best!)

2 eggplants
¼ cup eggbeaters
24 ozs. fat-free cottage cheese
¼ tsp. salt
black pepper to taste
14-oz. can tomato sauce
2-4 Tbsp. Italian seasoning, according to
   your taste preference

1. Peel eggplants and cut in ½"-thick slices.
Soak in salt-water for about 5 minutes to
remove bitterness. Drain well.
2. Spray slow cooker with fat-free cooking
spray.
3. Mix eggbeaters, cottage cheese, salt, and
pepper together in bowl.
4. Mix tomato sauce and Italian seasoning
together in another bowl.
5. Spoon a thin layer of tomato sauce into
bottom of slow cooker. Top with about one-
third of the eggplant slices, and then one-third
of the egg/cheese mixture, and finally one-third
of the remaining tomato sauce mixture.
6. Repeat those layers twice, ending with
seasoned tomato sauce.
7. Cover. Cook on high 4 hours. Allow to
rest 15 minutes before serving.

Per Serving: 120 calories (10 calories from fat), 1g total fat
(0g saturated, 0g trans), 30mg cholesterol, 940mg sodium,
17g total carbohydrate (4g fiber, 11g sugar), 11g protein,
15%DV vitamin A, 4%DV vitamin C, 8%DV calcium,
4%DV iron.

*Note: For more spice, add red pepper seasoning
to taste in Step 4.*

Eggplant & Zucchini Casserole

Jennifer Dzialowski
Brighton, MI

Makes 6 servings
(Ideal slow-cooker size: 5-quart)

2 egg whites
1 medium-sized eggplant
1 medium-sized zucchini
1½ cups bread crumbs
1 tsp. garlic powder
1 tsp. low-sodium Italian seasoning
48-oz. jar fat-free, low-sodium spaghetti
   sauce
8-oz. bag low-fat shredded mozzarella
   cheese

1. Beat egg whites in small bowl.
2. Slice eggplant and zucchini. Place in
separate bowl.
3. Combine in another bowl bread crumbs,
garlic powder, and Italian seasoning.
4. Dip sliced veggies in egg white and then
in bread crumbs. Layer in slow cooker,
pouring sauce and sprinkling cheese over each
layer. (Reserve ½ cup cheese). Top with sauce.
5. Cover. Cook on low 5-6 hours or until
vegetables are tender.
6. Top with remaining cheese during last 15
minutes of cooking.

Per Serving: 280 calories (100 calories from fat), 11g total
fat (4.5g saturated, 0g trans), 20mg cholesterol, 1380mg
sodium, 30g total carbohydrate (6g fiber, 15g sugar), 15g
protein, 20%DV vitamin A, 20%DV vitamin C, 30%DV
calcium, 15%DV iron.

*Note: For added flavoring, sprinkle chopped
onions and minced garlic over each layer of
vegetables.*

Zucchini Special

Louise Stackhouse
Benten, PA

Makes 4 servings
(Ideal slow-cooker size: 3-quart)

1 medium-to-large zucchini, peeled and
   sliced
1 medium-sized onion, sliced
1 qt. low-sodium stewed tomatoes with
   juice, or 2 14½-oz. cans low-sodium
   stewed tomatoes with juice
¼ tsp. salt
1 tsp. dried basil
8 ozs. fat-free mozzarella cheese, shredded

1. Layer zucchini, onion, and tomatoes in
slow cooker.
2. Sprinkle with salt and basil.
3. Cover. Cook on low 6-8 hours.
4. Sprinkle with cheese 15 minutes before
end of cooking time.

Per Serving: 170 calories (0 calories from fat), 0g total fat
(0g saturated, 0g trans), 5mg cholesterol, 620mg sodium,
20g total carbohydrate (5g fiber, 15g sugar), 19g protein,
20%DV vitamin A, 20%DV vitamin C, 90%DV calcium,
20%DV iron.

Zucchini Casserole

Rebecca Leichty
Harrisonburg, VA

Makes 6 servings
(Ideal slow-cooker size: 3-quart)

2-3 cups zucchini, thinly sliced
1 medium-sized onion, diced
2 large carrots, shredded (enough to make
   1 cup)
10¾-oz. can 98% fat free cream of celery
   soup

10¾-oz. can condensed cream of chicken
   soup
¼ tsp. salt
dash of black pepper
dash of ground cumin, if you like

1. Spray slow cooker with fat-free cooking
spray. Mix vegetables, soups, and salt together
gently in slow cooker. Cover.
2. Cook on high 4-6 hours, or until
vegetables are as crunchy or as soft as you
like.

Per Serving: 100 calories (40 calories from fat), 4.5g total
fat (1.5g saturated, 0.5g trans), 5mg cholesterol, 760mg
sodium, 12g total carbohydrate (2g fiber, 4g sugar), 3g
protein, 100%DV vitamin A, 6%DV vitamin C, 4%DV
calcium, 4%DV iron.

Zucchini in Sour Cream

Lizzie Ann Yoder
Hartville, OH

Makes 6 servings
(Ideal slow-cooker size: 3- or 4-quart)

4 cups zucchini, unpeeled, sliced
1 cup fat-free sour cream
¼ cup skim milk
1 cup onions, chopped
1 tsp. salt
1 cup grated low-fat sharp cheddar cheese

1. Parboil zucchini in microwave for 2-3
minutes. Turn into slow cooker sprayed with
non-fat cooking spray.
2. Combine sour cream, milk, onions, and
salt. Pour over zucchini and stir gently.
3. Cover. Cook on low 1-1½ hours.
4. Sprinkle cheese over vegetables 30 minutes
before serving.

Per Serving: 100 calories (20 calories from fat), 2g total fat (1g
saturated, 0g trans), 10mg cholesterol, 430mg sodium, 12g
total carbohydrate (1g fiber, 7g sugar), 8g protein, 10%DV
vitamin A, 0%DV vitamin C, 20%DV calcium, 4%DV iron.

Vegetable Acorn Squash

Janet Roggie
Lowville, NY

Makes 6 servings
(Ideal slow-cooker size: 4-quart)

1 large acorn squash
½ tsp. salt
¼ tsp. ground cinnamon
1 Tbsp. butter or margarine

1. Wash squash.
2. Cook on low for 8 hours.
3. Split and remove seeds.
4. Sprinkle with salt and cinnamon. Dot with butter.

Per Serving: 45 calories (20 calories from fat), 2g total fat (1g saturated, 0g trans), 5mg cholesterol, 0mg sodium, 7g total carbohydrate (1g fiber, 2g sugar), 1g protein, 6%DV vitamin A, 8%DV vitamin C, 2%DV calcium, 2%DV iron.

Squash and Apples

Sharon Miller
Holmesville, OH

Makes 6 servings
(Ideal slow-cooker size: 6-quart)

1 large butternut squash, peeled, seeded, and cut into ¼″ slices
2 medium-sized cooking apples, cored and cut into ¼″ slices
3 Tbsp. raisins, optional
3 Tbsp. reduced-calorie pancake syrup
dash of ground cinnamon and/or nutmeg
¼ cup apple cider or apple juice

1. Layer half of the following ingredients in slow cooker: squash, apples, and raisins.
2. Drizzle with half the syrup.

3. Repeat layers.
4. Pour cider over the top.
5. Cook on low 6-8 hours or until squash is tender.

Per Serving: 130 calories (0 calories from fat), 0g total fat (0g saturated, 0g trans), 0mg cholesterol, 10mg sodium, 34g total carbohydrate (8g fiber, 15g sugar), 2g protein, 200%DV vitamin A, 20%DV vitamin C, 10%DV calcium, 8%DV iron.

Broccoli Casserole

Jeanne Allen
Rye, CO

Makes 4 servings
(Ideal slow-cooker size: 4-quart)

2 10-oz. pkgs. frozen broccoli spears, thawed and cut in pieces
10¾-oz. can 98% fat-free cream of celery soup
1½ cups reduced-fat cheddar cheese, divided
¼ cup yellow onions, finely chopped
1 cup baked potato chips, crushed

1. Combine broccoli, soup, 1 cup cheese, and onions in slow cooker sprayed with non-fat cooking spray.
2. Cover. Cook on low 3-4 hours or on high 2 hours, or until broccoli is done to your liking.
3. Mix remaining ½ cup cheese and crushed potato chips together and sprinkle on top of casserole 30 minutes before end of cooking time. Leave cooker uncovered during this final half hour of cooking.

Per Serving: 390 calories (80 calories from fat), 8g total fat (3g saturated, 0.5g trans), 15mg cholesterol, 1200mg sodium, 61g total carbohydrate (9g fiber, 8g sugar), 22g protein, 40%DV vitamin A, 60%DV vitamin C, 50%DV calcium, 10%DV iron.

Broccoli Casserole

Dorothy Van Deest
Memphis, TN

Makes 6 servings
(Ideal slow-cooker size: 3-quart)

10-oz. pkg. frozen chopped broccoli
6 eggs, beaten
24-oz. carton fat-free small-curd cottage
  cheese
6 Tbsp. flour
8 ozs. fat-free mild cheese of your choice,
  diced
2 green onions, chopped
1/2 tsp. salt

1. Place frozen broccoli in colander. Run
cold water over it until it thaws. Separate into
pieces. Drain well.
2. Combine remaining ingredients in large
bowl and mix until well blended. Stir in
broccoli. Pour into slow cooker sprayed with
fat-free cooking spray.
3. Cover. Cook on high 1 hour. Stir well,
then resume cooking on low 2-4 hours.

Per Serving: 250 calories (40 calories from fat), 4.5g total
fat (1.5g saturated, 0g trans), 200mg cholesterol, 980mg
sodium, 20g total carbohydrate (4g fiber, 8g sugar), 32g
protein, 20%DV vitamin A, 20%DV vitamin C, 35%DV
calcium, 8%DV iron.

*Note: You can use fresh broccoli instead of
frozen.*

Broccoli Oriental

Frieda Weisz
Aberdeen, SD

Makes 8 servings
(Ideal slow-cooker size: 3 1/2- or 4-quart)

2 lbs. fresh broccoli, trimmed and chopped
  into bite-size pieces
1 clove garlic, minced
1 green or red bell pepper, cut into thin
  slices
1 onion, cut into slices
4 Tbsp. light soy sauce
1/2 tsp. salt
dash of black pepper
1 Tbsp. sesame seeds, optional, as garnish

1. Combine all ingredients except sesame
seeds in slow cooker.
2. Cook on low for 6 hours. Top with sesame
seeds.
3. Serve on brown rice.

Per Serving: 50 calories (10 calories from fat), 1 total fat (0g
saturated, 0g trans), 0mg cholesterol, 300mg sodium, 9g total
carbohydrate (4g fiber, 3g sugar), 4g protein, 50%DV vitamin
A, 150%DV vitamin C, 6%DV calcium, 15%DV iron.

Broccoli Delight

Nancy Wagner Graves
Manhattan, KS

Makes 4-6 servings
(Ideal slow-cooker size: 3 1/2- or 4-quart)

1-2 lbs. broccoli, chopped
2 cups cauliflower, chopped
10 3/4-oz. can 98% fat-free cream of celery
  soup
1/2 tsp. salt
1/4 tsp. black pepper

1 medium-sized onion, diced
2-4 garlic cloves, crushed, according to
   your taste preference
1/2 cup vegetable broth

1. Combine all ingredients in slow cooker.
2. Cook on low 4-6 hours or on high 2-3
hours.

Per Serving: 110 calories (20 calories from fat), 2.5 total fat
(0.5g saturated, 0.5g trans), 5mg cholesterol, 740mg
sodium, 19g total carbohydrate (5g fiber, 5g sugar), 6g
protein, 300%DV vitamin A, 100%DV vitamin C, 10%DV
calcium, 10%DV iron.

Julia's Broccoli and Cauliflower with Cheese

Julia Lapp
New Holland, PA

Makes 6 servings
(Ideal slow-cooker size: 3 1/2-quart)

5 cups raw broccoli and cauliflower, cut in
   bite-sized pieces
1/4 cup water
2 Tbsp. butter or margarine
2 Tbsp. flour
1/2 tsp. salt
1 cup fat-free milk
1 cup shredded fat-free cheddar cheese

1. Cook broccoli and cauliflower in
saucepan in water, until just crispy tender. Set
aside.
2. Make white sauce by melting the butter
in another pan over low heat. Blend in flour
and salt. Add milk all at once. Cook quickly,
stirring constantly until mixture thickens and
bubbles. Add cheese. Stir until melted and
smooth.
3. Combine vegetables and sauce in slow
cooker. Mix well.
4. Cook on low 1 1/2 hours.

Per Serving: 100 calories (30 calories from fat), 3g total fat
(0.5g saturated, 0g trans), 5mg cholesterol, 460mg sodium,
8g total carbohydrate (2g fiber, 4g sugar), 9g protein,
20%DV vitamin A, 40%DV vitamin C, 25%DV calcium,
4%DV iron.

*Note: If you like, substitute green beans and
carrots, or other vegetables, in place of the
broccoli and cauliflower.*

Broccoli and Rice Casserole

Virginia Graybill
Hershey, PA

Makes 6 servings
(Ideal slow-cooker size: 3 1/2- or 4-quart)

1 small onion, diced
1/4 cup margarine, melted
2 cups quick-cooking rice
2 cups water
10 3/4-oz. can 98% fat-free cream of
   mushroom soup
1/2 tsp. salt
5-oz. jar low-fat sharp cheese spread
2 10-oz. pkgs. frozen chopped broccoli,
   partially thawed

1. Combine all ingredients in slow cooker.
Stir thoroughly.
2. Cover. Cook on low 6-7 hours or on high
2-3 hours.

Per Serving: 210 calories (80 calories from fat), 9g total fat
(3g saturated, 0.5g trans), 10mg cholesterol, 660mg
sodium, 22g total carbohydrate (3g fiber, 4g sugar), 10g
protein, 30%DV vitamin A, 50%DV vitamin C, 25%DV
calcium, 8%DV iron.

Never Fail Rice

Mary E. Wheatley
Mashpee, MA

Makes 6 servings
(Ideal slow-cooker size: 1- or 2-quart)

1 cup uncooked long grain rice
2 cups water
1/2 tsp. salt
1/2 Tbsp. butter

1. Combine all ingredients in small slow cooker.
2. Cover. Cook on low 4-6 hours or on high 2-3 hours, or until rice is just fully cooked.
3. Fluff with a fork. Serve.

Per Serving: 120 calories (10 calories from fat), 1g total fat (0.5g saturated, 0g trans), 5mg cholesterol, 200mg sodium, 25g total carbohydrate (0g fiber, 0g sugar), 2g protein, 0%DV vitamin A, 0%DV vitamin C, 2%DV calcium, 8%DV iron.

Herb Rice

Frieda Weisz
Aberdeen, SD

Makes 6 servings
(Ideal slow-cooker size: 3 1/2-quart)

3 chicken bouillon cubes
3 cups water
1 1/2 cups uncooked long grain rice
1 tsp. dried rosemary
1/2 tsp. dried marjoram
1/4 cup dried parsley, chopped
1 Tbsp. butter or margarine
1/4 cup onions, diced
1/2 cup slivered almonds, optional

1. Mix together chicken bouillon cubes and water.
2. Combine all ingredients in slow cooker.
3. Cook on low 4-6 hours, or until rice is fully cooked.

Per Serving: 70 calories (20 calories from fat), 2g total fat (1g saturated, 0g trans), 5mg cholesterol, 610mg sodium, 10g total carbohydrate (0.5g fiber, 1g sugar), 1g protein, 4%DV vitamin A, 2%DV vitamin C, 2%DV calcium, 6%DV iron.

Note: If you prefer, you may use 24 ozs. (or 3 cups) fat-free low-sodium chicken broth instead of the bouillon cubes and water

Wild Rice

Ruth S. Weaver
Reinholds, PA

Makes 5 servings
(Ideal slow-cooker size: 3-quart)

1 cup wild rice, or wild rice mixture, uncooked
1/2 cup sliced fresh mushrooms
1/2 cup diced onions
1/2 cup diced green or red bell peppers
1 Tbsp. oil
1/2 tsp. salt
1/4 tsp. black pepper
2 1/2 cups fat-free, low-sodium chicken broth

1. Layer rice and vegetables in slow cooker. Pour oil, salt, and pepper over vegetables. Stir.
2. Heat chicken broth. Pour over ingredients in slow cooker.
3. Cover. Cook on high 2 1/2-3 hours, or until rice is soft and liquid is absorbed.

Per Serving: 180 calories (30 calories from fat), 3.5g total fat (0g saturated, 0g trans), 0mg cholesterol, 300mg sodium, 31g total carbohydrate (3g fiber, 2g sugar), 9g protein, 0%DV vitamin A, 10%DV vitamin C, 2%DV calcium, 10%DV iron.

Herbed Lentils and Rice

Sharon Miller
Holmesville, OH

Makes 4 servings
(Ideal slow-cooker size: 3-quart)

2³/₄ cups reduced-sodium fat-free chicken broth
³/₄ cup water
³/₄ cup dry lentils, rinsed
³/₄ cup onions, chopped
¹/₂ cup dry wild rice
¹/₂ tsp. dried basil
¹/₄ tsp. dried oregano
¹/₄ tsp. dried thyme
¹/₈ tsp. garlic powder
¹/₂ tsp. salt
¹/₄ tsp. black pepper
1 cup shredded reduced-fat Swiss cheese

1. Spray slow cooker with fat-free cooking spray.
2. Combine all ingredients except cheese in slow cooker.
3. Cook on low 6-8 hours, or until lentils and rice are tender. Do not remove lid until it has cooked at least 6 hours.
4. Stir in shredded cheese 5-10 minutes before serving.

Per Serving: 420 calories (130 calories from fat), 14g total fat (9g saturated, 0g trans), 35mg cholesterol, 500mg sodium, 41g total carbohydrate (10g fiber, 3g sugar), 33g protein, 15%DV vitamin A, 2%DV vitamin C, 60%DV calcium, 30%DV iron.

Elegant Carrots with Onions

Dorothy VanDeest
Memphis, TN
Marjorie Yoder Guengerich
Harrisonburg, VA

Makes 6 servings
(Ideal slow-cooker size: 3- or 4-quart)

1 cube chicken bouillon
1 cup boiling water
2 medium-sized onions, sliced
1 Tbsp. butter or margarine
1 Tbsp. flour
pinch of salt (optional)
6 carrots, pared and cut into julienne strips
1 Tbsp. sugar (optional)

1. Dissolve bouillon cube in boiling water. Set aside.
2. In a large skillet, sauté onions in butter or margarine until transparent, stirring to separate rings.
3. Add flour and salt to onions in skillet. Add slightly cooled bouillon. Cook until thickened.
4. Combine carrots and onion sauce in slow cooker, stirring to coat carrots
5. Cover and cook on high one hour, then turn to low for 2-6 hours.
6. If desired, add sugar just before serving.

Per Serving: 35 calories (15 calories from fat), 1.5 total fat (1g saturated, 0g trans), 5mg cholesterol, 330mg sodium, 5g total carbohydrate (1g fiber, 2g sugar), 1g protein, 2%DV vitamin A, 4%DV vitamin C, 2%DV calcium, 2%DV iron.

Orange Glazed Carrots

Cyndie Marrara
Port Matilda, PA

Makes 6-8 servings
(Ideal slow-cooker size: 3¹/₂-quart)

32-oz. pkg. baby carrots
¹/₄ cup packed brown sugar
¹/₂ cup orange juice
1 Tbsp. butter
¹/₂-³/₄ tsp. ground cinnamon, according to
   your taste preference
¹/₄ tsp. ground nutmeg
2 Tbsp. cornstarch
¹/₄ cup water

1. Combine all ingredients except cornstarch and water in slow cooker.

2. Cover. Cook on low 4-6 hours, or until carrots are done to your liking.

3. Put carrots in serving dish and keep warm, reserving cooking juices. Put reserved juices in small saucepan. Bring to boil.

4. Mix cornstarch and water in small bowl until blended. Add to juices. Boil one minute or until thickened, stirring constantly.

5. Pour over carrots and serve.

Per Serving: 130 calories (25 calories from fat), 3g total fat (1.5g saturated, 0g trans), 5mg cholesterol, 60mg sodium, 26g total carbohydrate (3g fiber, 18g sugar), 1g protein, 300%DV vitamin A, 20%DV vitamin C, 4%DV calcium, 8%DV iron.

Baked Tomatoes

Lizzie Ann Yoder
Hartville, OH

Makes 4 servings
(Ideal slow-cooker size: 2¹/₂- or 3-quart)

2 tomatoes, each cut in half
¹/₂ Tbsp. olive oil
¹/₂ tsp. parsley, chopped,
   or ¹/₄ tsp. dry parsley flakes
¹/₄ tsp. dried oregano
¹/₄ tsp. dried basil

1. Place tomato halves in slow cooker sprayed with non-fat cooking spray.

2. Drizzle oil over tomatoes. Sprinkle with remaining ingredients.

3. Cover. Cook on high 45 minutes-1 hour.

Per Serving: 30 calories (20 calories from fat), 2g total fat (0g saturated, 0g trans), 0mg cholesterol, 5mg sodium, 4g total carbohydrate (0.5g fiber, 2g sugar), 1g protein, 4%DV vitamin A, 10%DV vitamin C, 0%DV calcium, 2%DV iron.

Stewed Tomatoes

Michelle Showalter
Bridgewater, VA

Makes 12 servings
(Ideal slow-cooker size: 4-quart)

2 qts. low-sodium canned tomatoes
¼ cup sugar
1 tsp. salt
dash of black pepper
2 Tbsp. butter
2 cups bread cubes

1. Place tomatoes in slow cooker.
2. Sprinkle with sugar, salt, and pepper.
3. Lightly toast bread cubes in melted butter in skillet on top of stove. Spread over tomatoes.
4. Cover. Cook on high 3-4 hours

Per Serving: 90 calories (20 calories from fat), 2.5g total fat (1.5g saturated, 0g trans), 5mg cholesterol, 650mg sodium, 15g total carbohydrate (2g fiber, 9g sugar), 2g protein, 10%DV vitamin A, 10%DV vitamin C, 10%DV calcium, 4%DV iron.

Note: If you prefer bread that is less moist and soft, add bread cubes 15 minutes before serving and continue cooking without the lid.

Cranberry-Orange Beets

Jean Butzer
Batavia, NY

Makes 6 servings
(Ideal slow-cooker size: 6-quart)

2 lbs. medium-sized beets, peeled and quartered
½ tsp. ground nutmeg
1 cup cranberry juice
1 tsp. orange peel, finely shredded, optional
2 Tbsp. butter
2 Tbsp. sugar
4 tsp. cornstarch

1. Place beets in slow cooker. Sprinkle with nutmeg.
2. Add cranberry juice and orange peel. Dot with butter.
3. Cover. Cook on low 6-7 hours or on high 3-3½ hours.
4. In small bowl, combine sugar and cornstarch.
5. Remove ½ cup of cooking liquid and stir into cornstarch.
6. Stir mixture into slow cooker.
7. Cover. Cook on high 15-30 minutes.

Per Serving: 150 calories (35 calories from fat), 4g total fat (2.5g saturated, 0g trans), 10mg cholesterol, 120mg sodium, 26g total carbohydrate (4g fiber, 19g sugar), 2g protein, 4%DV vitamin A, 20%DV vitamin C, 2%DV calcium, 8%DV iron.

Harvard Beets

Marjorie Yoder Guengerich
Harrisonburg, VA

Makes 6 servings
(Ideal slow-cooker size: 3-quart)

⅓ **cup sugar**
2 **Tbsp. flour**
¼ **cup beet juice or water**
¼ **cup vinegar**
2 **16-oz. cans sliced beets, drained**

1. Mix sugar and flour. Stir in beet juice and vinegar. Mix well.
2. Place beets in slow cooker. Pour sugar and vinegar mixture over beets. Stir to coat.
3. Cover. Cook on high 1 hour. Turn to low until ready to serve.

Per Serving: 100 calories (0 calories from fat), 0g total fat (0g saturated, 0g trans), 0mg cholesterol, 75mg sodium, 24g total carbohydrate (3g fiber, 17g sugar), 2g protein, 0%DV vitamin A, 0%DV vitamin C, 0%DV calcium, 8%DV iron.

Brussels Sprouts with Pimentos

Donna Lantgon
Rapid City, SD

Makes 8 servings
(Ideal slow-cooker size: 3½- or 4-quart)

2 **lbs. brussels sprouts**
¼ **tsp. dried oregano**
½ **tsp. dried basil**
2-**oz. jar pimentos, drained**
¼ **cup, or 1 small can, sliced black olives, drained**
1 **Tbsp. olive oil**
½ **cup water**

1. Combine all ingredients in slow cooker.
2. Cook on low 6 hours.

Per Serving: 70 calories (20 calories from fat), 2.5g total fat (0g saturated, 0g trans), 0mg cholesterol, 25mg sodium, 11g total carbohydrate (3g fiber, 5g sugar), 3g protein, 20%DV vitamin A, 100%DV vitamin C, 4%DV calcium, 10%DV iron.

Baked Corn

Velma Stauffer
Akron, PA

Makes 8 servings
(Ideal slow-cooker size: 3-quart)

1 qt. corn (be sure to thaw and drain if using frozen corn)
2 eggs, beaten
1 tsp. salt
1 cup fat-free milk
1/8 tsp. black pepper
2 tsp. oil
2 Tbsp. sugar
3 Tbsp. flour

1. Combine all ingredients well. Pour into slow cooker sprayed with fat-free cooking spray.
2. Cover. Cook on high 3 hours.

Per Serving: 140 calories (25 calories from fat), 3g total fat (0.5g saturated, 0g trans), 45mg cholesterol, 320mg sodium, 25g total carbohydrate (2g fiber, 6g sugar), 5g protein, 0%DV vitamin A, 0%DV vitamin C, 4%DV calcium, 4%DV iron.

Cheesy Hominy

Michelle Showalter
Bridgewater, VA

Makes 14 servings
(Ideal slow-cooker size: 5- or 6-quart)

2 cups cracked hominy
6 cups water
2 Tbsp. flour
1 1/2 cups fat-free milk
4 cups fat-free sharp cheddar cheese, grated
1 1/2 tsp. salt
1/4 tsp. black pepper
2 Tbsp. butter

1. Combine hominy and water in slow cooker.
2. Cover. Cook on high 3-4 hours or on low 6-8 hours.
3. Stir in remaining ingredients.
4. Cover. Cook on high 30 minutes or on low 60 minutes.

Per Serving: 90 calories (15 calories from fat), 2g total fat (1g saturated, 0g trans), 10mg cholesterol, 620mg sodium, 7g total carbohydrate (0.5g fiber, 1g sugar), 12g protein, 10%DV vitamin A, 0%DV vitamin C, 30%DV calcium, 2%DV iron.

Cheesy Hominy is a nice change if you're tired of the same old thing. It's wonderful with ham, slices of bacon, or meatballs. Add a green vegetable and you have a lovely meal. Hominy is usually available at bulk-food stores.

Mushrooms in Red Wine

Donna Lantgen
Rapid City, SD

Makes 4 servings
(Ideal slow-cooker size: 2- or 3-quart)

1 lb. fresh mushrooms, stemmed,
    trimmed, and cleaned
4 cloves garlic, minced
1/4 cup onion
1 Tbsp. olive oil
1 cup red wine

1. Combine all ingredients in slow cooker.
2. Cook on low for 6 hours.

Per Serving: 110 calories (35 calories from fat), 4g total fat
(0.5g saturated, 0g trans), 0mg cholesterol, 10mg sodium,
7g total carbohydrate (2g fiber, 2g sugar), 4g protein,
0%DV vitamin A, 6%DV vitamin C, 2%DV calcium,
8%DV iron.

Notes:

1. You can serve this as a side dish or as a condiment.

2. You can also use it as the base for a sauce to which you could add steak tips or ground beef, as well as 2 cups chopped onions, 2 tsp. dried oregano, 1 1/2 tsp. salt, 1/2 tsp. black pepper, and 4 cloves minced garlic. You could also add a quart of spaghetti sauce and serve the mixture over a pound of your favorite pasta.

Wild Mushrooms Italian

Connie Johnson
Loudon, NH

Makes 5-7 servings
(Ideal slow-cooker size: 5-quart)

2 large onions, chopped
3 large red bell peppers, chopped
3 large green bell peppers, chopped
2 Tbsp. oil
12-oz. pkg. oyster mushrooms, cleaned
    and chopped
4 garlic cloves, minced
3 fresh bay leaves
10 fresh basil leaves, chopped
1 1/2 tsp. salt
1 1/2 tsp. black pepper
28-oz. can low-sodium Italian plum
    tomatoes, crushed or chopped

1. Sauté onions and peppers in oil in skillet until soft. Stir in mushrooms and garlic. Sauté just until mushrooms begin to turn brown. Pour into slow cooker.
2. Add remaining ingredients. Stir well.
3. Cover. Cook on low 6-8 hours.

Per Serving: 180 calories (60 calories from fat), 7g total fat
(1g saturated, 0g trans), 0mg cholesterol, 1040mg sodium,
29g total carbohydrate (8g fiber, 6g sugar), 7g protein,
50%DV vitamin A, 150%DV vitamin C, 8%DV calcium,
25%DV iron.

Note: This dish is good as an appetizer or on pita bread, or served over rice or pasta for a main dish.

Desserts

Baked Apples with Dates

Mary E. Wheatley
Mashpee, MA

Makes 8 servings
(Ideal slow-cooker size: 6-quart oval, or large enough cooker that the apples can each sit on the floor of the cooker, rather than being stacked)

8 medium-sized baking apples

Filling:
3/4 cup coarsely chopped dates
3 Tbsp. chopped pecans
1/4 cup, or less, brown sugar

Topping:
1 tsp. ground cinnamon
1/2 tsp. ground nutmeg
1 Tbsp. butter
1/2 cup water

1. Wash, core, and peel top third of apples.
2. Mix dates and chopped nuts with small amount of brown sugar. Stuff into centers of apples where cores had been.
3. Place apples in slow cooker.
4. Sprinkle with cinnamon and nutmeg. Dot with butter.
5. Add water around inside edge of cooker.
6. Cover. Cook on low 4-6 hours or on high 2-3 hours, or until apples are as tender as you like them.

Per Serving: 120 calories (20 calories from fat), 2g total fat (0g saturated, 0g trans), 0mg cholesterol, 0mg sodium, 26g total carbohydrate (2g fiber, 23g sugar), 1g protein, 0%DV vitamin A, 0%DV vitamin C, 0%DV calcium, 0%DV iron.

Baked Apples with Cranberries

Stacy Schmucker Stoltzfus
Enola, PA
Rebecca Meyerkorth
Wamego, KS

Makes 4 servings
(Ideal slow-cooker size: 5- or 6-quart oval)

¼ cup toasted chopped pecans or walnuts
3 Tbsp. dried cranberries or currants
3 Tbsp. brown sugar
¾ tsp. ground cinnamon, divided
¾ tsp. ground nutmeg
4 medium-sized Granny Smith apples, cored
1 cup brown sugar, packed
¾ cup apple cider
2 Tbsp. maple syrup, or 1 tsp. maple flavoring

1. Combine nuts, dried cranberries, and 3 Tbsp. brown sugar. Add ¼ tsp. cinnamon and all of nutmeg.
2. Peel the top third of each apple. Remove each apple's core, but keep apple whole. Place in slow cooker.
3. Spoon nut and fruit mixture into center of each apple, where the core had been.
4. Combine remaining cinnamon, 1 cup brown sugar, cider, and maple syrup in a small bowl. Stir well. Pour over apples.
5. Cover. Cook on low 2½-3 hours.
6. Remove apples with a spoon into serving bowls. Pour remaining juice over each apple.

Per Serving: 430 calories (50 calories from fat), 5g total fat (0.5g saturated, 0g trans), 0mg cholesterol, 35mg sodium, 99g total carbohydrate (4g fiber, 93g sugar), 1g protein, 0%DV vitamin A, 0%DV vitamin C, 8%DV calcium, 10%DV iron.

Note: *If you wish, and diets allow, serve the apples with low-fat frozen yogurt.*

Baked Apples with Raisins

Carol Findling
Princeton, IL

Makes 5-6 servings
(Ideal slow-cooker size: 4- or 5-quart)

5-6 apples (Winesap, Rome, Cortland, Jonathan, Gala, or other good baking apples)
⅓ cup raisins
½ cup unsweetened apple juice
½ cup boiling water
½ tsp. ground cinnamon
¼ tsp. ground nutmeg

1. Core apples and peel around top of apple. Arrange in slow cooker. (Note: If cooker is deep you may have to do 2 layers).
2. Fill center with raisins.
3. Combine juice, water, cinnamon, and nutmeg. Pour over apples.
4. Cook on low 2-4 hours, depending on size and variety of apples.
5. Serve warm or cool.

Per Serving: 110 calories (0 calories from fat), 0g total fat (0g saturated, 0g trans), 0mg cholesterol, 0mg sodium, 28g total carbohydrate (5g fiber, 22g sugar), 0g protein, 2%DV vitamin A, 4%DV vitamin C, 0%DV calcium, 4%DV iron.

Notes:
1. If your diet allows, you may want to substitute craisins for raisins.
2. If you like, and you can afford the calories, you may want to reduce the raisins to ¼ cup and add 2-3 Tbsp. finely chopped walnuts or pecans to Step 2.
3. If you're able to splurge on calories, you may want to top the apples with a small dip of frozen yogurt for each serving.

Country Apples

Betty K. Drescher
Quakertown, PA

Makes 8 servings
(Ideal slow-cooker size: 2¹/2-quart)

4-5 cups apples, peeled and sliced
2 Tbsp. flour
¹/4 cup sugar
¹/3 cup raisins
¹/4 tsp. ground cinnamon
²/3 cup dry oatmeal, rolled or quick
1 cup water
2 Tbsp. butter, melted
¹/3 cup brown sugar

1. Coat apples in flour and white sugar. Stir in raisins, cinnamon, and oatmeal.
2. Pour water into slow cooker. Add apple mix.
3. Pour melted butter over apples. Sprinkle with brown sugar.
4. Cover. Cook on low 5-6 hours.
5. Serve over vanilla ice cream as a dessert, over oatmeal for breakfast, or use as a filling for crepes.

Per Serving: 160 calories (30 calories from fat), 3g total fat (2g saturated, 0g trans), 10mg cholesterol, 5mg sodium, 35g total carbohydrate (2g fiber, 26g sugar), 1g protein, 0%DV vitamin A, 0%DV vitamin C, 2%DV calcium, 4%DV iron.

Chunk-Style Applesauce

Miriam Nolt, New Holland, PA
Judi Manos, West Islip, NY
Jean Butzer, Batavia, NY
Janet Roggie, Lowville, NY
Michelle Steffen, Harrisonburg, VA

Makes 8 servings
(Ideal slow-cooker size: 3¹/2-quart)

8 large cooking apples, peeled, cored, and sliced or cut into chunks
¹/2 cup water
1 tsp. cinnamon
¹/2 cup sugar

1. Combine all ingredients in slow cooker.
2. Cover. Cook on low 8 hours or on high 3-4 hours.
3. Serve warm. (This sauce is also delicious served chilled!)

Per Serving: 110 calories (0 calories from fat), 0g total fat (0g saturated, 0g trans), 0mg cholesterol, 0mg sodium, 30g total carbohydrate (3g fiber, 26g sugar), 0g protein, 0%DV vitamin A, 0%DV vitamin C, 2%DV calcium, 2%DV iron.

Dawn's Healthy Harvest Applesauce

Dawn Day
Westminster, CA

Makes 12 servings
(Ideal slow-cooker size: 5-quart)

10 medium-sized apples (Rome, McIntosh, Pippin, or a variety that holds its shape well)
3 fresh pears
1 cup fresh or frozen cranberries
½ cup unfiltered apple cider
3 tsp. ground cinnamon
¼ tsp. ground nutmeg
¼ tsp. ground cloves
juice of 1 lemon
½ cup brown sugar, optional

1. Peel and chop apples and pears into ¼" cubes. Place in slow cooker.
2. Mix in cranberries and remaining ingredients.
3. Cover. Cook on low 8 hours.

Per Serving: 100 calories (0 calories from fat), 0g total fat (0g saturated, 0g trans), 0mg cholesterol, 0mg sodium, 28g total carbohydrate (6g fiber, 20g sugar), 0g protein, 2%DV vitamin A, 2%DV vitamin C, 4%DV calcium, 4%DV iron.

Notes:
1. You may add a little more cider for a saucier consistency.
2. Serve hot or cold as a side dish with pork or chicken, or chilled as a dessert.

Spiced Apples

Shari and Dale Mast
Harrisonburg, VA

Makes 10-12 servings
(Ideal slow-cooker size: 6-quart)

16 cups sliced apples, peeled or unpeeled
½ cup brown sugar
3 Tbsp. minute tapioca
1 tsp. ground cinnamon

1. Layer half of sliced apples, sugar, tapioca, and cinnamon in slow cooker.
2. Repeat, making a second layer using remaining ingredients.
3. Cover. Cook on high 4 hours or on low 5 hours.
4. Stir before serving. Delicious hot or cold.

Per Serving: 130 calories (0 calories from fat), 0g total fat (0g saturated, 0g trans), 0mg cholesterol, 0mg sodium, 33g total carbohydrate (3g fiber, 27g sugar), 0g protein, 0%DV vitamin A, 0%DV vitamin C, 2%DV calcium, 2%DV iron.

Carmeled Pears 'n Wine

Sharon Timpe
Jackson, WI

Makes 6 servings
(Ideal slow-cooker size: 6-quart)

6 medium-sized fresh pears with stems
1 cup white wine (sauterne works well)
1/2 cup sugar
1/2 cup water
3 Tbsp. lemon juice
2 apple cinnamon sticks, each about
2 1/2-3″ long
3 whole dried cloves
1/4 tsp. ground nutmeg
6 Tbsp. fat-free caramel apple dip

1. Peel pears, leaving whole with stems intact.
2. Place upright in slow cooker. Shave bottom if needed to level fruit.
3. Combine wine, sugar, water, lemon juice, cinnamon, cloves, and nutmeg. Pour over pears.
4. Cook on low 4-6 hours, or until pears are tender.
5. Cool pears in liquid.
6. Transfer pears to individual serving dishes. Place 2 tsp. cooking liquid in bottom of each dish.
7. Microwave caramel dip for 20 seconds and stir. Repeat until heated through.
8. Drizzle caramel over pears and serve.

Per Serving: 290 calories (25 calories from fat), 2.5 total fat (0g saturated, 0g trans), 0mg cholesterol, 140mg sodium, 62g total carbohydrate (4g fiber, 42g sugar), 2g protein, 0%DV vitamin A, 4%DV vitamin C, 15%DV calcium, 6%DV iron.

Golden Fruit Compote

Cindy Krestynick
Glen Lyon, PA
Judi Manos
West Islip, NY

Makes 8 servings
(Ideal slow-cooker size: 3-quart)

1-lb. 13-oz. can light peach or pear slices,
undrained
1/2 cup dried apricots
1/4 cup golden raisins
1/8 tsp. ground cinnamon
1/8 tsp. ground nutmeg
3/4 cup orange juice

1. Combine undrained peach or pear slices, apricots, raisins, cinnamon, and nutmeg in slow cooker. Stir in orange juice. Completely immerse fruit in liquid.
2. Cover and cook on low 6-8 hours.
3. Serve cold with angel food cake or fat-free ice cream. Serve warm as a side dish in the main meal.

Per Serving: 70 calories (0 calories from fat), 0g total fat (0g saturated, 0g trans), 0mg cholesterol, 0mg sodium, 17g total carbohydrate (2g fiber, 13g sugar), 1g protein, 2%DV vitamin A, 10%DV vitamin C, 2%DV calcium, 4%DV iron.

Notes:
   If you prefer a thicker compote, mix together 2 Tbsp. cornstarch and 1/4 cup cold water until smooth. Stir into hot fruit 15 minutes before end of cooking time. Stir until absorbed in juice.

Hot Fruit Compote

Sue Williams, Gulfport, MS

Makes 4-6 servings
(Ideal slow-cooker size: 4-quart)

1 lb. dried plums
1 1/3 cups dried apricots
13 1/2-oz. can unsweetened pineapple
chunks, undrained
1-lb. can unsweetened pitted dark sweet
cherries, undrained
1/4 cup dry white wine
2 cups water
1/3 cup sugar

1. Mix together all ingredients in slow cooker.
2. Cover and cook on low 7-8 hours or high 3-4 hours.
3. Serve warm.

Per Serving: 600 calories (10 calories from fat), 1g total fat (0g saturated, 0g trans), 0mg cholesterol, 15mg sodium, 148g total carbohydrate (13g fiber, 112g sugar), 6g protein, 50%DV vitamin A, 10%DV vitamin C, 10%DV calcium, 40%DV iron.

Hot Fruit Salad

Judi Manos
West Islip, NY

Makes 16 servings
(Ideal slow-cooker size: 4-quart)

25-oz. can unsweetened chunky
applesauce
21-oz. can light cherry pie filling
20-oz. can light pineapple chunks,
undrained
15 1/4-oz. can light sliced peaches,
undrained

15 1/2-oz. can light apricot halves,
undrained
15-oz. can light mandarin oranges,
undrained
1/2 cup brown sugar, packed
1 tsp. ground cinnamon

1. Combine applesauce and all canned fruit in slow cooker. Stir gently.
2. Combine brown sugar and cinnamon. Sprinkle over fruit mixture.
3. Cover. Cook on low 3-4 hours.

Per Serving: 150 calories (0 calories from fat), 0g total fat (0g saturated, 0g trans), 0mg cholesterol, 25mg sodium, 37g total carbohydrate (2g fiber, 34g sugar), 1g protein, 10%DV vitamin A, 10%DV vitamin C, 2%DV calcium, 4%DV iron.

Note: This recipe is very easy. It is especially great around the holidays. The aroma it creates in the house is wonderful.

Hot Fruit Dessert

Pat Unternahrer
Wayland, IA

Makes about 8-9 servings
(Ideal slow-cooker size: 5-quart)

3 grapefruit, peeled and sectioned
11-oz. can mandarin orange segments,
drained
16-oz. can unsweetened sliced peaches,
drained
16-oz. can unsweetened fruit cocktail,
drained
20-oz. can unsweetened pineapple chunks,
drained
3 bananas, sliced
1 Tbsp. lemon juice
21-oz. can low-fat cherry pie filling

1. Combine all ingredients in slow cooker.
2. Cover. Cook on low 4 hours.
3. Chill and serve.

Per Serving: 120 calories (0 calories from fat), 0g total fat (0g saturated, 0g trans), 0mg cholesterol, 15mg sodium, 31g total carbohydrate (3g fiber, 24g sugar), 1g protein, 2%DV vitamin A, 30%DV vitamin C, 2%DV calcium, 2%DV iron.

Note: This is an excellent topping for angel-food cake, if diets allow.

Strawberry Rhubarb Sauce
Tina Snyder
Manheim, PA

*Makes 8 servings
(Ideal slow-cooker size: 3¹/₂-quart)*

6 cups sliced rhubarb
³/₄ cup sugar
1 cinnamon stick, optional
¹/₂ cup white grape juice
2 cups sliced strawberries, unsweetened

1. Place rhubarb in slow cooker. Pour sugar over. Add cinnamon stick, if you wish, and grape juice. Stir well.
2. Cover and cook on low 5-6 hours, or until rhubarb is tender.
3. Stir in strawberries. Cook 1 hour longer.
4. Remove cinnamon stick if you've used it. Chill.

Per Serving: 120 calories (0 calories from fat), 0g total fat (0g saturated, 0g trans), 0mg cholesterol, 10mg sodium, 29g total carbohydrate (3g fiber, 26g sugar), 1g protein, 0%DV vitamin A, 30%DV vitamin C, 10%DV calcium, 4%DV iron.

Note: Serve as is, or, if diets allow, over cake or ice cream.

Rhubarb Sauce
Esther Porter
Minneapolis, MN

*Makes 6 servings
(Ideal slow-cooker size: 4¹/₂-quart)*

1¹/₂ lbs. rhubarb
¹/₈ tsp. salt
¹/₂ cup water
¹/₂ cup sugar
pinch of baking soda

1. Cut rhubarb into ¹/₂-inch thick slices.
2. Combine all ingredients except baking soda in slow cooker. Cook on low 4-5 hours. Stir in baking soda.
3. Serve chilled.

Per Serving: 90 calories (0 calories from fat), 0g total fat (0g saturated, 0g trans), 0mg cholesterol, 55mg sodium, 22g total carbohydrate (2g fiber, 19g sugar), 1g protein, 0%DV vitamin A, 0%DV vitamin C, 10%DV calcium, 2%DV iron.

Note: You may want to add 1 pint sliced strawberries about 30 minutes before the end of the cooking time.

Pineapple Sauce

Elizabeth L. Richards
Rapid City, SD

Makes 8 servings
(Ideal slow-cooker size: 3-quart)

4 cups apple juice
15-oz. can light crushed pineapples,
undrained
1½ cups golden raisins
½ tsp. ground cinnamon
½ tsp. ground allspice
½ cup sugar
¼ cup cornstarch

1. Combine all ingredients in slow cooker. Mix well.
2. Cover. Cook on high 2 hours.
3. Serve as a topping for dessert, as a topping for baked ham, or as a side dish during the holidays.

Per Serving: 250 calories (0 calories from fat), 0g total fat (0g saturated, 0g trans), 0mg cholesterol, 10mg sodium, 63g total carbohydrate (2g fiber, 53g sugar), 1g protein, 0%DV vitamin A, 60%DV vitamin C, 2%DV calcium, 8%DV iron.

Apple Oatmeal Pudding

Sue Hamilton
Minooka, IL

Makes 6 servings
(Ideal slow-cooker size: 3½-quart)

½ cup flour
¼ tsp. salt
1½ tsp. pumpkin pie spice
1 cup Splenda
⅓ cup powdered skim milk
3 eggs, or 9 egg whites

2 tsp. baking powder
¾ cup rolled, or quick, oats
1½ tsp. vanilla
3 cups cooking apples, peeled and diced

1. Combine all ingredients in greased slow cooker. Mix well.
2. Cover. Cook on low 4 hours.
3. Serve hot or cold.

Per Serving: 190 calories (30 calories from fat), 3.5g total fat (1g saturated, 0g trans), 95mg cholesterol, 150mg sodium, 32g total carbohydrate (3g fiber, 9g sugar), 7g protein, 2%DV vitamin A, 2%DV vitamin C, 15%DV calcium, 8%DV iron.

Note: If your diet permits, you may want to serve this with a dollop of low-fat whipped topping or fat-free ice cream on each serving.

Vanilla Bean Rice Pudding

Michele Ruvola
Selden, NY

Makes 12 servings
(Ideal slow-cooker size: 4-quart)

6 cups fat-free milk
1½ cups uncooked converted rice
1 cup sugar
1 cup raisins
1 Tbsp. butter or margarine, melted
½ tsp. salt
1 vanilla bean, split
1 large egg
½ tsp. ground cinnamon
8-oz. carton fat-free sour cream

1. Combine milk, rice, sugar, raisins, butter, and salt in slow cooker. Stir well.
2. Scrape seeds from vanilla bean. Add seeds and bean to milk mixture.
3. Cover with lid and cook on high 2½-4 hours, or just until rice is tender and most of liquid is absorbed.

4. Place egg in small bowl. Stir well with a whisk and gradually add ½ cup hot rice mixture to egg.

5. Return egg mixture to slow cooker, stirring constantly with whisk. Cook 1 minute while stirring. Remove inner vessel from slow cooker.

6. Let stand 5 minutes. Mix in cinnamon and sour cream. Discard vanilla bean.

7. Serve warm, not hot, or refrigerate until fully chilled.

Per Serving: 270 calories (15 calories from fat), 2g total fat (1g saturated, 0g trans), 20mg cholesterol, 180mg sodium, 55g total carbohydrate (0.5g fiber, 33g sugar), 8g protein, 8%DV vitamin A, 2%DV vitamin C, 20%DV calcium, 8%DV iron.

Note: If your diet permits, you may top individual servings with light, or fat-free, vanilla-flavored whipped topping.

Just Rice Pudding

Mrs. Audrey L. Kneer
Williamsfield, IL

Makes 10 servings
(Ideal slow-cooker size: 5-quart)

1 cup long grain white rice, uncooked
1 cup sugar
8 cups skim milk
¾ cup fat-free, cholesterol-free egg product
1 cup skim milk
2 tsp. vanilla
¼ tsp. salt
¼ tsp. ground nutmeg or cinnamon

1. Combine rice, sugar, and 8 cups skim milk in slow cooker.

2. Cover. Cook on high 2 hours or just until rice is tender.

3. Beat together egg-substitute, 1 cup skim milk, vanilla, and salt. Add to slow cooker. Stir.

4. Cover. Cook on high 25-30 minutes.

5. Sprinkle with nutmeg or cinnamon and serve warm.

Per Serving: 200 calories (20 calories from fat), 2g total fat (0.5g saturated, 0g trans), 70mg cholesterol, 190mg sodium, 36g total carbohydrate (0g fiber, 30g sugar), 10g protein, 4%DV vitamin A, 0%DV vitamin C, 30%DV calcium, 4%DV iron..

Old-Fashioned Rice Pudding

Betty K. Drescher
Quakertown, PA

Makes 8 servings
(Ideal slow-cooker size: 2½-quart)

2 cups cooked rice
1½ cups fat-free evaporated milk
⅓ cup brown sugar
2 Tbsp. margarine
2 tsp. vanilla
½ tsp. ground nutmeg
¾ cup fat-free, cholesterol-free egg product
1 cup raisins

1. Combine rice thoroughly with all other ingredients in slow cooker sprayed with non-fat cooking spray.

2. Cover. Cook on low 2-4 hours. Stir after first hour.

Per Serving: 230 calories (40 calories from fat), 4.5g total fat (1g saturated, 0g trans), 80mg cholesterol, 120mg sodium, 42g total carbohydrate (1g fiber, 28g sugar), 8g protein, 0%DV vitamin A, 0%DV vitamin C, 15%DV calcium, 10%DV iron.

Note: If you like a creamier rice pudding, and if your diet allows, you may want to add another 1-1¼ cup fat-free evaporated milk before cooking, halfway through cooking, or just before serving.

Deluxe Tapioca Pudding

Michelle Showalter
Bridgewater, VA

Makes 16 servings
(Ideal slow-cooker size: 4-quart)

2 qts. fat-free milk
¾ cup dry small pearl tapioca
1 cup sugar
¾ cup eggbeaters
2 tsp. vanilla
3 cups fat-free frozen whipped topping,
   thawed

1. Combine milk, tapioca, and sugar in slow cooker.
2. Cook on high 3-4 hours, or until tapioca is tender.
3. Add a little of the hot tapioca-milk mixture to the eggbeaters. Stir. Whisk eggbeaters into tapioca-milk mixture. Add vanilla.
4. Cover. Cook on high 20-30 minutes.
5. Cool. Chill in refrigerator. When fully chilled, beat with hand mixer to fluff the pudding.
6. Fold in whipped topping.

Per Serving: 150 calories (10 calories from fat), 1g total fat (0g saturated, 0g trans), 40mg cholesterol, 80mg sodium, 29g total carbohydrate (0g fiber, 20g sugar), 5g protein, 0%DV vitamin A, 0%DV vitamin C, 15%DV calcium, 2%DV iron.

Tapioca Salad

Karen Ashworth
Duenweg, MO

Makes 12 servings
(Ideal slow-cooker size: 4-quart)

10 Tbsp. large pearl tapioca
⅓ cup sugar
dash salt
4 cups water
1 cup grapes, cut in half
1 cup crushed pineapple, drained of juice
1 cup fat-free frozen whipped topping,
   thawed

1. Mix together tapioca, sugar, salt, and water in slow cooker.
2. Cook on high 3 hours or until tapioca pearls are almost translucent.
3. Cool thoroughly in refrigerator.
4. Stir in fruit. When well mixed, fold in thawed whipped topping. Serve cold.

Per Serving: 70 calories (0 calories from fat), 0g total fat (0g saturated, 0g trans), 0mg cholesterol, 30mg sodium, 18g total carbohydrate (0g fiber, 9g sugar), 0g protein, 0%DV vitamin A, 0%DV vitamin C, 0%DV calcium, 0%DV iron.

Cinnamon Raisin Bread Pudding

Penny Blosser
Beavercreek, OH

Makes 8 servings
(Ideal slow-cooker size: 4-quart)

10 slices cinnamon bread, cut into cubes
1 cup raisins
1 cup fat-free, cholesterol-free egg product
1½ cups warm water
1 tsp. vanilla
½ tsp. ground cinnamon
16-oz. can fat-free sweetened condensed
  milk

1. Place bread cubes and raisins in greased slow cooker. Mix together gently.
2. Mix remaining ingredients together and pour over top.
3. Cover. Cook on high 30 minutes, then on low 2-2½ hours.

Per Serving: 360 calories (50 calories from fat), 6g total fat (1.5g saturated, 0g trans), 110mg cholesterol, 240mg sodium, 69g total carbohydrate (3g fiber, 53g sugar), 12g protein, 0%DV vitamin A, 0%DV vitamin C, 20%DV calcium, 10%DV iron.

Home-Style Bread Pudding

Lizzie Weaver
Ephrata, PA

Makes 6 servings
(Ideal slow-cooker size:
large enough to hold your baking insert)

⅓ cup eggbeaters
2¼ cups fat-free milk
½ tsp. ground cinnamon
¼ tsp. salt
⅓ cup brown sugar
1 tsp. vanilla
2 cups 1"-square bread cubes
½ cup raisins

1. Combine all ingredients in bowl. Pour into slow-cooker baking insert. Cover baking insert. Place on metal rack (or rubber jar ring) in bottom of slow cooker.
2. Pour ½ cup hot water into cooker.
3. Cover slow cooker. Cook on high 2-3 hours.
4. Serve pudding warm or cold.

Per Serving: 170 calories (15 calories from fat), 2g total fat (0.5g saturated, 0g trans), 50mg cholesterol, 70mg sodium, 33g total carbohydrate (0g fiber, 26g sugar), 6g protein, 0%DV vitamin A, 0%DV vitamin C, 15%DV calcium, 6%DV iron.

Cranberry Pudding Cake

Sue Hamilton
Minooka, IL

Makes 6 servings
(Ideal slow-cooker size: 2-quart)

1½ cups fresh or frozen cranberries
1¾ cups water
1 small box sugar-free orange gelatin
½ cup Splenda
1 cup flour
1½ tsp. baking powder
½ cup Splenda
1 tsp. vanilla extract
¼ tsp. baking soda
½ cup skim milk
½ tsp. almond extract

1. In a microwaveable bowl, combine cranberries and water.
2. Cook in microwave 4-5 minutes on high until cranberries pop.
3. Stir in gelatin and ½ cup Splenda until dissolved. Set aside.
4. In another bowl, combine flour, baking powder, ½ cup Splenda, vanilla extract, baking soda, milk, and almond extract. Mix until dry ingredients are moistened.
5. Pour batter into slow cooker sprayed with nonstick cooking spray. Top with hot cranberry mixture.
6. Cover. Cook on low 3-4 hours.
7. This is best served warm or cold rather than hot.

Per Serving: 180 calories (5 calories from fat), 0.5g total fat (0g saturated, 0g trans), 0mg cholesterol, 500mg sodium, 25g total carbohydrate (2g fiber, 3g sugar), 10g protein, 2%DV vitamin A, 2%DV vitamin C, 8%DV calcium, 6%DV iron.

Crockpot Pumpkin Pie Pudding

Sue Hamilton
Minooka, IL

Makes 8 servings
(Ideal slow-cooker size: 3-quart)

15-oz. can pumpkin
12-oz. can evaporated skim milk
¾ cup Splenda
½ cup low-fat buttermilk baking mix
2 eggs, beaten, or 6 egg whites
2 tsp. pumpkin pie spice
1 tsp. lemon zest

1. Combine all ingredients in slow cooker sprayed with cooking spray. Stir until lumps disappear.
2. Cover. Cook on low 3 hours.
3. Serve warm or cold.

Per Serving: 140 calories (30 calories from fat), 3.5g total fat (1g saturated, 0g trans), 50mg cholesterol, 220mg sodium, 21g total carbohydrate (2g fiber, 7g sugar), 7g protein, 200%DV vitamin A, 2%DV vitamin C, 15%DV calcium, 8%DV iron.

Note: If you like, and your diet permits, add a spoonful of low-fat whipped topping to each serving.

Apple Crisp
Mary Jane Musser
Manheim, PA

Makes 6 servings
(Ideal slow-cooker size: 3-quart)

6 cups cooking apples, peeled, cored, and sliced
1/2 cup dry quick oatmeal
1/2 cup brown sugar
1/2 cup flour
2 Tbsp. margarine
1/2 tsp. ground cinnamon

1. Place apples in slow cooker sprayed with non-fat cooking spray.
2. Combine remaining ingredients in a mixing bowl until crumbly.
3. Sprinkle mixture over apples.
4. Cover. Cook on low 4 hours or on high 2 hours.

Per Serving: 260 calories (40 calories from fat), 4.5g total fat (0.5g saturated, 0g trans), 0mg cholesterol, 55mg sodium, 53g total carbohydrate (4g fiber, 32g sugar), 3g protein, 0%DV vitamin A, 0%DV vitamin C, 2%DV calcium, 8%DV iron.

A hint from the recipe's submitter:
The next time you do a major cleaning in your kitchen, clear your kitchen shelves of those high-fat items you haven't used in a while. When they are out of the house they won't be a temptation.

Low-Fat Apple Cake
Sue Hamilton
Minooka, IL

Makes 8 servings
(Ideal slow-cooker size: 4-quart)

1 cup flour
3/4 cup sugar
2 tsp. baking powder
1 tsp. ground cinnamon
1/4 tsp. salt
4 medium-sized cooking apples, chopped
1/3 cup eggbeaters
2 tsp. vanilla

1. Combine flour, sugar, baking powder, cinnamon, and salt.
2. Add apples, stirring lightly to coat.
3. Combine eggbeaters and vanilla. Add to apple mixture. Stir until just moistened. Spoon into lightly greased slow cooker.
4. Cover. Bake on high 2 1/2-3 hours.
5. Serve warm.

Per Serving: 180 calories (10 calories from fat), 1g total fat (0g saturated, 0g trans), 35mg cholesterol, 85mg sodium, 41g total carbohydrate (2g fiber, 26g sugar), 3g protein, 0%DV vitamin A, 0%DV vitamin C, 6%DV calcium, 6%DV iron.

Slow-Cooker Berry Cobbler

Wilma Haberkamp
Fairbank, IA
Virginia Graybill
Hershey, PA

Makes 8 servings
(Ideal slow-cooker size: 5-quart)

1 1/4 cups all-purpose flour (divided)
2 Tbsp. sugar, plus 1 cup sugar (divided)
1 tsp. baking powder
1/4 tsp. ground cinnamon
1 egg, lightly beaten
1/4 cup skim milk
2 Tbsp. canola oil
1/8 tsp. salt
2 cups unsweetened raspberries, fresh, or thawed if frozen, and drained
2 cups unsweetened blueberries, fresh, or thawed if frozen, and drained

1. In a mixing bowl, combine 1 cup flour, 2 Tbsp. sugar, baking powder, and cinnamon.

2. In a separate bowl, combine egg, milk, and oil. Stir into dry ingredients until moistened. Batter will be thick.

3. Spray slow cooker with cooking spray. Spread batter evenly on bottom of slow cooker.

4. In another bowl, combine salt, remaining flour, remaining sugar, and berries. Toss to coat berries.

5. Spread berries over batter.

6. Cook on high 2-2 1/2 hours, or until a toothpick inserted into cobbler comes out clean.

Per Serving: 260 calories (40 calories from fat), 4.5g total fat (0g saturated, 0g trans), 25mg cholesterol, 50mg sodium, 52g total carbohydrate (4g fiber, 34g sugar), 3g protein, 2%DV vitamin A, 10%DV vitamin C, 6%DV calcium, 8%DV iron.

Note: If your diet permits, this is good served in soup bowls with cold milk poured over.

Cherry Cobbler

Penny Blosser
Beavercreek, OH

Makes 6 servings
(Ideal slow-cooker size: 3 1/2-quart)

21-oz. can low-fat, low-sodium cherry pie filling
1 cup flour
1/4 cup sugar
1/4 cup butter, melted
1/2 cup skim milk
1 1/2 tsp. baking powder
1/2 tsp. almond extract
1/4 tsp. salt

1. Pour pie filling into greased slow cooker.

2. Combine remaining ingredients. Beat until smooth. Spread over pie filling.

3. Cover. Cook on high 1 1/2-2 hours on high.

Per Serving: 230 calories (5 calories from fat), 0.5g total fat (0g saturated, 0g trans), 0mg cholesterol, 125mg sodium, 54g total carbohydrate (1g fiber, 33g sugar), 3g protein, 0%DV vitamin A, 0%DV vitamin C, 10%DV calcium, 8%DV iron.

Quick Yummy Peaches

Willard E. Roth
Elkhart, IN

Makes 6 servings

¹/₃ cup low-fat buttermilk baking mix
²/₃ cup dry quick oats
¹/₃ cup brown sugar
1 tsp. ground cinnamon
4 cups sliced peaches, canned or fresh
¹/₂ cup water

1. Mix together baking mix, dry oats, brown sugar, and cinnamon in greased slow cooker.
2. Stir in peaches and water.
3. Cook on low for at least 5 hours. (If you like a drier cobbler, remove lid for last 15-30 minutes of cooking.)

Per Serving: 270 calories (25 calories from fat) (0.5g saturated, 0g trans), 0mg cholesterol, 230mg sodium, 57g total carbohydrate (1g fiber, 42g sugar), 3g protein, 10%DV vitamin A, 0%DV vitamin C, 4%DV calcium, 6%DV iron.

Note: If your diet allows, serve with fat-free frozen yogurt or ice cream.

Hot Fudge Cake

Evelyn L. Ward
Greeley, CO

Makes 8 servings
(Ideal slow-cooker size: 3¹/₂-quart)

1³/₄ cups brown sugar, divided
1 cup flour
3 Tbsp., plus ¹/₄ cup, unsweetened cocoa, divided
1¹/₂ tsp. baking powder
¹/₂ tsp. salt
¹/₂ cup skim milk
2 Tbsp. butter, melted
¹/₂ tsp. vanilla
1³/₄ cups boiling water

1. In a mixing bowl, mix together 1 cup brown sugar, flour, 3 Tbsp. cocoa, baking powder, and salt.
2. Stir in milk, butter, and vanilla.
3. Pour into slow cooker sprayed with non-fat cooking spray.
4. In a separate bowl, mix together ³/₄ cup brown sugar and ¹/₄ cup cocoa. Sprinkle over batter in the slow cooker. Do not stir.
5. Pour boiling water over mixture. Do not stir.
6. Cover. Cook on high 1¹/₂-1³/₄ hours, or until toothpick inserted into cake comes out clean.

Per Serving: 280 calories (35 calories from fat), 3.5g total fat (2g saturated, 0g trans), 10mg cholesterol, 180mg sodium, 63g total carbohydrate (2g fiber, 48g sugar), 3g protein, 0%DV vitamin A, 0%DV vitamin C, 10%DV calcium, 15%DV iron.

Note: Serve with low-fat ice cream or fat-free whipped topping if you wish, and if diets allow.

Chocolate Mud Cake

Marci Baum
Annville, PA

Makes 8 servings
(Ideal slow-cooker size: 4-quart)

1 cup flour
2 tsp. baking powder
2 Tbsp. butter
2 ozs. semisweet chocolate,
   or 1/3 cup chocolate chips
1 cup sugar, divided
3 Tbsp. plus 1/3 cup Dutch-processed cocoa
1 Tbsp. vanilla extract
1/4 tsp. salt
1/3 cup skim milk
1 egg yolk
1/3 cup brown sugar
1 1/2 cups hot water

1. Coat inside of slow cooker with nonfat cooking spray.
2. In mixing bowl, whisk together flour and baking powder. Set aside.
3. In a large microwave-safe mixing bowl, melt the butter and chocolate in the microwave. Mix well.
4. Whisk in 2/3 cup sugar, 3 Tbsp. cocoa, vanilla, salt, milk, and egg yolk.
5. Add the flour mixture. Stir until thoroughly mixed.
6. Pour batter into slow cooker. Spread evenly.
7. Whisk together remaining sugar, cocoa, and hot water until sugar is dissolved. Pour over batter in slow cooker. Do not stir.
8. Cover. Cook on high 1-2 hours. The cake will be very moist and floating on a layer of molten chocolate when it's done. And you'll know it is done cooking when nearly all the cake is set and its edges begin to pull away from the sides of the pot.
9. Turn off slow cooker and remove lid. Try not to let the condensed steam from the lid drip onto the cake.

Let cool for 25 minutes before cutting and spooning onto individual plates.

Per Serving: 370 calories (60 calories from fat), 7g total fat (3.5g saturated, 0g trans), 35mg cholesterol, 150mg sodium, 72g total carbohydrate (2g fiber, 53g sugar), 9g protein, 0%DV vitamin A, 0%DV vitamin C, 25%DV calcium, 8%DV iron.

Note: *If diets permit, serve the cake with lowfat or fat-free frozen yogurt.*

Appetizers, Snacks, and Spreads

Prairie Fire Dip

Cheri Jantzen
Houston, TX

Makes 10 servings (about 1¼ cups total)
(Ideal slow-cooker size: 2-quart)

1 cup refried fat-free beans
  (half of a 15-oz. can)
½ cup shredded fat-free Monterey Jack
  cheese
¼ cup water
1 Tbsp. minced onion
1 clove garlic, minced
2 tsp. chili powder
hot sauce as desired

1. Combine all ingredients in slow cooker.
2. Cover. Cook on high 1 hour, or on low 2-3 hours.

Serve with baked tortilla chips

Per Serving: 45 calories (0 calories from fat), 0g total fat (0g saturated, 0g trans), 0mg cholesterol, 190mg sodium, 6g total carbohydrate (2g fiber, 0g sugar), 5g protein, 6%DV vitamin A, 0%DV vitamin C, 15%DV calcium, 4%DV iron.

Note: This recipe can easily be doubled.

Chili Cheese Dip

Vicki Dinkel
Sharon Springs, KS

Makes 8 servings
(Ideal slow-cooker size—2 quart)

1 onion, diced
8-oz. pkg. fat-free cream cheese, cubed
2 15-oz. cans lowfat vegetarian chili
  without beans
2 tsp. garlic salt
1½ cups salsa

1. Lightly brown onion in skillet sprayed with non-fat cooking spray. Transfer to slow cooker.
2. Stir in cream cheese, chili, garlic salt, and salsa.
3. Cover. Cook on low 4 hours, stirring occasionally.
4. Serve with baked tortilla chips.

Per Serving: 230 calories (15 calories from fat), 2g total fat (0g saturated, 0g trans), 0mg cholesterol, 1420mg sodium, 40g total carbohydrate (8g fiber, 2g sugar), 15g protein, 10%DV vitamin A, 4%DV vitamin C, 10%DV calcium, 10%DV iron.

Nacho Dip
Susan Tjon
Austin, TX

Makes 8 servings
(Ideal slow-cooker size: 3-quart)

8 ozs. fat-free cream cheese
1 cup shredded reduced-fat cheddar
   cheese
½ cup mild or medium chunky salsa
¼ cup fat-free or 2% milk
8-oz. bag baked tortilla chips or assorted
   fresh vegetables

1. Cut cream cheese into chunks.
2. Combine cream cheese, cheddar cheese, salsa, and milk in slow cooker.
3. Cook on low 2 hours. Stir to blend.
4. When smooth and hot, serve with baked tortilla chips or assorted fresh vegetables.

Per Serving: 170 calories (25 calories from fat), 2.5 total fat (1g saturated, 0g trans), 5mg cholesterol, 430mg sodium, 27g total carbohydrate (2g fiber, 1g sugar), 10g protein, 8%DV vitamin A, 4%DV vitamin C, 20%DV calcium, 4%DV iron.

Note: You may double this recipe successfully. Just be sure to allow extra cooking time.

Salsa
Wilma J. Haberkamp
Fairbank, IA

Makes 6-7 pints, or 48 or more 4-Tbsp.-size servings
(Ideal slow-cooker size—6 quart or larger)

13 tomatoes, peeled and seeded
1 tsp. salt
4 tsp. white vinegar
2 6½-oz. cans tomato paste
⅔ cup Louisiana Pure Hot Sauce
1 large yellow onion, chopped
1 large red onion, chopped
1 green bell pepper, seeded and chopped
1 red bell pepper, seeded and chopped
1 yellow bell pepper, seeded and chopped
1 or 2 hot peppers, seeded
3 banana peppers, seeded and chopped

1. Combine all ingredients in large bowl and mix well. Ladle into 6-qt., or larger, slow cooker.
2. Cook on high 1 hour, and then reduce to low for 2 hours.
3. Pour into sterilized jars and follow directions from your canner for sealing and preserving.

Per Serving: 25 calories (0 calories from fat), 0g total fat (0g saturated, 0g trans), 0mg cholesterol, 140mg sodium, 6g total carbohydrate (1g fiber, 2g sugar), 1g protein, 15%DV vitamin A, 40%DV vitamin C, 0%DV calcium, 2%DV iron.

A note from the tester: When I served the salsa, I stirred in some fresh chopped cilantro to add taste and lively green color. I served it as an appetizer and 8 people almost finished a pint jar!

Slow-Cooker Salsa

Joyce Shackelford
Green Bay, WI

Makes 2 cups or 8 servings
(Ideal slow-cooker size—1 or 2 quart)

10 plum tomatoes, cored
2 garlic cloves
1 medium-sized onion, cut in wedges
2 or 3 jalapeño peppers
half a medium-sized green bell pepper,
  chopped
1/4 cup cilantro or parsley leaves
1/2 tsp. salt
1/4 tsp. black pepper

1. Cut a small slit in two tomatoes. Insert a garlic clove in each slit. Place tomatoes and onions in slow cooker.

2. Cut stems off jalapeños. Remove seeds for a milder salsa. Place jalapeños in slow cooker. Add chopped bell pepper.

3. Cover. Cook on high 2½-3 hours. Cool.

4. In a blender, combine the tomato mixture, cilantro, and salt. Process until smooth.

5. Refrigerate leftovers.

Per Serving: 25 calories (0 calories from fat), 0 total fat (0g saturated, 0g trans), 0mg cholesterol, 150mg sodium, 5g total carbohydrate (1g fiber, 3g sugar), 1g protein, 10%DV vitamin A, 20%DV vitamin C, 0%DV calcium, 2%DV iron.

Use rubber gloves when cutting hot peppers.

Fruit Salsa

Joyce Shackelford
Green Bay, WI

Makes 4 cups or 16 servings
(Ideal slow-cooker size: 2- or 3-quart)

11-oz. can mandarin oranges
8½-oz. can unsweetened sliced peaches,
  undrained
8-oz. can unsweetened pineapple tidbits,
  undrained
1 medium-sized onion, chopped
half a medium-sized green bell pepper,
  chopped
half a medium-sized red bell pepper,
  chopped
half a medium-sized yellow bell pepper,
  chopped
3 garlic cloves, minced
3 Tbsp. cornstarch
4 tsp. vinegar

1. Combine all ingredients in slow cooker.

2. Cover. Cook on high 2 hours, stirring occasionally.

3. Serve with baked tortilla chips.

Per Serving: 35 calories (0 calories from fat), 0 total fat (0g saturated, 0g trans), 0mg cholesterol, 5mg sodium, 8g total carbohydrate (0.5g fiber, 6g sugar), 0g protein, 10%DV vitamin A, 20%DV vitamin C, 0%DV calcium, 2%DV iron.

Texas Dip
Donna Lantgen
Rapid City, SD

Makes 8 servings
(Ideal slow-cooker size: 1½-quart)

1 cup onions, chopped
1 small can diced green chilies
16-oz. can Rotel tomatoes, diced,
   or 2 cups fresh tomatoes, diced
1½ cups cubed Velveeta Light cheese

1. Combine all ingredients in slow cooker.
2. Cook on low 6 hours.

Per Serving: 120 calories (40 calories from fat), 4.5 total fat
(3g saturated, 0g trans), 20mg cholesterol, 900mg sodium,
11g total carbohydrate (2g fiber, 7g sugar), 9g protein,
15%DV vitamin A, 15%DV vitamin C, 30%DV calcium,
2%DV iron.

Serve with lowfat tortilla chips or cut-up fresh
vegetables.

Slim Dunk
Vera Smucker
Goshen, IN

Makes 3 cups or 12 servings
(Ideal slow-cooker size: 1½-quart)

2 cups fat-free sour cream
¼ cup fat-free miracle whip salad dressing
10-oz. pkg. frozen chopped spinach,
   squeezed dry and chopped
1.8-oz. envelope dry leek soup mix
¼ cup red bell pepper, minced

1. Combine all ingredients in slow cooker.
Mix well.

2. Cover. Cook on high 1 hour.
3. Serve with fat-free baked tortilla chips.

Per Serving: 70 calories (10 calories from fat), 1 total fat
(0.5g saturated, 0g trans), 5mg cholesterol, 310mg sodium,
11g total carbohydrate (0.5g fiber, 4g sugar), 3g protein,
25%DV vitamin A, 10%DV vitamin C, 10%DV calcium,
4%DV iron.

Broccoli Cheese Dip
Carla Koslowsky
Hillsboro, KS

Makes 6 cups dip, or about 23 2-oz. servings
(Ideal slow-cooker size: 3- or 4-quart)

1 cup chopped celery
½ cup chopped onions
10-oz. pkg. frozen chopped broccoli,
   cooked
1 cup cooked rice
10¾-oz. can fat-free, sodium-free cream of
   mushroom soup
16-oz. jar fat-free cheese spread

1. Combine all ingredients in slow cooker.
2. Cover. Heat on low 2 hours.
3. Serve with snack breads or crackers.

Per Serving: 60 calories (15 calories from fat), 1.5g total fat
(1g saturated, 0g trans), 5mg cholesterol, 110mg sodium,
7g total carbohydrate (0g fiber, 1g sugar), 6g protein,
0%DV vitamin A, 0%DV vitamin C, 15%DV calcium,
2%DV iron.

Notes:
   1. If you're an onion-lover, you may want to
increase the chopped onions to ¾ cup.
   2. If you prefer your vegetables soft rather than
crunchy, you may want to cook the onions and
celery before adding them to the cooker.

Artichoke Dip

Maryann Markano
Wilmington, DE

Makes 6-10 servings
(Ideal slow-cooker size: 2½ or 3-quart)

14-oz. can non-marinated artichoke hearts,
  chopped
10¾-oz. can cream of mushroom/roasted
  garlic condensed soup
1 cup fat-free cream cheese, broken into
  small pieces
¼ tsp. black pepper
⅛ tsp. crushed red pepper flakes
  (optional)
dash of salt
½ cup fat-free shredded Parmesan cheese
½ cup fat-free shredded mozzarella cheese
½ cup sliced green onions
½ cup roasted red peppers, chopped
baked pita or bagel chips (for dipping)

1. Spray inside of slow cooker with fat-free
vegetable spray.
2. Combine all ingredients except chips in
slow cooker. Mix well.
3. Cook on high 1½ hours. Reduce to low
and keep warm for serving.
4. Stir just before serving.

Per Serving: 170 calories (10 calories from fat), 1.5g total
fat (0.5g saturated, 0g trans), 5mg cholesterol, 600mg
sodium, 25g total carbohydrate (3g fiber, 2g sugar), 12g
protein, 10%DV vitamin A, 10%DV vitamin C, 30%DV
calcium, 8%DV iron.

Hot Artichoke Dip

Mary E. Wheatley
Mashpee, MA

Makes 7-8 cups, or 28 2-oz. servings
(Ideal slow-cooker size: 3-quart)

2 14¾-oz. jars marinated artichoke hearts,
  drained
1½ cups fat-free mayonnaise
1½ cups fat-free sour cream
1 cup water chestnuts, chopped
¼ cup grated Parmesan cheese
¼ cup finely chopped scallions

1. Cut artichoke hearts into small pieces.
Add mayonnaise, sour cream, water chestnuts,
cheese, and scallions. Pour into slow cooker.
2. Cover. Cook on high 1-2 hours or on low
3-4 hours.
3. Serve with crackers or crusty French
bread.

Per Serving: 60 calories (20 calories from fat), 2.5g total fat
(0g saturated, 0g trans), 5mg cholesterol, 240mg sodium,
8g total carbohydrate (2g fiber, 2g sugar), 2g protein,
0%DV vitamin A, 10%DV vitamin C, 4%DV calcium,
0%DV iron.

Mexican Dip

Marla Folkerts, Holland, OH

Makes 15 servings
(Ideal slow-cooker size: 3-quart)

1 lb. low-fat ground beef or turkey
8-oz. pkg. no-fat Mexican cheese, grated
16-oz. jar mild, thick and chunky picante
    salsa, or thick and chunky salsa
16-oz. can vegetarian refried beans

1. Brown meat. Do not drain.
2. Add remaining ingredients. Stir until mixed and hot.
3. Keep warm in slow cooker. Serve with lowfat tortilla chips.

Per Serving: 110 calories (25 calories from fat), 3g total fat (1g saturated, 0g trans), 15mg cholesterol, 400mg sodium, 7g total carbohydrate (2g fiber, 1g sugar), 12g protein, 6%DV vitamin A, 8%DV vitamin C, 25%DV calcium, 8%DV iron.

Hot Hamburger Dip

Kristi See
Weskan, KS

Makes 12 servings
(Ideal slow-cooker size: 4- or 5-quart)

1/2 lb. lean ground beef
2 small onions, chopped
1/2 lb. Velveeta Light cheese, cubed
10-oz. can green chilies and tomatoes
2 tsp. Worcestershire sauce
1/2 tsp. chili powder
1 tsp. garlic powder
1/2 tsp. black pepper
10³/4-oz. can low-sodium tomato soup
10³/4-oz. can 98% fat-free mushroom soup

1. Brown beef and onions in a nonstick skillet. Place in slow cooker.
2. Add remaining ingredients and stir well.
3. Cover. Cook on low until cheese is melted, about 2 hours.

Per Serving: 110 calories (40 calories from fat), 4.5g total fat (2.5g saturated, 1g trans), 15mg cholesterol, 620mg sodium, 9g total carbohydrate (0g fiber, 3g sugar), 8g protein, 6%DV vitamin A, 6%DV vitamin C, 15%DV calcium, 4%DV iron.

Chicken Cheese Dip

Sheridy Steele
Ardmore, OK

Makes 10 servings
(Ideal slow-cooker size: 1- or1¹/2 quart)

1/2 lb. Velveeta cheese
12-oz. can tomatoes with chilies
1 cup cooked skinless chicken breast,
    diced and shredded
1/2 cup bell peppers, chopped

1. Cube cheese. Melt.
2. Combine cheese, tomatoes, chicken, and peppers in slow cooker.
3. Cook on low 1-2 hours.
4. Serve with baked chips.

Per Serving: 270 calories (45 calories from fat), 5g total fat (2g saturated, 0g trans), 30mg cholesterol, 830mg sodium, 43g total carbohydrate (4g fiber, 2g sugar), 15g protein, 8%DV vitamin A, 10%DV vitamin C, 20%DV calcium, 6%DV iron.

Notes:
1. To add color, use a mixture of chopped red, yellow and green bell peppers.
2. For a thicker dip, drain the tomatoes with chilies before mixing them in.

Mexican Chicken Dip

Barb Yoder
Angola, IN

Makes 12 servings
(Ideal slow-cooker size: 3-quart)

15-oz. can fat-free chicken breast, roasted
1½ cups fat-free sour cream
10-oz. can cut-up tomatoes and green chilies
10¾-oz. can condensed cream of chicken soup
10¾-oz. can 98% fat-free cream of mushroom soup
¾ lb. Velveeta Light cheese, cubed and divided
10-oz. pkg. fat-free flour tortillas

1. In a large bowl, mix together chicken, sour cream, tomatoes and chilies, soups and about half of the cheese cubes.
2. With a kitchen shears, cut tortillas into 1"-1½" squares.
3. Place a thin layer of sauce mixture on bottom of slow cooker sprayed with non-fat cooking spray.
4. Add a thick layer of tortilla squares. Then add a thick layer of sauce.
5. Repeat layers.
6. Pour remaining cheese cubes over all.
7. Cover. Cook on low 5-6 hours. Do not stir for first 3 hours.
8. Stir about ½ hour before serving. Stir again just before serving.

Per Serving: 230 calories (60 calories from fat), 7g total fat (3g saturated, 1.5g trans), 35mg cholesterol, 1540mg sodium, 26g total carbohydrate (0.5g fiber, 6g sugar), 16g protein, 10%DV vitamin A, 2%DV vitamin C, 25%DV calcium, 8%DV iron.

Tangy Cocktail Franks

Linda Sluiter
Schererville, IN

Makes 12 servings
(Ideal slow-cooker size: 3-quart)

14-oz. jar currant jelly
¼ cup prepared mustard
3 Tbsp. dry sherry
¼ tsp. ground allspice
30-oz. can unsweetened pineapple chunks
6-oz. pkg. low-sodium cocktail franks

1. Melt jelly in slow cooker turned on high. Stir in seasonings until blended.
2. Drain pineapple chunks and any liquid in cocktail franks package. Discard juice. Gently stir pineapple and franks into slow cooker.
3. Cover. Cook on low 1-2 hours.
4. Serve and enjoy.

Per Serving: 160 calories (40 calories from fat), 4g total fat (2g saturated, 0g trans), 10mg cholesterol, 170mg sodium, 28g total carbohydrate (0.5g fiber, 25g sugar), 2g protein, 0%DV vitamin A, 0%DV vitamin C, 2%DV calcium, 4%DV iron.

Hot Crab Dip
Karen Waggoner
Joplin, MO

Makes 5 cups
(Ideal slow-cooker size: 2-quart)

1/3 **cup salsa**
1/2 **cup fat-free milk**
2 **8-oz. pkgs. imitation crabmeat, flaked finely**
3/4 **cup green onions, thinly sliced**
4-**oz. can chopped green chilies**
3 **8-oz. pkgs. fat-free cream cheese, cubed**
10 **ozs. stone wheat crackers**

1. Spray slow cooker with fat-free cooking spray.
2. Mix salsa and milk.
3. Stir in all remaining ingredients except crackers.
4. Cover. Cook on low 3-4 hours.
5. Stir approximately every half hour.
6. Serve with crackers or raw vegetables.

Per Serving: 520 calories (110 calories from fat), 12g total fat (3g saturated, 0g trans), 55mg cholesterol, 1410mg sodium, 65g total carbohydrate (8g fiber, 4g sugar), 38g protein, 20%DV vitamin A, 10%DV vitamin C, 35%DV calcium, 15%DV iron.

Seafood Dip
Joan Rosenberger
Stephens City, VA

Makes 24 servings of 2 Tbsp. each
(Ideal slow-cooker size: 3 1/2-quart)

10-**oz. pkg. fat-free cream cheese**
8-**oz. pkg. imitation crab strands, freeze-dried**

2 **Tbsp. onion, finely chopped**
4-5 **drops hot sauce**
1/4 **cup walnuts, finely chopped**
1 **tsp. paprika**

1. Blend all ingredients except nuts and paprika until well mixed.
2. Spread in slow cooker. Sprinkle with nuts and paprika.
3. Cook on low 3 hours.

Per Serving: 70 calories (10 calories from fat), 1.5g total fat (0g saturated, 0g trans), 5mg cholesterol, 370mg sodium, 7g total carbohydrate (0g fiber, 3g sugar), 7g protein, 6%DV vitamin A, 0%DV vitamin C, 4%DV calcium, 0%DV iron.

Serve with crackers.

Cheesy New Orleans Shrimp Dip
Kelly Evenson
Pittsboro, NC

Makes 3-4 cups dip or 24 servings
(Ideal slow-cooker size: 2-quart)

1 **slice lean turkey bacon**
3 **medium-sized onions, chopped**
1 **garlic clove, minced**
4 **jumbo shrimp, peeled and deveined**
1 **medium-sized tomato, peeled and chopped**
3 **cups low-fat Monterey Jack cheese, shredded**
4 **drops Tabasco sauce**
1/8 **tsp. cayenne pepper**
dash of black pepper

1. Cook bacon until crisp. Drain on paper towel. Crumble.
2. Sauté onion and garlic in bacon drippings. Drain on paper towel.
3. Coarsely chop shrimp.

4. Combine all ingredients in slow cooker.

5. Cover. Cook on low 1 hour, or until cheese is melted. Thin with milk if too thick.

6. Serve with chips.

Per Serving: 130 calories (5 calories from fat), 0.5g total fat (0g saturated, 0g trans), 10mg cholesterol, 520mg sodium, 12g total carbohydrate (1g fiber, 4g sugar), 18g protein, 10%DV vitamin A, 0%DV vitamin C, 60%DV calcium, 2%DV iron.

Pickled Whiting

Sue Hamilton
Minooka, IL

Makes 24 servings
(Ideal slow-cooker size: 6-quart)

2 onions, sliced
1 cup white vinegar
3/4 cup Splenda
1 tsp. salt
1 Tbsp. allspice
2 lbs. frozen individual whiting with skin

1. Combine onions, vinegar, Splenda, salt, and allspice in bottom of slow cooker.

2. Slice frozen whiting into 2" slices, each with skin on. Place fish in slow cooker, pushing it down into the liquid as much as possible.

3. Cook on low 3-4 hours.

4. Pour cooking liquid over fish, cover, and refrigerate. Serve when well chilled.

Per Serving: 45 calories (5 calories from fat), 0.5 total fat (0g saturated, 0g trans), 25mg cholesterol, 125mg sodium, 2g total carbohydrate (0g fiber, 1g sugar), 7g protein, 0%DV vitamin A, 0%DV vitamin C, 2%DV calcium, 0%DV iron.

Apple Butter – for Your Toast

Alix Nancy Botsford
Seminole, OK

Makes 9 cups
(Ideal slow-cooker size: 5- or 6-quart)

108-oz. can (#8 size) unsweetened applesauce
2 cups cider
1 Tbsp. ground cinnamon
1 tsp. ground ginger
1/2 tsp. ground cloves, or 1 tsp. ground nutmeg, optional

1. Combine applesauce and cider in slow cooker.

2. Cover. Cook on high 3-4 hours.

3. Add spices.

4. Cover. Cook 1 hour more.

5. Sterilize cup- or pint-size jars. Heat lids.

6. Fill jars with apple butter. Clean rim with damp paper towel. Put on lids.

7. Place in canner and cook according to manufacturer's instructions.

Per Serving: 180 calories (0 calories from fat), 0g total fat (0g saturated, 0g trans), 0mg cholesterol, 15mg sodium, 46g total carbohydrate (5g fiber, 38g sugar), 1g protein, 0%DV vitamin A, 60%DV vitamin C, 2%DV calcium, 4%DV iron.

This is better than any air freshener. When anyone comes home I receive a hug and then a question:"Where's the toast?"

It also tastes wonderful on plain yogurt!

Pear Butter

Betty Moore
Plano, Il

Makes 2 pints
(Ideal slow-cooker size: 5-quart)

10 large, well-ripened pears (4 lbs.)
2 Tbsp. frozen orange juice concentrate
2 cups sugar
1 tsp. ground cinnamon
1 tsp. ground cloves
1/2 tsp. ground allspice

1. Peel and quarter pears. Place in slow cooker.
2. Cover. Cook on low 12 hours. Drain thoroughly and then discard liquid.
3. Mash or puree pears. Add remaining ingredients. Mix well and return to slow cooker.
4. Cover. Cook on high 1 hour.
5. Place in hot sterile jars and seal. Process in hot water bath for 10 minutes. Allow to cool undisturbed for 24 hours.

Per Serving: 100 calories (0 calories from fat), 0g total fat (0g saturated, 0g trans), 0mg cholesterol, 0mg sodium, 26g total carbohydrate (2g fiber, 23g sugar), 0g protein, 0%DV vitamin A, 0%DV vitamin C, 0%DV calcium, 0%DV iron.

Note: *If the butter is too soupy after cooking on low 12 hours, you may want to cook it uncovered during Step 4 in order to create a stiffer consistency.*

Pear Butter

Dorothy Miller
Gulfport, MI

Makes 6 pints
(Ideal slow-cooker size: 5-quarts)

8 cups pear sauce
3 cups brown sugar
1 Tbsp. lemon juice
1 Tbsp. cinnamon

1. Combine all ingredients in slow cooker.
2. Cover. Cook on high 10-12 hours.

Per Serving: 40 calories (0 calories from fat), 0g total fat (0g saturated, 0g trans), 0mg cholesterol, 0mg sodium, 10g total carbohydrate (0g fiber, 10g sugar), 0g protein, 0%DV vitamin A, 0%DV vitamin C, 0%DV calcium, 0%DV iron.

Note: *To make pear sauce, peel, core, and slice 12 large, well-ripened pears. Place in slow cooker with 3/4 cup water. Cover and cook on low 8-10 hours, or until very soft. Stir to blend.*

Beverages

Hot Mulled Cider

Betty K. Drescher
Quakertown, PA

Makes 8 servings
(Ideal slow-cooker size: 3¹/2-quart)

1 tsp. whole cloves
¼ cup brown sugar
2 qts. cider
1 3"-long cinnamon stick
1 orange, sliced

   1. Tie cloves in cheesecloth or put in tea strainer.
   2. Combine all ingredients in slow cooker.
   3. Cover. Cook on low 3-6 hours.

Per Serving: 160 calories (0 calories from fat), 0g total fat (0g saturated, 0g trans), 0mg cholesterol, 30mg sodium, 39g total carbohydrate (0.5g fiber, 34g sugar), 0g protein, 0%DV vitamin A, 8%DV vitamin C, 2%DV calcium, 2%DV iron.

Hot Apple Cinnamon Drink

Marla Folkerts
Holland, OH

Makes 24 servings
(Ideal slow-cooker size: 6-quart)

1 gallon cider
2 liters diet ginger ale
4 ozs. hard candies—your choice of flavors
cinnamon sticks, optional

   1. Combine all ingredients in slow cooker.
   2. Cover. Simmer on low 3-5 hours.

Per Serving: 100 calories (0 calories from fat), 0g total fat (0g saturated, 0g trans), 0mg cholesterol, 30mg sodium, 25g total carbohydrate (0g fiber, 20g sugar), 0g protein, 0%DV vitamin A, 0%DV vitamin C, 0%DV calcium, 0%DV iron.

Spiced Cider

Loretta Weisz
Auburn, WA

Makes 20 5-oz. servings
(Ideal slow-cooker size: 4-quart)

2 qts. cider, or 3 6-oz. cans frozen cider
concentrate
5½-oz. pkg. hot cinnamon candies
3-oz. pkg. orangeade mix
1 qt. water
12 whole cloves

1. Combine all ingredients in slow cooker.
2. Cover. Cook on low 3-4 hours.
3. Remove whole cloves with slotted spoon before serving.

Per Serving: 80 calories (0 calories from fat), 0g total fat (0g saturated, 0g trans), 0mg cholesterol, 15mg sodium, 20g total carbohydrate (0g fiber, 17g sugar), 0g protein, 0%DV vitamin A, 10%DV vitamin C, 2%DV calcium, 0%DV iron.

Wassail Punch

Marcia S. Myer
Manheim, PA

Makes 18 servings
(Ideal slow-cooker size: 4-quart)

2 qts. apple cider
2 cups orange juice
2 cups pineapple juice
½ cup lemon juice
⅓-½ cup sugar, according to your taste
preference
12 whole cloves
4 cinnamon sticks
orange slices, or clove-studded orange
slices (optional)

1. Combine all ingredients in slow cooker. Mix well.
2. Cover. Cook on low 2-3 hours.
3. Remove cloves and cinnamon sticks before serving.

Per Serving: 140 calories (0 calories from fat), 0g total fat (0g saturated, 0g trans), 0mg cholesterol, 15mg sodium, 34g total carbohydrate (0.5g fiber, 31g sugar), 0g protein, 2%DV vitamin A, 20%DV vitamin C, 2%DV calcium, 2%DV iron.

Christmas Wassail

Linda Sluiter
Schererville, IN

Makes 8 servings
(Ideal slow-cooker size: 3-quart)

1 qt. apple cider
½ cup orange or pineapple juice
2 cups water
3 orange pekoe tea bags
¼ cup brown sugar
¼ tsp. ground cinnamon
¼ tsp. ground cloves
oranges

1. Combine all ingredients except oranges in slow cooker.
2. Cover. Cook on high 1-2 hours.
3. Slice oranges to float on top. Serve in mugs.

Per Serving: 160 calories (0 calories from fat), 0g total fat (0g saturated, 0g trans), 0mg cholesterol, 20mg sodium, 45g total carbohydrate (7g fiber, 35g sugar), 1g protein, 2%DV vitamin A, 100%DV vitamin C, 8%DV calcium, 4%DV iron.

Peachy Spiced Cider

Joyce Shackelford
Green Bay, WI

Makes 8 small servings
(Ideal slow-cooker size: 2-quart)

4 5½-oz. cans peach nectar
2 cups unsweetened apple juice
½ tsp. ground ginger
¼ tsp. ground cinnamon
¼ tsp. ground nutmeg
4 fresh orange slices, cut ¼" thick and then halved

1. Combine peach nectar, apple juice, ginger, cinnamon, and nutmeg in slow cooker.
2. Top with orange slices.
3. Cover. Cook on low 4-6 hours.
4. Remove orange slices and stir before serving.

Per Serving: 180 calories (0 calories from fat), 0g total fat (0g saturated, 0g trans), 0mg cholesterol, 15mg sodium, 44g total carbohydrate (3g fiber, 41g sugar), 1g protein, 6%DV vitamin A, 100%DV vitamin C, 4%DV calcium, 6%DV iron.

Dawn's Spicy Cranapple Cider
Dawn Day
Westminster, CA

Makes 12 servings
(Ideal slow-cooker size: 4-quart)

1/2 gallon unfiltered apple cider
1 qt. cranberry juice
2 tsp. ground cinnamon
1/4 tsp. ground cloves
1/4 tsp. ground nutmeg
cinnamon sticks for garnish

1. Combine all ingredients in slow cooker.
2. Cover. Cook on low 4-5 hours or until drink is heated through.
3. Serve in a mug with cinnamon sticks.

Per Serving: 50 calories (0 calories from fat), 0g total fat (0g saturated, 0g trans), 0mg cholesterol, 0mg sodium, 12g total carbohydrate (0g fiber, 12g sugar), 0g protein, 0%DV vitamin A, 40%DV vitamin C, 0%DV calcium, 2%DV iron.

Cranberry Punch
Betty B. Dennison
Grove City, PA

Makes 8 servings
(Ideal slow-cooker size: 4-quart)

8 whole cardamom pods
2 sticks cinnamon
12 whole cloves
4 cups dry red wine
2 6-oz. cans frozen cranberry concentrate
2 2/3 cups water
1/2 cup honey (or to taste)
1 orange sliced into 8 thin crescents

1. Make a spice packet of the following items: Pinch open cardamom pods to release seeds and place them on a piece of cheesecloth or paper coffee filter. Add cinnamon sticks and cloves. Tie with a string to make a bag.
2. Pour wine, cranberry concentrate, water, and honey into slow cooker. Heat on low.
3. Submerge spice packet in the liquid and heat but do not boil.
4. Let punch steep on low for up to 4 hours.
5. To serve, remove and discard spice bag. Divide punch among cups. Float an orange slice in each cup. Serve warm.

Per Serving: 240 calories (0 calories from fat), 0g total fat (0g saturated, 0g trans), 0mg cholesterol, 30mg sodium, 40g total carbohydrate (3g fiber, 33g sugar), 2g protein, 4%DV vitamin A, 20%DV vitamin C, 8%DV calcium, 10%DV iron.

Spiced Apricot Cider
Joyce Shackelford
Green Bay, WI
Mary Longenecker
Bethel, PA

Makes 6 servings
(Ideal slow-cooker size: 2 1/2-quart)

2 12-oz. cans apricot nectar
2 cups water
1/4 cup lemon juice
1/4 cup sugar
2 whole cloves
2 3"-long cinnamon sticks

1. Combine all ingredients in slow cooker.
2. Cover. Cook on high 2 hours.
3. Remove cloves and cinnamon sticks before serving.

Per Serving: 140 calories (0 calories from fat), 0g total fat (0g saturated, 0g trans), 0mg cholesterol, 40mg sodium, 35g total carbohydrate (1g fiber, 27g sugar), 1g protein, 20%DV vitamin A, 80%DV vitamin C, 2%DV calcium, 4%DV iron.

Orange Ginger Tea

Jeanne Heyerly
Chenoa, IL

Makes 8-10 servings
(Ideal slow-cooker size: 2¹/2-quart)

2 qts. water
3 1"-squares fresh gingerroot, sliced
3 Tbsp. brown sugar or honey
1 orange, sliced

1. Place water and gingerroot in slow cooker.
2. Cover. Cook on high 2 hours; then on low 2-4 hours.
3. Add sugar or honey and sliced orange 1 hour before serving.

Per Serving: 20 calories (0 calories from fat), 0g total fat (0g saturated, 0g trans), 0mg cholesterol, 10mg sodium, 6g total carbohydrate (0g fiber, 5g sugar), 0g protein, 0%DV vitamin A, 8%DV vitamin C, 2%DV calcium, 0%DV iron.

This tea makes cold-sufferers feel better!

Mint Tea

Leona Miller
Millersburg, OH

Makes 8 servings
(Ideal slow-cooker size: 3-quart)

2 quarts hot water
Splenda to taste
8 tea bags
2 drops mint extract

1. Combine water and Splenda in slow cooker. Mix well until Splenda is dissolved.
2. Add the tea bags and mint extract.
3. Cook on high 2 hours.

Per Serving: 0 calories (0 calories from fat), 0g total fat (0g saturated, 0g trans), 0mg cholesterol, 5mg sodium, 0g total carbohydrate (0g fiber, 0g sugar), 0g protein, 0%DV vitamin A, 0%DV vitamin C, 0%DV calcium, 0%DV iron.

This is nice for hot breakfast buffets.

Almond Tea

Frances Schrag
Newton, KS

Makes 10-11 servings
(Ideal slow-cooker size: 4¹/2-quart)

10 cups boiling water
1 Tbsp. instant tea
2/3 cup lemon juice
6 Tbsp. sugar
1 tsp. vanilla
1 tsp. almond extract

1. Mix together all ingredients in slow cooker.
2. Turn to high and heat thoroughly (about 1 hour). Turn to low while serving.

Per Serving: 30 calories (0 calories from fat), 0g total fat (0g saturated, 0g trans), 0mg cholesterol, 5mg sodium, 8g total carbohydrate (0g fiber, 7g sugar), 0g protein, 0%DV vitamin A, 0%DV vitamin C, 0%DV calcium, 0%DV iron.

Spiced Coffee

Joyce Shackelford
Green Bay, WI

Makes 8 servings
(Ideal slow-cooker size: 3-quart)

8 cups brewed coffee
1/3 cup sugar
1/4 cup low-fat chocolate syrup
1/2 tsp. anise extract
4 cinnamon sticks, halved
1 1/2 tsp. whole cloves

1. Combine coffee, sugar, chocolate syrup, and anise extract in slow cooker.
2. Place cinnamon sticks and cloves in cheesecloth bag. Place in slow cooker.
3. Cover. Cook on low 2-3 hours.
4. Discard spice bag.
5. Ladle coffee into mugs. Garnish each with half a cinnamon stick.

Per Serving: 70 calories (10 calories from fat), 1g total fat (0g saturated, 0g trans), 0mg cholesterol, 20mg sodium, 17g total carbohydrate (0.5g fiber, 14g sugar), 0g protein, 6%DV vitamin A, 2%DV vitamin C, 2%DV calcium, 10%DV iron.

Mocha Eggnog

Char Hagner
Montague, MI

Makes 8 servings
(Ideal slow-cooker size: 2-quart)

1 qt. low-fat eggnog
1 Tbsp. instant decaf French vanilla coffee granules
1/4 cup coffee-flavored liqueur

1. Combine eggnog and coffee granules in slow cooker.
2. Cover. Cook until mixture is hot and coffee granules dissolve.
3. Add coffee liqueur just before serving.
4. Ladle into mugs.

Per Serving: 170 calories (40 calories from fat), 4.5g total fat (2.5g saturated, 0g trans), 50mg cholesterol, 85mg sodium, 24g total carbohydrate (0g fiber, 22g sugar), 6g protein, 4%DV vitamin A, 0%DV vitamin C, 15%DV calcium, 0%DV iron.

Note: If you like, and if your diet allows, you may want to serve the eggnog topped with a spoonful of low-fat whipping cream and a sprinkling of shaved chocolate.

Breakfast Dishes

Overnight Apple Oatmeal

Frances Musser, Newmanstown, PA
John D. Allen, Rye, CO

Makes 4 servings
(Ideal slow-cooker size: 2-quart)

2 cups skim or 2% milk
2 Tbsp. honey, or ¼ cup brown sugar
1 Tbsp. margarine
¼ tsp. salt
½ tsp. ground cinnamon
1 cup dry rolled oats
1 cup apples, chopped
½ cup raisins, optional
¼ cup walnuts, chopped
½ cup fat-free half-and-half

1. Spray inside of slow cooker with non-fat cooking spray.
2. In a mixing bowl, combine all ingredients except half-and-half. Pour into cooker.
3. Cover and cook on low overnight, ideally 6-8 hours. The oatmeal is ready to eat in the morning.
4. Stir in the half-and-half just before serving.

Per Serving: 240 calories (60 calories from fat), 6g total fat (1g saturated, 0g trans), 0mg cholesterol, 240mg sodium, 37g total carbohydrate (4g fiber, 21g sugar), 10g protein, 8%DV vitamin A, 6%DV vitamin C, 20%DV calcium, 8%DV iron.

Almond-Date Oatmeal

Darla Sathre, Baxter, MN

Makes 8 servings
(Ideal slow-cooker size: 3-quart)

2 cups dry rolled oats
1/2 cup dry Grape-Nuts cereal
1/2 cup almonds, slivered
1/4 cup dates, chopped
4 cups water

1. Combine all ingredients in slow cooker.
2. Cook on low 4-6 hours.
3. Serve with fat-free milk.

Per Serving: 160 calories (45 calories from fat), 5g total fat
(0g saturated, 0g trans), 0mg cholesterol, 50mg sodium,
26g total carbohydrate (4g fiber, 5g sugar), 5g protein,
2%DV vitamin A, 0%DV vitamin C, 2%DV calcium,
15%DV iron.

Breakfast Apple Cobbler

Virginia Graybill
Hershey, PA

Makes 8-10 servings
(Ideal slow-cooker size: 5- or 6-quart)

8 medium-sized tart apples
1/2 cup sugar
2 Tbsp. fresh lemon juice
1-2 tsp. grated lemon rind
dash of ground cinnamon
1/4 cup butter, melted
1 1/2 cups natural fat-free cereal mixed with
fruit and nuts

1. Spray interior of cooker lightly with nonfat cooking spray.
2. Core, peel, and slice apples into slow cooker.
3. Add sugar, lemon juice, rind, and cinnamon.
4. Mix cereal and melted butter together.
5. Add to ingredients in slow cooker. Mix thoroughly.
6. Cover. Cook on low 6 hours or high 2-3 hours.

Per Serving: 210 calories (45 calories from fat), 5g total fat
(3g saturated, 0g trans), 10mg cholesterol, 105mg sodium,
43g total carbohydrate (6g fiber, 25g sugar), 2g protein,
6%DV vitamin A, 10%DV vitamin C, 2%DV calcium,
30%DV iron.

Note: You can serve this with fat-free milk for breakfast. If diets permit, you can also serve it as a dessert with fat-free frozen yogurt instead.

Breakfast Fruit Compote

Betty K. Drescher
Quakertown, PA

Makes 8-9 servings
(Ideal slow-cooker size: 3- or 4-quart)

12-oz. pkg. dried apricots
12-oz. pkg. pitted dried plums
11-oz. can mandarin oranges in light
  syrup, undrained
29-oz. can sliced peaches in light syrup,
  undrained
1/4 cup white raisins
10 maraschino cherries

1. Combine all ingredients in slow cooker. Mix well.
2. Cover. Cook on low 6-7 hours or on high 2-3 hours.

Per Serving: 300 calories (0 calories from fat), 0g total fat (0g saturated, 0g trans), 0mg cholesterol, 40mg sodium, 74g total carbohydrate (5g fiber, 42g sugar), 3g protein, 30%DV vitamin A, 10%DV vitamin C, 4%DV calcium, 15%DV iron.

Note: If the fruit seems to be drying out as it cooks, you may want to add up to 1 cup water.

Blueberry Apple Waffle Topping

Willard E. Roth
Elkhart, IN

Makes 10-12 servings
(Ideal slow-cooker size: 3 1/2- or 4-quart)

1 qt. natural applesauce, unsweetened
2 Granny Smith apples, unpeeled, cored,
  and sliced
1 pt. fresh or frozen blueberries
1/2 Tbsp. ground cinnamon
1/2 cup pure maple syrup
1 tsp. almond flavoring
1/2 cup walnuts, chopped

1. Stir together applesauce, apples, and blueberries in slow cooker sprayed with non-fat cooking spray.
2. Add cinnamon and maple syrup.
3. Cover. Cook on low 3 hours.
4. Add almond flavoring and walnuts just before serving.

Per Serving: 130 calories (35 calories from fat), 3.5g total fat (0g saturated, 0g trans), 0mg cholesterol, 0mg sodium, 25g total carbohydrate (3g fiber, 20g sugar), 2g protein, 0%DV vitamin A, 20%DV vitamin C, 2%DV calcium, 4%DV iron.

Note: If your diet allows, this is also delicious served over cake or fat-free frozen yogurt.

Cornmeal Mush

Betty K. Drescher
Quakertown, PA

Makes 10 servings
(Ideal slow-cooker size: 3½- or 4-quart)

2 cups cornmeal
5 cups cold water, divided
1½ tsp. salt
1 Tbsp. butter or margarine

1. In a mixing bowl, stir cornmeal, 2 cups cold water, and salt together. When smooth, add remaining water. Stir well.
2. Spray slow cooker with low-fat cooking spray. Pour cornmeal mixture into slow cooker.
3. Cover. Cook on low 7-8 hours.

Per Serving: 110 calories (10 calories from fat), 1.5g total fat (0g saturated, 0g trans), 0mg cholesterol, 370mg sodium, 21g total carbohydrate (2g fiber, 0g sugar), 2g protein, 2%DV vitamin A, 0%DV vitamin C, 0%DV calcium, 6%DV iron.

Enjoy a bowl of hot mush for milk or supper with fat-free milk and Splenda. Pour remaining mush into a container to cool. Refrigerate overnight. Slice and brown in a skillet until browned on each side. Serve with apple butter or maple syrup.

Breads

Boston Brown Bread

Virginia Graybill
Hershey, PA

Makes 1 loaf
(Ideal slow-cooker size: tall 4- or 5-quart cooker)

½ cup flour
½ tsp. baking powder
½ tsp. baking soda
½ tsp. salt
½ cup yellow cornmeal
½ cup whole wheat flour
¼ cup walnuts, chopped
6 Tbsp. unsulfured molasses
1 cup low-fat buttermilk, or sour milk
½ cup raisins

1. Sift flour with baking powder, baking soda, and salt.
2. Stir in cornmeal and whole wheat flour.
3. Add remaining ingredients. Beat well.
4. Pour batter into greased and floured 2-lb. coffee can.
5. Pour 2 cups water into slow cooker. Set can inside cooker.
6. Place aluminum foil over top of can, folding it down around the edge of the can. Cover cooker.
7. Cook on high 4-5 hours, until a skewer inserted in center of bread comes out clean.
8. Remove can from cooker. Lay it on its side to cool. Keep can covered one hour before unmolding.
9. Slice and serve.

Per Serving: 80 calories (10 calories from fat), 1g total fat (0g saturated, 0g trans), 0mg cholesterol, 105mg sodium, 16g total carbohydrate (0.5g fiber, 7g sugar), 2g protein, 0%DV vitamin A, 0%DV vitamin C, 4%DV calcium, 4%DV iron.

Parmesan Garlic Quick Bread

Leona Miller
Millersburg, OH

Makes 8 servings
(Ideal slow-cooker size: 2- or 3-quart)

1 1/2 cups reduced-fat buttermilk baking
  mix
2 egg whites
1/2 cup skim milk
1 Tbsp. minced onions
1 Tbsp. sugar
1 1/2 tsp. garlic powder
1/4 cup reduced-fat Parmesan cheese

1. Combine baking mix, egg whites, milk, onions, sugar, and garlic powder in a mixing bowl.
2. Spray slow cooker with cooking spray. Spoon dough into cooker.
3. Sprinkle dough with Parmesan cheese.
4. Cook on high 1 hour.

Per Serving: 120 calories (20 calories from fat), 2g total fat (1g saturated, 0g trans), 0mg cholesterol, 330mg sodium, 19g total carbohydrate (0g fiber, 4g sugar), 4g protein, 0%DV vitamin A, 0%DV vitamin C, 4%DV calcium, 4%DV iron.

This bread is great with hot soup, Italian dishes, or salads.

Cottage Cheese Bread

Leona Miller
Millersburg, OH

Makes 8 servings
(Ideal slow-cooker size: 3-quart)

1 cup fat-free cottage cheese
4 egg whites
1 cup sugar
3/4 cup fat-free or 2% milk
1 tsp. vanilla
2 3/4 cups reduced-fat buttermilk baking
  mix
1/2 cup raisins or dried cranberries
1/2 tsp. orange zest

1. Combine all ingredients in a mixing bowl.
2. Pour into greased slow cooker.
3. Cook on high 2 hours.

Per Serving: 320 calories (25 calories from fat), 3g total fat (0.5g saturated, 0g trans), 0mg cholesterol, 510mg sodium, 63g total carbohydrate (0.5g fiber, 34g sugar), 10g protein, 0%DV vitamin A, 0%DV vitamin C, 6%DV calcium, 10%DV iron.

Index

About the Author

Phyllis Pellman Good is a *New York Times* bestselling author whose books have sold more than 6 million copies.

Good has authored or co-authored many cookbooks, including the national #1 bestselling cookbook (with Dawn J. Ranck) *Fix-It and Forget-It Cookbook: Feasting with your Slow Cooker* and, also in the series, *Fix-It and Forget-It Recipes for Entertaining: Slow Cooker Favorites for All the Year Round* (also with Ranck). Good's other cookbooks include *The Best of Amish Cooking, The Best of Mennonite Fellowship Meals, The Central Market Cookbook,* and *Favorite Recipes with Herbs.*

Phyllis Pellman Good is Senior Editor at Good Books. She received her B.A. and M.A. in English from New York University. She and her husband, Merle, live in Lancaster, Pennsylvania. They are the parents of two young-adult daughters.

For a complete listing of books by Phyllis Pellman Good, as well as excerpts and reviews, visit www.goodbks.com.